Postcolonial Theory and Francophone Literary Studies

Florida A&M University, Tallahassee
Florida Atlantic University, Boca Raton
Florida Gulf Coast University, Ft. Myers
Florida International University, Miami
Florida State University, Tallahassee
University of Central Florida, Orlando
University of Florida, Gainesville
University of North Florida, Jacksonville
University of South Florida, Tampa
University of West Florida, Pensacola

Postcolonial Theory and Francophone Literary Studies

Edited by H. Adlai Murdoch and Anne Donadey

University Press of Florida
Gainesville · Tallahassee · Tampa · Boca Raton
Pensacola · Orlando · Miami · Jacksonville · Ft. Myers

Printed in the United States of America on recycled, acid-free paper

09 08 07 06 05 04 6 5 4 3 2 1

Library of Congress Cataloging-in-Publication Data
Postcolonial theory and Francophone literary studies / edited by
H. Adlai Murdoch and Anne Donadey.
p. cm.
Includes bibliographical references and index.
ISBN 0-8130-2776-4 (alk. paper)
1. French literature—French-speaking countries—History and criticism.
2. Postcolonialism—French-speaking countries. 3. Postcolonialism in literature.
I. Murdoch, H. Adlai. II. Donadey, Anne.
PQ3897.P67 2005
840.9'358—dc22 2004051287

The University Press of Florida is the scholarly publishing agency for the State University System of Florida, comprising Florida A&M University, Florida Atlantic University, Florida Gulf Coast University, Florida International University, Florida State University, University of Central Florida, University of Florida, University of North Florida, University of South Florida, and University of West Florida.

University Press of Florida
15 Northwest 15th Street
Gainesville, FL 32611-2079
http://www.upf.com

Contents

1

Introduction

Productive Intersections

Anne Donadey and H. Adlai Murdoch

This collection of original essays takes a comparative approach to the discrete but intersecting fields of postcolonial theory and francophone studies, and maps the productive cross-fertilization that emerges from this doubling of discourses. Indeed, as Farid Laroussi and Christopher L. Miller point out in their introduction to a recent issue of *Yale French Studies* that analyzes various aspects of the francophone literature phenomenon, the inclusion of francophone studies in French departments has engendered "the most significant change in the field of French Studies since the theoretical and feminist revolutions of the 1970s . . . and . . . the necessity of reappraising the discipline as a whole" (1). Along these lines, *Postcolonial Theory and Francophone Literary Studies* offers postcolonial reformulations of francophone studies and francophone reformulations of postcolonial studies. It evaluates the contributions of postcolonial theory to francophone studies, as well as the impact of francophone theory and literature on postcolonial studies.

In recent years, both areas of study have risen to prominence in the U.S. academy, mostly in departments of English and French literature respectively. Both fields focus on similar issues, such as: diaspora and hybridity, nationalism and transnationalism, gender and race, multilingualism, opposition and ambivalence, and the need to rewrite colonial history. Both areas of study follow parallel tracks to develop similar trajectories and analogous theoretical frameworks. The works of early francophone thinkers such as Aimé Césaire and especially Frantz Fanon have shaped postcolonial theory to a significant degree, an endeavor that, as Ronnie Scharfman puts it, "challenged from the margins the authority, institutions and ideology of the French metropolitan center in an effort to decolonize the mind" ("Before" 10). In spite of all this, specific and exact points of intersection between the two fields are fewer than one might expect. Rather, what we often see in both fields is a growing appropriation of specific discursive sites, a continual expansion of boundaries that seeks to fix francophone and postcolonial studies as fields of inquiry that share certain attributes. *Postcolonial Theory and Francophone Literary Studies* fills the need to broaden the dialogue between postcolonial theory and francophone studies. Although several chapters engage literary texts, this book is not primarily literary criticism. Rather, it makes a theoretical contribution to both postcolonial and francophone studies.

We define postcolonial studies as an interdisciplinary field of scholarship that developed out of Commonwealth studies in the 1980s and 1990s in the United Kingdom and out of the revelations of "orientalism" in the United States. Postcolonial theorists, many of whom are Indian, British, and Australian scholars working in Anglo-Saxon universities, proposed a reinterpretation of literature and history that would account for the colonial experience while insisting on its centrality. The field of postcolonial studies tends to focus largely on anglophone literature and contexts and to be heavily indebted to French poststructuralist theory; further, as Celia Britton and Michael Syrotinski point out in their introduction to a special issue of *Paragraph* on "Francophone Texts and Postcolonial Theory," "there has until recently been a marked resistance to reading francophone writing in conjunction with the texts and concepts that have become common theoretical currency in anglophone studies" (1). As a result of this double bind, only a few scholars not writing in English have made an impact on the field of postcolonial studies, and their works are usually taken out of context and read only in English translation, a process that can sometimes foster misinterpretations. An excellent analysis of this phenomenon is provided by E. Anthony Hurley in this volume, when he points out that the English translation of Fanon's central chapter in *Black Skin, White Masks*, "L'Expérience vécue du Noir" [The lived experience of the black person] has long been mistranslated as "The Fact of Blackness." Replacing *experience* with *fact* and *black person* with *blackness* moves the reader away from the subjective experience of black individuals. It connotes a unitary conception of what it means to be black and makes Fanon appear more rigidly essentialist than he in fact is. We are not arguing against the use of works in translation here. Later in this introduction, we actually make the opposite claim. As Spivak has often stated, we are simply indicating that when academics are not familiar with a particular language and are working from a translation, they should remain aware of the provisional nature of their analysis and should make an effort to seek out secondary sources written by scholars working from the original text to clarify nuances and ambiguities.

Francophone studies has progressively drawn on postcolonial studies as a field of knowledge. However, as Michael Dash cogently suggests, even the early Caribbean context of what would become *francophonie* functioned through a "transnational perspective . . . [that] firmly established as a new literary project, what could previously have been seen as merely an adjunct to writing in French" ("Caraïbe" 94). The field as a whole has built upon and enlarged this tradition, such that francophone studies is currently understood specifically to be the study of French-language literature, film, and culture from regions and countries outside mainland France. We focus particularly on the problematics of cultural production and the articulation of cultural identity in former French colonies and by immigrants from these sites living in France. Francophone studies may be said to be generally more textually based than postcolonial studies and tends to refer primarily to the inflections and transformations of a French and francophone theoretical and literary tradition.

An emergent field within French departments since the 1980s, francophone studies has now become a central part of French studies in the U.S. academy, helping to curb dwindling enrollments in French through its varying cultural and geopolitical foci. Until fairly recently, only a limited number of scholars (such as Françoise Lionnet and Robert Young) worked specifically at the intersection of the postcolonial and francophone fields. While the increased overlapping and centrality of these areas of study—owing in part to a renewed focus on multicultural perspectives in the U.S. academy—have, on the one hand, produced "some institutional and individual sense of confusion, gain, and loss," as Mireille Rosello claims (128), it has on the other also provoked drastic changes in scholarship, syllabi, and the structure of academic French departments. Indeed, Françoise Lionnet goes so far as to say that "francophone studies has presided over what might be called the 'becoming-transnational' of French studies" ("Introduction" 784). The present volume inscribes itself in the current push to retheorize and reframe French and francophone studies (see also Le Hir and Strand).

Francophone studies, then, represents a rapidly burgeoning academic field that came into its own in the 1990s and now encompasses the literary and cultural output of, inter alia, the geographical areas of the Caribbean, the Maghreb, sub-Saharan Africa, and Quebec. With the literatures of many of these regions coming into their own either in tandem with or in opposition to overt political domination by the colonial *métropole*, it is increasingly clear that the creative fragmentation and pluralism that ground them, the result of their varying ethnic and colonial histories, cultures, and political realities—ranging from independence to departmentalization, from Berbers to Creoles—produce a variety of different readings of the term *francophonie*.

In its turn, postcolonial studies, a field often accused of adopting a monolithic, totalizing, and undifferentiated attitude toward the subjects of its discourses, collapsing histories, political structures, and ethnic formations into a single, homogenized whole, has been unequivocally and unalterably shaped by this abundance of francophone voices. The goal of this book, then, is to reassess the varied impact and scope of these reformulations, to examine the range of subsets of postcolonialism informed by *francophonie*, and to define new boundaries and future parameters of study for those regions where both fields intersect (see, for example, Brière on Quebec and Larrier on Haiti in this volume; see also, in works cited, Dash's "Postcolonial Thought," on Haiti).

Both postcolonial and francophone studies are marked by considerable debates that attach to their nomenclature. For example, postcolonial criticism is largely seen as having a homogenizing effect on its subjects; as Bart Moore-Gilbert puts it in his book *Postcolonial Theory*, it has "significantly altered . . . modes of analysis" and "has helped to undermine the traditional conception of disciplinary boundaries." In fact, it might not be going too far to claim, as some have, that postcolonial criticism "is now itself betraying a tendency to 'colonize' an evergrowing number of historical periods, geographical locations and disciplinary fields" (Moore-Gilbert, *Postcolonial Theory* 8–9). Even the very scope of the term *postcolonial* is itself at issue, since, as Moore-Gilbert, Stanton, and Maley point out, "postcolonialism remains an elusive and contested term. It designates at one and the same time a chronological moment, a political movement, and an intellectual activity, and it is this multiple status that makes exact definition difficult" (1). Following these lines of argument to their logical conclusion, Quayson and Goldberg conclude, in the introduction to their collection, *Relocating Postcolonialism*, that "a crucial question for Postcolonial Studies concerns how to shape itself from the standpoint of its imagined future irrelevance" (xiii).

Francophone studies, on the other hand, finds itself riven by debates over location, exclusion, creolization, *métropole*/periphery, French universalism, and the French relationship to the rest of the French-speaking world, as well as related issues of ethnicity, nation, migration, and ethnic and cultural stereotyping. Recent essays by David Murphy and Gabrielle Parker, as well as chapters by Eloise Brière and by Coursil and Perret in this volume, highlight the politically problematic aspects of *francophonie* as an institution with a colonial history and clear neocolonial potential today, in part because of its continuing reliance on a center-periphery model. A more generous reading of the resonances of *francophonie* would be inclusive of many of the issues mentioned above in a nonhierarchical way, "foregrounding," as Françoise Lionnet puts it, "the liberating potential of counternarratives" (*Postcolonial*

Representations 20). For example, in this volume, Michel Laronde deconstructs the French versus francophone binary opposition by proposing that we include "Franco-French" literature and cultural production, together with postcolonial work in French, under the label *francophone*. Similarly, David Murphy uses "the term 'Francophone postcolonial studies' to refer to the study of postcolonial issues in *all* literature (as well as other cultural forms) in French, not just texts by non-French writers" (185, n. 56). In particular, he calls for a reassessment of French history and literature through the prism of postcolonial studies (178).

While aware of these paradoxes and potential pitfalls, we have chosen to keep the terms that are currently used to refer to each area of study, not because we do not agree with the critiques of the terms, but because we are seeking to make an intervention into both fields as they are constituted today and to make a case for increased cross-pollination between the two. It should be clear that we are arguing for transnational intersections among fields that have a natural affinity but are still too often separated by disciplinary and linguistic barriers.

Influential theorists writing in languages other than English have radically reshaped concepts of *francophonie* and its relationship with postcolonialism. French poststructuralist theorists have had an influence in both areas of study. Chapters by Erickson and Scharfman in this volume testify to the productive intellectual intersections between poststructuralism and postcolonialism in the francophone context. Indeed, the decentralization of the subject and of its agency in poststructuralism appears to find uncanny echoes in the deconstruction of assumptions of metropolitan mastery in both *francophonie* and postcolonialism, confronting and subverting, as Ronnie Scharfman claims, "tensions and resistances that still challenge the traditional hexagonal curriculum organized by century or genre" ("Before" 9). One might also mention the discursive and intellectual connections between Derrida and Spivak, Khatibi and Derrida, and the psychoanalytical triad Lacan/Fanon/Bhabha. Further, the francophone Caribbean theorist of decolonization Frantz Fanon has emerged as a leading precursor of postcolonial studies. Other important voices are the francophone Caribbean poet-theorist Aimé Césaire, Portuguese political theorist Amilcar Cabral, and Spanish Caribbean scholar Antonio Benitez-Rojo. Additionally, the analytical writings of Martinique's Edouard Glissant, the Caribbean *créolistes* Bernabé, Chamoiseau, and Confiant, Morocco's Abdelkebir Khatibi, and the work of French anthropologist Jean-Loup Amselle on such subjects as cultural creolization, ethnic pluralism, and immigration in a wider postcolonial French-speaking world have assumed increasing importance. Yet, except for work by scholars such as Robert Young and John McLeod, recent postcolonial criticism has made little more than a few basic references to any structural or perspectival role played by such contributions from French and francophone studies.

This is all the more surprising as postcolonial studies, at its inception, was a comparative endeavor that did include the French-speaking world. Edward Said in the ur-text of postcolonial studies, *Orientalism*, as well as Homi Bhabha and Gayatri Spivak in their 1980s and early 1990s work, based their theories on comparisons of the anglophone and francophone spheres, from French orientalist scholars to Baudelaire, Fanon, and the Algerian writer Assia Djebar. Not surprisingly, the postcolonial scholars who have been most influential in highlighting connections between francophone and anglophone contributions to postcolonial studies have been academics with comparative training that included the francophone sphere (such as Spivak, Lionnet, and Young).

Reasons for postcolonial studies' current lack of engagement with the francophone space are many and varied, and while theorists in Britain, Canada, and Australia certainly have their own reasons for (non)engagement with French studies, this phenomenon may be related to the convergence of two paradoxical tendencies in U.S. academia: the loss of interest in multilingual competency (except for Spanish, which is now the de facto second national language) and an increased commitment to internationalizing the curriculum (see Thomas in this volume). This paradox is due in part to the fact that efforts toward internationalizing curricula are generally envisioned in the context of a homogenized global economy in which the lingua franca is expected to be English. To these two tendencies, one might add the loss of economic and political power of Europe in general, which militates in favor of the loss of postcolonial theory's comparative edge outside of the field circumscribed by the English language.

International political power determines to a certain extent which languages will be accorded prominence, as Coursil and Perret argue in this volume. In this respect, it is interesting to note that cultural production in indigenous postcolonial languages is even more absent from postcolonial theory's concerns than works in other former colonial languages such as French or Spanish. If postcolonial studies does not want to become a major avenue through which the dominance of English as a U.S.-based imperializing and globalizing technology of power reinvents and reestablishes itself, it will need to go back to its comparative roots and expand its areas of study, including not only work done in other European languages but also cultural production performed in national and ethnic languages. This is the reason Gayatri Spivak argues that postcolonial studies is more accurately positioned in an interdisciplinary and/or cross-disciplinary framework than solely in English, and that the graduate curriculum should include the in-depth study of at least one language indigenous to the postcolonial world in order to contravene "the very *imperium* of English" ("Scattered Speculations" 277). This is equally true for francophone studies, and it resonates with Thomas's call for the need to pay more attention to African theorists in the development of postcolonial theory.

In this context, the role of translation emerges as central to bringing into focus the work of theorists writing in languages other than English (see Apter, "On Translation"). For example, one of the reasons for the fact that Edouard Glissant's work has had relatively more influence on the anglophone field of study than Khatibi's is that his major works have been translated into English, which is not the case for Khatibi's central 1983 study, *Maghreb pluriel*. Similarly, the recent availability in English of Achille Mbembe's *On the Postcolony* signals perhaps the first time in a decade that a francophone theorist's intervention is influencing postcolonial theory (Thomas). In turn, the perceived need for translation is often linked to the presence of particular scholars such as Maryse Condé, V. Y. Mudimbe, Edouard Glissant, Achille Mbembe, and Assia Djebar in the U.S. academy. Once again, theorists such as Abdelkebir Khatibi are marginalized in this context. It can only be hoped that some of his works, such as *Maghreb pluriel* and *Penser le Maghreb*, will be translated soon.

Just as contemporary postcolonial theory has a tendency toward linguistic parochialism, one of the factors that have made it difficult for francophone studies specialists in France to take the insights of anglophone postcolonial theory into account has been the fact that few of these texts have found their way into French translation (Murphy 174). Furthermore, too many francophone studies practitioners (even in the United States) have failed to incorporate the insights of scholars such as Gayatri Spivak, even though she is a comparatist whose work in French is crucial, if undervalued. Indeed, it seems that in French studies—except for Young's work—Spivak is primarily of interest for her translation of Derrida's *Of Grammatology*. The contrast between anglophone and francophone studies in this regard is striking. In anglophone postcolonial studies, Spivak has been enshrined as part of what some might humorously refer to as the "holy trinity" of Said, Bhabha, Spivak (see Varadharajan; Young, *White Mythologies*; Moore-Gilbert, "Spivak and Bhabha"). A reassessment of the centrality of Spivak's insights for French and francophone studies is clearly needed (see Donadey, "Francophone"). Such a reassessment might reorient Spivak's readings of transnationalism and postcolonial culture to address the complexities and ambiguities of the French imperial presence and its aftermath through an analysis of the pervasive paradoxes in postcolonial writing in French: a task arguably begun with the chapters by Brière, Larrier, and Coursil and Perret included in this volume.

In France, there is a general reluctance to consider the relevance of postcoloniality to French studies (Thomas, chapter 14; Apter, "French"; Murphy). However, as Eloise Brière's chapter in this volume makes clear, this perception is beginning to change slowly.[1] Outside of France, most works of criticism published on francophone literary and cultural production continue to inscribe themselves in the "francophone studies" model of close reading of texts with references to primarily French and francophone sources. Yet critics analyzing the works of francophone women writers often rely on a variety of feminist frameworks with regard to the analysis of specific texts. Particularly appropriate theories that are cited with some frequency include the intersectional theories of U.S. feminists of color such as Patricia Hill Collins and Mae Henderson, postcolonial feminist texts such as Chandra Talpade Mohanty's and Trinh Minh-ha's, and French/francophone feminist works such as those of Hélène Cixous (born in Algeria) and Luce Irigaray (born in Belgium). The impact of feminist theory on francophone studies has generally been greater than that of postcolonial theory to date. In other words, the point of entry of postcolonial theory into francophone studies has been primarily through postcolonial feminist theory. In the 1990s, few francophone studies scholars took up the term *postcolonial*, and when they did, it was often simply as a temporal marker in which *colonial* and *postcolonial* were used to refer to the periods before and after formal independence, respectively (see Sherzer 19, n. 29). For example, Green et al.'s *Postcolonial Subjects* uses the term *postcolonial* but not the theoretical apparatus it implies.

Only recently (with the exception of notable work by Françoise Lionnet and Robert Young) have scholars tried to bring together the insights of both fields. Chris Bongie's *Islands and Exiles*, for example, examines patterns of cultural identity and cultural mixing, using the work of several postcolonial theorists on hybridity, *métissage*, and transnationalism to show the extent of the imbrication of the colonial and the postcolonial worlds, centering on a "shifting middle ground of divergence and convergence" that he terms the "'creole continuum' of post/colonial identity politics" (52). On the other hand, Celia Britton's thoroughgoing engagement with the work of Martinican theorist and novelist Edouard Glissant provides a long-overdue extended analysis of the complex contribution made by this important contemporary thinker. In her *Edouard Glissant and Postcolonial Theory*, Britton juxtaposes anglophone and Glissantian theory to better elucidate the latter's principle of the *contrepoétique* [counterpoetics] that necessarily emerges from an analysis of the Martinican conundrum based on its status as a French *département*, that is, as part and parcel of the French territory. Similar in form and scope to the notion of counterdiscourse, Glissant's *contrepoétique* enables the elaboration of subversive strategies of language and resistance through techniques of narrative representation (on Glissant, see also Dash, "Postcolonial Thought," as well as Prabhu and Quayson in this volume). Similarly, in their coedited collection, *Postcolonial Theory and Criticism*, Laura Chrisman and Benita Parry contest the tendency to derive postcolonial conceptualizations from antinomial argumentation; indeed, they argue strongly for "more dialectical as well as relational approaches" and specifically engage Bhabha's concept of hybridity for its "inflexibility and partiality" (x). Britton and Syrotinski also address the need for less entrenched approaches and positions in this area, suggesting that "[p]ostcolonialism's longstanding concern with hybridity needs, perhaps, to become more reflexive" (3). Along similar theoretical lines, Anne Donadey's recent *Recasting Postcolonialism* engages and theorizes a number of power structures that imbricate Algerian women's writing and the postcolonial paradigm. More specifically, issues such as oppositionality and agency are problematized and critiqued from a multiplicity of perspectives whose very pluralism aims to subvert the hegemonic hold of theory. Adlai Murdoch's *Creole Identity in the French Caribbean Novel* uses a variety of theoretical approaches to exploit the creative ambiguities of departmentalism inscribed in a number of French Caribbean novels. Finally, Forsdick and Murphy's superb edited volume, *Francophone Postcolonial Studies: A Critical Introduction*, proposes to "decolonize" the term *francophone* though a dialogue with postcolonial studies ("The Case" 7). The volume provides a welcome historical emphasis, discusses linguistic issues, "tensions between nation and globalization," and specific regional considerations ("The Case" 4).

Like Forsdick and Murphy's volume, *Postcolonial Theory and Francophone Literary Studies* is necessarily a comparative and interdisciplinary venture. It goes beyond entrenched boundaries, be they linguistic and national (French versus English) or artificially induced political and temporal categories (anglophone versus francophone, pre- and postcolonial writing). Because both postcolonial and francophone studies rely on interdisciplinary models, this volume brings together insights and methods taken from literary criticism and theory, history (Mudimbe-Boyi, Harrow), film studies (Harrow, Woodhull), philosophy and linguistics (Coursil and Perret). Through conceptual, theoretical, and procedural revision, the range of discourses and approaches engendered by this conjunction of categories gains a new analytical footing.

This book is grouped thematically into four sections, each of which draws together a subcategory of francophone interests usefully illuminated and interrogated by postcolonial critique. The first, "Rethinking Theoretical Beginnings," looks back beyond the appearance of Edward Said's *Orientalism* in 1978 to displace and disprove the centrality of the metropolitan French context. Here, emphasis is placed on the tensions and teleologies of the early decolonization period, demonstrating the imbrication of the colonial presence not only with Fanon but with structuralism and the specter of Haiti as well, so important as we recognize the 200th anniversary of its independence in 2004. The first essay, E. Anthony Hurley's reading of Fanon, titled "Power, Purpose, the Presumptuousness of Postcoloniality, and Frantz Fanon's *Peau noire, masques blancs*," proposes to challenge the framework of the present volume by asserting that the "postcolonial" contains connotations that paradoxically match the ideologies of colonization; as a result, he argues, the effective subtext of postcoloniality is aimed at determining who will have power in postcolonial studies. Elisabeth Mudimbe-Boyi's "Unfathomable Toussaint" claims that the apparent ambiguities and contradictions in Toussaint Louverture's persona are in fact nodal points on an evolutionary arc that counts on its subject's inscrutability. Alec G. Hargreaves's "A Neglected Precursor" analyzes the tensions and limitations of Roland Barthes's work on semiology and its theoretical contribution to postcoloniality. As Chela Sandoval suggests, "There is a permeable boundary . . . between Fanon's work and that of Barthes" (130). Her work traces both the similarities and the differences between these two theorists' contributions to a methodology of emancipation. Read together, Hurley's and Hargreaves's chapters point to the differences between Fanon's and Barthes's contributions. Whereas Hargreaves argues for Barthes's inclusion in the postcolonial field as a precursor, Hurley provocatively contends that to place Fanon under the rubric of the postcolonial is to dull the revolutionary edge of his writings.

The essays in Part II, grouped under the rubric "Postcolonialism, Modernity, and French Identities," engage and revise many commonly held assumptions regarding French identity. For example, in "Nomadic Thought, Postcolonialism, and Maghrebian Writing," John D. Erickson explores key aspects of Maghrebian literature in French through the concept of nomadic thought and its impact on notions of nationalism and pluralism in a postcolonial context. In "Narratives of Internal Exile," Ronnie Scharfman examines the challenge posed by an Algerian background for such "French" writers as Hélène Cixous and Jacques Derrida, the impossiblity of autobiography for dispossessed subjects, and the resulting role of what she terms "privileged difference" in taking a stand against various forms of oppression. In "*Mémoires d'Immigrés*," Kenneth W. Harrow engages the role of film in assessing the impact of postwar Algerian immigration into France and the resulting transformation of the HLMs [subsidized housing] of the *banlieues* [poor suburbs] by male immigrants and their families. In "French Interwar Cinema," Winifred Woodhull analyzes French film of the period as a form of "vernacular modernism" that drew on the transnational flows of capital, labor, commodities, gendered ideologies, and culture to breach the boundaries of the French imperial project. The continually shifting definitions of postcolonialism and identity in the francophone world are thus shown to be increasingly applicable both to France and to its former colonies, as patterns of ethnicity, culture, and visual and narrative representation remain in constant flux.

Part III, "Displacing *Francophonie*: Migration and Transcultural Identities," examines the scope of postwar demographic shifts and their consequences. In "Quebec and France," Eloise A. Brière analyzes the paradoxes of Québécois exceptionalism, the extent to which it is (not) a distinct society, different from the rest of Canada and from France, and the resulting revision of issues of center and periphery. In "Displaced Discourses," Michel Laronde deconstructs the complex intersection of literatures of immigration, the francophone diaspora, and postcoloniality; the simultaneous presence of such myriad influences in contemporary France demands a redefinition and reconception of these initiatory categories. And in their survey of "The Francophone Postcolonial Field," Jacques Coursil and Delphine Perret revisit key historical moments to look more closely at such terms as *colonization*, *decolonization*, and *globalization*; since postcolonial theory stresses forms of language use, the conflicted intersection of theoretical concepts and historical tropes becomes a key issue. The in-depth interrogations of the term *francophonie* undertaken here, then, expose the trenchant ambiguities that stymie most attempts at definition and complicate the relationship to the *métropole*. Ultimately, the impossibility of fixing any of these terms is firmly foregrounded.

Finally, in Part IV, "Theorizing the Black Atlantic," the historico-cultural roles and relationships that link Haiti, Guadeloupe and Martinique, and Africa to France are redefined along new lines that move us away from a French center-periphery model. In "Borders, Books, and *Points de Repère*," Renée Larrier examines issues of border crossing involving Haitian writers and the broader questions of identity, language production, location, and transnationalism that Haitian literature raises. In "Francophone Studies/Postcolonial Studies," Anjali Prabhu and Ato Quayson reconsider a number of theoretical questions arising out of hybridity's central role in postcolonial theory. Through close readings of Homi K. Bhabha and Edouard Glissant, they posit the former's notion of hybridity as a discursive space giving rise to the possibility of figuring difference, over against Glissant's more radical notion of the other of thought, generating an explicative encounter that marks a key move toward the larger project of postcolonializing. And in

"Intersections and Trajectories," Dominic Thomas invites us to reconsider our understanding of postcoloniality by underscoring the importance of African theoretical models, by interrogating France's long and complicated history with Africa, and by foregrounding African concepts of and contributions to francophone studies. Through these broadly ranging discussions of language use in "French" literary history, assumptions of uniformity, unidirectionality, hierarchy, and the purity or porousness of cultural practices are subverted and ultimately thrown into disarray. New paradigms for the postcolonial and its related linguistic expression are established through the exploration of alternative geographical and cultural axes. Finally, in her afterword, Françoise Lionnet uses the prism of gender to highlight the ways in which difference, in its several guises, compounds the shape and substance of the francophone postcolonial field. She argues that feminist theory, in particular, should be a central element in the new configuration of the field.

The future of francophone as well as postcolonial studies is thus clearly both interdisciplinary and comparative. Some have questioned whether francophone studies belongs primarily to French departments, or if it may find a more ideal home elsewhere. Larrier in this volume as well as Réda Bensmaïa, Leslie Rabine, and Nelly Furman agree that the academic division of departments based on national literatures no longer reflects geopolitical realities because of transnational and global circuits of exchange (Bensmaïa 275; Rabine 296; Furman 69). Francophone studies scholars have been interdisciplinary from the beginning, whether working on anthropological approaches to African literature or placing literature in its multiple historical and cultural contexts. Indeed, Bensmaïa's description of the postcolonial writer as "simultaneous translator" and "professional foreigner," seems a fitting designation for the francophone studies scholar as well (305–06). The most exciting and insightful scholarship, both in postcolonial and in francophone studies, has been interdisciplinary and comparative (Spivak, Lionnet). In particular, several critics are now moving toward a conceptualization of transnational/transcolonial studies that better represents the current geopolitical situation, avoids the political pitfalls of terms such as *postcolonial* and *francophone*, and allows critics to bypass arbitrary disciplinary and linguistic divisions (see Larrier, Brière, and Thomas in this volume; in works cited, Gilroy, Lionnet "Transnationalism").

As this book makes clear, both postcolonial theory and francophone studies will benefit from developing a sustained comparative engagement with each other, "by demonstrat[ing]," as Britton and Syrotinski put it, "the potential gain to be had from acknowledging postcolonial theory's internal tensions and contradictions, and from opening its frontiers to greater cross-border activity between postcolonialism and other theories" (5). For example, postcolonial studies may be reminded of the importance of attending closely to the specificities of text and context of production. It can learn to pay more attention to the mediation provided by translations of texts into English in order to avoid misinterpretations by taking into account the interpretations of scholars working with the original texts. In this way, it will reach a better understanding of decolonization through a reassessment of precursors to postcolonial theory such as Fanon, Barthes, and Sartre (see Hurley and Hargreaves in this volume; in works cited, Haddour, Williams). In particular, the poststructuralist bent of much postcolonial theory may have prevented it from taking into account the anticolonial work of the Marxist Sartre (Williams) or of the structuralist early Barthes (Hargreaves in this volume). Finally, new transnational paradigms make a knowledge of the francophone context necessary for scholars interested in writers living in English-speaking countries and writing in English but hailing from (at least partly) francophone areas of the world, such as the Haitian-American writer Edwidge Danticat (see Larrier in this volume).

Similarly, francophone studies will benefit from the mature theoretical and ethical constructs of thinkers such as Spivak and Bhabha. A sustained engagement with the concerns of postcolonial theory could help France work through its colonial history and revisit its ideology of universalism and assimilation (Thomas in this volume; Apter, "French" 171–72; Murphy 178–79). Finally, such an engagement will help question naturalized and homogenized views of Frenchness that were created historically in opposition to France's constructed "others" and that still enjoy wide currency today (Brière in this volume).

Postcolonial theory is now beginning to take into account the insights of U.S. ethnic studies, and important advancements in knowledge are evident in the work of scholars such as Singh and Schmidt, Jenny Sharpe, and Christine MacLeod, who are addressing the growing parallels, connections, and mergings, as well as the points of divergence, between multicultural and postcolonial studies. Similar productive intersections are called for between postcolonial theory and francophone studies, and the call is fortunately beginning to be heeded. The field of francophone studies is currently evolving so quickly that it is not an exaggeration to say that it is at a new juncture in its history. An increasing number of researchers in the United Kingdom, the United States, and France are now bridging the gap between francophone and postcolonial studies. They are theorizing "francophone postcolonial studies" (Murphy 185) and are thus reconfiguring the field. To take the year 2003 only as an example, a new journal, *Francophone Postcolonial Studies*, has been launched; special issues of *Yale French Studies* and of *MLN* as well as two edited book collections, *Francophone Postcolonial Studies: A Critical*

Introduction by Charles Forsdick and David Murphy and *Les Etudes littéraires francophones: Etat des lieux* by Lieven D'hulst and Jean-Marc Moura, have been published. In particular, the creation of a journal entirely devoted to "an approach that highlights a distinctive but reciprocal relationship between Francophone Studies and Postcolonial Studies" is an important sign of recognition by a critical mass of academics that these intersecting fields would benefit from developing sustained connections (*Francophone Postcolonial Studies* 6). We are pleased to witness and participate in current reconceptualizations of the field and hope that this book will contribute to and inspire further research in these areas.

Note

1. Scholars in other European studies fields are similarly beginning to take stock of the impact of colonization on nations as disparate as Germany, Russia, and Italy (Zantop, Layton, Palumbo). There is still room for further study on this topic in Europe, especially with regard to Belgium.

Works Cited

Apter, Emily. "French Colonial Studies and Postcolonial Theory." *SubStance* 76/77 (1995): 169–80.

———. "On Translation in a Global Market." *Public Culture* 13.1 (Winter 2001): 1–12.

Bensmaïa, Réda. "Political Geography of Literature: On Khatibi's 'Professional Traveller.'" *French Cultural Studies: Criticism at the Crossroads*. Ed. Marie-Pierre Le Hir and Dana Strand. Albany: State University of New York Press, 2000. 295–308.

Bongie, Chris. *Islands and Exiles: The Creole Identities of Post/Colonial Literature*. Stanford, Calif.: Stanford University Press, 1998.

Britton, Celia M. *Edouard Glissant and Postcolonial Theory: Strategies of Language and Resistance*. Charlottesville: University Press of Virginia, 1999.

Britton, Celia M., and Michael Syrotinski. "Introduction." *Paragraph* 24.3 (November 2001): 1–11.

Chrisman, Laura, and Benita Parry, eds. *Postcolonial Theory and Criticism: Essays and Studies 1999*. Cambridge, U.K.: Brewer, 2000.

Dash, J. Michael. "Caraïbe fantôme: The Play of Difference in the Francophone Caribbean." *Yale French Studies* 103 (2003): 93–105.

———. "Postcolonial Thought and the Francophone Caribbean." *Francophone Postcolonial Studies: A Critical Introduction*. Ed. Charles Forsdick and David Murphy. London: Arnold, 2003. 231–41.

Derrida, Jacques. *Of Grammatology*. Trans. Gayatri Chakravorty Spivak. Baltimore: Johns Hopkins University Press, 1976.

D'hulst, Lieven, and Jean-Marc Moura, eds. *Les Etudes littéraires francophones: état des lieux*. Lille, France: Editions du Conseil scientifique de l'Université Lille III, 2003.

Donadey, Anne. "Francophone Women Writers and Postcolonial Theory." *Francophone Postcolonial Studies: A Critical Introduction*. Ed. Charles Forsdick and David Murphy. London: Arnold, 2003. 202–10.

———. *Recasting Postcolonialism: Women Writing between Worlds*. Portsmouth, N.H.: Heinemann, 2001.

Forsdick, Charles, and David Murphy. "The Case for Francophone Postcolonial Studies." *Francophone Postcolonial Studies: A Critical Introduction*. Ed. Charles Forsdick and David Murphy. London: Arnold, 2003. 1–14.

Forsdick, Charles, and David Murphy, eds. *Francophone Postcolonial Studies: A Critical Introduction*. London: Arnold, 2003.

Francophone Postcolonial Studies 1.1 (Spring/Summer 2003).

Furman, Nelly. "French Studies: Back to the Future." *Profession* 1998: 68–80.

Gilroy, Paul. *The Black Atlantic: Modernity and Double Consciousness*. Cambridge, Mass.: Harvard University Press, 1993.

Green, Mary Jean, Karen Gould, Micheline Rice-Maximin, Keith L. Walker, and Jack A. Yeager, eds. *Postcolonial Subjects: Francophone Women Writers*. Minneapolis: University of Minnesota Press, 1996.

Haddour, Azzedine. "The Camus-Sartre Debate and the Colonial Question in Algeria." *Francophone Postcolonial Studies: A Critical Introduction*. Ed. Charles Forsdick and David Murphy. London: Arnold, 2003. 66–76.

Khatibi, Abdelkebir. *Maghreb pluriel*. Paris: Denoël, 1983.

———. *Penser le Maghreb*. Rabat, Morocco: Société marocaine des éditeurs réunis, 1993.

Laroussi, Farid, and Christopher L. Miller. "Editors' Preface: French and Francophone: The Challenge of Expanding Horizons." *Yale French Studies* 103 (2003): 1–6.

Layton, Susan. *Russian Literature and Empire: Conquest of the Caucasus from Pushkin to Tolstoy*. Cambridge, U.K.: Cambridge University Press, 1994.

Le Hir, Marie-Pierre, and Dana Strand, eds. *French Cultural Studies: Criticism at the Crossroads*. Albany: State University of New York Press, 2000.

Lionnet, Françoise. *Autobiographical Voices: Race, Gender, Self-Portraiture*. Ithaca, N.Y.: Cornell University Press, 1989.

———. "Introduction." *MLN* 118.4 (2003): 783–86.

———. *Postcolonial Representations: Women, Literature, Identity*. Ithaca, N.Y.: Cornell University Press, 1995.

———. "Transnationalism, Postcolonialism or Transcolonialism? Reflections on Los Angeles, Geography, and the Uses of Theory." *Emergences* 10.1 (2000): 25–35.

MacLeod, Christine. "Black American Literature and the Postcolonial Debate." *The Yearbook of English Studies* 27 (1997): 51–65.

Mbembe, Achille. *On the Postcolony*. Berkeley: University of California Press, 2001.

McLeod, John. "Contesting Contexts: Francophone Thought and Anglophone Postcolonialism." *Francophone Postcolonial Studies: A Critical Introduction*. Ed. Charles Forsdick and David Murphy. London: Arnold, 2003. 192–201.

MLN 118.4 (2003). Special issue on "Francophone Studies: New Landscapes." Ed. Françoise Lionnet and Dominic Thomas.

Moore-Gilbert, Bart. *Postcolonial Theory: Contexts, Practices, Politics*. London: Verso, 1997.

———. "Spivak and Bhabha." *A Companion to Postcolonial Studies*. Ed. Henry Schwarz and Sangeeta Ray. Oxford, U.K.: Blackwell Publishers, 2000. 451–66.

Moore-Gilbert, Bart, Gareth Stanton, and Willy Maley, eds. "Introduction." *Postcolonial Criticism*. London: Longman, 1997. 1–72.

Murdoch, H. Adlai. *Creole Identity in the French Caribbean Novel*. Gainesville: University Press of Florida, 2001.

Murphy, David. "De-centring French Studies: Towards a Postcolonial Theory of Francophone Cultures." *French Cultural Studies* 13.2 (June 2002): 165–85.

Palumbo, Patrizia, ed. *A Place in the Sun: Africa in Italian Colonial Culture from Post-Unification to the Present*. Berkeley: University of California Press, 2003.

Parker, Gabrielle. "'Francophonie' and 'universalité': Evolution of Two Notions Conjoined." *Francophone Postcolonial Studies: A Critical Introduction*. Ed. Charles Forsdick and David Murphy. London: Arnold, 2003. 91–101.

Quayson, Ato, and David Theo Goldberg. "Introduction: Scale and Sensibility." *Relocating Postcolonialism*. Ed. David Theo Goldberg and Ato Quayson. Oxford, U.K.: Blackwell Publishers, 2002. xi–xxii.

Rabine, Leslie. "Interdisciplinarity, Knowledge, and Desire: A Reading of Marcel Griaule's *Dieu d'eau*." *French Cultural Studies: Criticism at the Crossroads*. Ed. Marie-Pierre Le Hir and Dana Strand. Albany: State University of New York Press, 2000. 275–94.

Rosello, Mireille. "Unhoming Francophone Studies: A House in the Middle of the Current." *Yale French Studies* 103 (2003): 123–32.

Said, Edward W. *Orientalism*. New York: Pantheon Books, 1978.

Scharfman, Ronnie. "Before the Postcolonial." *Yale French Studies* 103 (2003): 9–16.

Sharpe, Jenny. "Postcolonial Studies in the House of US Multiculturalism." *A Companion to Postcolonial Studies*. Ed. Henry Schwarz and Sangeeta Ray. Malden, Mass.: Blackwell Publishers, 2000. 112–25.

Sherzer, Dina. "Introduction." *Cinema, Colonialism, Postcolonialism: Perspectives from the French and Francophone World*. Ed. Dina Sherzer. Austin: University of Texas Press, 1996. 1–19.

Singh, Amritjit, and Peter Schmidt. "On the Borders Between U.S. Studies and Postcolonial Theory." *Postcolonial Theory and the United States: Race, Ethnicity, and Literature*. Ed. Amritjit Singh and Peter Schmidt. Jackson: University Press of Mississippi, 2000. 3–69.

Spivak, Gayatri Chakravorty. "Scattered Speculations on the Question of Culture Studies." *Outside in the Teaching Machine*. New York: Routledge, 1993. 255–84.

Varadharajan, Asha. *Exotic Parodies: Subjectivity in Adorno, Said, and Spivak*. Minneapolis: University of Minnesota Press, 1995.

Williams, Patrick. "'Faire peau neuve'—Césaire, Fanon, Memmi, Sartre and Senghor." *Francophone Postcolonial Studies: A Critical Introduction*. Ed. Charles Forsdick and David Murphy. London: Arnold, 2003. 181–91.

Yale French Studies 103 (2003). Special issue on "French and Francophone: The Challenge of Expanding Horizons." Ed. Farid Laroussi and Christopher L. Miller.

Young, Robert J. C. *Postcolonialism: An Historical Introduction.* Oxford, U.K.: Blackwell Publishers, 2001.

———. *White Mythologies: Writing History and the West.* London: Routledge, 1990.

Zantop, Susanne. "Colonial Legends, Postcolonial Legacies." *A User's Guide to German Cultural Studies.* Ed. Scott Denham, Irene Kacandes, and Jonathan Petropoulos. Ann Arbor: University of Michigan Press, 1997. 189–205.

I

Rethinking Theoretical Beginnings

2

Power, Purpose, the Presumptuousness of Postcoloniality, and Frantz Fanon's *Peau noire, masques blancs*

E. Anthony Hurley

This chapter proposes to challenge the very framework in which the present volume is set—the masked ideological assumptions of the discourse of postcoloniality.[1] In my view, adopting or even accepting postcoloniality as a frame for discussing the literary and artistic productions of people who for centuries endured the horrors of slavery and colonization is not without presumption, since the hierarchized structures, social, political, and psychological, of colonial societies are still firmly in place even in those territories whose political status officially signals the end of the colonial era. I contend that such a frame contains a hidden purpose—that of determining who will have power in the neocolonial empires of postcolonial studies.

Frantz Fanon's experience, both his lived experience and his experience as the subject or object of literary discourse, as expressed in *Peau noire, masques blancs*, exemplifies some of the complex linkages and tensions that exist between the (successfully?) colonized subject and the (ex)colonial power. What I propose is not a specific rereading or reexamination of *Peau noire, masques blancs*, but rather a meditation on the somewhat mythical Fanon that first emerged in this text and the response to this person and persona by literary commentators in the context of the following questions: What purpose does the reading or critiquing of Fanon and *Peau noire* serve in the context of postcoloniality? What images of Fanon emerge from postcolonial critics? What groups, what ideas seek or find power in the critical appropriation of Fanon? These questions will form a backdrop for the larger frame of the following question: Who gains power and who loses from the propagation of the existence of postcoloniality? I am very aware that my own discussion of this topic is both problematical and presumptuous, since I cannot engage in such a discussion without to some extent compromising my own integrity, without becoming enmeshed in the same mystification that I am claiming to challenge. I am also very much aware that part of this process necessitates my becoming involved, or embroiled, in the "politics of mention," (an expression attributed to Hortense Spillers), unavoidably validating or enhancing the "authority" of commentators whose ideological positions conflict with my own.[2]

Since the concept of postcoloniality depends for its very existence on its historical precedent, let us first look at the Fanon of *Peau noire* within the context of colonialism. The Fanon of this text is patently a deeply conflicted individual, assuming (unintentionally) the superiority of French culture (linguistic, intellectual, aesthetic practices and traditions) even when attempting to devise an alternative psychological and cultural independence. This assumption is reflected, for instance, in his judgment of the literary productions "en patois" of a writer such as fellow Martinican Gilbert Gratiant. In Fanon's view, "La valeur poétique de ces créations est fort douteuse" [The poetic value of these creations is very questionable] (42).[3] A similar assumption of French cultural superiority is most directly and tellingly articulated in his reaction to a Dr. Michel Salomon, a Jew whom Fanon characterizes as a racist despite his long experience of antisemitism: "Qu'est-ce que cette histoire de peuple noir, de nationalité nègre? Je suis Français. Je suis intéressé à la culture française, à la civilisation française. . . . Je suis intéressé personnellement au destin français, aux valeurs françaises, à la nation française. Qu'ai-je à faire, moi, d'un Empire noir?" [What's all this about a black people, about black nationality? I am French. I am involved in French culture, in French civilization. . . . I am personally involved in the destiny of France, in French values, in the French nation. What does a black Empire have to do with me?] (184).

Fanon's purpose, nevertheless, as expressed in the introduction, is "libérer l'homme de couleur de lui-même" [to liberate the man of color from himself] (26). He is careful, however, to indicate the importance of the socioeconomic dimension to this liberation: "[L]a véritable désalienation du Noir implique une prise de conscience abrupte des réalités économiques et sociales" [True disalienation of the black man involves an abrupt awareness of economic and social realities] (28). Fanon further specifies, in the first chapter, that though in the first instance he is talking about "le Noir Antillais" [Antillean blacks], "par delà l'Antillais nous visons tout homme colonisé" [beyond Antilleans, we are aiming at all colonized people] (34). Throughout the text, Fanon remains attuned to the significance of the harsh sociopolitical realities with which many blacks are confronted: "Nous ne poussons pas la naïveté jusqu'à croire que les appels à la raison ou au respect de l'homme puissent changer le réel. Pour le nègre qui travaille dans les plantations de canne de Robert, il n'y a qu'une solution: la lutte" [We are not so naïve as to think that reality can be changed by appeals to reason or to respect for mankind. For the nigger working in the sugar cane plantations of the Robert region, there is only one solution: struggle] (201).[4]

Despite this awareness, by the end of the text, which is self-exploratory, cathartic, even tentative, a no less conflicted Fanon emerges, still a colonized subject, but determined to continue his personal decolonization process. He can confirm his distance from the Aimé Césaire persona of *Cahier d'un retour au pays natal* with the assertion: "Ma peau noire n'est pas dépositaire de valeurs spécifiques" [My black skin is not the guardian of specific values] (204). Fanon concludes his meditation with the often-quoted prayer that echoes, but proclaims his separation from, the Cesairian position: "O mon corps, fais de moi toujours un homme qui interroge!" [O body of mine, make me always a man who questions!] (208). We note that the process of rigorous self-examination, which Césaire's poetic persona undergoes and narrates in the course of the *Cahier*, leads him to adopt a position of sacred commitment and dedication to his native land and its people: "Faites de ma tête une tête de proue / et de moi-même, mon coeur, ne faites ni un père, ni un frère, / ni un fils, mais le père, mais le frère, mais le fils, / ni un mari, mais l'amant de cet unique peuple. . . . / Faites-moi commissaire de son sang / Faites-moi dépositaire de son ressentiment / faites de moi un homme de terminaison / faites de moi un homme d'initiation / faites de moi un homme de recueillement / mais faites aussi de moi un homme d'ensemencement" [Make my head a prow's head / and of me, my heart, make neither a father, nor a brother / nor a son, but the father, but the brother, but the son, / not a husband, but the lover of this unique people. . . . / Make me commissioner of its blood / make me guardian of its resentment / make me a man of termination / make me a man of initiation / make me a man of contemplation / but make me also a man of implantation] (123). Fanon, still at the stage of questioning, evidently becomes uncomfortable with Césaire's expressions of certitude, of righteous conviction and focused dedication. And we know where this questioning leads him: to a geographical displacement to North Africa and to a more direct political, anticolonial activism that justifies physical violence as a response to the physical and psychic violence that for him is part and parcel of colonialism.

Within the past few decades we have seen the emergence within British and North American academic circles of a discourse, even perhaps an ideology, of postcoloniality that claims Fanon as one of its apostles. Robert J. C. Young, in *Postcolonialism: An Historical Introduction*, attributes the birth of contemporary postcolonial theory first to Fanon and later to Edward Said: "Edward W. Said . . . demonstrated that the historical practices and the full range of effects of colonialism on the colonized territories and their peoples, could be analyzed conceptually and discursively, and it was this that created the academic field of postcolonialism. . . . Apart from Said, postcolonial theory is predominantly based on the work of Frantz Fanon, and it was Fanon who developed the analysis of colonialism as a single formation" (18).

While Said's judgment of Fanon relates more specifically to the later Fanon of *Sociologie d'une révolution* (first published in 1959) and *Les Damnés de la terre* (first published in 1961), it is clear even in *Peau noire* that Fanon, in his critique of Octave Mannoni's *Psychologie de la colonisation*, is thinking of colonialism as a form of institutionalized exploitation. The view of Fanon as an apostle of decolonization is expanded by Roger Berger, who, in his 1990 review article "Contemporary Anglophone Literary Theory: The Return of Fanon," invokes Fanon as a significant marker of literary theory, equating Fanon's politics of decolonization to a critical positionality. Berger alludes to the significant division in African literary theory to be found in what he calls the Fanonist "threshold" that "divides 'accommodation' with existing western textual strategies and rejection of Eurocentric methodologies in the search for an Afrocentric means of reading and understanding texts" (142). To consider Fanon as Afrocentric (in the sense proposed by Molefi Asante), however attractive such a view might be to some of us, is to distort Fanon's ideological tendency. Fanon has never explicitly or implicitly rejected European intellectual traditions or methodologies. Berger implies, nevertheless, that Fanon, because of his own intellectual and practical initiatives, provides postcolonial literary theorists with a choice of attitude and approach. Similarly, Nicholas Harrison, in his 1998 article "Positioning (Fanon)," while recognizing the complexity of even situating Fanon because of his physical and intellectual movement, and the different signals Fanon gives about his own "situatedness" (in the context of his somewhat contradictory allegiance to and support of Martinique, the French Resistance movement during World War II, and Algeria, as well as his similarly contradictory stances on anticolonialism and on universalism) (58), asserts nevertheless that Fanon is "one of the key figures of postcolonial theory" (57).

These assumptions, apparently innocent and transparently beyond dispute, which undergird the representations of Fanon in relation to postcoloniality, need, however, to be challenged. At the very least, we need to pose and respond to this question: What are the semantic and sociopolitical applications and implications of the elusive terminology of postcoloniality that includes *postcolonial*, *postcolonialism*, and *postcoloniality*?

Young relates the concept of postcoloniality directly to documented historical and political occurrences: "The postcolonial is a dialectical concept that marks the broad historical facts of decolonization and the determined achievement of sovereignty—but also the realities of nations and peoples emerging into a new imperialistic context of economic and sometimes political domination" (57). This accurate but limited definition does not account for the more elusive applications that surround the term, particularly in the context of literary theory. Jeanie Suk, in *Postcolonial Paradoxes in French Caribbean Writing*, underlines the problematic nature of the term *postcolonial.* Suk rightly observes that "it possesses an uneasily defined temporality, politics, and institutional location. . . . [It has] myriad possible designations—among them a historical period, a political status, a geographical area, a critical stance, an intellectual development" (1). Despite this acknowledgment of the fluidity of the term, however, Suk finds herself later espousing the view that "'[p]ostcolonial' then, becomes a contractual indicator of a practice of reading that accentuates the commonality of the problems that arise from colonialism, its aftermath, and continuation, regardless of formal political status" (19). Suk thereby attests to the inevitability of the link that postcoloniality has to colonialism and thus to the enduring traces of colonialism within postcolonial literary practices.

It needs to be recognized, however, that Suk's definition, which attempts to mediate among the apparently conflicting designations of postcoloniality, cannot do so without acknowledging the undeniability of a subtextual "post-ness" that has political and ideological implications and suggests a status different from, maybe even better than, that of the colonial. It needs to be realized, also, that postcoloniality, as an abstract referent, avoids explicit ideological positioning (unlike, for example, decolonization or anticolonialism). It operates in a region of opacity that blunts edges, that conceals certainties, that permits misunderstandings and even distortions. Postcoloniality is effectively PC, safe.

In the entry on *post-colonialism/postcolonialism* in *Key Concepts in Post-colonial Studies*, Bill Ashcroft, Gareth Griffiths, and Helen Tiffin suggest that "the term 'post-colonial' per se was first used to refer to cultural interactions within colonial societies in literary circles. . . . This was part of an attempt to politicize and focus the concerns of fields such as Commonwealth literature and the study of the so-called New Literatures in English which had been initiated in the late 1960s. The term has subsequently been widely used to signify the political, linguistic and cultural experience of societies that were former European colonies" (186). Indeed, there has emerged a whole body of theory that centers on the postcoloniality of the United States, Canada, Australia, and New Zealand. Amritjit Singh and Peter Schmidt, in *Postcolonial Theory and the United States*, discuss the contradictory situation of the United States in this context: "The U.S. may be understood as the world's first postcolonial *and* neocolonial country. . . . While the U.S. defined itself as the world's first independent and anti-colonial nation-state it simultaneously incorporated many of the defining features of European colonial networks—including the color line—into its economic and cultural life" (5).

Deborah L. Madsen, in the opening essay, "Beyond the Commonwealth," of her edited volume *Post-Colonial Literatures: Expanding the Canon*, references Helen Tiffin and Diana Brydon's reminder in *Decolonizing Fictions* (1993) that "the United States, in particular, as the only ex-British colony fully to become an imperial power in its own right, can no longer easily be grouped with countries whose cultures are still largely determined by dependency" (4). Even more to the point, Karen Piper, in her article "Post-Colonialism in the United States?" in the same Madsen volume, clarifies that "The US, then, is post-colonial in the sense that its fundamental identity is wrapped in a colonizing project—whether settler or indigenous, the inhabitants of the US have been impacted by the colonial ideal of resource 'development' or exploitation" (19). Similarly, C. Richard King, in *Postcolonial America*, attempts a rereading of postcoloniality to include the United States. He observes "in the contemporary United States . . . a shift from the celebration, comfortable acceptance, and largely unquestioned appropriateness of conquest and colonization to the predicaments associated with living through the illegitimate, uncomfortable, conflicted aftermath of an irreversible conquest" (7). King cautions, however, that "[r]eformulating postcoloniality and American empire . . . demands a sensitivity to the contradictions of 'the American experience'" (8).

Lawrence Buell, in "Postcolonial Anxiety in Classic U.S. Literature," observes that "the argument has been pressed, by Canadian and Australian scholars particularly for a kind of postcolonial dynamic operating in the vexed relation of settler or white creole cultures . . . to the cultures of their respective imperia" (196). Stephen Slemon, in an essay entitled "Post-colonial Critical Theories," remarks that the term *post-colonial state* "begs the question of the difference between, on the one hand, 'white' or 'invader-settler' 'post-colonial' nations like Australia, Canada, New Zealand, or South Africa and, on the other hand, 'Third-World' 'post-colonial' nations like Ghana, Pakistan, Vanuatu, or Barbados" (181).

Alan Lawson and Chris Tiffin, in their conclusion to *De-scribing Empire*, consider it "one of the apparent paradoxes of the field" that "post-colonialism is often seen to attempt to construct and analyse colonialism as an overarching, transhistorical practice, whereas at all levels its constitutive marker is one of heterogeneity" (230). The focus of Lawson and Tiffin is primarily with the "settler subject" (231) (i.e., white?), both male and female, to the point that they contend, with illuminating and ironic frankness, that "[t]he very diversity of colonial experience with its Eurocentred hierarchies has fathered a shadowing counter-hierarchy in which he or she who can most plausibly claim the kiss of the whip is accorded the pre-eminent speaking position" (232).

In his 1996 article "When Was the Post-colonial?" Stuart Hall poses a series of questions that suggest some of the complexities of the competing claims of postcoloniality:

> Is Britain "post-colonial" in the same sense as the U.S.? Indeed, is the U.S. usefully thought of as "postcolonial" at all? Should the term be commonly applied to Australia, which is a white settler colony, and to India? Can Algerians living at home and in France, the French and the *pied noir* settlers, all be "postcolonial"? Is Latin America "post-colonial" even though its independence struggles were fought early in the nineteenth century, long before the recent stage of "decolonization" to which the term more evidently refers, and were led by descendants of Spanish settlers who had colonized their own "native people"? (245)

It must be recognized that the focus of critics such as Diana Brydon and Stephen Slemon on/from Canada and Helen Tiffin on/from Australia exemplifies the extent to which attitudes to and interpretations of postcoloniality are informed by the nature of the colonizing experience to which one has been exposed and to which one, consciously or unconsciously, subscribes.

In general, however, there is, in the application of postcoloniality to contemporary literary discourse, a tendency to focus on the accession to independence in the mid-twentieth century of "former" colonies of European powers, largely in regions characterized as the Third World. As Young asserts, "[p]ostcolonial . . . critique is united by a common political and moral consensus towards the history and legacy of western colonialism. It presupposes that the history of European expansion and the occupations of most of the global land-mass between 1492 and 1945 mask a process that was both specific and problematic" (5). *Postcolonial* thus implies a difference, at the sociopolitical and historical levels, between those western European practitioners of colonialist expansionism (including Euro-America) and the societies and peoples (of Africa, the Caribbean, South America, Asia, and even within the United States) who were and are the victims and inheritors of this expansionism. It is this oppression-liberation dialectic that plays itself out at the level of literary critical theory and practice under the umbrella of postcolonialism. It is difficult, therefore, to deny the political dimensions of postcoloniality. As Young asserts: "Postcolonial critique focuses on forces of oppression and coercive domination that operate in the contemporary world; the politics of anti-colonialism and neocolonialism, race, gender, nationalism, class and ethnicities define its terrain" (11).

At the same time, the term *postcolonial* in its very abstractness includes connotations of transcendence, even of superiority, that match the ideology of colonization. Kwame Anthony Appiah, in defining postcoloniality, relates it to the context of world capitalism and the role that intellectuals (such as ourselves, contributors to this volume) play in supporting the capitalistic enterprise: "Postcoloniality is the condition of what we might ungenerously call a comprador intelligentsia: of a relatively small, Western-style, Western-trained, group of writers and thinkers who mediate the trade in cultural commodities of world capitalism at the periphery. . . . Postcolonial intellectuals in Africa . . . are almost entirely dependent for their support on two institutions: the African university—an institution whose intellectual life is overwhelmingly constituted as Western—and the Euro-American publisher and reader" (149). Appiah's deliberate use of the vocabulary of Third World (Chinese) revolutionary socialism, with its suggestion of native agents in the pay of foreign powers, raises issues of political commitment and loyalty. Appiah's definition reinforces the notion of complicity with a colonial or colonizing ideology or power and encourages us to ask ourselves questions such as the following: To what extent do we consider ourselves part of this "comprador intelligentsia"? To what extent are we participating, consciously or unconsciously, as mediators in the trade in cultural commodities such as the real and symbolic "Fanon"? To what extent do we consider ourselves, in embracing postcoloniality, complicitous with neocolonizing powers?

Another dimension of postcolonialism that must be considered is its link to the related problem of racism. Eileen Julien, in a recent article that discusses convergences between Césaire, Fanon, and Wright in relation to culture and decolonization, reminds us that, in Fanon's view, colonialism is synonymous with racism (157). In *Peau noire* Fanon makes a series of quasi-syllogistic propositions that underscore the association he finds between European civilization, expansionism, and racism: "Une société est raciste ou ne l'est pas" [A society is either racist or not] (89); "Le racisme colonial ne diffère pas des autres racismes" [Colonial racism is not different from any other racism] (91); "l'Europe a une structure raciste. . . . La France est un pays raciste" [Europe has a racist structure. . . . France is a racist country; emphasis in the original] (94). Albert Memmi has made the same connection in relation to the Tunisian experience: "*Le racisme résume et symbolise la relation fondamentale qui unit colonialiste et colonisé*" [Racism epitomizes and symbolizes the fundamental relationship between colonialist and colonized] (92). Memmi, expanding on the connection expressed by Fanon, further insists: "Le racisme apparaît, ainsi, non comme un détail plus ou moins accidentel mais comme un élément consubstantiel au colonialisme. Il est la meilleure expression du fait colonial, et un des traits les plus significatifs du colonialiste" [Thus, racism appears, not as a more or less fortuitous detail, but as an element that is consubstantial to colonialism. It is the best expression of the phenomenon of colonialism, and one of the most significant characteristics of the colonialist] (95).

If, therefore, we extend the logic of the assertions shared by Fanon and Memmi, postcolonialism would necessarily embrace the notion of postracism. This would imply that the area of postcolonial theories and studies is one that somehow bypasses, avoids, overlooks, and negates race. When Julien comments that Fanon "unmasks racism behind its various guises" (157), we are impelled to ask a further question: Can the discourse of postcoloniality be another of these guises?

Julien's emphasis supports that of Mary Ann Doane, who has underscored the importance of racism in the relationships examined by Fanon: "The work of Frantz Fanon (particularly *Black Skin, White Masks*) constitutes one of the few attempts to activate psychoanalysis in the examination and indictment of the relation between colonizer and colonized—a relation subtended by racism" (217). What is particularly persuasive about the conclusions Doane draws from Fanon's investigations of colonialism and particularly from Fanon's exclusion of the relationship between white women and black women (while examining relations between black men and white women, black women and white men, and white men and black men), is that she relates the literary form used by Fanon to colonialist discourse. Doane reminds us that the "colonialist discourses of photography, poetry, and the essay frequently equated the African woman and the African continent—the conquest of the former signified the successful appropriation of the latter" (213). It must be admitted, as Young has observed, that "colonialism operated not only as a form of military rule but also simultaneously as a *discourse* of domination" (383). And in this context, we can accept Foucault's view, cited by Young, that "discourse always involves a form of violence in the way it imposes its linguistic order on the world; knowledge has to conform to its paradigms in order to be regarded as legitimate" (386). The question that arises, therefore, is: To what extent is the discourse of postcoloniality a permutation of colonialist discourse? To what extent is this discourse seeking to appropriate the African and colonized diaspora?

The recognition of Fanon as the unmasker of some of the hidden purposes and effects of colonialism lies at the root of Homi Bhabha's judgment of Fanon. In his 1989 article, "Remembering Fanon," Bhabha stresses the urgent need to remember Fanon: "Urgent, in order to remind us of that crucial engagement between mask and identity, image and identification, from which comes the lasting tension of our freedom and the lasting impression of ourselves as others" (147). This rather noncommittal judgment may be contrasted with that of Gautam Premnath, the title of whose book article plays with deliberate subversive intent on Bhabha's "Remembering Fanon," replacing "the Colonial Condition" of Bhabha's original title with his own "Decolonizing Diaspora." The change in title underscores a movement from Bhabha's implicit passivity (accepting the colonial condition) to Premnath's more explicit ideological activism (decolonization), which more closely reflects Fanon's activist experiences and practices. Premnath claims specifically that moments in Homi Bhabha's reading of Fanon (particularly in *Nation and Narration*) "combine to diminish the project of decolonization that animated Fanon's intellectual production" (59). The fact that this article by Premnath appears in a volume titled *Postcolonial Theory and Criticism* is significant. It implies to some extent that Premnath views postcolonial theory in its political potential—as a mechanism for decolonization.

It is here that the dilemma that lies at the root of the adoption of the postcoloniality frame rises to the surface. To what extent can, or should, the purpose of postcoloniality be politically activist? To what extent does this discourse permit or encourage political activism? Nigel Gibson, in a 1999 article, "Thoughts about Doing Fanonism in the 1990s," warns that "we should be wary of the way the cultural studies of Fanon have shied away from engaging politically or philosophically with Fanon as a revolutionary and political actor" (97). Gibson therefore approaches Appiah's reading of the potential or actual complicity between the intellectual activity of postcolonial studies and strategies of neocolonial capitalism. According to Young, "it was Fanon who articulated militant anti-colonial activism with the tradition of psychological redemption and black empowerment central to the traditions of Garvey and Negritude. The development of a distinctive postcolonial epistemology and ontology does not conflict with political activism" (275). As we have seen, Berger had already broached this attitudinal choice between activism and passivism. This aspect of Fanon's ideas and actions is particularly relevant to the situating of Fanon within the frame of postcoloniality.

Another of the concealed dangers of the postcoloniality frame is revealed unwittingly by Nicholas Harrison, who, as I showed earlier, considers Fanon as one of the key figures of postcolonial theory but who reaches the following illuminating conclusion: "[T]o 'situate' Fanon by saying that he thinks such-and-such a thing *because* he is West Indian, for example, may make a perfectly legitimate starting point or even conclusion for certain types of discourse, of which the intellectual biography would be one; but within a discourse that one might properly call critical, such a proposition, even if it is true, is neither here nor there" (66). It may be neither here nor there in situating the opinion of this critic and theorist to note that this article appears in *Paragraph*, a journal whose subtitle is *A Journal of Modern Critical Theory*. One of the underlying assumptions or implications of Harrison's opinion is that postcoloniality, which is widely recognized as a modern critical discourse, should, in judging Fanon, devalorize or even completely discount the fact that he is Caribbean. This may just be an aberrant view, not at all representative of the mainstream of postcolonial theorists. In its aberration, however, it points to what may very well be a masked (to echo Fanon's imagery) implication of postcoloniality: the tendency to minimize the lived experience of past and present colonization.

It is relevant here to stress the importance of the term *lived experience*, since the popularity of Charles Lam Markmann's translation of the title of the fifth chapter of *Peau noire*, "L'expérience vécue du Noir," literally "the lived experience of the black person" as "The Fact of Blackness" (a postcolonial translation?) has tended to privilege the abstract over the concrete and distract attention away from the weight Fanon gives throughout the text to the actual experience of people of color and from his constant questioning of the theoretical formulations that seek to explain and explain away that experience.[5]

David Macey, in his recent biography of Fanon, remarks that "Fanon came to be seen as the apostle of violence"(2). It is undeniable that Fanon's life and work exemplify the struggle of a colonized individual to resist colonial domination, through psychological and political action, and who came to believe, out of his own lived experience, that so great was the violence of colonialism that violence might be the only viable answer. Macey further observes that "[o]ver seventy years [*sic*] after his death, Fanon remains a surprisingly enigmatic figure.[6] Whether he should be regarded as 'Martinican,' 'Algerian,' 'French,' or simply 'black' is not a question that can be decided easily" (7). It may be argued that judgment of Fanon depends to some extent on the relative weight given to these components or aspects of Fanon's identity as well as on the perspective and identity of the judge. Thus, I contend that, within the context of postcoloniality, any judgment of Fanon will shed light not merely on Fanon, but more significantly on the judge, in relation to attitudes and approaches to and interpretations of postcoloniality. This idea has been hinted at by Henry Louis Gates Jr., who introduced his "Critical Fanonism" article with an epigraph from Fanon's *Black Skin, White Masks*, which provided the motif for developing the concept of a dynamics of reflectivity at work in critical approaches to Fanon: "This book, it is hoped, will be a mirror" (457). This potentially fruitful insight, however, is undermined by Gates's characterization of Fanon as "a Rorschach blot with legs" (458), an image which, clever as it is, reveals a subtle (unconscious, masked?) purpose of dehumanizing and belittling Fanon.

What is at issue is the recognition that many if not all of the choices we make, however innocently, in relation to scholarly activities serve purposes within a wider framework of ideology, economics, and politics. Christopher L. Miller underscores the political and economic implications of intellectual activity in western academic arenas, particularly in relation to Africa and things African: "What is designated as 'theory' in Western academies is the most prestigious and valued mode of production. . . . [T]heory is simply that which is labeled as theory by the institutions that empower themselves to do so. 'Theory' therefore stands as a figure for the role that Westerners have assigned themselves in their relation to Africa—detached, objective, universal, synthesizing, and, most of all, powerful" (7). Miller reminds us, "Theory maintains an inherent tend[e]ncy to universalism, which ineluctably erases differences. In academic circles, theory is power, and power is never easy to control" (296). Similarly, Gareth Griffiths underscores the point that "the study of post-colonial societies and texts has been recruited to the politics of the metropolitan academies" (167). Stephen Slemon also cautions, in "The Scramble for Post-Colonialism," about the tendency "to understand 'post-colonialism' mostly as an object of desire for critical practice; as a shimmering talisman that in itself has the power to confer political legitimacy onto specific forms of institutionalized labour, especially by ones that are troubled by their mediated position within the apparatus of mediated power" (17). Furthermore, there is more than a grain of truth in the assertion by Maureen Konkle, in "Indian Literacy, U.S. Colonialism, and Literary Criticism," that "[m]odern colonialism is a struggle for territory that takes place in part through the production of knowledge" (153). Barbara Christian's reminders in her 1987 article "The Race for Theory" are still relevant: "Some of our most daring and potentially radical critics (and by *our* I mean black, women, Third World) have been influenced, even coopted, into speaking a language and defining their discussion in terms alien to and opposed to our needs and orientation" (52).

Bearing all this in mind, we can now pose other questions: To what extent does postcoloniality represent a position of power? To what extent does it seek to mask or erase differences? To what extent does an examination of Fanon within this frame constitute a project of appropriation?

Macey points out that "Fanon 'lived, fought and died Algerian,' but he was also a product of French culture and French colonialism. He was also born a native son of Martinique" (30). This Martinican experience, Macey insists, constitutes the bedrock of Fanon's later explorations and activities: "For the Martinican Fanon, the experience of coming under the white gaze reproduces the primal experience of his island's history: slavery and a colonization so brutal as to be a form of trauma or even annihilation" (168).

The common factor in the rival affiliations that constitute the Fanon persona (Martinican, Algerian, French, black, etc.) is French colonial practice. It is against this backdrop that every aspect of Fanon's life (his awareness, education, marriages, career, politics, and writings) evolves. In his first published work, *Peau noire, masques blancs*, he is struggling to make sense of his experiences as a colonized black man confronted with the reality of French colonial racism, using, as Macey points out (162), every available intellectual tool at his disposal, including Sartre, Merleau-Ponty, and Césaire as well as his other fragmentary philosophical, psychiatric, and psychoanalytical readings.

In our reading of Fanon, therefore, it is perfectly legitimate, particularly for critics who form part of what Appiah has dubbed the "comprador intelligentsia," to indicate the contradictions, inadequate scholarship, the lack of consistency, the omissions, overstatements, and exaggerations of Fanon's self-exploration. These so-called weaknesses and contradictions are convincing illustrations of the power of colonial indoctrination. As Macey points out, the basis of Fanon's thesis in *Peau noire* was his realization that "in Martinique, mental illness is the result of a cultural situation determined by the existence of colonialism" (194). The challenge, therefore, is to examine Fanon's life and writings without in so doing being complicitous in the neocolonial project of undermining the validity of his anticolonial stances, of minimizing his determination to dismantle colonialism, of erasing his exposure of the severe and traumatic consequences (psychological, existential) of abusive colonialism. In other words, Fanon can most legitimately be approached critically, not in the context of postcoloniality, but in that of anticolonialism. The dimension that must not be diminished is the political, where realities of power (economic, social, and cultural, as well as military) are applied to transform forcibly the very self-concept of people, to bring them to the point of accepting the rightness of the force used to abuse them. Postcoloniality is a code for the presumptuous enterprise of masking this political dimension.

I am well aware that I am beating a dead horse, since the western academy of which I am a part, however reluctantly, has already embraced and enshrined postcolonial studies as a frame for examining Fanon's life and writings. Nothing I have to say will affect this display of power. I can, however, point to the irony, the arrogance, the presumptuousness of using such a frame to judge someone whose primary life work was to challenge and dismantle the very system of power that now seeks to erase or distort his real contributions. I can also point to the need for a discussion on the nexus between sincerity and complicity in what is called postcolonial studies.

And here I would like to interject a non-PC reading of Fanon. What I find most endearing about him is his imperfection, his flaws, his uncertainties, his contradictoriness, his vulnerability, his incompleteness. What I respect most is the direction of his interrupted trajectory, the fact that his life did have a trajectory. He is, in this respect, reminiscent of Malcolm X, if such an anachronistic comparison is permissible. The vocabulary in which Fanon's trajectory is expressed (of Negritude, psychiatry, existentialism, and violence, as well as universal humanism) is linked to the sociopolitical and intellectual conventions of the period in which he lived. His trajectory takes him toward greater self-honesty, increasing rejection of insularity, of narrowness, of confinement, to seek to fulfill an inner aspiration toward total liberation (psychological, ideological, social, political, but also spiritual). This trajectory, however, ensures that it is difficult to limit Fanon to any period and particularly to any imperialistic intellectual trend, such as postcoloniality, however well its recolonizing tendency may be masked.

Literary scholars and academic humanities theorists in general find it difficult to accept the implications of a Fanon, someone who moves, however tentatively and contradictorily, toward recognizing the violence of colonialism and the necessity for similar violence to counteract colonialism's traumatic and devastating effects. Fanon recognized early the limitations of discourse. Even in *Peau noire* he could express his awareness that reason and intelligence do not help solve the urgent problems faced by those who endure or have endured the violence of colonization. Part of the problem posed by colonization is the imbalance of power between colonizer and colonized. Within the academic field of so-called postcolonial studies, it is important to consider the relative positions of practitioners. Who forms part of the group of colonizers, and who forms part of the group of colonized? Who is seeking to maintain power, and who is seeking to gain power? The discourse of postcoloniality itself is both weapon and contested territory. The purpose of the discourse as applied by colonizers is fundamentally different from that as used by the colonized. It is for this reason that any discussion of Fanon, particularly within the context of a discourse of postcoloniality, that masks, avoids, or minimizes his fierce anticolonial activism (ideological and discursive, as well as military) is fundamentally flawed and presumptuous.

Macey's assessment of Fanon's first book bears reflection: "*Peau noire* was and is an elusive book, not least because it is so difficult to categorize in terms of genre. It is difficult to think of any precedent for it, and it did not establish any new genre or tradition. It had no sequel" (161). Does postcoloniality presume to constitute such a sequel?

Notes

1. An earlier version of this chapter was presented as a paper at the African Literature Association Conference, San Diego, California, 3–7 April 2002, under the title "Judging Fanon: Presumptions of Postcoloniality."

2. See Stephen Slemon, "The Scramble for Post-colonialism" 31.

3. All translations, unless otherwise indicated, are my own.

4. I choose the term *nigger* advisedly to render *nègre*, in spite of the understandable

resistances it will undoubtedly create. Fanon is making a class distinction that is difficult to render into English as there is no exact equivalent. *Nigger* is stronger than, but closer to, Fanon's *nègre* than is *Negro*, which is too bland. Fanon is alluding to the different responses that result from the reality of a hierarchical system of domination and exploitation (economic, class, psychic). What other term translates this reality? Clayton Eshleman and Annette Smith also render *nègre* as *nigger* in their translation of Césaire's *Cahier*. According to them, educated upper-class Antilleans of the time would have considered *nègre* as the most insulting way of referring to a black person (even though the term might have been considered neutral by the general public). For this reason, Eshleman and Smith state that from "the point of view of the translator, it is therefore important to translate 'nègre' as 'nigger'" (Césaire, *Notebook* 60).

5. Recent commentators/critics such as Gibson and Macey have drawn attention to the dangerous implications of Markmann's creative translation.

6. Since Fanon died in 1961, this is evidently an editorial oversight.

Works Cited

Appiah, Kwame Anthony. *In My Father's House: Africa in the Philosophy of Culture*. New York: Oxford University Press, 1992.

Ashcroft, Bill, Gareth Griffiths, and Helen Tiffin. *Key Concepts in Post-colonial Studies*. London: Routledge, 1998.

Berger, Roger. "Contemporary Anglophone Literary Theory: The Return of Fanon." *Research in African Literatures* 21.1 (Spring 1990): 141–51.

Bhabha, Homi K. "Remembering Fanon: Self, Psyche, and the Colonial Condition." *Remaking History*. Ed. Barbara Kruger and Phil Mariani. Seattle: Bay Press, 1989. 131–48.

Buell, Lawrence. "Postcolonial Anxiety in Classic U.S. Literature." *Postcolonial Theory and the United States*. Ed. Amritjit Singh and Peter Schmidt. Jackson: University Press of Mississippi, 2000. 196–219.

Césaire, Aimé. *Cahier d'un retour au pays natal*. Paris: Présence africaine, 1971.

———. *Notebook of a Return to the Native Land*. Trans. and ed. Clayton Eshleman and Annette Smith. Middletown, Conn.: Wesleyan University Press, 2001.

Christian, Barbara. "The Race for Theory." *Cultural Critique* 6 (Spring 1987): 51–63.

Doane, Mary Ann. *Femmes Fatales*. New York: Routledge, 1991.

Fanon, Frantz. *Black Skin, White Masks*. Trans. Charles Lam Markmann. New York: Grove Weidenfeld, 1967.

———. *Les damnés de la terre*. Paris: Maspéro, 1968.

———. *Peau noire, masques blancs*. Paris: Seuil, 1952.

———. *Sociologie d'une révolution: l'an V de la révolution algérienne*. Paris: Maspéro, 1972.

Gates, Henry Louis, Jr. "Critical Fanonism." *Critical Inquiry* 17 (Spring 1991): 457–70.

Gibson, Nigel. "Thoughts about Doing Fanonism in the 1990s." *College Literature* 26.2 (Spring 1999): 96–117.

Griffiths, Gareth. "The Post-colonial Project: Critical Approaches and Problems." *New*

National and Post-Colonial Literatures: An Introduction. Ed. Bruce King. Oxford, U.K.: Clarendon Press, 1996. 164–77.

Hall, Stuart. "When Was 'the Post-colonial'? Thinking at the Limit." *The Post-Colonial Question: Common Skies, Divided Horizons*. Ed. Iain Chambers and Lidia Curti. London: Routledge, 1996. 242–60.

Harrison, Nicholas. "Positioning (Fanon)." *Paragraph* 21.1 (March 1998): 57–68.

Julien, Eileen. "Terrains de rencontre: Césaire, Fanon, and Wright on Culture and Decolonization." *Yale French Studies* 98 (2000): 149–66.

King, Bruce, ed. *New National and Post-Colonial Literatures: An Introduction*. Oxford, U.K.: Clarendon Press, 1996.

King, C. Richard, ed. *Postcolonial America*. Urbana: University of Illinois Press, 2000.

Konkle, Maureen. "Indian Literacy, U.S. Colonialism, and Literary Criticism." *Postcolonial Theory and the United States*. Ed. Amritjit Singh and Peter Schmidt. Jackson: University Press of Mississippi, 2000. 151–75.

Lawson, Alan, and Chris Tiffin. "Conclusion: Reading Difference." *De-Scribing Empire: Post-colonialism and Textuality*. Ed. Chris Tiffin and Alan Lawson. London: Routledge, 1994. 230–35.

Macey, David. *Frantz Fanon: A Biography*. New York: Picador, 2001.

Madsen, Deborah L. "Beyond the Commonwealth: Post-Colonialism and American Literature." *Post-Colonial Literatures: Expanding the Canon*. Ed. Deborah L. Madsen. London: Pluto Press, 1999. 1–13.

Mannoni, Octave. *Psychologie de la colonisation*. Paris: Seuil, 1950.

Memmi, Albert. *Portrait du colonisé, précédé du portrait du colonisateur*. Paris: Gallimard, 1985.

Miller, Christopher L. *Theories of Africans: Francophone Literature and Anthropology in Africa*. Chicago: University of Chicago Press, 1990.

Piper, Karen. "Post-Colonialism in the United States: Diversity or Hybridity?" *Post-Colonial Literatures: Expanding the Canon*. Ed. Deborah L. Madsen. London: Pluto Press, 1999. 14–28.

Premnath, Gautam. "Remembering Fanon, Decolonizing Diaspora." *Postcolonial Theory and Criticism*. Ed. Laura Chrisman and Benita Parry. Cambridge, U.K.: Brewer, 1999. 57–73.

Singh, Amritjit, and Peter Schmidt, eds. *Postcolonial Theory and the United States*. Jackson: University Press of Mississippi, 2000.

Slemon, Stephen. "Post-colonial Critical Theories." *New National and Post-Colonial Literatures: An Introduction*. Ed. Bruce King. Oxford, U.K.: Clarendon Press, 1996. 178–97.

———. "The Scramble for Post-Colonialism." *Describing Empire: Post-colonialism and Textuality*. Ed. Chris Tiffin and Alan Lawson. London: Routledge, 1994. 15–32.

Suk, Jeanie. *Postcolonial Paradoxes in French Caribbean Writing: Césaire, Glissant, Condé*. New York: Oxford University Press, 2001.

Young, Robert J. C. *Postcolonialism: An Historical Introduction*. Oxford, U.K.: Blackwell, 2001.

3

Unfathomable Toussaint

The (Un)Making of a Hero

Elisabeth Mudimbe-Boyi

> Il flatte l'oeil, mais il perce l'âme. Comme dans tout ce style on sent, malgré l'adresse, la main prête à frapper sous la main qui caresse.
> [He flatters the eye, but pierces the soul. As in this whole style, one senses, despite the skill, the hand ready to strike beneath the hand that caresses.]
> **(Lamartine, *Toussaint Louverture* 45)**

> Restez dans une fausse et douteuse attitude;
> Aïez pour les Français des visages amis,
> L'oeil ouvert du serpent et des coeurs ennemis.
> [Remain in a false and doubtful attitude
> Have for the French friendly faces,
> The open eye of the serpent and enemy hearts.]
> **(Lamartine, *Toussaint Louverture* 52)**

On 7 April 1803, a black prisoner in the fort of Joux in the French Alps, was found dead in his cell, "sur une chaise, près du feu, la tête appuyée contre la cheminée, le bras droit pendant, sans mouvement" [sitting on a chair, next to the fire, his head leaning against the chimney, his right arm hanging straight down, motionless](Pluchon 535–36). As reported by his jailer, his body had been in pain, degrading day by day: headaches, vomiting, stomachaches, dry cough, surges of fever, lack of appetite. The post mortem medical report summarily concluded after examination that "l'apoplexie, la pleuropéri-pneumonie sont les causes de mort de Toussaint Louverture" [apoplexy and pleuritic pneumonia are the causes of the death of Toussaint Louverture] (Pluchon 536). So passed away this personage, so described in a quotation by one of his biographers, Pierre Pluchon. This man indeed was François Dominique Toussaint Bréda, immortalized in history and literature as Toussaint Louverture. Toussaint's ultimate attitude finds an echo in Claude McKay's poem a century later: "If we must die, O let us nobly die" (Baker 165).[1] Despite the humiliation of his captivity, Toussaint wanted, perhaps, to die "sitting" and not lying down. Keeping an upright posture could be seen as a way of asserting his invincibility in prison and in death until the ultimate moment, and of thus actualizing the words he had pronounced when brought into captivity: "En me renversant, vous n'avez abattu à Saint-Domingue que le tronc de l'arbre de la liberté des Noirs, il repoussera par les racines, car elles sont profondes et vivaces" [In overthrowing me, you have only chopped down at Saint-Domingue the trunk of the tree of black liberty, it will grow back by its roots, because they are deep and enduring].[2]

As a confirmation of Toussaint's prophetic words, his collaborator Jean-Jacques Dessalines would continue the struggle, defeating the French general Leclerc, responsible for Toussaint's arrest, and leading Saint Domingue to independence and to the proclamation of the Haitian nation on 1 January 1804. Napoleon, who was defeated later, also died exiled and in captivity. In the conclusion of his biography of Toussaint, Pluchon confirms Toussaint as the major victor (544).

I

J. A. Ferguson summarizes the different ways in which Toussaint has been represented in nineteenth-century history and literature. She distinguishes various categories of works on Toussaint, on the basis of their locus of enunciation: there are abolitionists who are rather "hagiographic" and Bonapartists who tend to be "demonological" (395). The abolitionists tend to present a rather positive image of Toussaint, emphasizing his commitment to and struggle for liberty, while the Bonapartists vilify him.

Toussaint Louverture has also been iconized as a mythical figure of the Haitian Revolution and featured in the works of francophone and anglophone writers. There are, from the nineteenth century to the beginning of this century, numerous books and articles, biographies, and literary works in all genres on Toussaint Louverture.[3] In *Orientalism* Edward Said and his critics have debated the question of representation and its ideological subtext. Representations of Toussaint are certainly informed by the intersection of visions based on different loci of enunciation: contemporary contexts, political views, and the authors' national or ethnic resonances. I would like to suggest that the ambivalent and apparently contradictory representations of Toussaint are shaped by much more than ideology. On the one hand, they should be related to his mimetic reproduction of the ambiguities of the French abolitionists' discourse and, on the other hand, to a legacy of slavery: the exercise of dissimulation as a defense mechanism developed by slaves in plantation society. The culture of the plantation combined with trends from the *métropole* lay at the foundation of Toussaint's political strategy and charted his trajectory to becoming a well-trained and skillful navigator in the space of ambiguities. Thus, Toussaint's contradictory images are not in fact contradictory: they underscore the behavior of a character who evolves as an ambiguous, elusive, and inscrutable subject enclosed in his unfathomableness.

In *Toussaint Louverture*, Aimé Césaire, grounding his demonstration in abundant references to various texts, showed how, despite all the liberal discourses and stated commitment to the cause of slaves, post-Revolution French institutions were still locked in timidity and tergiversation, reluctant to abolish slavery (159–70). He points equally to some ambiguities in La Société des Amis des Noirs, which was nevertheless in the vanguard of the promotion of the emancipation of blacks (85–86). With passion, caustic irony, and references to the texts, Louis Sala-Molins also brings to light the ambiguities and the limitations of the 1685 Code Noir, as well as of the abolitionists' discourse, denouncing "les subtilités des 'Amis des Noirs'" [the subtleties of the "Friends of the Blacks"] (261–74) and "les élégances de Montesquieu" [the elegances of Montesquieu] (221–36), and situating "Le Code Noir à l'ombre des Lumières" [The Black Code in the shadow of the Enlightenment] (205). Joseph Jurt, for his part, underlines the ambivalence of Condorcet's opposition to slavery (385–95).[4] Condorcet was the *secrétaire perpétuel* of L'Académie des Sciences and would become a prominent and active member of La Société des Amis des Noirs, taking strong positions against slavery in his writing. Yet, as Jurt reminds us, "Si Condorcet est inflexible en ce qui concerne les principes, il se montre très prudent—le terme revient à plusieurs reprises sous sa plume—quant aux modalités, quant au 'choix des moyens et du temps.' . . . Ses propositions témoignent d'une certaine timidité empreinte d'un ton protectionniste" [If Condorcet is inflexible with respect to principles, he proves to be very prudent—the term reappears several times in his writing—when it comes to modalities and the choice of methods and timing. . . . His propositions show a certain timidity marked by a protectionist tone] (Jurt 390). Adding his voice to the contemporary critique of the Enlightenment, Jurt connects Condorcet's ambiguity to the Lumières' idea of "progress": "Mais ce libéralisme politique va de pair avec un paternalisme évident. Condorcet envisage, comme le remarque Marcel Merle, l'évolution du progrès comme une conversion aux valeurs européennes. . . . Ce type de discours est caractéristique de l'argumentation des philosophes du Siècle des Lumières; s'ils plaident pour des droits de l'homme, la raison et la liberté, ils présentent ces valeurs européennes comme universelles et ne reconnaissent pas l'altérité des systèmes culturels extra-européens" [But this political liberalism goes hand in hand with an obvious paternalism. As Marcel Merle observes, Condorcet envisions the evolution of progress as a conversion to European values. . . . This type of discourse is characteristic of the argumentation of the philosophers of the Enlightenment; if they argue for human rights, reason and liberty, they present these European values as universal and do not recognize the otherness of extra-European cultural systems] (393–94).

As for the culture of the plantation, another Afro-American poet, Paul Laurence Dunbar, in his poem "We Wear the Mask," alludes to the smiling face of the slave: "We wear the mask that grins and lies" (Baker 116–17).[5] In his *Black Liberator*, Stephen Alexis, a Haitian biographer of Toussaint, summarizes this behavior of dissimulation, voluntary or forced, when he recalls Toussaint's trajectory:

> His life was one of work, suffering, and pride—the secret pride of humble folk. He was saddened by all the servile, mechanical tasks which the Negroes had to perform, and which filled the bright sunlit land with unbound affliction. . . . Day after day he would watch the slaves at work on the sugar plantations, toiling under the constant threat of the lash. But he hid his feelings, smiled at the overseer, and gave the impression that he was a contented youngster, in whom the seed of rebellion could never germinate. He played his role so well that his masters were completely deceived for forty years, every day holding him up as an example to the other slaves. (14)
>
> During the first years of his married life Toussaint appeared to be perfectly happy. He continued to give the impression to his master of an apathetic slave who had achieved his ideal and wished for nothing more. But already he was shaping in his mind the broad outlines of the strategy he would employ in what was to be his phenomenal ascent to power. He would lull his adversary into a false state of security, and then, at the right time, turn and crush him utterly, swiftly, and relentlessly. (16)

In *All Souls' Rising*, a fictionalized rendition of the Haitian Revolution, Madison Smartt Bell points out Toussaint's ability to play with words and evade univocity even in writing, leaving the door open to multiple interpretations and shifting signification: Toussaint was "making words on paper for the *colon* white-men to read. But Toussaint was learning the way to make the words in knots instead of lines, so that they twisted like mating snakes upon each other and would say more than one thing" (275). "I saw that Toussaint had learned a way to make his words march in more than one direction" (287). In the course of time, Toussaint quietly cultivated and progressively crafted his nonrevealing attitude into a political strategy: he became a master of words and double talk, cunning and ambiguity.

II

From the nineteenth century to the contemporary period, Toussaint has remained an intriguing character who elicits a fascination that goes beyond linguistic, national, and racial boundaries. The diversity and abundance of writings on Toussaint Louverture clearly testify to the acknowledgment on the part of writers within and outside of the Hexagon of his relevance to the history of the Caribbean in general and of Haiti in particular. Whether they depict him in a positive or negative light, and whether they treat him as an objectively historical or as a constructed character, they speak to the importance of the legacy of Toussaint Louverture.

The overview that follows aims to show points of intersection and different sites of enunciation from which Toussaint's literary representations emerge. In Alphonse de Lamartine's play *Toussaint Louverture*, paratextual features such as the title indicate the centrality of Toussaint in the drama.[6] Upon closer analysis, one finds that, through Toussaint, Lamartine actually showcases his own social romanticism. Toussaint functions as a pretext, providing Lamartine with a channel for the political views he forcefully defended at the French Chambre des députés [house of representatives]. Indeed, Lamartine proudly gives himself credit as he recalls this public act in the preface to his poetic drama: "Je ne dissimule aucune de ses nombreuses imperfections; ce n'était dans mon intention qu'un discours en vers et en action en faveur de l'abolition de l'esclavage. L'esclavage est à jamais aboli; aujourd'hui, qu'on me pardonne le drame en faveur de l'acte. Si mon nom est associé dans l'avenir de la race noire aux noms de Wilberforce et des abolitionnistes français, ce ne sera pas pour ce poëme, *ce sera pour le 27 février 1848, où ma main signa l'émancipation de l'esclavage au nom de la France!*" [I am not concealing any of his numerous imperfections; a discourse in verse and in action in favor of the abolition of slavery was my sole intention. Slavery is forever abolished; today, may I be forgiven the drama in favor of the act. If my name is associated in the future of the black race with the names of Wilberforce and of French abolitionists, it will not be for this poem, *it will be for the 27th of February, 1848, when my hand signed the emancipation of the slaves in the name of France!*] (10, my emphasis). In the same preface, Lamartine denounces Bonaparte's action against Toussaint, casting Toussaint as a hero for black people, and calling for reparations: "L'histoire et la France doivent réparation tardive de ces ostracismes du héros des noirs"

[History and France owe belated reparations for ostracizing the hero of the blacks] (9).

With his play *Monsieur Toussaint*, Edouard Glissant brings on stage several characters connected with the Haitian Revolution or the Caribbean slaves' revolt: Boukman, Mackandal, Delgrès, Christophe, Dessalines, Rigaud. The play embodies a concern with the history of the Caribbean: to bring the past into the present (apparitions of the dead and of specters throughout the play) in order to examine, revisit, and interpret it from a different vantage point and through different lenses, those of the postcolonial subject. For Glissant, "dévoiler le passé, par d'autres dénaturé ou oblitéré, permet parfois de mieux toucher l'actuel. . . . Renouer avec son histoire, c'est se vouer aux saveurs du présent; lesquelles, dépouillées de cet enracinement dans le temps, ramènent à de vaines délectations" [To unveil the past, distorted or obliterated by others, allows us sometimes to better affect the present. . . . To reconnect with one's history is to devote oneself to the savors of the present which, stripped of this rootedness in time, are but empty delights] (26).

With *Toussaint Louverture* and *Iles de tempête*, Aimé Césaire from Martinique and Bernard Dadié from the Ivory Coast display a critical, but rather sympathetic, point of view on Toussaint, while framing him as a liberator. The aim is to establish a correlation between the past of slavery and the present of colonization in order to draw lessons for the present: a present in which Africa and the Caribbean are linked by a similar history of colonial dominance. By choosing as a title *Toussaint Louverture: la Révolution française et le problème colonial*, Césaire clearly links the two moments: the French Revolution and the decolonization process.[7] In both Dadié and Césaire, Toussaint is the positive and negative catalyzing force between the master society and the slaves, the colonizer and the colonized.

Dadié's play delineates topics similar to those in Césaire's *Toussaint*. Before bringing Toussaint on stage, Dadié introduces a whole range of characters, tracing the genealogy of the Haitian Revolution and marking its founding moment with Toussaint's revolutionary endeavor. One hears Raynal's voice offstage and sees Mirabeau, Jefferson and Washington, Makandal, and Toussaint himself. Characters from the past and the present, nationals and expatriate experts, all interact on stage. Through his characters and historical figures from the past, Dadié conveys a critique of today's independent African governments, of pervasive neocolonialism, of dictatorships and false democracies, and of the so-called *Coopération Technique* [technical cooperation] between ex-colonies and the former colonizing *métropoles*. His play is perhaps the best to exemplify Toussaint's mimicry embedded in parody and tropes such as repetition and parallelism.[8] To underscore the dimension of mimicry, Dadié blurs the historical chronology and the geographical lines by creating a simultaneity between Toussaint's confinement in the fort of Joux and Napoleon's exile and captivity on the island of Saint Helena. Dadié's play and its dialogues point out the parallelism of both characters' situations and their missions: "Toussaint Louverture: M'en voudrait-il, le General Bonaparte, d'être dans l'histoire, tout comme lui, un repère? N'est-ce pas l'identité de notre destin? Ici, je brise les chaînes et là-bas, il brise les trônes" [Toussaint Louverture: Does General Bonaparte hold it against me that I am a point of reference in history, just like him? Isn't it our identical destiny? Here, I am breaking chains and over there, he is breaking thrones] (85). "Napoléon (*après un long silence*): Nous étions tous deux des ïles. Nous avons tous deux eu à lutter contre les mêmes puissances. Il est mort sur le continent" [Napoleon (*after a long silence*): We were both islands. We both had to struggle against the same forces. He died on the continent] (134).

Toussaint's nephew, Moyse, emerges as the voice against mimicry: "Notre révolte doit balayer le passé, tout le passé; il nous faut une société nouvelle, d'hommes travaillant dans la joie, et *non une caricature de société occidentale*" [Our revolt must sweep away the past, all of the past; we need a new society of men working in joy, and *not a caricature of western society*] (81, my emphasis).

Contemporary Haiti's history provides another frame for the reading of Toussaint's centrality and legacy. In his inauguration ceremony in 2001, the twice-elected president of Haiti, Bertrand Aristide, stated: "Le 29 août 1793, Toussaint Louverture déclara: 'Je suis Toussaint Louverture. Je veux que la liberté et l'égalité règnent à Saint Domingue.' Aujourd'hui, 2 mars 2001, si Toussaint Louverture se trouvait ici, au Palais National, il aurait sans doute déclaré: 'Je suis Toussaint Louverture. Je veux que la paix règne en Haïti' [On 29 August 1793, Toussaint Louverture declared: "I am Toussaint Louverture. I want liberty and equality to reign in Saint Domingue." Today, 2 March 2001, if Toussaint Louverture were here, at the National Palace, he would undoubtedly have declared: "I am Toussaint Louverture. I want peace to reign in Haiti"].[9]

Aristide's reference marks the contextual difference between then and now. If, in Toussaint's time, what was at stake was freedom, in today's Haiti, injured and handicapped by continuous internal struggles and violence, peace is the priority. As an acknowledgment of a legacy or, rather, a political strategy, Aristide's words are meaningful, and they carry a symbolic value. By repeating Toussaint's words "*Je suis* [my emphasis] Toussaint Louverture," Aristide actually impersonates the historical hero of the Haitian struggle for liberation through a form of ventriloquism. Aristide wants to stress a historical legacy. As the new president of Haiti, he is narrating his political genealogy and inscribing himself in the lineage of the Haitians' mythologized hero. The explicit reference to Toussaint as a "liberator" provides a subtext in which Aristide implicitly introduces himself as Toussaint's heir. He thus legitimates his position as the new leader of Haiti, backed by the exemplary and emblematic figure of Toussaint, with whom he identifies. On the other hand, by opposing "freedom" in the past and "peace" in the present as the major goal, Aristide points to the difference between yesterday's and today's contexts, which leaves him with the grounds to follow a different path and means, but also to shift trajectory. In Toussaint's footsteps, Aristide defines a politics of ambivalence, inscribed in an ambiguous discourse. In his inaugural speech, one could read a desire for both filiation and identification, as well as an affirmation of political self-assertion and strategic independence.

The conflict in representations of Toussaint only reflects his inscrutable attitudes, conflicting political allegiances, and the ambiguous discourses that he had himself exercised. Possible oxymorons such as proud humiliation or, to follow Pluchon, victorious defeat might reproduce the mimicry, the contrasts, the contradictions, and the ambiguities that characterized Toussaint's public life.

Convergence and divergence, inversion and subversion constitute the tropes through which Toussaint's politics of ambiguity and mimicry were made possible, creating the evading subject. In the representations of Toussaint, hexagonal and nonhexagonal interpretations are intertwined; color, class, and economic interests conflate and conflict, history and literary imagination intersect. Portraits of Toussaint converge and diverge according to their locus of enunciation and their vantage points, their ideological or political intention. What remains unchanged is the emergence of an evading subject, used to the politics of ambiguity and mimicry, and shifting alliances between French and Spaniards, between blacks, mulattoes, and whites, wanting to emulate Bonaparte. The question to which the answer remains unclear is, Was this an inherent trait in Toussaint's personality, or was it a deliberate strategy to elude and delude in order to acquire and maintain power? A similar ambiguity and uncertainty mark even the very name with which Toussaint is framed by history. The origin of *Louverture* is uncertain. Is *Louverture* a self-ascription or a given surname? The variations in spelling give it the same elusive and unseizable dimension as the name bearer himself: Toussaint Louverture, Toussaint L'Ouverture, Toussaint-Louverture. The nominal expansion implied in *Louverture* definitely raises Toussaint to the status of an epic hero.

III

As a revolutionary, Toussaint Louverture unquestionably marks a major postcolonial moment in history: that is, a political and ideological questioning and contestation of the hegemonic power, as well as the will or action for resistance and destabilization of that power. Interestingly enough, the different representations of Toussaint, whether historical or literary, tend to validate both a postcolonial reading of texts and a critique, or at least a relativization, of the postcolonial concept.[10] In fact, these representations of Toussaint deconstruct some assumptions of the postcolonial, such as: the ideological imperial gaze, the concern with cultural identity, the opposition between center and periphery, race as a locus of enunciation, and, in a cursory note, the predominance of the postcolonial in the Anglo-Saxon world. This brings us to the following reflections.

Although it is not inscribed in the hegemonic position and stereotypes found in the imperial gaze and its discourses, ideology is not necessarily absent from the postcolonial gaze. Dadié's Toussaint, for example, carries a political message, as does Glissant's. The literature surveyed for this chapter shows that a positive image of Toussaint is not the prerogative of Africa or the Caribbean. The Ivorian Dadié is more critical of Toussaint than is the French Pierre Pluchon. Where does one draw the borders of the postcolonial? French abolitionist discourse, despite the reluctance and the ambiguities signaled earlier, somehow contested the established order of the Republic and disrupted its relation to the colonies. Like the Martinican Césaire, the French Schoelcher, in his biography of Toussaint, took certain critical stands against him. At the same time, however, he relativized his critiques by pointing to the historical context in which Toussaint had to perform.

Toussaint understood the value of education, as proven by his own situation in the Bréda household and by his desire to attend to his sons' education, sending them to study in France. If Toussaint's great dream was the liberation of blacks, however, nothing in the numerous biographies and other studies of him points to the question of culture, or to its corollary, cultural identity, as formulated in the Negritude movement or later in the concepts of *antillanité* and *créolité*. Toussaint's focus was the emancipation of blacks, and, in an apparent contradiction, the acknowledgment of his Frenchness. For him, though, there was no contradiction in being French and leading a black revolution. On the contrary, Frenchness and freedom meant recognition, equality, and thus the actualization of the French Revolution's ideals of liberty, fraternity, and equality. Questions about culture were not present in Toussaint's plans. If they were, they seem to have been diluted in a more general preoccupation with the emancipation of blacks. This absence of concern about a black identity or culture only bolsters Toussaint's ambiguous positions. On the one hand, unlike the Negritude movement, Toussaint's priority was political change and its consequences at the social level. This priority was dictated by the primary social context of the time, slavery.

A comparison reveals an inversion of the situation with the later Negritude movement. For the founding fathers of Negritude and the group gravitating around the journals *L'Etudiant noir* and *Présence africaine*, the urgency and the primary struggle had to be in the realm of culture and identity. Political claims could be established, they thought, only if they were grounded in a culture, even if mythical, and a recovered racial identity. On the other hand, through the process of appropriation, Toussaint and the Negritude movement came together. The Negritude poets of the twentieth century appropriated the French language and their experience of French culture, considered, to borrow Césaire's title for one of his collections of poetry, as "armes miraculeuses" [miraculous weapons]. These weapons were put to work to undermine colonial power and to assert claims for cultural identity, followed by a claim for political emancipation. Toussaint's struggle for the emancipation of slaves was grounded in the very basic principles of the French Revolution. He recuperated and appropriated these principles in order to rise up against the political domination of Saint Domingue by metropolitan power and the submission of blacks through slavery.

One of the ambiguities in the 1685 Code Noir of Louis XIV, as well as in the abolitionist discourse of La Société des Amis des Noirs, is conveyed by the constant fluctuation in description between "noirs," "mulâtres," "hommes de couleur," and "hommes de couleur libres" [blacks, mulattoes, colored men, and free colored men]: that is, between race, color, and class. Where is Toussaint located on this scale? A former slave born around May 1743, he was freed by his master, Bayon de Libertat of the Bréda plantation. Toussaint, a free man, went on to own twenty hectares of a coffee plantation cultivated by slaves (Donnadien 59). It is this same Toussaint, a liberated slave and slave owner himself, who then became an antislavery revolutionary. As noted by David Geggus in *A Turbulent Time*, "It is significant that Toussaint Louverture was not a slave, but a member of the lower rank of the free colored section" (12). This intermediary position could be compared to that of the "évolués" of the French colonies. It allowed Toussaint to navigate between the different classes and color groups, being and not being a member of both the dominant and the subaltern groups. As recorded in history, the plantation societies were highly stratified in terms of color. Toussaint was aware of both the whites' and the mulattoes' contempt. When the imperatives of his political and military goals required it, Toussaint contracted alliances with either faction. If color played a role in the general configuration of the Haitian

Revolution, the struggle for emancipation and Toussaint's politics sometimes blurred the color lines, successively creating coalitions with the class of whites, who dominated the means of production, with mulattoes, with the class of nonfree blacks, and with the *petits blancs*.[11]

If one had to situate him, Toussaint would belong to French colonial history. The body of works generated by his persona goes far beyond the borders of the francophone world, colonies or *métropole*. As shown in the succinct bibliography presented in this chapter, Toussaint as a revolutionary figure has inspired European, Caribbean, and African writers in general. His pan-Caribbean and transnational presence, especially among African writers or writers such as Césaire, might point in a two-way transatlantic direction. Thus, Toussaint's figure, as Paul Gilroy states in *The Black Atlantic*, transcends "both the structures of the nation state and the constraints of ethnicity and national peculiarity" (19). The printed book has replaced the "image of ships in motion across the spaces between Europe, America, Africa and the Caribbean as a central organizing symbol" (4). Lamartine's, Césaire's, Glissant's, and Dadié's writings on Toussaint display a tricontinental crosscurrent and exchange of ideas, suggesting a possible expansion of the black Atlantic in which the intellectual context of African and francophone Europe, sites and heirs of the Atlantic trade, might also be analyzed.

IV

Toussaint's life ended in solitary confinement. He died exiled from the country for which he had fought. Through his search and struggle for freedom, he rose to the status of a legendary figure and national hero. Writers and biographers have compared him to Christ or Moses the savior, have called him a black Spartacus, a black Napoleon, or the George Washington of the Caribbean. Toussaint, appropriating the French Revolution's ideals, inscribes himself in the politics and ideology of the postcolonial. Yet, in his *Toussaint Louverture*, one of Toussaint's biographers, Pluchon, completely plays down the role of the French Revolution in the making of Toussaint. Pluchon rather grounds him in the sphere of influence of the Ancien Régime (553–60).[12]

Toussaint is now framed by history, by the world literary imagination, and by the Caribbean collective memory as an emblematic, synecdochal figure. In the words of Rochambeau when proposing a strategy against Toussaint: "Cet homme est une nation," "ce peuple est un enfant: sa force est celle d'un homme. Ne combattez qu'en lui toute sa nation" [This man is a nation, this people is a child: its force is that of a man. Fight in him alone his entire nation] (qtd. in Lamartine 84). What matters is the image of grandeur left by Toussaint. With or without a mandate, he did represent the Saint Domingue slaves and *stood up* for them and their liberation. In the closing of *Cahier d'un retour au pays natal*, Aimé Césaire underscores this grandeur when he salutes and celebrates in Toussaint Haiti, as the country "où la négritude se mit *debout* pour la première fois et dit qu'elle croyait à son humanité" (24, my emphasis) [where Negritude *stood up* for the first time and swore by its humanity] (Césaire, *Return* 47).

The image that emerges from this stance tells of Toussaint's legacy, alive in

> la négraille assise
> inattendument debout
> debout dans la cale
> debout dans les cabines
> debout sur le pont
> debout dans le vent
> debout sous le soleil
> debout dans le sang
> debout
>   et
>   libre
>
> (Césaire, *Cahier* 61–62)

> [the seated "poor-old-Negro"
> unexpectedly standing
> upright in the hold
> upright in the cabins
> upright on the bridge
> upright in the wind
> upright under the sun
> upright in the blood
> upright
>   and
>   free]
>
> Césaire, *Return* 133–35

It is in this capacity that Toussaint has been framed in the literary imagination. As a synecdochal figure, Toussaint, glorified or demonized, victorious or defeated, remains the initiator of the Haitian Revolution and the quintessential exemplary figure who fought for black liberation. He belongs to narratives of the past from which national myths originate.

Notes

My thanks to Libby Murphy for her editorial assistance and for translating some quotations from the French. Unless indicated otherwise, translations from the French are hers.

1. Original in McKay, *Selected Poems.*

2. These words of Toussaint's have become legendary and are quoted with slight variations in his biographies and literary representations. Bernard Dadié gives this version: "En m'arrêtant, vous avez seulement abattu le tronc de l'arbre de la Liberté de Saint Domingue. Les racines repousseront car elles sont nombreuses et profondes" (Dadié 2) [In stopping me, you have only chopped down the trunk of the tree of the Liberty of Saint Domingue. The roots will grow again because they are numerous and deep.] For biographies of Toussaint, see Pluchon, James, Schoelcher, Alexis, Pauléus Sannon, and Césaire.

3. There is an abundant literature on the Haitian Revolution with a focus on Toussaint and the Haitian Revolution, or on the French Revolution in relation to the Haitian Revolution. The works listed here are a few examples consulted to find a direction for this chapter. Among literary works in French, see Lamartine, Glissant, Dadié, Dorsinville, Pasquet, and Leloup. Gordon Collier quotes several works of literature by Haitians in which Toussaint is the dominant character (see also Clark). The works cited section displays a list of plays on the Haitian Revolution, and several of them are centered around the figure of Toussaint.

Among literary works in English inspired by Toussaint, see Martineau. For a discussion of this work, see Belasco, in which she underlines the relevance of Martineau's fictional history to American abolitionists. Sonnets by William Wordsworth also feature Toussaint (in particular, see his "To Toussaint L'Ouverture"). See also Lamming.

Less known perhaps than the earlier quoted landmark works by Schoelcher, Pluchon, James, Césaire, Glissant, and Dadié, a vast literature on Toussaint attests to the fascination he has exercised through time and space. See for example, Waxman, Tyson, Brutus, Nemours, Pierre-Charles, Benjamin, and Célestin. Among articles and book chapters, see Auguste, Benn, Bourke, Ferguson, Mouralis, Onyeoziri, Carter, Freeman, Dupuy, Court, Fick, and Gaspar and Geggus. Among other literary works, see also Carpentier, Walcott, and Bell. For the most recent works, see Fombrun, Jean-Pierre, and Moïse. It would go beyond the scope of this limited study to investigate oral literature in Haiti or elsewhere in the Caribbean for the examination of Toussaint's representations in popular culture manifestations such as songs, stories, and iconography.

4. For the Enlightenment and race, see Eze.

5. Original in Dunbar, *Complete Poems.*

6. I use as a reference the volume edited by Léon-François Hoffmann.

7. Césaire's theater is a *théâtre de la décolonisation* [theater of decolonization], as actualized in his other plays. See *La Tragédie du Roi Christophe* and *Une Saison au Congo.* For Césaire and decolonization, see Jones, Kesteloot, and Oddon.

8. See "Of Mimicry and Man," the well-known text by Homi Bhabha. Particularly relevant to Toussaint is Bhabha's assertion that mimicry is threatening. Also relevant is the quote from Jacques Lacan used by Bhabha as an introduction, "The effect of mim-

icry is camouflage" (85). I would like to make a point here that all his life, Toussaint had been in theatrical representation, thus playing roles: as a docile slave in the house of the Bréda, as a general in the French army, and as a public figure. In Lamartine's play, Toussaint is disguised as a blind man. The disguise functions precisely as a "camouflage," concealing the identity of the person and reinforcing Toussaint's image as an elusive character. Moreover, the disguise mimics something else, making the person same and not quite same. As elusive as he was, Toussaint was indeed a threat to the representatives of the dominant power. Toussaint's political representation, that is, his standing for the whole group of slaves, was threatening as well.

9. Aristide's speech on the Internet is provided by the Haitian Embassy in Washington, D.C. One cannot fail to notice the similarity between Aristide's and Toussaint's words, as reproduced by Percy Waxman quoting from a letter by Toussaint, in which he explains his allegiance to and alliance with Spain: "Brothers and Friends: I am Toussaint Louverture; my name is perhaps known to you. I have undertaken to avenge your wrongs. It is my desire that liberty and equality shall reign in San Domingo. I am striving to this end. Come and unite with us, and fight with us for the same cause. Toussaint Louverture" (qtd. in Waxman 100–101).

Dadié, in *Iles de tempête*, uses the same letter, but in a different context, when Toussaint is confronted by Dessalines, who reports to him about the peasants' discontent with his new rule: "Paysans de Saint Domingue, mes frères, je veux que la liberté et l'égalité règnent à Saint Domingue. Je travaille à les faire exister. J'ai besoin de votre confiance. Unissez-vous à moi, frères, et combattez avec moi pour la même cause" [Peasants of Saint Domingue, my brothers, I want liberty and equality to reign in Saint Domingue. I am working to bring them into existence. I need your confidence. Unite with me, brothers, and fight with me for the same cause] (63).

10. See *Social Text*, Moore-Gilbert, Meddeb, and, more recently, Ashcroft and also Young.

11. In *The Black Jacobins*, C.L.R. James, without ignoring or downplaying race or color, sometimes seems to place greater emphasis on the category of class. For a discussion of his position, see Farred and also Geggus.

12. It is worth quoting Pluchon at length because he shows particularly well Toussaint's ambiguities, as well as how adept Toussaint was at manipulating situations:

> Toussaint Louverture ne se réclame pas de 1789 et des années qui ont suivi; ce sont les héritiers de la Révolution française qui le revendiquent et lui désignent un piédestal dans le Panthéon des grands ancêtres. . . . Et c'est ici que le vieux chef montre son génie. Lui, le profiteur du système colonial, lui qui n'a pas inventé l'affranchissement général, se taille un destin héroïque: celui de défenseur de la liberté des Noirs. . . . Le vieux Toussaint . . . n'est pas le produit du tumulte et des cris qui agitent le monde du prétoire français en 1789. Non, il a été formé à l'école de cet ordre et de cette tradition qu'honore l'Ancien Régime. . . . [I]l reste fidèle aux valeurs et au système colonial qui ont consacré son *mérite* en lui procurant la liberté par affranchissement et qui lui ont permis de devenir un petit colon apprécié, maître d'esclaves et de biens. Cet homme, au crépuscule de sa vie, doit ce qu'il est et ce qu'il possède à son talent, à son travail, à sa conscience, dans le respect de l'ordre socio-économique de l'île, dont il est un bénéficiaire après en

avoir été un rouage servile. . . . Le premier général noir de l'histoire française est un héritier de l'Ancien Régime, par toutes les facettes de sa personnalité. Il n'est pas une création ni un disciple de la Révolution française, à laquelle il se sent profondément étranger, sentiment qu'il ne cachera ni dans sa vie quotidienne ni dans les grandes affaires. (547–54)

[Toussaint Louverture does not claim to draw his inspiration from 1789 and from the years that followed it; it is, rather, the heirs of the French Revolution who claim him and put him on a pedestal in the pantheon of great forefathers . . . And it is here that the old leader reveals his genius. Toussaint, who profited from the colonial system, Toussaint, who did not come up with the idea of a widespread emancipation, fashions a heroic destiny for himself: that of the defender of black freedom. . . . The old Toussaint . . . is not the product of the tumult and the cries that trouble the world of the French Praetorium in 1789. No, he was trained within an order and tradition that the Ancien Régime held in high esteem. . . . (H)e remains faithful to colonial values and to the colonial system which has consecrated his *merit* in procuring his freedom through emancipation and which has allowed him to become an appreciated petty colonist, a master of slaves and of property. This man, in the twilight of his life, owes what he is and what he possesses to his talent, his labor, his conscience; he is respectful of the socioeconomic order of the island, of which he is now a beneficiary, after having once been a servile cog in its wheel. The first black general in French history is an heir of the Ancien Régime in every facet of his personality. He is neither a creation nor a disciple of the French Revolution, with which he feels no identification whatsoever, a sentiment that he hid neither in his daily life nor in matters of public concern.]

Works Cited

Alexis, Stephen. *Black Liberator: The Life of Toussaint Louverture.* Trans. William Stirling. London: Ernest Benn, 1949.

Aristide, Jean-Bertrand. "Discours du Président de la République Son Excellence Jean-Bertrand Aristide à l'occasion de la prise de fonction du nouveau gouvernement." Haitian Embassy, Washington, D.C. (March 2, 2001). <http://www.haiti.org/jba-discours-02-03-01.htm>, accessed 16 February 2003.

Ashcroft, Bill. *Post-Colonial Transformation.* London: Routledge, 2001.

Auguste, Claude. "Toussaint Louverture et la Révolution française." *Jahrbuch für Geschichte von Staat, Wirtschaft und Gesellschaft Lateinamerikas* 28 (1991): 53–83.

Baker, Houston A., Jr. *Black Literature in America.* New York: McGraw-Hill, 1971.

Belasco, Susan. "Harriet Martineau's Black Hero and the American Antislavery Movement." *Nineteenth-Century Literature* 55.2 (September 2000): 157–94.

Bell, Madison Smartt. *All Souls' Rising.* New York: Pantheon, 1995.

Benjamin, Robert C. O. *Life of Toussaint L'Ouverture.* Los Angeles: Evening Express Print, 1888.

Benn, Christine. "O Miserable Chieftain! Toussaint Louverture in der Englischsprachigen Lyrik." *Jahrbuch für Geschichte von Staat, Wirtschaft und Gesellschaft Lateinamerikas* 28 (1991): 391–406.

Bhabha, Homi K. "Of Mimicry and Man." *The Location of Culture*. London: Routledge, 1994. 85–92.

Bourke, Thomas E. "Toussaint L'Ouverture and the Black Revolution of St. Domingue as Reflected in German Literature from Kleist to Buch." *History of European Ideas* 11 (1989): 121–30.

Brutus, Edner. *Révolution dans Saint-Domingue*. Paris: Panthéon, 1970.

Carpentier, Alejo. *El Reino do este mundo*. Mexico City: Edición Iberoamericana, 1949.

Carter, Steven R. "Lorraine Hansberry's Toussaint." *Black American Literature Forum* 1 (Spring 1989): 139–48.

Célestin, Délinois Martin. *La Politique humaniste de Louis XVI et la volonté indépendantiste de Toussaint Louverture*. Paris: Editions du Panthéon, 1997.

Césaire, Aimé. *Les Armes miraculeuses*. Paris: Gallimard, 1946.

———. *Cahier d'un retour au pays natal*. Paris: Présence africaine, 1983.

———. *Return to My Native Land*. Trans. Emile Snyders. Paris: Présence africaine, 1968.

———. *Une Saison au Congo*. Paris: Seuil, 1966.

———. *Toussaint Louverture: la Révolution française et le problème colonial*. Paris: Présence africaine, 1962.

———. *La Tragédie du Roi Christophe*. Paris: Présence africaine, 1963.

Clark, VèVè A. "Haiti's Tragic Overture: (Mis)Representations of the Haitian Revolution in the World Drama (1796–1975)." *Representing the French Revolution: Literature, Historiography, and Art*. Ed. James A. W. Heffernan. Hanover, N.H.: University Press of New England, 1992. 237–60.

Collier, Gordon. "The 'Noble Ruins' of Art and the Haitian Revolution: Carpentier, Césaire, Glissant, James, O'Neill, Walcott, and Others." *Fusion of Cultures?* Ed. Peter O. Stummer and Christopher Balme. Amsterdam: Rodopi, 1996. 269–328.

Court, Antoine. "Lamartine et Césaire, deux regards sur Toussaint Louverture." *Oeuvres et critiques* 19.2 (1994): 267–80.

Dadié, Bernard B. *Iles de tempête: pièce en sept tableaux*. Paris: Présence africaine, 1973.

Donnadien, Jean-Louis. "Le Comte et l'affranchi; destins croisés." *Historia* 80 (November–December 2002): 54–59.

Dorsinville, Roger. 1965. *Toussaint Louverture, ou, La vocation de la liberté*. Reprint, Montreal: Editions du Centre International de Documentation et d'Information Haïtienne Caraïbéenne et Afro-Canadienne (CIDIHCA), 1987.

Dunbar, Paul Laurence. "We Wear the Mask." *The Complete Poems of Paul Laurence Dunbar*. New York: Dodd, Mead, 1968. 190–92.

Dupuy, Alex. "Toussaint Louverture and the Haitian Revolution: A Reassessment of C. L. R. James's Interpretation." *C.L.R. James: His Intellectual Legacies*. Ed. Selwyn R. Cudjoe and William E. Cain. Amherst: University of Massachusetts Press, 1995. 106–17.

Eze, Emmanuel Chukwudi, ed. *Race and Enlightenment: A Reader.* Oxford, U.K.: Blackwell, 1997.

Farred, Grant. "First Stop, Port-au-Prince: Mapping Postcolonial Africa through Toussaint Louverture and His Black Jacobins." *The Politics of Culture in the Shadow of Capital.* Ed. Lisa Lowe and David Lloyd. Durham, N.C.: Duke University Press, 1997. 227–47.

Ferguson, J. A. "Le Premier des Noirs: The Nineteenth-Century Image of Toussaint Louverture." *Nineteenth-Century French Studies* 15.4 (Summer 1987): 394–406.

Fick, Carolyn E. *The Making of Haiti: The Saint Domingue Revolution from Below.* Knoxville: University of Tennessee Press, 1990.

Fombrun, Odette R. *Toussaint Louverture, tacticien de génie: la Constitution indépendantiste de 1801.* Port-au-Prince: Maison Henri Deschamps, 2001.

Freeman E. "From Raynal's 'New Spartacus' to Lamartine's 'Toussaint Louverture': A Myth of the Black Soul in Rebellion." *Myth and Its Making in the French Theatre: Studies Presented to W. D. Howarth.* Ed. E. Freeman et al. Cambridge, U.K.: Cambridge University Press, 1988. 136–57.

Gaspar, David B., and David P. Geggus, eds. *A Turbulent Time: The French Revolution and the Greater Caribbean.* Bloomington: Indiana University Press, 1997.

Geggus, David P. "The French and the Haitian Revolutions, and Resistance to Slavery in the Americas: An Overview." *Revue française d'histoire d'Outre-Mer* 56 (1989): 107–24.

Gilroy, Paul. *The Black Atlantic: Modernity and Double Consciousness.* Cambridge, Mass.: Harvard University Press, 1993.

Glissant, Edouard. *Monsieur Toussaint.* Paris: Seuil, 1961.

James, C.L.R. *The Black Jacobins: Toussaint L'Ouverture and the San Domingo Revolution.* New York: Random House, 1963.

Jean-Pierre, Jean Reynold. *Et Toussaint Louverture émerge: 1793–1802.* Port-au-Prince: Editions presses nationales d'Haïti, 2000.

Jones, Foster T. "Césaire's Toussaint: A Metahistorical Reading." *Studies in the Humanities* 11.1 (June 1984): 44–49.

Jurt, Joseph. "Condorcet: l'idée de progrès et l'opposition à l'esclavage." *Condorcet, mathématicien, économiste, philosophe, homme politique.* Ed. Pierre Crépel Christian Gilain. Paris: Minerve, 1989. 385–95.

Kesteloot, Lilyan. "*La Tragédie du Roi Christophe* ou les indépendances africaines au miroir d'Haïti." *Présence africaine* 51 (1964): 131–45.

Lamartine, Alphonse de. *Toussaint Louverture.* Ed. Léon-François Hoffmann. Exeter, U.K.: University Press of Exeter, 1998.

Lamming, George. *The Pleasures of Exile.* London: M. Joseph, 1960.

Leloup, Jacqueline. *Le Précurseur: Toussaint Louverture.* Brazzaville: Editions du NIC, 1989.

Martineau, Harriet. *The Hour and the Man: A Historical Romance.* London: E. Moxon, 1841.

McKay, Claude. *Selected Poems.* New York: Bookman, 1953.

Meddeb, Abdelwahab. "Ouverture/argument." *Dédale* 5–6 (Spring 1997): 12–14.

Moïse, Claude. *Le Projet national de Toussaint Louverture et la Constitution de 1801*. Montreal: Editions du Centre International de Documentation et d'Information Haïtienne Caraïbéenne et Afro-Canadienne (CIDIHCA), 2001.

Moore-Gilbert, Bart. *Postcolonial Theory: Contexts, Practices, Politics*. London: Verso, 1997.

Mouralis, Bernard. "L'Image de l'indépendance haïtienne dans la littérature négro-africaine." *Revue de littérature comparée* 48.4 (1974): 504–35.

Nemours, Alfred. *Histoire de la captivité et de la mort de Toussaint-Louverture: notre pélerinage au fort de Joux*. Paris: Berger-Levrault, 1992.

Oddon, Marcel. "Les Tragédies de la décolonisation: Aimé Césaire et Edouard Glissant." *Le Théâtre moderne*. Ed. Jean Jacquot. Vol. 2. Paris: Centre National de la Recherche Scientifique, 1967. 85–101.

Onyeoziri, Gloria. "Le Toussaint d'Aimé Césaire: réflexions sur le statut d'un texte." *L'esprit Créateur* 32.1 (Spring 1992): 87–96.

Pasquet, Fabienne. *La Deuxième mort de Toussaint-Louverture*. Arles, France: Actes sud, 2001.

Pauléus Sannon, H. *Histoire de Toussaint Louverture*. 3 vols. Port-au-Prince: Imprimerie Héraux, 1920–1933.

Pierre-Charles, Gérard. *Vision contemporaine de Toussaint Louverture*. Port-au-Prince: Centre de recherche et de formation économique et sociale pour le développement, 1992.

Pluchon, Pierre. *Toussaint Louverture: un révolutionnaire noir d'Ancien Régime*. Paris: Fayard, 1989.

Said, Edward W. *Orientalism*. New York: Vintage Books, 1978.

Sala-Molins, Louis. *Le Code noir, ou, Le calvaire de Canaan*. Paris: Presses Universitaires de France, 1987.

Schoelcher, Victor. *Vie de Toussaint-Louverture*. Paris: P. Ollendorff, 1889.

Social Text 31/32 (1992). Special issue on "Third World and Post-Colonial Issues." Ed. Bruce Robbins and Andrew Ross.

Tyson, George F. Jr., ed. *Toussaint L'Ouverture*. Englewood Cliffs, N.J.: Prentice-Hall, 1973.

Walcott, Derek. *The Haitian Trilogy*. New York: Farrar, Straus and Giroux, 2002.

Waxman, Percy. *The Black Napoleon. The Story of Toussaint Louverture*. New York: Harcourt, Brace, 1931.

Wordsworth, William. *Poems, in Two Volumes and Other Poems, 1800–1807*. Ed. Jared Curtis. Ithaca, N.Y.: Cornell University Press, 1983.

Young, Robert J. C. *Postcolonialism: An Historical Introduction*. Oxford, U.K.: Blackwell, 2001.

4

A Neglected Precursor

Roland Barthes and the Origins of Postcolonialism

Alec G. Hargreaves

The general slowness of French scholars to embrace the problematic of what is now known as postcolonialism stands in paradoxical contrast with the pervasive influence of French and francophone writers and theorists among many of those who have helped to make postcolonial studies such a vibrant field of inquiry in the anglophone world. In recent years, these early influences have been increasingly recognized by anglophone scholars. Huggan, for example, describes postcolonial criticism as "the provisional attempt to forge a working alliance between the—often Marxist-inspired—politics of anti-colonial resistance, exemplified in the liberationist tracts of Fanon, Césaire and Memmi, and the disparate, allegedly destabilizing poststructuralisms of Derrida, Lacan, Althusser and Foucault" (260).

The absence of Roland Barthes from this list is not unusual. In a recent guide to francophone studies, the entry on "postcolonialism" includes an almost identical list of French and francophone influences, again without any reference to Barthes (Majumdar 206). Scholars such as Young, Knight, and Sandoval are unusual in highlighting the significance of Barthes's work in the genealogy of postcolonial studies. Yet the articles collected by Barthes in *Mythologies*, which remains one of his most widely read works, frequently focus on the process of decolonization and in doing so develop one of the earliest and most sophisticated critiques of colonial discourse to have emerged from France. This chapter examines the contribution of Barthes to the field of postcolonial studies and attempts to explain the neglect from which he has suffered.

The earliest intellectuals of French expression generally cited in the genealogy of postcolonialism—Fanon, Césaire, Memmi, etc.—had their origins among the colonized peoples of the overseas empire. While the perceived excesses of French colonialism had sometimes been criticized by writers and intellectuals of French descent such as André Gide and Albert Camus, their vision was generally reformist in nature. At the height of the empire, the surrealists had been virtually alone in France in opposing the principle of colonization, notably in the counterexhibition that they organized during the 1931 Colonial Exhibition in Paris (Nadeau 325–27). It was not until the 1950s that thinkers such as Sartre and Barthes began to elaborate more sustained critiques of the foundations of colonialism. As Sandoval observes, "Barthes's *Mythologies* represents one of the first efforts to critique and outline 'white' forms of consciousness by a member of the colonizing class responding to the decolonizing processes going on at the time he was writing" (126). Borrowing the term "de-coloniality" from Helen Tiffin, Sandoval argues that Barthes's work "can be seen to pre-figure, and in many cases go beyond, the critical categories and contradictions that are central to the intellectual processes of decoloniality" (3).

At the same time, Sandoval sees "Barthes's great manifesto on semiology . . . as both advancing de-colonial interests and inadvertently extending relations of cultural center and periphery in the formation of the canon of literary theory" (90). Viewed in a postcolonial perspective, the articles collected in *Mythologies* do contain important ambiguities and tensions that, as I will show in this chapter, help to explain the relative infrequency with which they are cited by theorists of postcolonialism. Similar tensions are also evident in later phases of Barthes's work and personal life, which Sandoval passes over but to which Knight draws attention. These are especially visible in his increasing emphasis on the notion of personal pleasure in parallel with an apparent neglect of politics, a dynamic exemplified in a string of sexual encounters in postcolonial Morocco through which, Knight suggests, "sexual politics . . . tie Barthes to an Orientalism that he seeks, in other ways, to go beyond" (123). In this context, the salient element of those encounters is not that they were homosexual but that the pleasure which they afforded to Barthes was facilitated by unequal power relations which were neocolonial in nature.

To fully appreciate the extent and the limitations of Barthes's contribution to postcolonial theory, it is important to note that as widely (though not universally) understood, postcolonial studies is taken to embrace "all the culture affected by the imperial process from the moment of colonization to the present day" (Ashcroft, Griffiths, and Tiffin 2). Within this broad space, exponents of postcolonial studies have focused on two main tasks: the critique of colonial discourse and the analysis of work by writers originating among colonized peoples, including diasporic groups now settled in the former colonial heartland. *Mythologies* makes an early and extremely incisive contribution to the first of these fields. The semiological theory of sociocultural myths advanced by Barthes with special (though not exclusive) reference to French colonialism is arguably more subtle and more rigorous than the analysis of European orientalism published two decades later by Edward Said. Yet it is Said's *Orientalism* that is customarily seen as the founding text of what would later become known as postcolonial studies, though Said does not himself use that phrase.

Said describes orientalism as a western discourse or style "for dominating, restructuring, and having authority over the Orient," the Orient being understood in this context as the Islamic world (3). In developing his argument, Said draws extensively on a number of French and francophone thinkers, most notably Foucault. By contrast, Said makes only two passing references to Barthes. In the first of these Said notes that Barthes sees all linguistic formations as deformations of the objects that they purport to represent; in the second Said refers to Barthes's demonstration of the fact that through myths, such deformations may take multiple forms (273, 308). Said makes no reference to the fact that in *Mythologies* Barthes had explicitly applied his theory of myths to certain forms of orientalism and associated western discourses central to the processes of colonial domination.

Among the many texts in *Mythologies* exploring these discourses are "Continent perdu" [The lost continent], "Bichon chez les Nègres" [Bichon and the Negroes], "Le Biftek et les frites" [Steak and fries], and "Le Mythe aujourd'hui" [Myth today], the last of which contains Barthes's most elaborate exposition of his semiological methodology for the study of myths. In "Continent perdu," Barthes sets out to deconstruct "un grand documentaire sur 'l'Orient'" [a major documentary on "the East"], which, he says, "éclaire bien le mythe actuel de l'exotisme" [throws a clear light on the current myth of exoticism] (163/94).[1] The Orient depicted in the movie is Asian, not the Islamic Orient on which Said focuses. But in his critique of the film, Barthes lays bare processes of representational deformation that in large degree replicate those highlighted in Said's account of orientalism and in the wider field of colonial discourse within which orientalism may be located. As Knight correctly notes, "the early Barthes was a quite exemplary demystifier of Orientalist discourse" (93).

The analysis of colonial discourse is at the very heart of texts such as "Grammaire africaine" [African grammar], showing how official and journalistic declarations about the colonies attempted to mask and travesty the tide of events pushing inexorably toward decolonization. And in "Le Mythe aujourd'hui," the principal example through which Barthes illustrates his theory of myths is the front cover of an issue of the French magazine *Paris-Match* featuring a photograph of a young African dressed in French military uniform, saluting with eyes raised toward an object out of frame that is presumed to be the French tricolor flag. Beyond this immediate or surface level of meaning, Barthes sees a second, more ideological thrust. Through the apparent fidelity of the young African to the French flag, the photograph is seen by Barthes to be spinning a mythical vision of French colonialism aimed at neutralizing those who claim it is an oppressive system, for the youth's salute seems to show that French colonial rule is respected and defended by those whom its opponents portray as its victims. In this way, the seemingly simple meaning of the magazine cover is shown to be deformed in the service of an underlying message serving the interests of colonial domination.

The centrality of ideological domination in the production and consumption of myths is such that Barthes sees colonization as a veritable synonym for these processes. A myth, he says, is nothing other than "un vol par colonisation" [a robbery by colonization] (219/132). But what exactly is being stolen from whom? It seems clear that myths involve the theft of meaning. Barthes writes: "Le mythe est toujours un vol de langage. Je vole le nègre qui salue" [Myth is always a language-robbery. I rob the Negro who is saluting] (217/131). At first sight it might appear that an original meaning is being stolen from the young African depicted on the cover of *Paris-Match*. But if that had been the thrust of Barthes's analysis, he would rather have written: "Je vole au nègre qui salue le sens de l'image" [I steal from the saluting Negro the meaning of the image]. Barthes is instead suggesting that a semantic charge already attaching to but not constructed by the African in the photograph's first level of meaning is being plundered and warped in the service of a second level of meaning, which he describes as the myth of "l'impérialité française" [French imperiality] (211/125). Within this analysis, the African soldier features as part of a stolen image, "le nègre qui salue" [the Negro who is saluting], but not as the maker of any of the stolen meaning (217/131). In other words, the African seems to lack any kind of agency in the discursive processes being described here by Barthes.

This assumption emerges more clearly elsewhere in *Mythologies*. "Statistiquement, le mythe est à droite," writes Barthes. "Là, il est essentiel: bien nourri, luisant, expansif, bavard, il s'invente sans cesse" [Statistically, myth is on the right. There, it is essential; well fed, sleek, expansive, garrulous, it invents itself ceaselessly] (236/148). In contrast, "la gauche se définit toujours par rapport à l'opprimé, prolétaire ou colonisé. Or, la parole de l'opprimé ne peut être que pauvre, monotone, immédiate: son dénuement est la mesure même de son langage: il n'en a qu'un, toujours le même, celui de ses actes; le méta-langage est un luxe, il ne peut encore y accéder." [the left always defines itself in relation to the oppressed, whether proletarian or colonized. Yet when the oppressed speak, they are able to do so only in poor, monotonous, immediate ways; their destitution is the very yardstick of their language, which is always one and the same: that of their actions; metalanguage is a luxury to which they do not yet have access] (236/148). These remarks are consonant with the idea that while the African soldier may have the potential to destabilize or overthrow the colonial system at the level of praxis, he is incapable of generating any discourse worthy of note.

It is here that we approach a major dividing line within postcolonial studies, that between the study of colonial discourse and the study of discourses produced by colonized or formerly colonized subjects. In marking that transition, Gayatri Spivak famously asked: "Can the subaltern speak?" Exponents of postcolonial studies responded by working vigorously to uncover traces of meaning inscribed by the colonized in the works of the colonizer and by celebrating the marks of anticolonial resistance seen in the works produced by writers, filmmakers, and other artists originating in colonized peoples. Barthes never made this transition. While consistently aligning himself with the disempowered against a class enemy whom he generally describes as "bourgeois" or still more dismissively as "petit bourgeois," he speaks for but never enables us to hear the voice of the dominated Other.

In "Le Mythe aujourd'hui," Barthes identifies two main forces of opposition to myths and the dominant class that weaves them. One of these is poetic invention, which "s'affirme toujours comme un meurtre du langage, une sorte d'analogue spatial, sensible, du silence. La poésie occupe la position inverse du mythe" [always asserts itself as a murder of language, a kind of spatial, tangible analogue of silence. Poetry occupies a position that is the reverse of that of myth] (220/134). This kind of poetry is the work of an avant-garde that resists the bourgeoisie through art rather than politics (226/139). Political resistance to myths and the class whose domination they support is the work of a "parti révolutionnaire. Mais [c]e parti ne peut constituer qu'une richesse politique: en société bourgeoise, il n'y a ni culture ni morale prolétarienne, il n'y a pas d'art prolétarien" [revolutionary party. But this party is a purely political resource: in a bourgeois culture, there is neither proletarian culture nor proletarian morality, there is no proletarian art] (226/139). In Barthes's thinking there is a sharp disjuncture between these two forms of resistance to the ruling class, both at home and in the overseas empire. One, operating in the sphere of material praxis, is seen as the work of an oppressed class that is incapable of producing any significant discourse or culture. The other, discursive and cultural in nature, is the work of a dissident, politically impotent fraction of the dominant class. This disjuncture is a major feature in the vision of the colonized Other inscribed in *Mythologies*.

The importance of the colonial arena in this early phase of Barthes's work is underlined in his assertion that "[c]'est aujourd'hui le colonisé qui assume pleinement la condition éthique et politique décrite par Marx comme condition du prolétaire" [today it is the colonized peoples who fully embody the ethical and political condition described by Marx as being that of the proletariat] (236/148, n. 25). The political action of the colonized flies in the face of the myths supporting French colonialism, shaking it to its foundations. This action is illustrated in "Continent perdu," which takes its title from that of a documentary movie shot among the islands of Southeast Asia. At almost the same moment in time, representatives of the new African and Asian states emerging from European colonial rule had met in the Indonesian city of Bandung in 1955 to lay the foundations for the nonaligned movement. Barthes concludes mischievously that "les 'belles images' de *Continent perdu* ne peuvent être innocentes: il ne peut être innocent de *perdre* le continent qui s'est retrouvé à Bandoeng" [the "beautiful pictures" of *The Lost Continent* are never innocent: it is by no means an innocent act to *lose* the continent which has just found itself at Bandung] (165/96).

A similar reversal of perspectives, in which European colonial discourse is challenged and subverted by the political action of the Third World, is found in the conclusion to another of the texts in *Mythologies*, "Bichon chez les Nègres," a further exposure of the workings of colonial discourse in the columns of *Paris-Match*. This time the magazine article is about the exploits of a young French couple and their baby, Bichon, who set off to explore an unnamed African country. The stereotypes recycled in the article produce a familiar picture but through a novel lens, the eyes of Bichon, which reduce the behavior of Africans to the level of an exotic Punch and Judy show. This, says Barthes, is symptomatic of the infantile nature of the petit bourgeois mythmaking critiqued in this and other articles. Such mythmaking is unable to envision otherness. As depicted in the *Paris-Match* reportage, Africans are mere sources of entertainment. After exposing these images, Barthes concludes by lamenting that mythmaking of this kind helps to maintain readers of *Paris-Match* in a pre-eighteenth-century mode. Enlightenment figures such as Montesquieu and Voltaire are cited by Barthes as examples of more sophisticated minds capable of challenging the self-satisfied assumptions of petit bourgeois thinking through imaginative writings in which Europe is critiqued through foreign eyes. Had Voltaire lived in the twentieth century, says Barthes, instead of writing Bichon's adventures in the manner of *Paris-Match*, "il imaginerait plutôt quelque Bichon cannibale (ou coréen) aux prises avec le 'guignol' napalmisé de l'Occident" [he would have rather imagined a cannibal or Korean Bichon locked in combat against the napalmed figure of a Western marionette] (67). Here we find the division of labor noted earlier between two types of resistance to colonial domination. In a reversal of the American use of napalm during the Korean War (1950–53), Barthes imagines the west being napalmed by Korean insurgents. While Asians are seen as the political agents of anticolonial struggle, they appear nevertheless to be incapable of challenging colonial domination at a discursive level. In Montesquieu's *Les Lettres persanes* (1721), as in Voltaire's *L'Ingénu* (1767), Europe is seen through the eyes of outsiders from Persia and North America respectively, but their trenchant critiques are voiced by European authors. In the same way, it is apparently assumed that only another European, some latter-day Montesquieu or Voltaire—in whose role we are implicitly invited to see Barthes himself—might now be capable of correcting the myths spun by popular media such as *Paris-Match*.

A similar disjuncture is apparent in "La Grande famille des hommes," where Barthes engages in a merciless critique of an exhibition of photographs from around the world purporting to show the essential commonality shared by a Great Family of Man, far outweighing any differences of class, nationality, or ethnicity. In a parenthetical reference to the lynching of a young African American, Emmet Till, in 1955, Barthes asks, "[M]ais pourquoi ne pas demander aux parents d'Emmet Till, le jeune nègre assassiné par des blancs, ce qu'ils pensent, eux, de *la grande famille des hommes*?" [But why not ask the parents of Emmet Till, the young Negro assassinated by Whites, what *they* think of *The Great Family of Man*?] (175/101). In another parenthesis, he enjoins the reader, "Demandons aussi aux travailleurs nord-africains de la Goutte d'or ce qu'ils pensent de *la grande famille des hommes*" [Let us also ask the North African workers of the Goutte d'Or district in Paris what they think of *The Great Family of Man*] (176/102). These are incisively formulated and highly pertinent questions. Yet Barthes seems to have made no attempt to seek answers from those who might have been able to provide them. He appears to have assumed that African Americans such as Emmet Till's parents or migrant workers like those in la Goutte d'or lacked any discourse worth listening to.

Barthes makes no secret of this conviction: "L'opprimé n'est rien, il n'a en lui qu'une parole, celle de son émancipation; l'oppresseur est tout, sa parole est riche, multiforme, souple, disposant de tous les degrés possibles de dignité: il a l'exclusivité du métalangage" [The oppressed is nothing, he has only one language, that of his emancipation; the oppressor is everything, his language is rich, multiform, supple, with every possible degree of dignity at his disposal: he alone accedes to the realm of metalanguage] (237/149). It is a curious paradox that Barthes, who frequently denounced the petit bourgeois inability to imagine the Other (239/151), seems to have suffered a similar failure in the face of the racialized and colonial Other. If, as Knight observes, "Barthes has not always received the political credit he deserves . . . both for tracking down many examples of pro-colonial myths and for relating them to other forms of mystification" (95), this is no doubt in part because he failed to move beyond that first phase of the postcolonial dialectic to fully embrace the cultures of postcolonial subjects.

More fundamentally, the apparently seamless union between the political tide of decolonization in the 1950s and the pleasure Barthes took in applying his critical faculties to dominant discourses soon began to appear as a temporary conjunction of circumstances from which his later work grew increasingly detached. While numerous social movements subsequently attempted to redistribute power through the breach opened up within western societies by the end of empire overseas, Barthes concentrated increasingly on textual and other pleasures. Hence Sandoval's judgment: "Barthes's territorial range of control ended at the location where his semiotic theory of resistance should have met in coalition with those theories of resistance that have been generated by oppressed and colonized peoples. Unable to negotiate that leap, Barthes constructed instead a view of semiotics, of 'mythology,' and of resistance where the individual practitioner can only act alone, isolated and in despair" (113).

The magnitude of Barthes's later detachment from the kinds of coalitions to which his early career might have been expected to bind him is exemplified in his preface to a 1971 Italian edition of Pierre Loti's novel *Aziyadé* (1879). Set in Turkey, the novel is saturated in the literary clichés and inequalities of power that are characteristic of orientalism. The Barthes who wrote *Mythologies* could scarcely have resisted the opportunity to demonstrate the textual workings of orientalist myths. By contrast, the Barthes who writes about *Aziyadé* in 1971 makes little more than a passing reference to orientalism, choosing instead to revel in outing the novel's homosexual subtext, which is celebrated as a hippie-style form of dandyism of the kind practiced by late-twentieth-century westerners in exotic locations such as Tangiers, "où la débauche règne sans s'y prendre au sérieux" [where debauchery reigns without ever taking itself seriously] ("Pierre Loti" 184). This image of the seemingly innocent pleasures enjoyed by hippie travelers detached from normal social conventions cuts little ice today, when global tourism has made the blurring of the lines between hedonism, sexual tourism, prostitution, and neocolonialism ever more troubling. Barthes's reference, with no apparent irony, to the harmlessness of debauchery in a city such as Tangiers, long known for blurred boundaries of that kind, seems to implicitly draw a parallel between his own experiences in Morocco at around the time he wrote this preface and those of Loti a century earlier in Istanbul. As I have argued elsewhere, Loti's writings exemplify a form of literary imperialism that is entirely of a piece with other contemporaneous forms of colonial discourse (Hargreaves, *Colonial Experience*). After the incisiveness displayed by Barthes in his critique of colonial discourse in *Mythologies*, it is ironic and disturbing to see his later celebration of "la dérive" [drifting] leading him to revel in the company of such dubious figures as Loti ("Pierre Loti" 184). Unusually, Barthes thus exemplifies on the one hand some of the most trenchant early analyses of colonial discourse and on the other some of the ways in which attitudes and power relations inherited from the colonial period continue to structure neocolonialist thinking and behavior.

Note

1. Whenever two page numbers are listed, the first refers to the French original and the second to the published English translation. Some translations have been modified for clarity.

Works cited

Ashcroft, Bill, Gareth Griffiths, and Helen Tiffin. *The Empire Writes Back: Theory and Practice in Post-Colonial Literatures*. London: Routledge, 1989.

Barthes, Roland. 1957. *Mythologies*. Paris: Seuil, 1970.

———. *Mythologies*. Trans. Annette Lavers. New York: Hill and Wang, 1972.

———. "Pierre Loti: 'Aziyadé.'" *Le Degré zéro de l'écriture*. Suivi de *Nouveaux essais critiques*. Paris: Seuil, 1972. 170–87. [First published as Barthes's preface to Pierre Loti, *Aziyadé*, Parma, Italy: Franco-Maria Ricci, 1971.]

Hargreaves, Alec G. *The Colonial Experience in French Fiction: A Study of Pierre Loti, Ernest Psichari and Pierre Mille*. London: Macmillan; Atlantic Highlands, N.J.: Humanities Press, 1981.

Huggan, Graham. *The Post-Colonial Exotic: Marketing the Margins*. London: Routledge, 2001.

Knight, Diana. *Barthes and Utopia: Space, Travel and Writing*. Oxford, U.K.: Clarendon Press, 1997.

Loti, Pierre. *Aziyadé*. Paris: Calmann-Lévy, 1879.

Majumdar, Margaret A. *Francophone Studies: The Essential Glossary*. London: Arnold, 2002.

Nadeau, Maurice. *Histoire du surréalisme*. Suivi de *Documents surréalistes*. Paris: Seuil, 1964.

Said, Edward W. *Orientalism*. London: Routledge and Kegan Paul, 1978.

Sandoval, Chela. *Methodology of the Oppressed.* Minneapolis: University of Minnesota Press, 2000.

Spivak, Gayatri Chakravorty. "Can the Subaltern Speak?" *Marxism and the Interpretation of Culture.* Ed. Cary Nelson and Lawrence Grossberg. Houndmills, U.K.: Macmillan Education, 1988. 271–313.

Young, Robert J. C. *White Mythologies: Writing, History and the West.* London: Routledge, 1990.

II

Postcolonialism, Modernity, and French Identities

5

Nomadic Thought, Postcolonialism, and Maghrebian Writing

John D. Erickson

Mieux vaut la liberté que le ventre plein
[Better to be free than to have a full stomach]
Tuareg adage

The concept of nomadic thought and the relationship between authors/theorists and their environment have had a strong impact on Maghrebian writing in French and postcolonial theory in recent years, particularly since Deleuze and Guattari elaborated the concept, first in *Anti-Oedipe*, then in *Mille plateaux*. It has come to stand for a mode of differentiation in regard to nationalist/fundamentalist/nativist social and religious strictures, on the one hand, and the global politics of western culture on the other. It has come to connote becoming, movement, and pluralist values as opposed to the static, totalistic, reductionist ideology and strategies of statist and theocratic institutions. I shall examine how the term "nomadic thought" has informed theoretical and cultural traditions, with reference to the postcolonial vocabulary and to the fictional work of a representative Maghrebian writer, Tahar Djaout.

The Characteristics of Nomadism (Defining the Term)

The word *nomad*, from the Latin *nomad-, nomas,* signifying a person belonging to a wandering pastoral people, derives etymologically from the Greek *nemein*, to pasture. *Webster's Third* gives the following as its first usage: "a member of a people that has no fixed residence but wanders from place to place usu. seasonally and within a well-defined territory for the purpose of securing its supply of food either by gathering of plants and hunting of animals, by using suitable grounds for quick crops, or esp. by finding grazing lands and water for its herds." The penetration of pastoral groups into fertile agricultural lands in the Western Sahara has occurred continuously for nearly a thousand years. "Beginning with the Almoravid explosion out of the Mauritanian desert in the eleventh century, the major thrust of these movements has been from the fringes of the Sahara northward into the Atlas and beyond to the fertile Atlantic coast plains" (Dunn 85). These areas proved vulnerable to pastoral penetration. "[I]n many parts of the Maghreb no state was able to provide an extended period of security during which the pressure by pastoralists on partially settled peoples was controlled and moderated" (Meeker 214–15). Even the sedentary peoples, retaining their political customs and attitudes from their pastoralist origins, helped to create a situation necessarily undermining "the basis for any routinized and systematic form of legitimate political organization," thus inherently resisting "the development of the state as an instrument of public administration" (Meeker 214–15).

The segmentary design of nomadic tribal groups, in which the role of the leader is essentially nominal and weak, and whose power depends on persuasion, reflects a structural form that diminishes control. Consequently among nomads a question arises about "the very possibility of a conception of a legitimate political community or a legitimate political authority" (Meeker 221). Thus, while the segmentary structure made the former pastoral groups, once sedentarized, susceptible to hegemonic incursions, its difference also resulted in an innate opposition against any dominant political system, against statist and global systems that work to perpetuate their power.

The tendency of the state to "domesticate" the people under its rule has led to strong forces of resistance in the Maghreb. The sociologist Michel Maffesoli speaks of just such a domestication:

> L'histoire est connue. Par contre ce qui reste à analyser c'est la lointaine origine d'une telle domestication. En prenant ces termes en leur sens le plus large, on peut dire que celle-ci se trouve dans le glissement du nomadisme vers la sédentarité. Nombreuses sont les monographies, ethnographiques en particulier, qui montrent que le passage des communautés aux communes, puis de celles-ci aux entités administratives plus grandes, pour en arriver à l'État-nation, va de pair avec la naissance d'un pouvoir d'autant plus abstrait qu'il est plus éloigné. Le nomadisme est totalement antithétique à la forme de l'État moderne. Et celui-ci s'emploie, avec constance, à supprimer ce qu'il considère comme une survivance d'un mode de vie archaïque. En fixant l'on peut dominer. Il s'agit là d'une bonne illustration de ce "fantasme de l'un," qui est le propre de la violence totalitaire moderne. (22)

> [Its history is known. What remains to be analyzed is the distant origin of such a domestication. In considering these terms in their broadest

sense, we can say that domestication lies in the movement of nomadism toward sedentariness. Numerous studies, especially those of ethnographers, show that the transition from [tribal] communities to municipalities, then to greater administrative entities, to emerge finally as Nation-States, takes place concurrently with the engendering of power all the more abstract because it is remote. Nomadism is totally antithetical to the form of the modern State, which constantly works to suppress what it considers to be the survival of an archaic mode of existence. In delimiting one can dominate. It is a good example of the "delusion of oneness" that is the essence of modern totalitarian violence.]

The "delusion of oneness" rests on the authoritarian/totalitarian urge toward homogeneity, toward a unitary structure that seeks to domesticate the masses, to make of the many one. "Oneness" in this sense inveighs against pluralism and multiculturalism, against the diversity of opposing ideas and frames of thought. Fixation and reduction to the Same serve as mileposts marking the way to a uniformizing utopia in which the narrative of self-identity is sanctioned and "a world system of barriers, maps, frontiers, police forces, customs and exchange controls" (Said 307) is put in place.

In his essay "Le voyage et l'écriture" Michel Butor speaks of the effect of nomadic cultures meeting and merging with long established sedentary cultures. The inexorable shock accompanying the change from errancy to fixation that occurs as the former culture adopts the latter's customs, myths, and monuments is tantamount to death (15). Jeffrey Peters speaks of one of these monuments as being cartographic production: "The map must be counted among the western monuments that contribute to the death of nomadic cultures. The act of naming and the correlative processes of textualization that are part of making maps equate to a colonialist flattening that seeks the erasure of cultural difference" (100). Such erasure works toward a homogeneous communization leading to stasis and settlement that negate itinerancy and movement.

Mapping, the establishment of frontiers, surveying, territorial division into geographical boundaries (counties, parishes, and cantons), laying of grids, drawing of borders, and road building all represent delimitation, containment, and stagnation. In regard to the nomad the aim of the State is to sedentarize. In the fourteenth century, historian and sociologist Ibn Khaldûn contrasted the Bedouin way of life as being closer to the natural state and far removed from the degenerate habits of sedentary people who exist in the final stage of civilization in which decay has set in. He argued that the latter's reliance upon arbitrary, fixating social laws resulted in the destruction of their moral and physical strength and power to resist the impingement of external forces, as opposed to observance of religious laws whose moral restraints are intrinsic (94–97). Ibn Khaldûn saw the Bedouins as an undomesticated nation marked by freedom from authority and given over to wandering and movement—the antithesis and negation of sedentarization and stationariness, which are at the root of civilization, which he saw as a degeneration of culture (118).

Inasmuch as nomadic movement, whether physical or mental, is marked by displacement—movement from point to point in space without possessing any point of that trajectory—it contravenes statist authority, based on immobilization, enclosure, and appropriation (possession). Despite the adherence of nomads to a place where they can trade their goods for supplies, to a place of departure and uncertain return (they may return elsewhere), nomadic tribal groups are deterritorialized. In contrast to the migrants, they have no definitive destination. For them there is no reterritorialization at the end of their trajectory; there is instead instinctive rejection of sedentarization, attachment to the earth that is mediated by the property laws of a State apparatus. On the contrary, deterritorialization constitutes the nomads' relation to the earth, in which land ceases to be reified and remains what it is fundamentally: ground over which to move. Nomads are localized, not bounded. What is bounded, limited and limiting, is what Deleuze and Guattari call striated space, "the *relative global*" (*Thousand* 382).

Nomadic space differs radically from State space. "[E]ven though the nomadic trajectory may follow trails or customary routes, it does not fulfill the function of the sedentary [and fixed, undeviating] road, which is to *parcel out a closed space to people*, assigning each person a share and regulating the communication between shares. The nomadic trajectory does the opposite: it *distributes people (or animals) in an open space*, one that is indefinite and non-communicating, . . . a space without borders or enclosure" (Massumi, *Thousand* 380).

The desert nomad can be said to be nowhere and everywhere. As Maffesoli observes, he simultaneously occupies a specific place and tends toward a non-place (80). Nomadic wandering or movement is a process and not an end, for the journey itself is the object, "the shaping fact of existence" (Rushdie, "On Adventure" 225).

D. N. Rodowick has recently raised a fundamental question that has preoccupied postcolonial and francophone theorists: "Comment créer des valeurs nouvelles . . . qui échappent aux binarismes de l'opposition, politique, social, sexuelle? . . . Comment créer des identifications . . . impensables parce qu'elles ne sont plus maîtrisées par l'opposition et la représentation mais qui sont, au contraire, libérées par la différence pure?" [How can one create new values . . . that go beyond the binaries of political, social, and sexual opposition? . . . How can one create identities . . . [that are] unthinkable because they are no longer determined by opposition and representation but are, on the contrary, liberated by pure difference?] (117). Nomadic thought goes beyond mere binary opposition, for like the nomadic journey it is in a constant state of flux, unfixed, varying, unidentifiable with a defined and regulated system of thought. Resistance and opposition come about but only from the vantage point of the dominant master discourse. Nomadic thought is indeed marked by "pure difference." Moreover, in occupying spaces that are nowhere and everywhere, it problematizes representation.

In his foreword to *A Thousand Plateaus*, Brian Massumi speaks of just those new values offered by Deleuze and Guattari's conceptualization of nomadic thought, which supplant the closed system of representation inherent in ruling discourses: "Rather than analyzing the world into discrete components, reducing their manyness to the One of identity, and ordering them by rank, [nomadic thought] . . . synthesizes a multiplicity of elements without effacing their heterogeneity or hindering their potential for future rearranging (to the contrary). *The modus operandi of nomad thought is affirmation, even when its apparent object is negative*" (xiii, my emphasis). Massumi distinguishes between the "force" of nomadic thought as opposed to the "power" of authoritarian thought. The former exerts itself from the exterior in challenging and breaking constraints in order to open up new fields of vision, while the latter erects barriers and enclosures. Massumi speaks of a qualitative difference between nomadic space and State space: "State space is 'striated,' or gridded. Movement in it is confined as by gravity to a horizontal plane, and limited by the order of that plane to preset paths between fixed and identifiable points. Nomad space is 'smooth,' or open-ended. One can rise up at any point and move to any other. Its mode of distribution is the *nomos*: arraying oneself in an open space (hold the street), as opposed to the *logos* of entrenching oneself in a closed space (hold the fort)" (xiii). *A Thousand Plateaus* thus proposes the substitution of a "smooth" or open-ended mode of intellection for all closed systems of thought.

The Antilogic of Nomadic Thought

The way one perceives the world fashions the way one thinks about it. It goes without saying that owing to their way of life, their needs and desires in relation to empirical reality, and how they register such "reality," nomads' thought unequivocally deviates from the way mainstream western thought functions. Nearly a century ago Isabelle Eberhardt, who spent the latter part of her brief life of twenty-seven years in the Sahara, speaking of the Saharan *ksar* (town) of M'sila, wrote, "Nous sommes dans la nouvelle, de construction récente, où les rues sont larges, où il n'y a pas de coins d'ombre et de mystère, et où tout—même la commodité—est sacrifié au goût du *Roumi* pour les lignes droites" [We are in the new (town), recently constructed, where the streets are wide, where there are no dark and mysterious corners, and where everything—even places of comfort—is sacrificed to the taste of the European for straight lines] (114). The Euclidean nature of western architecture, reflecting Cartesian logic and binary thinking, stems from a mode of conceptualization that contrasts with the character of nomadic thought. Positivist architecture, marked by geometric precision and straight lines, differs not only from the free form architecture, if we may call it that, of nomad encampments, but from the spatial displacement of nomads in their movement, which follows no straight line but zigzags from oasis to oasis, from watering place to watering place.

Nomadic thought is antilogical in nature (marked by what one might call collective disparity). The art or operation of "antilogic" (from the Greek *antilogike*), attributed primarily to the Sophists, as defined by G. B. Kerford "consists in causing the same thing to be seen by the same people now as possessing one predicate and now as possessing the opposite or contradictory predicate" (63). It is a technique whereby, in opposing one *logos* (argument) to another *logos*, one's opponent is led either to accept both *logoi* or to abandon the original proposition. The affirmation of nomadic thought, which permeates the works of such Maghrebian writers as Tahar Djaout, Assia Djebar, Tahar Ben Jelloun, and Abdellatif Laâbi, to mention but a few, is most effective when it works within the system in order to affirm its difference by subverting the functioning mechanisms of the system, by turning them to one's own use so as to bring about a process I have elsewhere termed "leveling," which delegitimates so-called inside (privileged) discourses by putting them on the same level as other discourses (*Islam* 19).

In "Theatrum philosophicum," as if to anticipate Rodowick's question about creating new values, Michel Foucault speaks of difference with reference to the concept of the nomadic: "*Pour libérer la différence, il nous faut une pensée sans contradiction, sans dialectique, sans négation: une pensée qui dise oui à la divergence; une pensée affirmative dont l'instrument est la disjonction*; une pensée du multiple—de la multiplicité dispersée et nomade que ne limite et ne regroupe aucune des contraintes du même" [*To free difference, we need a thought without contradiction, without dialectic, without negation: a thought that says yes to divergence; an affirmative thought whose operation is disjunctive*; a thought of the multiple—of dispersed and nomadic multiplicity that none of the constraints of the Same limit or rearrange] (90, my emphasis).

In their "Treatise on Nomadology" in *A Thousand Plateaus* Deleuze and Guattari speak of nomadic thoughts as counterthoughts that are by nature violent, redolent of the steppe and the desert, destructive of images. The images these "sand thoughts" destroy are the myths propagated by the State apparatus. Deleuze and Guattari term nomadic thought outside thought, that is, thought freed from the restraints of system, thought that does not just put forward another image to oppose the image devised by the State apparatus. Rather, it is a power that destroys the image as well as its copies, the model as well as its reproductions—the tendency to subordinate thought to "a mode of the True, the Just, or the Right (Cartesian truth, Kantian just, Hegelian right, etc.)." Deleuze and Guattari see the nature of outside thought as "truly a *pathos* (an *antilogos* and an *antimythos*)" (*Thousand* 377). These "sand thoughts" appear everywhere in Maghrebian writing. In *L'Interdite*, Malika Mokeddem's child character Dalila speaks of the sand that shifts incessantly: "Il bouge, il va partout. . . . La dune, elle se déplace. Elle change de forme" (71) [It moves, goes everywhere. . . . The dune continuously displaces itself and changes shape]. It is like the very movement of pastoral herders.

Deleuze and Guattari liken nomadology to a War Machine in terms of its concerted resistance that wards off the power of the State and positions itself outside State apparatus. That apparatus creates binary oppositions and forms that frame everything in inclusiveness and interiority (*Thousand* 351–52). The War Machine, on the other hand, opposes State apparatus in all respects. Deleuze and Guattari equate chess with the State and the Japanese game of Go with nomadic thought (*Thousand* 352–53). While chess pieces have intrinsic properties that require them to move unswervingly in a precise geometric network, Go pieces possess "no intrinsic properties, only situational ones. . . . [W]hat is proper to Go is war without battle lines, with neither confrontation nor retreat, without battles even" (353). The Go pieces work from the outside, and the War Machine is itself a form of pure exteriority as contrasted with the State apparatus, which is a form of pure interiority (354).

The notion of resistance need not entail mere opposition through simple negation, as Benita Parry suggests, but rejection of the arbitrary ground of opposition inherent in the statist position itself, which negates nonstatist discourse by locating it as marginal or outside. In fact, the question/opposition of inside-outside would appear to be moot, or at least a provisional way of naming what constitutes a different space. To invoke the notion of margin, marginals, or outsidedness when speaking of nomads, as critics from Ibn Khaldûn to Deleuze and Guattari have, is, in fact, to utilize the language of the dominant group. Jean-François Lyotard observes that "[i]l n'y a pas de marge du tout. Ce qui parle des marges, c'est l'Empire qui réfléchit ses bords, ses frontières, ses marches (régions à conquérir)" [there is no such thing as a margin. What speaks of margins is the Empire that reflects its boundaries, its borders, its marches (regions to be conquered)] ("Sur la force" 6). The implied resistance of marginal discourses such as that of nomadic thought is less oppositional in a negative sense than differentiating in a fully positive sense, which heralds a change of positionality of the dominant discourse. It is not a question of erasure, negation, or replacement so much as the recognition that all discourses compose a plurality of discourses, each equal, such that none warrants being privileged over another. The so-called dominant discourse becomes revealed as just another discourse insofar as all hierarchical systems, including faith systems, valorizing a specific discourse do so according to arbitrary, nonuniversal principles.

The Maghrebian author, Tahar Djaout, to whom I shall refer later, like several francophone authors, writes (with) in the very language of the colonizer but wields it in such a way as to unground and thus sap the ideological underpinnings of colonial discourse, as well as the discourses of the Islamic fundamentalists (the *intégristes*) and the State.

Postmodernism, Postcolonialism, Nomadic Thought

How do the postmodern and postcolonial narrative modes relate to one another and in turn to nomadic thought? Kwame Anthony Appiah, in speaking of postmodernism, sees a variety of postmodernisms—in the plural—which are distinguished by how "their theories of contemporary social, cultural, and economic life relate to the actual practices that constitute that life," and he adds: "Where the practice is theory—literary or philosophical—postmodernism as a *theory* of postmodernity can be adequate only if it reflects to some extent the realities of that practice, because the practice itself is fully theoretical" (142). Appiah points out that these various postmodernisms hold in common a rough consensus to the effect that there exists "an antecedent practice that laid claim to a certain exclusivity of insight and in each of them postmodernism is a name for the rejection of that claim to exclusivity" (142). Deleuze and Guattari incontestably reject a mode of exclusivity such as we find in statist and theocratic discourse. And indeed their theoretical positioning has been called postmodernist, as well as postcolonial.

Postmodern narratives, such as I see them, like postcolonial narratives are marked by spatial and temporal disjunction. Both narrative modes have devised local tactics to counter prevailing hegemonies, whatever their source, so as to ward off totalizing fields of force.[1] Among traits the postcolonial and postmodern modes share is a questioning of absolute systems that lay claim to universality and claim legitimation tautologically through referral to a set of principles that they themselves have arbitrarily implemented. Both modes reject the binaries and dualisms of dominant discourse (subject-object, fiction-reality, self-other, literature-criticism, etc.), as we observe in the alternative process of *métissage* at work in the pluralist dynamics of their narratives. Some particular characteristics they share are the following:

(1) Both modes challenge the sharp distinction between the work of art and empirical reality as drawn by Kantian aesthetics and modernist theory. They reject formalism that creates of the work of art a closed, stratified world. As opposed to the notion of art as universal and exclusively concerned with aesthetic representation of morally elevated (high) art, they view art rather as a local response to particular situations—the situation of women in the patriarchal cultures of the Maghreb, for instance, or that of nonwestern immigrants in London examined in the postcolonial narratives of Salman Rushdie.

The two modes similarly challenge the regulation of literary subject matter in terms of an exclusive, limited concept of what is proper to art, and expand the horizons of art by a mixture of genres and the introduction of popular or "low" art into literature. One of the specific ways the nonwestern authors modify the traditional narrative is by the insertion into the subject matter of magical realist elements that blur the traditional distinction in literary realist texts between fantasy and reality (see Erickson, "*Metoikoi*"). Such a differential mode of literary expression valorizes a discourse whose perceptual field is essentially nontraditional in terms of western narrative.

(2) Both modes have opened up the narrative by intertextuality in the narrower sense of the term, that is, by abundant recourse to works of other authors. Their intertextual foraging assumes less the form of an attempt to organize and unify a mass of disparate events, moreover, than that of a type of *bricolage* by which they "make do" with fragments and disordered parts to forge something pragmatically (a text, a thought process) that responds to a local situation, need, or desire (Lyotard, *Postmodern* 76).[2]

(3) Irony is of unquestionable importance as a perceptual mode for postcolonial as well as postmodern writers. It lies, according to Ross Chambers, in the "production of difference" between narrative function and textual function (Chambers 45). The notion of irony derives from the figure of the *Eiron*, who, for Aristotle, denoted a personage who was always more or less than what he seemed to be. The use of irony comes out most dramatically in the revisiting of the past and a reworking of history filtered through a divergent, distanced perspective, rather than the (his) story imposed by authoritarian narratives, whether Islamic, European, or patriarchal. Albert Memmi and Frantz Fanon have spoken of the willed forgetfulness of the colonized peoples intent on wiping from their memory the history of their oppression, and

Benjamin Stora has examined this forgetfulness on the part of the French people and the Algerian war of liberation.[3]

Authors of both modes are for the most part intent on combating this amnesia, by instituting a process of recovery through the memory or re-membering of the past that replaces official histories of dominant cultures by reinscribing a new historical version. This reinscription has taken the form of historically verifiable past events such as those surrounding the French occupation of Algeria subsequent to the fall of Algiers in 1830 up to the Algerian war of independence (1954–62), or of a history largely imagined, as in the "pre-history" of love contemplated by Assia Djebar, who becomes the amanuensis for the silent and silenced voices of her Algerian sisters, past and present (*L'Amour, la fantasia*). Such authors have also written an alternate history of the traditional western narrative through the destructuration of temporal and spatial elements.

Irony in postmodern and postcolonial narratives is directed as often toward self as toward other, such that both narratives are marked by authorial self-reflexivity and self-referentiality—an acutely conscious attitude toward the act of artistic creation that results in the author focusing on the writing process rather than on the narrative elements of character, plot, and setting. This is one reason why the worlds of postcolonialism and postmodernism tend to be chaotic and disorderly. There is, if not a celebration of disorder, a lack of concern about the nicely laid-out plot lines and stylistic coherence of traditional art. We witness considerable fragmentation. The disorderliness of narrative comes out in a type of "pure" event, where narrative is born from enunciation, grows out of its own procedures so that it may be said to be self-generating. This disorderliness has to do with an "ironic" belief in the discontinuity of experience and the undecidability of things, their relationships, and meaning. The irony here lies in the distance between the effort to fix meaning and the inherent futility of that effort.

(4) Finally, rhetorical positioning characterizes both postcolonialism and postmodernism: a sophistic tendency to persuade by bridging the divide between diction (what must be said) and contradiction (what must not be said). The aim of such positioning is, I believe, partly derivative of the desire to avoid appropriation by master discourses, but is also partly derivative in the case of Maghrebian authors from the love of rhetoric and persuasive speech found in Arabic, which feeds into the rhetorical emphasis extant in the European tongues they elaborate. Persuasion also appears as ploy to a desire to build community, but in the case of postcolonial and postmodern authors not a settled, sedentary community, rather a particularized one: the community of misfits or outcasts in Thomas Pynchon's *Vineland*; the community of migrants in Rushdie's *Satanic Verses*; the community of real or imagined female

historical figures in Christa Wolf's *Cassandra* and Djebar's *Loin de Médine*; or the community of ostracized characters of Khatibi and Ben Jelloun. The communities may be those of the mad Cynics, the wild Megarites, the Sophist clowns, the slaves, women, barbarians, and gays described by Lyotard ("Sur la force" 6); of the nomads, the deterritorialized, the inferior races, the animals and "niggers" described by Deleuze and Guattari (*Capitalisme* 125); of the Hogarthian nether world, the *Lumpenproletariat* so despised by Marx, or the anarchist outcasts of the 1890s—all communities in perceived or unperceived solidarity against the encroachments of hegemonic forces.

In *Amour bilingue* Abdelkebir Khatibi describes the authors of such narratives as seeking "[u]n pays retrouvé [qui] s'offre pour ce qu'il est, sans clôture et sans totalité" [a rediscovered country [that] offers itself as what it is, without closure or totality] (114). Postcolonial narratives, like postmodern narratives, often cannot be categorized; their edges blur and their purposes are often crossed; they are marked by the disparate, incommensurable, unclassifiable, and indeterminate, as are their authors, narrators, characters: "[E]lle se rendait inclassable" [She rendered herself unclassifiable] (Khatibi, *Amour bilingue* 120).

What about nomadism? I see nomadism as reflective of both postcolonial and postmodern, as I have chosen to define these terms, not in the sense of coming after but of responding to colonial and modernist systems of whatever time period.

Christopher Miller characterizes nomadic thought as an alternative to "identity" seeking and "one of the most compelling models of postidentitarian thinking available in the marketplace of theoretical ideas today, a way 'to conceive of individuality free from the confines of Identity, to think difference in itself, without any reference to the Same.'" The nomadology of Deleuze and Guattari as put forth in *Mille Plateaux* "represents a startling departure from the old notions of identity and difference" (173). But Miller, like some other critics, questions Deleuze and Guattari's theory of nomadology.

Winifred Woodhull, for instance, speaking of Maghrebian writers, distinguishes between "textual nomadism [that] stands in relation to real changes in the writers' geographical location" and the theoretical nomadism of Deleuze/Guattari or Foucault (89). Alluding to the same distinction, Christopher Miller states that "when hybridity or nomadology or any other model becomes the critic's ideology instead of a tool for the analysis of real problems, questions arise" (4). What has nomadology to do with "real *and* 'actual' nomads," he asks (177). The reference of critics like Woodhull and Miller to "real" changes and "real" nomads stresses the lack of relationship between theory and practice.

Deleuze and Guattari's justification for theorizing a nomadology lies in their insistence on the fact that "[h]istory is always written from the sedentary point of view and in the name of a unitary State apparatus, at least a possible one, even when the topic is nomads" (*Thousand* 23). They propose nomadology as the opposite of history, as a means to preserve the difference of nomadism. As Miller points out, however, an "epistemological paradox" arises, namely, that "nomads don't represent themselves in writing, they must be represented" (176). This supposition places Deleuze and Guattari on the same quasi-imperialist level as Marx, who, speaking of small peasant landowners in his work on Bonaparte, asserted that such "others" possess no means for political expression but need someone to represent their interests. Indeed, Deleuze and Guattari have taken over the task of speaking that otherness for the nomads, while on the contrary the latter's very otherness should speak for them. Finally, in claiming that nomadology is nonrepresentational and nonanthropological while citing a spate of ethnographical works, Deleuze and Guattari, as Miller sees them, straddle "the fence between purely intellectual nomadism and anthropological nomadism" (i.e., "real" nomads) (178–79). This is not the only example of Deleuze and Guattari "straddling the fence." Their drawing of distinctions between inside and outside also clashes with their own nonrepresentational and nonidentitarian theory.

In criticizing Deleuze and Guattari for theorization that replaces the "real," however, it appears to me that critics such as Miller and Woodhull stop short of examining the broader implications of that theorization and how it fundamentally challenges nationalism, which often rests on identity politics. Speaking of Frantz Fanon, Edward Said sees him as having projected a "cultural shift from the terrain of nationalist independence to the theoretical domain of liberation" (268). The importance of Deleuze and Guattari's theorization, to use Said's terms, lies in the fact that it counters the "theoretical elaborations produced by the culture of late western capitalism," which brought about "a culture of oppression and colonial enslavement" (268). The history nomadology rejects is history propagated by the great myths of western imperialism and the mercantilism of colonialism perpetuated in the enterprise of globalization.

The balancing and shifting between the poles of theory and "authenticity," representation and nonrepresentation, while appearing to be contradictory impulses in Deleuzian and Guattarian theory, do indeed serve a useful purpose in developing a comprehensive view of nomadic antilogical thought and an understanding of it as a cultural system marked by pure difference.

Nomadic Thought and Maghrebian Literature

The characters and situations in Maghrebian novels are often linguistic markers for an excluded, repressed discourse. Like Rushdie, the authors of these novels seek the repossession of the poisoned wells of language through a discourse that constitutes itself on the very basis of its otherness while discarding the binary other/self (Rushdie, *Satanic* 52), and which neutralizes master narratives by the leveling of hegemonic discourses (statist, patriarchal, theocratic). The latter come to be seen as just so many discourses, on equal footing with all other discourses, and are consequently delegitimated.

Nomadic thought marks the discourse of several Maghrebian writers. Lisa Lowe reads Deleuze and Guattari's use of the term *nomadic* as a series of wanderings that traverse a multitudinous network of intersecting plateaus, which each mediate different moments and forms of relations between that which is fragmented and destratified, immobilized and in motion, measured and in unrestrained abundance (Lowe 46). Read in this way, the nomadic forms the basis of a strategic move in terms of the creation of narrative that shifts spatially from site to site, from other text to other text, from plateau to plateau that mediates meaning.

Le Dernier été de la raison, the posthumously published (1999) novel of Algerian writer Tahar Djaout, assassinated in 1993 by the Muslim Brotherhood, is symptomatic of nomadic thought occurring in Maghrebian writing.[4] Djaout's novel presents the portrait of a dystopic society in which the religious fundamentalists, having taken power, set out to destroy the past, memory, and history itself, by replacing them with religious sovereignty. Djaout goes beyond differences and conflict between the *intégristes* and the central government: his work reflects how the sociopolitical situation of present-day Algeria represents a continuum—from colonial rule, to nominal independence, to the rise of a nationalistic, totalitarian government opposed by the *intégristes*, to the growing inroads of globalization, which through mercantilism and technology determines specific ways of thinking and acting that generally reject local culture. All these forces have brought about and continue to bring about a distortion and suppression of the cultural memory of the Algerian people. Postcolonialism has given way to an international neocolonialism, growing out of an internationalization of the market economy, a universalizing commodification controlled and directed by a new breed of European and American cultural imperialism.

Djaout's political geography consisted of mapping the Algeria of his time and restoring in the Algerian people a consciousness of history. His position or location resembles that of the bilingual writer personified by the Moroccan author Abdelkebir Khatibi's "professional voyager" (as Réda Bensmaïa aptly calls him) in *Un Eté à Stockholm*, and described by Bensmaïa as "a writer who, living between two languages, two borders, and therefore between different temporalities, can no longer belong to *one* history, *one* people, *one* country, but who belongs instead to a new time-space, which, though it is the product of an artistic creation, cannot be reduced to pure 'fiction' or 'myth'" (295).

Khatibi asks, "Quelle est la patrie d'un écrivain? Est-ce uniquement sa langue . . . ? Est-ce l'unité idéelle entre un terroir, une langue et une identité culturale [*sic*] d'esprit et du corps? Est-ce la mosaïque d'un exil et d'une trans-nation universelle?" [What is the homeland of a writer? Is it uniquely his language . . . ? Is it the ideal unity between his soil, language and a cultural identity of the mind and body? Is it the mosaic of an exile and of a universal trans-nation?] ("Nationalisme" 206). For Khatibi, the "homeland" of the writer emerges from a state of displacement, a nomadic movement between different lands, cultures and languages. The writer remains unattached to a specific territory or homogeneous culture. The concept of nation itself changes, becoming a cultural pluralism, a cultural mosaic that comprises a discourse interwoven with a multiplicity of voices.

The "Third World" intellectual experiences the need to seize from the totalitarian discourse control of the sign, to remake the world into an alternative image, to redefine national, cultural, and ethnic borders with reference to that "transnational" space of identity of which Bensmaïa speaks. Djaout's *Dernier été* contributes to this task. We witness the deterioration of the social and cultural fabric and Djaout's resistance to totalitarian domination throughout his works: from *L'Exproprié* (1981, definitive version 1991), *Les Chercheurs d'os* (1984), *L'Invention du désert* (1987), and *Les Vigiles* (1991) to *Le Dernier été*. His narrators are expropriated; they cross physical and mental borders; they encounter the denial of memory and history by an imposed fundamentalist version of the past, reinforced by the indifference of a people more and more immersed in consumerism and the acquisition of wealth; they search for their past, history, and remembrance in a country that has emerged from a war of liberation.

Le Dernier été recounts the ordeal of Boualem Yekker, a proprietor of a small bookstore, under the rule of the *Islamistes* who have taken power. Djaout describes Boualem as someone lost between the desert of faith and a paradise of books (124). Under a regime that attempts to ban all pleasure except that of obedience to the will of God, to banish the arts and beauty, which distract the populace, to banish dream, remembrance of the past, and history itself, Boualem refuses the imposition of power and turns toward the past in an attempt to forget the present.

Midway through *Le Dernier été*, Djaout introduces an extended contrast between secular texts in Arabic and the Text, signifying at once the Qur'an (the Book), the totalitarian State, and fundamentalist dogma. Boualem is enchanted by "[l]es textes arabes à la ponctuation lâche, textes ignorant les guillemets et où toutes les voix dialoguent et se mélangent" [the Arab texts with their loose punctuation, which ignore quotation marks and in which multiple voices dialogue and mix] (59). The spirals of words, the arabesque swirls of the letters, and the abstraction of language fascinate him. He describes how reading them provides an uncertain and aimless adventure as one follows twisting paths, trying to glimpse the face of words and restore to them a meaning. The reader of these secular Arab texts faces a bewildering forking, intertwining, and dividing of paths (59). He fights to rein in the words, which like bolting horses struggle to flee. The paths recall the forking paths of Jorge Luis Borges in his short story "The Garden of Forking Paths," where his character describes the project of the learned provincial governor Ts'ui Pên to compose a book filled with a maze of twists, turns, and contradictions, a veritable garden of forking paths, an infinite labyrinth. In reading Ts'ui Pên's book the reader chooses all alternatives simultaneously. "*He creates*, in this way, diverse futures, diverse times which themselves also proliferate and fork" (26). In Ts'ui Pên's book "all possible outcomes occur; each one is the point of departure for other forkings" (26). The character calls Ts'ui Pên's novel "an incomplete, but not false image of the universe [composed of] an infinite series of times, . . . a growing, dizzying net of divergent, convergent and parallel times. This network of times . . . embraces *all* possibilities of time" (28).

Djaout's bifurcating paths, like those of Borges, metaphorize that alternate, nomadic, transnational space of identity, problematize borders and limits, move like the words in and out of a multiplicity of temporal and spatial meanings, and introduce an expanding plurality of cultural signification. Djaout contrasts the loose, meandering writing and meaning of the Arab texts with the Text of Boualem's youth, the Qur'an, with the Truth that it laid down and to which he submitted. The Text of his youth removed him from an exciting universe, bewitching and dangerous, replete with miraculous machines, colorful monsters, and boats bobbling up as they go out to sea (62). In the multifaceted universe of the Arabic texts, "qui tourne comme une noria, circulent des sages et des fous, des hommes de bien et des individus pervers et dangereux, des hommes qui prêchent, d'autres qui vocifèrent ou blasphèment. Dans cet univers-kaléidoscope foisonnent des arbres qui nourissent, rafraîchissent et ombragent, des plantes ornementales, des oiseaux en cage et des oiseaux en liberté liés par l'amour du chant, des cafés où l'on discute et rit, des lieux où l'on s'amuse et danse. Il suffit de sortir de l'école-geôle pour s'engouffrer dans cet univers tourbillonnant" [which turns like a waterwheel, wise men and fools circulate, men of means, perverse and dangerous individuals, preachers, others who shout and blaspheme. In that kaleidoscopic universe trees that nourish, refresh and shade flourish, ornamental plants, caged and free birds linked by the love of song, cafés where people talk and laugh, frolic and dance. All one has to do is to break out of the school-jail (the Koranic school of his youth) to be swallowed up in that turbulent universe] (62).

Djaout closes these descriptive passages with the remark that blocking one's entry into the magical universe of secular books is not only the Qur'anic Master but society itself, blinded and fanaticized by the Book, the Text, held in check by the Word that weighs on it (61). The novel ends with the description of the growing repression of the *intégristes*, who have burned all books, having come to recognize the danger of words, for "tous les mots qu'ils n'arrivaient pas à domestiquer et à anesthésier" [all words they have not succeeded in domesticating and anesthetizing] brought doubt and change (124). "Il ne faut surtout pas que les mots entretiennent l'utopie d'une autre forme de vérité, de chemins insoupçonnés, d'un autre lieu de la pensée. . . . Ceux qui, défiant l'injonction, s'agrippent aux mots incontrôlés, doivent être mis hors d'état de nuire. Par le bâillonnement, la liquidation si nécessaire" [Above all it's necessary that words not hold out the false hope of another form of truth, of unknown paths, of another place of thought. . . . Those who, defying the injunction, cling to uncontrolled speech must be eliminated. By gagging, by liquidation if necessary] (124).

Homi K. Bhabha, in his essay on cultural difference, speaks of a structure of indeterminateness inherent in forms of cultural hybridity that allows for the development of an alternative discourse (312). The aleatory nature of language, its unpredictability and proclivity to escape us, owing to what Michel Foucault calls its "fearful materiality" (*Ordre* 10–11), threatens institutionalized discourse that attempts to smooth the rough edges of speech, to purge it of unwonted expression and of any explicit sign of the totalizing intent of institutions themselves. Tahar Djaout and several other postcolonial writers have seized on the potential of discourse for disruption, its dangerously exhilarating tendency to explode, by exposing its sharp edges, uncovering its asperities, introducing into it the unexpected and ungovernable.

Tahar Ben Jelloun considers each society as possessing a screen on which appear the authorized signs. Everything extending beyond these signs is proscribed. For Maghrebian society, he says, the totality of such authorized signs is a book (21)—the Qur'an, which delimits what subjects and forms of expression are acceptable. It is by the power of the sign that hegemonic apparatuses process information so as to regulate and organize the ways individuals perceive and "know," the ways in which they interpret and map their environment as a basis for their actions. All such apparatuses arrogate the power of the sign to themselves through systems of collective mapping, of exclusion, limitation, and appropriation, to use Michel Foucault's terms, that impose strategies to attenuate or assimilate all contestatory discourses, that rigorously assert and stabilize their ideology and seek to control the meaning of all forms of discourse.

Djaout's postcolonial text, *Le Dernier été*, depicts the sociopolitical situation of fin-de-siècle Algeria as the product in significant part of the colonial heritage being played out again in the process of religious conflict and globalization. Moreover, we find in it manifold elements of nomadic thought, rejection of hegemonic apparatuses, and insistent valorization of a new transnational time and space, marked by pluralism and heterogeneity, as opposed to globalizing imports that impose uniform thinking. In *L'Invention du désert* Djaout speaks of how modern consumer society imported from the west has debased traditional customs. He gives the example of an imaginary ludicrous substitution of pneumatic projectiles for stones in the Meccan custom of the lapidation of Satan. The customary casting of stones is outworn [*caduc*]: "C'est le monde moderne consommateur de polymères qui s'acharne sur l'image de Satan: bouteilles de Pepsi, bouts de ferraille ou fragments de plastique, tous les déchets de l'industrie clament en dévalant vers la décharge que c'est désormais au tour de l'Oncle Sam d'empoigner le collet de Satan" [What's in play is the modern consumer society of polymers that furiously smites Satan's image: Pepsi Cola bottles, bits of scrap iron and fragments of plastics, all the industrial garbage crying out as it gushes toward the garbage dump that henceforth it's the turn of Uncle Sam to seize Satan] (79). The metonymic rapprochement of Uncle Sam and Satan implicitly directs our interpretation.

Djaout's novels, like the writing of the many Maghrebian intellectuals in whose work we encounter the expression of nomadic values, parallel the few representative critical works I have mentioned here, which, while in occasional conflict, have all sought and seek to theorize a mode of existence expressed by nomadic "sand thoughts" that counter the ever-present menace of hegemonic domination.

The connection between nomadic thought and postcolonial and postmodern theory bearing on the literature and culture of the Maghreb is the refusal to be Other to/for hegemonic forces, whether nationalism, cultural imperialism, or religious fundamentalism. Nomadic authors are *bricoleurs* who take their material wherever it befits their purpose, whether it is a European language, technological constructs or genres, or tribal customs, just as the polyglot figure of a *Yoruba Man with a Bicycle* selected by James Baldwin for a show put on by the Center for African Art in New York was "produced by someone who does not care that the bicycle is the white man's invention—it is not there to be Other to the Yoruba Self," but because it is useful to the creative vision of the artist (Appiah 157).

The postcolonial mode of nomadic thought, like postmodernism, is the refusal of monistic thinking and the rejection of the "delusion of oneness" (Maffesoli 22). The form it takes reflects "the blurring of neat, dichotomous boundaries—*which does not mean the end of power differentials or the end of oppositionality*" (Donadey xxv, author's italics). Indeed, nomadic thought in its differentiality is inherently oppositional, in a positive sense. Like postcolonial and postmodern thinking in the sense I have characterized them, it rejects exclusivity and domestication, engages in a reinscription of history, of the forgotten past, and, to repeat Khatibi's words, carries on an incessant search for a "pays retrouvé [qui] s'offre pour ce qu'il est, sans clôture et sans totalité" [rediscovered country (that) offers itself for what it is, without closure or totality] (*Amour bilingue* 114).

Notes

1. My use of the concept "postmodernism" coincides fundamentally with that set forth by Linda Hutcheon in such works as *A Poetics of Postmodernism: History, Theory, Fiction* and *The Politics of Postmodernism*, as well as with the somewhat variant conceptions of Jean-François Lyotard elaborated in a number of texts. For a useful overview of the varied understandings of the term, see Allan Megill's essay, "What Does the Term 'Postmodern' Mean?"

2. Lyotard speaks of this phenomenon of "bricolage" in regard to postmodern architecture in *The Postmodern Explained* 76.

3. See Albert Memmi, *Portrait du colonisé, précédé du portrait du colonisateur*; *Portrait d'un juif*; and *L'Homme dominé*. For Frantz Fanon see *Peau noire, masques blancs* and *Les Damnés de la terre*.

4. The Muslim Brotherhood is referred to variously as the *Islamistes* or *intégristes*, who belong to the Front Islamique du Salut (FIS). Djaout referred to them as the Frères Vigilants in *Le Dernier été*.

Works Cited

Appiah, Kwame Anthony. *In My Father's House. Africa in the Philosophy of Culture*. New York: Oxford University Press, 1992.

Ben Jelloun, Tahar. *Harrouda*. Paris: Denoël, 1978.

Bensmaïa, Réda. "Political Geography of Literature: On Khatibi's 'Professional Traveller.'" *French Cultural Studies: Criticism at the Crossroads*. Ed. Marie-Pierre Le Hir and Dana Strand. Albany: State University of New York Press, 2000. 295–308.

Bhabha, Homi K. "DissemiNation: Time, Narrative, and the Margins of the Modern Nation." *Nation and Narration*. Ed. Homi K. Bhabha. London: Routledge, 1990. 291–322.

Borges, Jorge Luis. "The Garden of Forking Paths." *Labyrinths: Selected Stories & Other Writings*. New York: New Directions, 1964. 19–29.

Butor, Michel. "Le Voyage et l'écriture." *Répertoire IV*. Paris: Editions de Minuit, 1974. 9–29.

Chambers, Ross. *Room for Maneuver: Reading (the) Oppositional (in) Narrative*. Chicago: University of Chicago Press, 1991.

Deleuze, Gilles, and Félix Guattari. *Capitalisme et schizophrénie: l'anti-Oedipe*. Paris: Editions de Minuit, 1972.

———. *A Thousand Plateaus: Capitalism and Schizophrenia*. Trans. and foreword by Brian Massumi. Minneapolis: University of Minnesota Press, 1987.

Djaout, Tahar. *Les Chercheurs d'os*. Paris: Seuil, 1984.

———. *Le Dernier été de la raison*. Paris: Seuil, 1999.

———. *L'Exproprié*. 1981. Paris: François Majault, 1991.

———. *L'Invention du désert*. Paris: Seuil, 1987.

———. *Les Vigiles*. Paris: Seuil, 1991.

Djebar, Assia. *L'Amour, la fantasia*. Paris: Jean-Claude Lattès, 1985.

———. *Femmes d'Alger dans leur appartement*. Paris: Editions des femmes, 1980.

———. *Loin de Médine*. Paris: Albin Michel, 1991.

Donadey, Anne. *Recasting Postcolonialism: Women Writing between Worlds*. Portsmouth, N.H.: Heinemann, 2001.

Dunn, Ross E. "Berber Imperialism: The Ait Atta Expansion in Southeast Morocco from 1870–1970." *Arabs and Berbers: From the Tribe to Nation in North Africa*. Ed. Ernest Gellner and Charles Micaud. London: Duckworth, 1973. 85–107.

Eberhardt, Isabelle. *Oeuvres complètes*. Vol. 1: *Ecrits sur le sable (récits, notes et journaliers)*. Paris: Grasset, 1988.

Erickson, John D. *Islam and Postcolonial Narrative*. Cambridge, U.K.: Cambridge University Press, 1998.

———. "*Metoikoi* and Magical Realism in the Maghrebian Narratives of Tahar Ben Jelloun and Abdelkebir Khatibi." *Magical Realism: Theory, History, Community*. Ed. Lois Parkinson Zamora and Wendy B. Faris. Durham, N.C.: Duke University Press, 1995. 427–50.

Fanon, Frantz. *Les Damnés de la terre*. Preface by Jean-Paul Sartre. Paris: François Maspéro, 1961.

———. *Peau noire, masques blancs*. 1952. Reprint, Paris: Seuil, 1958.

Foucault, Michel. *L'Ordre du discours*. Paris: Gallimard, 1971.

———. "Theatrum philosophicum." *Dits et écrits: 1954–1988*. Vol. 2., 1970–1975. Ed. Daniel Defert and François Ewald. Paris: Gallimard, 1994. 75–99.

Hutcheon, Linda. *A Poetics of Postmodernism: History, Theory, Fiction*. New York: Routledge, 1988.

———. *The Politics of Postmodernism*. New York: Routledge, 1989.

Ibn Khaldûn. *The Muqaddimah: An Introduction to History*. Trans. Franz Rosenthal. Ed. N. J. Dawood. Princeton, N.J.: Princeton University Press, 1967.

Kerford, G. B. "Dialectic, Antilogic and Eristic." *The Sophistic Movement*. Cambridge, U.K.: Cambridge University Press, 1981. 59–67.

Khatibi, Abdelkebir. *Amour bilingue*. Montpellier, France: Fata Morgana, 1983.

———. *Un Eté à Stockholm: roman*. Paris: Flammarion, 1990.

———. "Nationalisme et internationalisme littéraires." *Figures de l'étranger dans la littérature française*. Paris: Denoël, 1987. 201–14.

Krebser, Markus, and Federica de Cesco, eds. *Touareg: Nomades du Sahara*. Lausanne: Editions Mondo, 1971.

Lowe, Lisa. "Literary Nomadics in Francophone Allegories of Post-colonialism: Pham Van Ky and Tahar Ben Jelloun." *Yale French Studies* 82 (1993): 43–61.

Lyotard, Jean-François. *The Postmodern Explained*. Trans. Don Barry et al. Minneapolis: University of Minnesota Press, 1993.

———. "Sur la force des faibles." *L'Arc* 64 (1976): 4–12.

Maffesoli, Michel. *Du nomadisme: vagabondages initiatiques*. Paris: Librairie Générale Française, Le Livre de poche, 1997.

Massumi, Brian, trans. "Translator's Foreword: Pleasures of Philosophy." *A Thousand Plateaus: Capitalism and Schizophrenia*. Gilles Deleuze and Félix Guattari. Minneapolis: University of Minnesota Press, 1987. ix–xv.

Meeker, Michael E. *Literature and Violence in North Arabia*. Cambridge, U.K.: Cambridge University Press, 1979.

Megill, Allan. "What Does the Term 'Postmodern' Mean?" *Annals of Scholarship* 6.2–3 (1989): 129–51.

Memmi, Albert. *L'Homme dominé*. Paris: Gallimard, 1968.

———. *Portrait du colonisé, précédé du portrait du colonisateur*. Preface by Jean-Paul Sartre. Paris: J. J. Pauvert, 1957.

———. *Portrait d'un Juif*. Paris: Gallimard, 1962.

Miller, Christopher L. *Nationalists and Nomads: Essays on Francophone African Literature and Culture*. Chicago: University of Chicago Press, 1999.

Mokeddem, Malika. *The Forbidden Woman*. Trans. K. Melissa Marcus. Lincoln: University of Nebraska Press, 1998.

———. *L'Interdite*. Paris: Grasset et Fasquelle, 1993.

Parry, Benita. "Problems in Current Theories of Colonial Discourse." *Oxford Literary Review* 9.1–2 (1987): 27–58.

Peters, Jeffrey. "The Cartographic Eye/I: Champlain and the Uses of Early Modern Geographic Discourse." *Genre* 30.1 (1997): 79–103.

Pynchon, Thomas. *Vineland*. Boston: Little, Brown, 1990.

Rodowick, D. N. "Personnages conceptuels et l'image-temps: 'gender' et l'histoire." *L'Esprit Créateur* 42.1 (Spring 2002): 107–21.

Rushdie, Salman. "On Adventure." *Imaginary Homelands: Essays and Criticism 1981–1991*. London: Granta, 1991. 222–25.

———. *The Satanic Verses*. New York: Viking, 1988.

Said, Edward W. *Culture and Imperialism*. New York: Vintage, 1994.

Stora, Benjamin. *La Guerre invisible: Algérie, années 90*. Paris: Presses de Sciences po, 2001.

Wolf, Christa. *Cassandra: A Novel and Four Essays*. Trans. Jan van Heurck. New York: Farrar, Straus and Giroux, 1984.

Woodhull, Winifred. *Transfigurations of the Maghreb: Feminism, Decolonization, and Literatures*. Minneapolis: University of Minnesota Press, 1993.

6

Narratives of Internal Exile

Cixous, Derrida, and the Vichy Years in Algeria

Ronnie Scharfman

> Toutes les biographies comme toutes les autobiographies comme tous les récits racontent une histoire à la place d'une autre histoire.
> [Biographies, autobiographies, and narratives, all tell one story/history instead of another story/history.]
> **Hélène Cixous, "Albums et légendes"**

Playing with words, playing on words, these are forbidden games in the tragic context of Algeria's current political and cultural crisis where, since 1992, intellectuals and writers have been gunned down simply for using the French language.[1] Yet it is precisely under the aegis of very serious wordplay that I shall place my investigation of some of the recent writings of those two Franco-Algerian ur-intellectuals, Hélène Cixous and Jacques Derrida, as I interrogate the genealogy of wordplay in relation to an ethics of solidarity. The Cixous texts that inform my inquiry are: "My Algeriance, in other words: to depart not to arrive from Algeria," which first appeared in *Les Inrockuptibles* and was translated in a collection of her texts published by Routledge, entitled *Stigmata*; "Letter to Zohra Drif," which appeared in a special issue of the British journal *parallax*, on "Translating 'Algeria'"; "Albums et légendes," a short autobiographical piece that closes the book she cowrote with Mireille Calle-Gruber, *Hélène Cixous: Photos de racines*, and a further elaboration of the themes that emerge in those three pieces in the "scènes primitives" of her autobiographical *Les Rêveries de la femme sauvage*. Those by Derrida include: "Taking a Stand for Algeria," in the same issue of *parallax*; "Circonfession," published in tandem with Geoffrey Bennington's essay on his work, "Derridabase," in the book *Jacques Derrida*; and his autobiographical essay on growing up in Algeria as alienated consciousness, *Le Monolinguisme de l'autre*. I shall also analyze a roundtable discussion hosted by Michel Casenave on the radio station France Culture, with Cixous, Derrida, and the Tunisian writer Abdelwahab Meddeb, on the question of Maghrebians writing in French, and the role of writing in the current Algerian catastrophe (Casenave).

Those familiar with the writings of Cixous and Derrida, whether literary or philosophical, know that wordplay is one of the defining characteristics of their respective styles. Cixous, after all, wrote her dissertation on James Joyce, and Derrida's signature theory and praxis, deconstruction, springs from and depends on doing things with and to words, breaking them down, turning them inside out to suggest multiple meanings, sometimes at war with each other.

Why then choose to emphasize wordplay in my exploration now? All the texts mentioned share two common characteristics: they were all written in the 1990s (Cixous's *Rêveries* in 2000), most since 1993, and they all return to the troubled Franco-Judeo-Maghrebian past of the authors, specifically to that painful and cruel moment when, in 1940, the Jews of Algeria were stripped of their French citizenship by Vichy's anti-Jewish laws. "Si jamais on avait voulu croire à la nationalité, alors là on a pris une leçon" [If ever we had wanted to believe in nationality, we sure learned our lesson then], says Cixous bitterly on France Culture's radio program (Casenave). In 1940 Jacques Derrida was ten years old, living in Algiers, and Hélène Cixous was three, living in Oran. Both were indelibly marked by this experience and claim its trace as constitutive of the very stuff of their writing. As recently as October 2002, in a lecture given at New York University, Derrida declared, in speaking of this time in his childhood: "Apprendre à lire, c'était apprendre à déconstruire l'anti-sémitisme" [Learning to read meant learning to deconstruct anti-semitism]. Until recently, both authors have shunned conventional autobiographical narratives, and, one might argue, the pieces in question address themselves to the impossiblity of autobiography for subjects dispossessed, displaced, by history, politics, racism. At the same time, I hope to demonstrate that what I choose to term their "privileged difference," which I read as an ethical stance, derives from this originary wound and its perpetual call to vigilance against all forms of oppression.

The question I would like to ask, then, is, What might be the political implications of returning to the troubling, troubled issue of their Franco-Judeo-Maghrebian identity, and why now? The French historian Henry Rousso, in his book *The Vichy Syndrome* demonstrated the dialectical relationship between contemporary Vichy historiography and renewed Franco-Jewish memory where, as he says, the historical research serves as a vector of memory. Similarly, it seems to me, two recent developments, one in France, the other in Algeria, could be read as vectors of memory in the cases of Cixous and Derrida. In France, historians have begun to turn to the history of colonialism and, in particular, to the Algerian conflict. The research of the Franco-Algerian Benjamin Stora of course springs to mind, as does that of historians working specifically now on Maghrebian Jewry, such as Michel Abitbol, as well as Jacques Taïeb, Shmuel Trigano, and Richard Ayoun. The peculiar status of Algeria's Jews under Vichy, no longer citizens of France but not yet citizens of that nonexistent independent state that would come to be known as Algeria, has become, in Pierre Nora's terms, a "lieu de mémoire."

Secondly, the recent terrorism in Algeria—which began in 1992 when the government cancelled elections in which it appeared that the FIS, the Islamic fundamentalists, would come to power, and which has resulted in the savage murder of thousands of Algerian Arabs and Berbers and the exodus, especially to France, but also to Canada and the United States, of thousands more seeking refuge and asylum—this terrorism also seems to be a catalyst for memory, compelling Cixous and Derrida to return to the native land, to revisit the traumatic, complex, multiple shifting identities that were theirs growing up as Jews in colonial and Vichy Algeria. My argument here is that by implicating themselves in a directly personal way in these recent narratives, by foregrounding the suffering implied by their exclusion, as Jews, between 1940 and 1943, from an already problematic French identity, both writers effect an identification with contemporary Algeria from which they were excluded, paradoxically and painfully, when they lived there as children and were perceived by the Arabs and Berbers as part of the French colonial regime.

Writing specifically now about Algeria, writing to, for, with, from, alongside Algeria, becomes a way to write Algeria otherwise, to transgress the interdictions and limitations of the current regime, whose policies Derrida refers to as a form of neocolonial violence and oppression, an internal one that imitates the ex-colonizer in its efforts to impose a monocultural "homohegemony" on a once pluralistic society. Derrida compares this mutilation of memory to the one imposed by Vichy France. Both Cixous and Derrida have a long history of political activism, fighting against racism, xenophobia, misogyny, torture, oppression, terrorism; signing petitions, forming committees, speaking out in public. But these writings constitute a specific response, an engagement with and resistance to past and present injustices. "L'écriture n'est pas ici un ailleurs littéraire" [Writing here is not a literary elsewhere], Derrida declared during the France Culture roundtable (Casenave). The "trouble de l'identité" [uneasiness of identity] from which he writes, the genealogical interruption that resulted in his making his life in France, constitute both a freedom and a responsibility to find new forms that render explicit the diverse heritage of any society. The corpus of his work bears the wound of memory and the memory of the wound.

To return to the opening remarks on the function of wordplay for these two writers, I would like to relate them to the two versions they give of their linguistic situations at the time of their exclusion from French schools in Algeria after 1941. Bear in mind that in 1941, Cixous was four years old; Derrida, eleven.

Cixous, Hispano-Moroccan-Sephardic on her father's side, whose family had been in Algeria since 1867, and German and Austro-Hungarian Ashkenaz on her mother's side, traces what I would call the "native land of her writing" to this vast stretch of times and lands where her childhood unfolds according to a double memory, two geographies, multiple languages:

> We played at languages in our house, my parents passed with pleasure and deftness from one language to another, the two of them, one from French, the other from German, jumping through Spanish and English, one with a bit of Arabic and the other with a bit of Hebrew. When I was ten years old my father gave me at the same time an Arabic and a Hebrew teacher. That translinguistic and loving sport sheltered me from all obligation or vague desire of obedience to one mother-father tongue. ("My Algeriance" 168–69)

Though early attuned to the polymorphic pleasures of a plurality of languages, which she clearly lived as a positive factor, Cixous nonetheless invests the mastering of the French language for several idiosyncratic reasons. When Vichy's anti-Jewish racist laws concerning the *numerus clausus* in schools went into effect in 1941, they included the expulsion of Jewish professors and teachers as well. These same laws deprived Cixous's father of his right to practice medicine. The Jewish communities throughout Algeria immediately responded by setting up makeshift schools, where excluded Jewish children could be taught by excluded Jewish teachers: "It was in the un-Frenchified Jewish dining room that I had my first franco-linguistic ecstasies. . . . I heard these prophetic words: 'adjectif qualificatif' . . . One day I will have the keys to the qualifying adjective. . . . At school I always wanted to beat the French in French, to be the best 'in French' as they said, to honor my father, who had been driven out" ("My Algeriance" 168–69).

Cixous insists on her "Algeriance," a French word she invents to articulate her particular individual sense of identity and identification with a country where she was born, which has nonetheless never been hers, but whose sensuality permeates her writing. This "Algeriance," which resonates with alliance and allegiance is, on the one hand, due to the sheer "chance" of her history and genealogy, through whose "accidence" she happened to be born there. On the other hand, she also seems to suggest that the condition of possibility of this identification lay in her leaving. Within the colonial context, mastering French meant an alienating identification with the French master. After the war, in the French secondary schools in Algiers where she is the only Jew, albeit now one reintegrated in "France," she "smells the strong odor of French racism," at the same time that she makes the painful discovery that for the three Muslim girls in her class whom she longs to befriend, she incarnates the despised French colonizer. "I let myself be hated by the Arabs and it was the smoothest, most mute, the most passive form of love I have ever known" (171).

In this double bind where to be inside is to be outside, for the young girl who had just experienced the suffering of exclusion herself, Cixous longs to remain "illegitimate" or, at least, to extricate herself from that position where she felt forced to walk over "les gens que j'aimais" [those I loved] (Casenave).

In a psychologically complicated vignette entitled "Pieds nus," published in the volume *Une Enfance algérienne*, where Cixous also talks about her Algerian childhood, she reconstructs a scene that we might call "the rape of the sandal." In this memory, little Hélène, beginning to feel strangely, vaguely exculpated and justified as a pariah by the antisemitic laws that demoted her father but brought the family closer to the oppressed Arabs, soon finds herself victimized, violated, metaphorically, by a little Arab shoeshine boy because she has new white sandals. The painful ambiguity of her ethnic position and statelessness is compounded by her very slight social and economic privilege. There is no place for her to belong. This instability of her subject position will alert her to the pitfalls of all belonging, at the same time sensitizing her to her own confused hunger for it.

The French language is what permits her to depart from such an impossible situation. Not being French since, as she points out, nobody in her diasporic family ever considered themselves French, and having been "spit out" by France in 1940 with Vichy's abrogation of the 1870 Crémieux decree, which had granted French citizenship to Algeria's Jews, showed Cixous forever just how precarious the very concept of nationality was. "The stormy, intermittent hospitality of the State and of the Nation. But the infinite hospitality of the language," she says, echoing Edmond Jabès ("My Algeriance" 153). Living in the French language, accepting the "legal fiction" of her French passport, Cixous allows herself to benefit from the liberty of what she calls, neologizing, France's "passporosity" (155), leaving her impossible position in her native Algeria in 1955, but not in order to "arrive" in France. She plays on the notions of "arrivance" and "partance," progressive forms that reveal her never having broken with Algeria, despite her departure, and her never having settled anywhere else.

This precarious identification, which only exile can reveal, is, of course, an inaugural moment for Cixous as writer, one who sees in mourning a form of benediction. "And in the end, a certain writing is engendered that does not settle in, it does not inhabit its house, it escapes, it goes off without turning back. . . . No regrets. Freedom, an inconvenient, intolerable freedom, a freedom that obliges one to let go. I felt perfectly at home, nowhere" ("My Algeriance" 163, 155). Writing as un-settling, then. Cixous claims she never lost Algeria, because it was never hers. Yet the flesh of her writing is indelibly marked by her love for it, not only as the land of her birth, but also as a maternal body. But as she remarks in the radio roundtable, there is no love without abandonment and the song, that is, writing, that results from it. Algeria will return to Hélène, in the form of a "newly-born woman" on the French side of the Mediterranean now. I shall discuss this monumental reconciliation in my conclusion.

The linguistic picture that Jacques Derrida paints in *Le Monolinguisme de l'autre*, a book concerned with the same Franco-Judeo-Maghrebian community in Algeria during the Vichy years, functions as the obverse of Cixous's, yet presents the same textual symptomology in its inscription of trauma and mutilation on the very stuff of writing.

To Cixous's almost celebratory polyglot positioning of herself as a little child in the paradise of what the Moroccan writer Khatibi characterizes as "Maghreb pluriel," Derrida opposes the provocative, even shocking opening pages of his scathing indictment of French colonial practices in Algeria in general, and in relation to the Jewish community in particular. From Cixous's analysis of the multiplicity of language choices that circulated in her household, we move to Derrida's declaration of linguistic paucity:

> Je n'ai qu'une langue, ce n'est pas la mienne. . . . Je suis monolingue. Mon monolinguisme demeure, et je l'appelle ma demeure, et je le ressens comme tel, j'y reste et je l'habite. Il m'habite. . . . Il me constitue. . . . Or jamais cette langue, la seule que je sois ainsi voué à parler . . . jamais ce ne sera la mienne. Jamais elle ne le fut en vérité. Tu perçois du coup l'origine de mes souffrances, puisque cette langue les traverse de part en part, et le lieu de mes passions, de mes désirs, de mes prières, la vocation de mes espérances. Mais j'ai tort, j'ai tort à parler de traversée et de lieu. Car c'est au bord du français, uniquement, ni en lui ni hors de lui, sur la ligne introuvable de sa côte que, depuis toujours, à demeure, je me demande si on peut aimer, jouir, prier, crever de douleur ou crever

tout court dans une autre langue ou sans rien en dire à personne, sans parler même. Mais avant tout et de surcroît, voici le double tranchant d'une lame aiguë que je voulais te confier presque sans mot dire, je souffre et je jouis de ceci que je te dis dans notre langue dite commune: "Oui, je n'ai qu'une langue, or ce n'est pas la mienne."

[I have only one language, it is not mine. I am monolingual. My monolingualism remains, and I call it my domain, and I experience it as such, I stay there and I inhabit it. It inhabits me. . . . It constitutes me. . . . Now this language, the only one that I am thus destined to speak . . . will never be mine. It never was to tell the truth. You immediately perceive the origin of my sufferings because this language traverses them from beginning to end, and the locus of my passions, of my desires, of my prayers, the vocation of my hopes. But I'm wrong, wrong to speak of crossing and locus. Because it's on the border of French only, neither in it nor outside it, on the unlocatable line of its coast that since forever, I have been questioning whether one can love, climax, pray, die of pain or just plain die in another language or without saying anything to anybody, without even speaking. But above and beyond all, here is the double edge of a sharpened blade that I wanted to entrust to you almost without saying a word, I suffer and I rejoice in this that I'm telling you in our so-called common language. Yes, I have only one language, now, it isn't mine.] (*Le Monolinguisme* 13–15, translation mine)

By seeing himself deprived of a mother tongue and, by extension, a motherland, learning quickly in school that "c'était de Paris que venait la normativité" [normativity came from Paris], by invoking the blade's double-edged valence as source of both suffering and orgasm, Derrida articulates a relationship to the French language that, he claims, was both "le mal et son remède" [the malady and its remedy] (Casenave). Derrida deconstructs and recrafts the French language to make it multilingual, what Abdelkebir Khatibi characterizes as translating French into French in his illuminating essay on Meddeb's novel *Talismano* (188).

In his text "Circonfession," the neologism Derrida coined that both joins and cuts off circumcision from confession, his mark of Jewish identity as wound and his desire to dialogue with his fellow North African, St. Augustine, Derrida reminds us: "Circoncision, je n'ai jamais parlé que de ça, considérez le discours sur la limite, les marges, marques, marches, etc., la clôture, l'anneau, alliance et don, le sacrifice, l'écriture du corps, le *pharmakos* exclu ou retranché, la coupure/couture de "Glas" [Circumcision, I never spoke about anything but that, consider my discourse on the limit, the margins, marks, steps, closure, the ring as alliance and gift, sacrifice, writing of the body, the *pharmakos*, excluded or suppressed, the cutting and sewing in *Glas*] (70, translation mine). The key here is that, until this text appeared in the Bennington book in 1991, circumcision made itself felt in Derrida's trenchant use of language but was not thematized explicitly as the wound of Jewishness. For one of the disastrous effects of assimilation, "francisation" resulting from the 1870 Crémieux law was, according to Derrida, to void Jewish identity of its difference. "Jewish" came under erasure, we might say: "Dans ma famille et chez les juifs d'Algérie, on ne disait presque jamais la 'circoncision' mais 'le baptême,' non la Bar Mitzwa mais 'la communion' avec les conséquences de l'adoucissement, de l'affadissement, par acculturation apeurée, dont j'ai toujours souffert plus ou moins consciemment, d'événements inavouables, ressentis comme tels, pas 'catholiques,' violents, barbares, durs, 'arabes,' circoncision circoncise, accusation de meurtre rituel intériorisée, secrètement assumée" [In my family, and among the Jews of Algeria, we almost never said "circumcision," but rather "baptism," not Bar Mitzvah, but "communion" with the consequence of softening, rendering bland, through a fearful acculturation, from which I always suffered more or less consciously, such unspeakable events, felt as such, not "catholic," violent, barbaric, tough, "Arab," circumcision circumcised, accusation of ritual murder internalized, secretly borne out] ("Circonfession" 72).

Through a kind of contamination by the values of "les Français de France," even less universalist and more antisemitic among the *pieds-noirs*, the French colonials of Algeria, Derrida experienced being cut off from the deeper meaning of belonging to an ancient community that this circumcision ritual symbolizes. Thus excised from Frenchness as a Jew, and from Jewishness by the French, Derrida will choose, according to his own narrative, to act out and act upon this genealogical interruption as well as this diverse heritage. He accomplishes this by marrying exogamically and refusing to circumcise his sons in the personal realm, and by inflecting the French language from the position of his own ambivalent and complicated affect, as his version of historical responsibility in the intellectual realm. In the ethical realm, Derrida, like Cixous, was, perhaps paradoxically, rendered vigilant against the mystification of any identity tyranny by the suffering of this exclusion, alert with what he characterized, in his NYU talk, as "la vigilance inquiète de l'étranger intérieur" [the worried vigilance of the internal stranger].

The text of "Circonfession," cut and spliced with Latin quotes from Augustine's "Confessions," functions as yet another mode of foregrounding North Africa's diverse and plural heritages—here Roman and Christian—at the same time as it circumvents and evokes the suffering of Derrida's mother's agony. As she lies dying, mirroring Augustine's mother, Saint Monica, Derrida makes multiple attempts to extract from his mother's tongue the answer to his question concerning his identity. "Who am I?" he queries, desperately hoping for her answer. But aphasiac and amnesiac, she cannot respond. Her silence here is emblematic of the secrets surrounding naming in Algeria's Jewish community, as it is only late in life that "Jackie" discovers his repressed Hebrew name, "Eliahou"—Elijah the Prophet.

Let us return now to *Le Monolinguisme de l'autre*. Derrida traces the causes of what he defines as his "trouble de l'identité" [identity turmoil], such that a text like "Circonfession" can be read as its effect. According to his analysis, a Franco-Maghrebian-Jew in Vichy Algeria was triply bereft:

(1) Because an indirect result of the Crémieux decree was a colonial version of "divide and conquer" that made Algerian Jews—but not Arabs or Berbers—citizens of France, the Jewish community found itself cut off from its languages and culture. One could study Arabic as an elective in the secular French public school. But as an academic subject and a "foreign" language, nobody did. And Berber was not even offered, nor was Hebrew, of course.

(2) Because of Vichy, the community found itself cut off from the French language and culture to which they aspired, abandoned in a political and juridical no-man's land. Having swallowed the myth of "francisation," they were then brutally spit out by France.

(3) And lastly, or, really, firstly, they were cut off from Jewish memory as well as the language and history that should have been theirs but at a certain moment were no longer: "[C]es jeunes 'Juifs indigènes' restaient de surcroît . . . étrangers à la culture juive: aliénation de l'âme, étrangement sans fond, une catastrophe, d'autres diraient aussi une chance paradoxale. Telle aurait été en tout cas l'inculture radicale dont je ne suis jamais sorti." [Moreover, young indigenous Jews were . . . strangers to Jewish culture: alienation of the soul, strangely without grounding—a catastrophe, others would say, also, paradoxical luck. Such would have been in any case the radical "unculture" from which I have never broken away] (*Monolinguisme* 87–95).

Derrida further bemoans the lack of any refuge-language, any familiar idiom within the Jewish community that might have provided a kind of intimate protection from this alienated linguistic situation. But Yiddish was the language of Europe's Jews, and they were not European, while, he says, Ladino was not spoken in the Algeria he knew. "En un mot, voilà une 'communauté' désintégrée" [In one word, here we had a disintegrated community] (92).

The assimilationist strategy Derrida denounces in these pages is not unlike the Arabization and Islamization strategy imposed on generations of post-independence Algerian children. In his remarks on Michel Casenave's France Culture program, he points out the disastrous effects of the Algerian educational strategy, which, like the French colonial one that preceded it and which, ironically, it imitates, is attempting to homogenize the population and induce a kind of cultural and linguistic amnesia by violently enforcing the use of the monolanguage—in this case, Arabic.

Derrida's scrupulous and painstaking analysis of his culturally traumatized childhood in *Le Monolinguisme de l'autre* is far from a self-serving, self-pitying revelation about his personal psychopathology and his anguished and inventive relationship to the French language. Rather, I would argue that it constitutes a responsible gesture of solidarity, what Nancy Wood characterizes as "a will to solidarity among former Jews of Algeria" (182 n. 54). It functions at once as an identification, a clarification, and a warning about the dangers for Algeria today, but also for France and any other multicultural society, inherent in efforts to repress, yet again, the diversity of memories and histories that should represent Algeria's chance to establish a democratic society, in the image of its plural precolonial past. Such a response also voices a hope, it seems to me, for the future of this beleaguered country, a hope shared by all displaced Algerians, and which Derrida refers to in *Le Monolinguisme de l'autre* as "Nostalgérie" (86).

A close reading of recent Cixous texts will demonstrate how these observations, which may appear merely descriptive, are operative in the writing itself, and how they point to issues of feminist solidarity in a postcolonial frame. During the Casenave France Culture roundtable cited above, Cixous explained that until 1993 she had never allowed Algeria to be the object of her writing. It was "une loi morale que je me faisais" [a moral law that I imposed on myself]. If claiming French identity has always seemed to her like a lie, claiming Algerian identity seemed like theft—robbing the Algerians of their suffering: "[C]hacun a la sienne, j'en ai une autre. Elles étaient mitoyennes" [Each one has his or hers, I have another. They were joint, but partitioned]. What changed radically for Cixous was the arrival in France of Algerian women seeking political asylum after the assassinations began in 1993. In a text entitled "Letter to Zohra Drif," which is, in fact, the narrative of her unwritten letter to the Arab girl she yearned to befriend in the French *lycée* [high school] and who went on to become an important fighter in the Battle of Algiers and a heroine of the war for independence, Cixous finally achieves, as an Algerian woman, her longed-for identification with her native land: "When I met Hamida in 1993, my first Algerian to come close to me, in reality, sitting beside me sitting beside her at a table as if absolutely nothing separated us, no mountains, no colonial infamy, neither religion nor wall nor secular silence, when I found myself and she Hamida speaking trembling to me about severed heads, the slit throats, the Assassination that has taken over this country, and nothing shut me in and I was not driven out, within that first hour that united us, I asked Hamida for news of Zohra Drif. As if my silent letter had waited forty years for Zohra to answer" (194).

This passage moves us because of Cixous's marvelously effective use of language to erase barriers: "Hamida sitting beside me sitting beside her" realizes a reciprocity and reversibility of subject/object positions where permeability replaces separation and simultaneity of gesture and desire replaces fearful hesitation. By bearing witness, she can share in the country's tragedy, neither imprisoned by it nor excluded from it—"nothing shut me in and I was not driven out." Cixous's freedom to leave Algeria, the painful freedom of privileged difference that had such an indelible effect on Derrida, too, seems to have come full circle with these recent narratives that textualize Algeria specifically. The return of the distressed has made it possible for Cixous to embrace her Algeriance as a moral imperative. Her plural identifications, with denigrated, excised Jew, colonized Arab, and oppressed woman, continue to evolve. But these positions are not mutually exclusive; quite the contrary. Perhaps the only repatriation possible from the internal exile of childhood trauma is this coming home of solidarity.

I am suggesting, then, that it is, paradoxically, out of the multiplicity of subject positions that have been Cixous's since childhood, the un-belonging for/in Algeria that she characterizes in *Les Rêveries* as "malgérie," that an ethics of dialogue, established as early as "Le Rire de la méduse," is reiterated here. Cixous's experience of Hamida is not that of a First World feminist assimilating a Third World feminist into her struggle but, rather, enacts, in the language itself, the ways in which she aligns herself with the endangered women of Algeria. In the passage above, Cixous is positioned beside Hamida but also beside herself at having found herself.

In similar terms, in a passage from *Les Rêveries de la femme sauvage*, she evokes the arrival in her French *lycée* in Algiers of three Arab girls in the early 1950s (one of whom is the Zohra Drif of the letter). Her own presence in that *lycée* is problematic, because, ever since Vichy, it avoided taking Jewish girls. Mistakenly enrolled there by her father, Cixous's perception of the *lycée* has everything to do with French antisemitism, on the one hand, and colonial practices of exclusion on the other. It is precisely because she is both Jewish and not French that Cixous is sensitized to the *lycée*'s "disguise," to its having usurped for its premises a magnificent Moorish palace and, to its racist colonial program, "un plan d'effacement de l'être algérien" [a plan of erasure of the Algerian subject] (124). Having experienced under Vichy "le plan d'effacement de l'être juif" [the plan of erasure of the Jewish subject] (126), the now adolescent Cixous is vigilant about the suppression, exclusion, substitution, excision of "l'être algérien" [the Algerian subject], and she conceives this first in ethical terms, as the urgency to denounce: "Dans le lycée, ici, c'est la France, or ce n'était qu'un immense mensonge. . . . [T]out ce que je voulais dire au lycée c'était: 'ce n'est pas vrai'" [In this high school, here, it's France, yet this was only an immense lie. . . . All I wanted to say in this high school was: "this is not true"] (150, translation mine). At the same time, she is kept apart from her best friend, Françoise, "et le nom de cette coupure radicale entre nos maisons était l'antisémitisme" [and the name of this radical division between our houses was antisemitism] (150).

When Gayatri Spivak, in her essay "French Feminism Revisited," plays off Cixous and Marie-Aimée Hélie Lucas as correctives to each other's postcolonial feminist projects, she does not trace the thrust of Cixous's solidarity to the specific moment I am focusing on here. By characterizing Cixous, like Derrida, as "in the strictest sense a Creole, a Frenchwoman born and raised in early childhood in Oran in the days before the Revolution" (Spivak 69), Spivak misses an important point. She cannot illuminate what it felt like for Cixous precisely *not* to be French or Arab *and* to be Jewish simultaneously, her inaugural experiences of wound as a young girl in Algeria. It is from these that I contend here that Cixous's passion, and her passion for social justice, arises.

Cixous revisits this terrain over and over in her *Rêveries*, neologizing that until she left Algeria at the age of eighteen, she was "inséparabe" [insep-Arable/inseparable] (45) in relation to the country of her birth, the coinage operating as an umbilical cord of attachment. Yet at the same time, she claims throughout this text, as she states in the opening lines, "Tout le temps où je vivais en Algérie je rêvais d'arriver un jour en Algérie, j'aurais fait n'importe quoi pour y arriver, je ne me suis jamais trouvée en Algérie" [The entire time that I lived in Algeria I dreamt of arriving in Algeria, I would have done anything to get there, I never found myself in Algeria] (9, translation mine).

How can we read this paradox if not through the lens of the painful, exclusionary difference of being Jewish under Vichy? This fact of birth, the mark of the perpetual outsider desiring to be fused with Algeria, with the Algerian Other, with Algeria as Mother's body, contributed to Cixous's eventual feminist stance its passion that is both ecstasy and suffering. For the young girl, this passion is displaced onto surrogate female figures expressed in her wanting to possess the family's housekeeper Aicha, the one Arab woman in her life with whom she shares a physical, if not erotic, intimacy. Similarly, in another childhood memory in *Rêveries*, Cixous gazes longingly at a beautiful Arab doll in a shop window, a doll with which she falls in love.

Forever separated by/from that which she is most attached to, Cixous evolves and matures, it seems to me, away from these pre-Oedipal fantasies of fusion when the three Arab girls arrive in her *lycée*. Although she immediately recognizes the reality of being condemned to separateness from them, one could argue that this represents her coming to a truly ethical and political stance, the recognition of individualities, of autonomies, of (secret) Algerian sisters, beside whom she is only too happy to be named. Her understanding of the importance of their symbolic infiltration of the *lycée*-that-is-France should not be underestimated. At the same time, the uncanny, almost ecstatic acceptance of her being near/far is predictive of a future Algeria from which she must, by definition, be excluded sacrificially, but which she embraces as both giving meaning to her dilemma and just. By placing her name beside theirs, she again effects a kind of solidarity of presence rather than one of nostalgia. Cixous's engagement, like Derrida's, must be sought out in the very stuff of her writing, in its neologisms and illuminating contradictions, in its breathless rhythms that seem to incarnate a little girl's running toward herself and toward those she would love:

> Elles ont été inoubliables, dès le premier jour elles étaient futures et nécessaires. . . . Cela n'a pas de nom ce qui m'arrive. C'est une salvation sans aucun dieu. . . . [J]'étais avec elles tenue loin d'elles. . . . [J]'étais avec elles sans elles moi qui à moins d'elles ne pouvais être moi. . . . [E]lles ont été instantanément tout l'autre pour moi, tout l'être prochain, j'ai tout de suite eu l'impression donc la certitude d'avoir reçu ma réponse. D'ailleurs elles étaient vraiment là. Le professeur faisait l'appel et on répondait cixous drif khaled lakdari présentes.
>
> [They were unforgettable, from the first day they were future and necessary . . . This has no name, what's happening to me. It is salvation without god. . . . I was with them held far from them. . . . I was with them without them, I who without them couldn't be me. . . . They were instantly the entire other for me, the whole neighbor, I immediately had the impression therefore the certainty of having received my answer. Besides, they were really present. The teacher called the roll and we answered cixous drif khaled lakdari here.] (*Les Rêveries*, 151–52, translation mine)

What makes this passage so satisfying, imbuing it with the sense both of completion and letting go, is what is compelling about all of Cixous's recent revisitings of Algeria. Her writing articulates a very personal, singular experience of suffering whose memory functions as her bridge of solidarity with those women now suffering in/from Algeria, forming the very basis, as Spivak reminds us, of the ethical relationship with the Other.

While totally consistent with both Derrida's and Cixous's ethical and political stances across the span of their intellectual trajectories, the revival of a more autobiographical Algerian memory in their recent works under investigation in this chapter was not predictable. Derrida's ongoing meditations on hospitality and Cixous's continued engagement with feminist issues of equality have been heightened and challenged by the violence and repression that continue to tear apart Algeria. Their return to their own painful histories in Algeria, the implicit and explicit connections they make between antisemitism and colonial violence, on the one hand, and the suppression of Algeria's hybrid past and neo- or postcolonial violence on the other, articulate a solidarity beyond mere ideology. By putting themselves on the line, by tracing the lines of wounds that never healed, Derrida and Cixous join the front lines of vigilance and protest against intolerance, oppression, and violence in Algeria. The writings in question encourage us all to examine the complicity of passivity. There can be no more urgent lesson in today's times.

Note

1. An earlier version of this chapter was in a speech given at the University of Pennsylvania, May 1999.

Works Cited

Abitbol, Michel. *Les Juifs d'Afrique du Nord sous Vichy*. Paris: Maisonneuve et Larose, 1983.

Ayoun, Richard. "Une Présence plurimillénaire." *Les Juifs d'Algérie: images et textes*. Ed. Jean Laloum and Jean-Luc Allouche. Paris: Editions du Scribe, 1987. 8–23.

Casenave, Michel. "Table ronde sur l'Algérie" with Hélène Cixous, Jacques Derrida, and Abdelwahab Meddeb. France Culture radio station, Paris, 23 March 1998.

Cixous, Hélène. "Letter to Zohra Drif." Trans. Eric Prenowitz. *parallax* 4.2 (1998): 189–96.

———. "Mon Algériance." *Les Inrockuptibles* 115 (20 August–2 September 1997): 71–74.

———. "My Algeriance, in Other Words: to Depart Not to Arrive from Algeria." Trans. Eric Prenowitz. *Stigmata: Escaping Texts*. Hélène Cixous. London: Routledge, 1998. 153–72.

———. "Pieds nus." *Une Enfance algérienne*. Ed. Leïla Sebbar. Paris: Gallimard, 1997. 53–63.

———. *Les Rêveries de la femme sauvage*. Paris: Galilée, 2000.

———. "Le Rire de la Méduse." *L'Arc* 61 (1975): 39–54.

Cixous, Hélène, and Mireille Calle-Gruber. "Albums et légendes." *Hélène Cixous: photos de racines*. Paris: Des femmes, 1994. 177–210.

Derrida, Jacques. "Abraham, l'autre." Lecture given at New York University, 28 October 2002.

———. *Le Monolinguisme de l'autre*. Paris: Editions Galilée, 1996.

———. "Parti pris pour l'Algérie." *Temps modernes* 580 (January–February 1995): 233–41.

———."Taking a Stand for Algeria." Trans. Boris Belay. *parallax* 4.2 (1998): 17–23.

Derrida, Jacques, and Geoffrey Bennington. "Circonfession." *Jacques Derrida*. Paris: Seuil, 1991. 7–291.

Khatibi, Abdelkebir. "Bilinguisme et littérature." *Maghreb pluriel*. Paris: Denoël, 1983. 177–207.

parallax 4.2 (1998). Special issue on "Translating 'Algeria.'" Ed. Joanne Morra and Marq Smith.

Rousso, Henry. *The Vichy Syndrome*. Trans. Arthur Goldhammer. Cambridge, Mass.: Harvard University Press, 1991.

Spivak, Gayatri Chakravorty. "French Feminism Revisited." *Feminists Theorize the Political*. Ed. Judith Butler and Joan W. Scott. New York: Routledge, 1992. 54–85.

Taïeb, Jacques. "Tumulte autour d'un décret: le décret Crémieux ou la première logique coloniale." *Nouveaux cahiers* 123 (Winter 1995–96): 69–79.

Trigano, Shmuel. "L'Avenir d'un déracinement." *Les Juifs d'Algérie: images et textes*. Ed. Jean Laloum and Jean-Luc Allouche. Paris: Editions du Scribe, 1987. 308–13.

Wood, Nancy. "Remembering the Jews of Algeria." *parallax* 4.2 (1998): 169–83.

7

Mémoires d'Immigrés

Bougnoul for What?

Kenneth W. Harrow

Mémoires d'immigrés was filmed in 1997 by Yamina Benguigui, a second-generation descendant of Algerian immigrants to France. Benguigui's project consists in bringing to life the memories of the men and women who constituted the first wave of Maghrebian immigration after the Second World War, and to evoke the reactions of their children to the current conditions they are experiencing, usually within the context of the HLMs (subsidized housing) where they are living.

The structure of *Mémoires d'immigrés* is provided by a series of talking heads who are responding to an interlocutor we do not see and who poses questions that we do not hear. A history of struggle unfolds, depicting all the difficulties the new immigrants had to face in creating new lives for themselves and their families. The more the design of the history is revealed, the more the presence of the filmmaker is effaced. The thread of the responses leads us ineluctably toward its conclusion, its closure. In an interview with Olivier Barlet, Benguigui indicates the reasons for the erasure of her presence: "Oui, c'est ma façon de réaliser mes documentaires. Je crois ainsi, la personne est avec vous: il n'y a pas quelqu'un au milieu, pas d'intermédiaire! De la même façon, il n'y a pas de commentaires" [Yes, it's my way of making documentaries. I think that that way the person {being interviewed} is with you: there isn't anyone in the middle, no intermediary! In the same way, there aren't any commentaries] (Barlet 38). Thus Benguigui affirms that she is creating a film that is "cinématographique" [artistic] rather than "reportage" [journalistic], and that in effacing her presence she allows the spectators to "rentre[r] comme dans un film" [feel involved as if it were a film]. In avoiding the sins of egotistical filmmakers like Mireille Dumas, who, for Benguigui, presents nothing but the image of herself, Benguigui opts for a strategy in which the obvious nature of the truth emerges, rather than being given directly by the filmmaker. What she may not consider is that the obvious, naturalized traits of her version of the truth emerge with all the more force precisely because the truth, like her presence, is veiled. The interviews are constructed with responses that become soliloquies marked by dissolves. At one point one of the interviewees has exhausted what she has to say. She turns to her sister and says, "Say something."

We can inscribe the issues generated by Benguigui's position as the film's unseen, unheard, implied narrator within the framework of Spivak's famous question, "Can the subaltern speak?" Spivak was interested in the relationship between the power of those who assigned themselves the position of spokespersons for the proletariat, the disempowered, the subaltern, and the subaltern's lack of access to authoritative discourse. Insisting on the mediation required for a discourse to be made public, to provide the conditions of possibility for agency, Spivak addressed the question of ideology, that is, of the *interested position* that spoke through dominant mechanisms of social mediation. What that leads us to is the oft-repeated question of what it means for the subaltern to speak, what relationship there is between the critic, theorist, intellectual, and the subalterns whose economic and social status and interests differ widely from those of the globalized specialists whose field of study is alterity—that is, the world of the other, the problems and needs of the other.

In women's studies this issue has been seen to be aggravated by the twin features of racism and sexism. That is, the question, "Can the subaltern speak?" becomes, à la Spivak, the collective fantasy expressed in the sentence "white men are saving brown women from brown men" (Spivak 92). Alternatively, we can redirect the question to *Mémoires* and ask whether the assimilated daughter can save the uneducated fathers and mothers from the white man. More precisely, can the "Beur" daughter speak for her parents within the context of their immigrant status in France? (Children of North African immigrants in France are often referred to as Beurs.) What appears to be the daughter's investigation into the conditions of the parents' story of their arrival in France, their lives as immigrants struggling in a new land, becomes, when seen through this optic, the story of the subaltern's daughter's voice.

The place of Beur literature within the canons of French literature can be seen in its treatment as either testimonial or sociological literature, or a literature of immigration, thus setting it apart from the body of French literature. French literature is regarded as what is "genuine" literature in French, with the understanding that French literature is the site for "literature" as a generic and unproblematic category.[1] The issue of difference, alterity, and sameness applies to the literature in the same way that it has been applied to the Beurs themselves—are they part of France, or apart from France; newly formed French or immigrant others? The textuality of being "part of France" implies a limpidity of language that would obviate the markers of dialectical difference. Being "part of France" is expressed in terms of a text that requires no subtitles, no act of translation of difference: it is expressed in the neutrality that patriarchal normalizing functions assign to the symbolic order and in conventional filmic terms has been transcribed as the conventional documentary form in which the talking head is presented as an unmediated voice. If "la petite Yamina" [little Yamina] erases herself from the stories of the Maghrebian men and women whose memories she has them reconstruct before the camera, it is so as to inscribe the subaltern voice into an unproblematic space of representation, one ostensibly free from ideology, difference, interest. However, that intention cannot be realized: that space has been the construct of a patriarchal order and, more particularly, that of a late capitalist order whose normalizing functions have worked to sustain the dominant values that undergird their order.[2]

Simultaneously, the formulation of Beur history, a reified and overdetermined immigrant narrative, has also been presented within the context of the notion of the "Beur" created through the ascription of fixed historical markers, through the constitution of a single historical trajectory whose well-defined beginning, voyage, arrival, settling in, problematic existence, etc., have been stabilized in the format of a single theme with variations. There is a subject, understood as unified and instantiated in the account given to this story, and there is the arrangement of voices around one generic narrative. These are the conditions that have been established so as to permit the subaltern to speak. We can call these formal elements the conditions of empowerment, as they permit the reconstruction of memories and provide for the accounting of historical actions. When the conditions of empowerment do not come under scrutiny in the act of filming, we are then subjected to the ideological exigency of the classical realist narrative.

What makes this issue salient is the context within which the film is made. On the one hand, it is ostensibly the project of the generation of Beur children to bring to light the conditions under which their parents came to France in the 1950s, and the difficult circumstances under which they lived. On the other, it is the project of the left, led by the filmmaker as child of those immigrants, to expose to a French audience the conditions to which they had subjected the immigrants in the past as an explanation for the present conflict and oppression facing the second generation. It is also a validation for that young second generation in their struggle to establish a subject position that they can define for themselves. In short, it is a "memory" put to use for political purposes.

That is why the issue of voice and representation is critical. The empowerment of the subaltern does not come from above; the voice that speaks for the subaltern is neither transparent nor free of its own interests. The "concealed Subject" (Spivak 66) is expressed as it interpellates the viewer, generating the "unrecognized contradiction within a position that valorizes the concrete experience of the oppressed, while being so uncritical about the historical role of the intellectual" (69). The subaltern speaks and is seen in *Mémoires*, but only within the field of representation, within the reflection of the camera's image, within the scope of its gaze, within earshot of its microphones, within the concreteness of its textuality, its celluloid materiality. This is the question of the daughter of the subaltern, then: can she speak for her parents, and if so, can she speak within the concealed spaces of the veiled filmmaker?

The History

The history constructed by Benguigui takes the form of a narrative in which almost all the Algerians and French were inscribed. In brief, here are its outlines:

After the "guerre de 40" [World War II], France needed laborers to rebuild its society—especially its industrial base. This laboring force was comprised of OS (*ouvriers specialisés*), workers trained to perform one particular function on the line in automobile factories like Renault, as well as in mines and steel plants. Additionally, some were employed in road building or housing construction; others, in street cleaning or as farm laborers. Agreements between the colony and the *métropole* were promulgated. Recruiters left for the Maghreb, and especially for the overseas colony, Algeria, to find people in good physical condition but also easy to train and manipulate, and not too demanding—that is, not people from the city but from the countryside, from remote rural areas, like Kabylia. They, it was thought, were best suited for employment, while also being dependent, subordinate, and submissive. These men thus formed the first wave of immigrants and were the subject of the first chapter in this narrative. They arrived in the years after the war and continued to come despite the subsequent revolution, the "événements" [events] in Algeria—the bombs in their mountains, the torture and violence in the countryside and cities—as if none of that were occurring, since they always needed money and France always needed a malleable workforce.

During the 1950s and 1960s, they lived in barracks, often six to a room, at times sharing beds so that the ones who worked by day could sleep in the beds of those who worked by night. And they sent the majority of what they earned to their families in Algeria. Everything was temporary in their minds: they were there to find employment for a fixed term, to gain some "sous" [bucks] to send home, and to return at the end of their work contract. Every eighteen months or so they went home for one or two months, visiting their families, getting their wives pregnant once more, and then returning to France. It was life "on the line" without variation.

The only hitch in this French policy was that the needs of both groups, employers and Maghrebian employees, were never satisfied: the economic exigencies never reached a conclusion, even with the infusion of Spanish, Portuguese, and Italian workers. After twenty-five years of unbearable "temporary" lives as men-machines had passed, the government came to the realization that this could not continue indefinitely and began to formulate more humane policies. In any event, this was the official line of the Giscard government in the 1970s. It is not 100 percent clear that all the reasons for changing the public policies were quite so altruistic. In 1974 a policy of reuniting families was formulated. Families divided by work would be reconstituted in France, "regroupés" according to the official formula. The men, called "célibataires" [bachelors] until then (curiously termed as such, by one administrator of the period, meaning men, single or married, but without their wives), were finally permitted to send for their wives and children formerly left behind in the Maghreb. They were then accorded a legal extension of their residence permits. It was, in effect, the turning point in their change in residential status from temporary to permanent. And it provided another turning point in the "face of France" from a society that had seen itself as having a monolithic understanding of Frenchness to one that was now more variegated. The children and their mothers who left for France brought this change, willy-nilly, and the second chapter of the narrative began: that of the new life of the nation along with that of the mothers.

This part of the story, the most moving, traces the anguish and difficulties of women obliged to leave their family *foyer* [home], their village, and their family lives to join the men whom they were sometimes forced to marry and who were more or less strangers to their own families. At times these men were considerably older than their wives and, following Maghrebian cultural patterns, often found their social life in public spaces with other men rather than with wives. The film presents the women's arrival in France, like that of their husbands before them, as universally bringing disappointment. Thinking they were about to arrive in heaven, soon they learned it was not at all what they had expected. The conditions of lodging were highly incommodious and inadequate: the factories constructed temporary housing for their workers, while the government rushed to build HLMs—the projects. However, the policies of the day were opposed to the creation of permanent Maghrebian ghettos, and not only did poor Portuguese, Italian, and French families have the right to move into the HLMs, but they also often were given priority over North Africans. For the Maghrebians, residence in the "temporary" barracks or "bidonvilles"—in effect, slums—could last up to twenty years, and during this time, the need for foreign laborers dried up.

The political policies shifted again, and instead of recruiting workers, from 1976 on the Barre government decided not only to end immigration, but to encourage the Maghrebians, now become superfluous, to return to their country of origin, a policy of "*réinsertion.*" To make this plan work, the government offered each family the grand sum of 10,000 francs for repatriation. But for the majority of Maghrebians, despite their oft-expressed desire to return, it was too little, too late. First, they were now thoroughly accustomed to life in France, and above all there was the situation of their children to be considered: the latter were, in most cases, French citizens, even if they also had Algerian citizenship. Moreover, they had grown up in France, where they were formed and educated, and now considered themselves French. "Frenchness" now became a site for contestation as the logical consequences of colonial policies of assimilation and now late colonial and postcolonial immigration brought to the surface the economic implications of the colonial project. If assimilation was more a rhetorical strategy than an economic policy, then the rhetoric attached to Frenchness was more a conservative instrument for continued domination than a humanitarian gesture of inclusion.

Thus the inevitable third chapter, the children. In a sense, this is the true subject of the documentary, since the "mémoires d'immigrés," those of the fathers, mothers, those of the past and their stories of immigration, always wound up in the same place: here are our children who do not have a real place in Algeria, who often do not know their maternal language, and who are not, in general, practicing Muslims. They will have to forge their own stories, be they difficult stories of struggle, in France.

The history of this *périple* [journey] is thus constructed around these three components. Each component is grounded in a narrative that gives closure to the meaning of the lives that are presented. Each is, then, a story of a life embodied in the recollections of the interviewees, the talking heads whose past is explained by the various French administrators who had recruited and hired them or who had shaped the policies that affected their lives. As the meaning emerges, the identities and origins, seemingly revealed to the camera, are actually constructed before us in the most conventional of ways, through the testimonial first-person accounts.

The Fathers

The fathers' stories are of those who came to work but were afraid of falling on the bad side of the authorities and finding themselves expelled. The men were thus fearful, or at the least discreet and, at the worst, miserable and ready to sacrifice themselves for their children. We might see this as the story of a psychology of dependency generated by the economics of colonialism. Furthermore, as this entails the doubly dependent status of noncitizen immigrants granted temporary work permits with limited residency, the issue of political and economic subaltern status might have been foregrounded. But the film begins not with poverty or opportunity at the outset, as we might have expected, but with the fathers' awareness of the gaze of the children. Even before the opening credits are finished, two of the fathers, Abdellah Samate and Mohamed Toukal, address their concerns to the invisible interlocutor, looking roughly in the direction of the camera. What emerges is their sense of being misunderstood or unappreciated by their children, for whom they have become something of an embarrassment.

The camera focuses in a close-up shot of Samate: "Nos enfants là aujourd'hui, il faudra qu'ils sachent pourquoi on est ici, pourquoi on est venu et comment on est venu, dans quelles conditions on a travaillé. . . . Même s'il y a des reproches, pourquoi qu'on est ici, c'est pas de ma faute, c'est la faute de l'économie. Je dirais même que c'est de la misère" [Our children today must know why we are here, why we came and how we came, under what conditions we worked. . . . Even if there are things to reproach, the whys of our presence here, it isn't my fault. It's the fault of the economy. I would even say that it was the misery].[3]

Mohamed Toukal, the second father, also looks almost directly at the camera and, at the very outset of the film, speaks from a position of guilt and recrimination, addressing the children: "Les enfants, ils aiment pas à comprendre. Ils disent, papa, il déconne, mon père, il divague. Ils disent, ce n'est pas vrai ce qu'il me raconte. Ils veulent pas croire parce que quand ils sont venus au monde tout est là, ils n'ont pas souffert." There follows the memory, the need to excuse his choice to emigrate: "En ce moment-là, nous, on n'a pas de choix. Quand on nous proposait un boulot, je m'excuse l'expression, même dans les chiottes on va travailler, on est venu pour travailler" [Children, they don't like to understand. They say, papa, he's full of shit; my father doesn't know what he's talking about. They say, it isn't true what he's telling me. They don't want to believe because when they came into the world everything was there, they didn't suffer. . . . At that time, we didn't have any choice. When they proposed a job to us, excuse the expression, even in the shithouse, we went to work. We came in order to work].

Not everyone wound up working in the factories, although that was the itinerary most commonly sketched; not everyone may have experienced these defensive feelings or felt the burdens of the past as suffering. But Toukal's final sentence, "On est venu pour travailler" [We came in order to work], has a clarity that defined the entirety of the enterprise for the immigrants. And one must also add that they came because their families normally experienced constrained circumstances. They were "les fils du pauvre," and their dramas were all adventures in seeking, like Feraoun's hero, the path that would take them out of that misery. That was the script they were writing; or, more accurately, the text they were co-scripting for *Mémoires d'immigrés*.

The Mothers

It was not the script of the mothers. The mothers who were obliged to come, often unwillingly, found in France their freedom, their voices, their status as independent women, often freed from the authority and even the control of their husbands. These husbands often became dependent on their own wives, who were frequently younger than they; at times these independent women even divorced their husbands. This is not *Le fils du pauvre*, but *Femmes d'Alger dans leur appartement*. Freedom and voice, the two themes of Algerian feminism, emerge here in emotional tones. In one of the more striking stories, Yamina, a fifty-ish woman, recounts her life of immigration as a young girl, replete with arranged marriage, domesticity, and obedience to the father and then to the husband. At middle age, after having suffered her husband's beatings for years, when the children had grown up, she decided to find work and leave her husband. Her notebook records a poem by Paul Eluard, which she had copied: "On my school notebooks, on my desk and the trees, on the sand, on the snow, I write your name . . . Liberty!" (87). At the age of forty, she says, she finally understood the word *liberty*. She discovers her voice in rebellion against her father. When he summons her to rebuke her, she speaks up: "Tu m'as fait partir d'Algérie à six ans, tu m'as fait quitter l'école à 13 ans; tu m'as fiancée à 14 et mariée à 16! Ce jour-là, il pleurait autant que je pleurais. J'ai vécu la vie du bled en plein coeur de la France. Et je me suis toujours tue. Aujourd'hui, j'ai quatre grands enfants, j'ai 40 ans, et je ne veux plus jamais me taire. Je peux enfin te dire non!" [You made me leave Algeria at the age of six; you made me leave school at 13; you made me get engaged at 14 and married at 16! That day, he cried as much as I cried. I lived the life of the old country here in the heart of France. And I always was silent. Today I have four grown-up children, I am 40 years old, and I will never again be silent. I can finally tell you no!] (88).

The Children

Finally, the children raised in the *bidonvilles*, children whose dreams were grounded in their status of permanent residency, in the HLMs. Children, conscious of being objects of the racist sentiments of the French people and of the iron-fisted policies of the police; children embarrassed by their fathers' fearfulness, closer to their suffering mothers, and filled with hatred toward Le Pen, leader of the far-right National Front party, and the police. Children between two worlds. What story better than that of the contested "Beur" author Leïla Sebbar's Shérazade, the purest figure of the marginal, to complete the triad. Like the other two, this is again a story of modernism's price, again paid by the different generations in different ways, but always as an ironic tale of the immigrant's dream turned bitter.[4]

This is a familiar, even too facile, narrative. How can we judge and critique its programmatic character without calling into question the foundations of the antiracist struggle in France? The difficulty lies with the approach that views this three-chaptered trajectory as ineluctable—and that relies upon a language and images already charged with loaded significance. The conflation of the many individual stories results generally in one comprehensive history, essentially that of the postwar Algerians. Even if there are references to Moroccans or Tunisians, there lies at the core of the narrative the story of the Algerian Benguigui family, the perspective provided by the child Yamina and her self-effaced drama. Notably, what is hidden in the act of filming is given presence in the written text: at the end of the introduction to the book, Benguigui the author merges herself into the split subject of the *énoncé*, as if the ambiguities of the film were sutured in the act of writing: "Ce livre est le récit de mon voyage au coeur de l'immigration maghrébine en France. L'histoire des pères, des mères, des enfants, l'histoire de mon père, de ma mère. Mon histoire" [This book is the account of my voyage to the heart of Maghrebian immigration to France. The history of the fathers, the mothers, the children; the story of my father, my mother. My story] (11).

However, if it is true that every story is unique, that all the stories of the immigrants are not the same, it is also true that this particular story is inscribed in a pattern that informs the relationships of work and power between states and peoples, and is oriented more toward the present than the past. In *Mémoires d'immigrés*, the immigrants' history ends with the drama of racism and the failure to incorporate Beurs into the wealthy, modern, closed French society. However, seen from the perspective of globalization, that is, taking into account the structural relationship between wealthy and poor countries, the fundamental questions might be quite different. Rather than scrutinizing the malleable character of the Kabyles, one would need to examine the system of production that continues the conditions of slavery while proclaiming its modernity. Not what does it mean to be Algerian or French, not where do we come from, what national identity do we have, but what are the conditions that cross both global and local lines that frame the parameters of economic and social relations.

The relationship between the idea of modernity and immigration is not coincidental or marginal. When the French and other Europeans arrived in Africa for the slave trade, and later developed policies for colonization, it was in the name of a "modern" civilization: the colonialists proclaimed their goals of ending tribal wars and slavery in Africa. But with forced labor, the draft into military service, and a thousand other colonial exactions, they continued the old practices of involuntary servitude in new clothing. Worse, they installed what Mahmood Mamdani (1996) identified as despotic regimes, thus abrogating African political systems of relative or limited power that existed before their arrivals. The modernism of Europeans could not exist without the idea of the Other, a backward, even barbaric Other, whose existence as such legitimated the Europeans' conquest and subsequent cultural, political, and economic forms of dominations. The "gens civilisés" and "évolués" [civilized and evolved people] needed their "bougnouls."

Bougnoul

The pattern of the Maghrebian immigrants resembled that of other economically deprived peoples, although the Maghrebians experienced in a few brief decades what others experienced over much longer periods. When slaves initially were exported from Africa, young male slaves were favored, because they had the strength needed for the hard work in the plantations. It was centuries before slave owners in the New World began to favor a policy of reproducing their workforce by having slave families produce children.[5]

For the Maghrebians, French policy changed in 1974, roughly thirty years after the end of World War II, and about twenty years after young Maghrebian men were recruited as laborers. With this shift in policy came new, unforeseen issues. The joining of separated families immediately created a housing crisis, since the older use of all-male barracks was no longer acceptable. Despite the Barre government's attempts to put in place a policy of paid *refoulement* [sending back], most Maghrebian families stayed in France, and the question of the wives' situation arose. In some instances, the women remained at home to raise their children, following the customs in North Africa whereby the men would go to work and socialize in the public spaces while the women made their lives in the family compounds or homes, or even apartments.

But France, or the idea of "France," meant freedom and opportunity for the women as well—freedom from the strict control of their fathers and husbands, opportunity to work in the public sphere. Benguigui chooses to present stories of women who divorced their husbands or, if not seeking such extreme independence, at least took courses in literacy, found jobs, and in some instances became successful entrepreneurs. Some of the women could be said not to have met the challenge and remained impoverished, dependent, and unintegrated into French society, unhappily dreaming of an impossible return home. Others—most—made new homes and new lives for themselves in France, even as they maintained enough of a tie to home and family in the Maghreb to regard it as the only possible resting place for their bones, the only location to which the word *home* had a permanent resonance. They remained first-generation immigrants, even if they had assimilated. And they regarded themselves as different from the French, from French women, French wives, French mothers, without considering how they themselves might have been factors in the changes occurring in France, or how they might have provided something of the foil against which a French sense of modernism would set itself off. In short, they had become one of the defining poles of French modernism, and Benguigui's footage of interviews with young women in the 1960s and 1990s reveals clearly how issues of dating, marriage, style, and family relations were given definition by the setting of Maghrebian standards against French ones. One of many examples would be that of the educated young Algerian woman Naima, who decided to take up the veil as a mark of her oppositional identity. Naima, however, was second-generation.

This leads us to the children who are presented, again and again, as the point of focalization for the "histoire." For generations of immigrants—first slave, then industrial worker—the imaginary relations of the workers to the system of production were radically altered as children born in the new lands entered into their lives; that is, the ideological norms and the interpellations of state regulatory agencies changed. Beginning with school the changes were dramatic. Shots of first-generation adult male workers studying French at evening school were replaced by second-generation adolescents who had been educated in French schools and by young second-generation adults who were in the process of making careers for themselves on the basis of French academic degrees. Again Benguigui is interested in how the Algerian or other Maghrebian second-generation immigrants experienced their situation in France, not considering how France itself might have changed, how the sense of a French identity or imaginary of modernism was being forged. The ideology of modernism governs here, even in the attempt to forge a counterhistory.

In the Caribbean, the term *Creole* came to signify those born on the islands rather than those immigrating to the islands. The term was employed in Jamaica to signify a class of whites born into that slave-heated outerbank of the empire, and who were therefore considered inferior to native-born English. In Portuguese- and French-speaking lands *Crio*, *Criollo*, *Creole* came to signify those who were the product of mixed African and European cultural roots: language, culture, and identities could all be termed *Creole*. Social status, political and economic positions all shifted with the influence of Creole populations. Similarly, second-generation, "Beur" Maghrebians brought into being new understandings of the immigrant situation. Benguigui gives us primarily those understandings from the point of view of those who considered the issues bearing on the Beur children themselves, not on their French schoolmates, not on the French world around them that was somehow assumed to be a fixed entity. Modernism's gaze fell on the Beur children, their problems, their lives and attitudes as the new, unforeseen problem.

Beur exceptionalism, the flip side of French racism, was born of this one-sided *regard* [gaze]. Benguigui's story of the children, the focal point of *Mémoires* in the final analysis, is the real story of French racism, of the birth of modern anti-Arab racism in French—the story of *bougnoulism*.

The term *bougnoul* has an interesting history, which Michel Séguy details:

> Connaissez-vous l'origine du mot "bougnoule"? Et bien, c'est la francisation du nom de famille provençal "Bounhoul," le NH étant l'équivalent du français du nord GN ou NI. "Bounioule" donc était un nom de famille très répandu dans l'arrière-pays de Marseille, et quand les Marseillais "de souche" voyaient débarquer ce qu'ici on appelle un "paysan de la Corrèze" il se trouvait que bon nombre d'entre eux se nommaient "Bounioule." C'est devenu un adjectif à l'époque (1850) pour des étrangers un peu rustres!
>
> Dans les années 1920–1930 devant l'afflux d'asiatiques à Marseille (terminus de la ligne d'extrême orient), cet adjectif fut réservé aux asiatiques . . . et après guerre, devant l'immigration arabe, ce terme leur fut réservé; on peut taquiner un ami arabe, vraiment ami, par bien des termes, mais pas celui là! Ça, c'est vraiment le terme qui fâche!
>
> [Do you know the origin of the word "bougnoul"? Well, it is the French rendering of the Provençal surname "Bounhoul," the "nh" being the equivalent of "gn" or "ni" for French spoken in the north of France. "Bounioule" was thus a widespread surname in the inland regions of Marseilles, and when the native residents of Marseilles saw the arrival

> of what one calls here a "peasant from the Corrèze region," it turned out that many of them were named Bounioule. That became an adjective at the time (1850) for foreigners who were a bit rustic!
>
> In the period 1920–1930, with the influx of Asians to Marseilles (the end of the line for the Far East route), this adjective was reserved for Asians . . . and after the war, given the Arab immigration, this term was reserved for them. One could tease an Arab friend, a real friend, with many terms, but not with that one! That was truly the term that caused anger].

The *Robert* gives the standard definition to *bougnoul*, *bougnoule*, or *bounioul*: "1890 Esnault, 'celui qui fait les corvées,' argot; du Wolof bougnoul 'noir.' 1. 1932. Nom donné par des Blancs du Sénégal aux Noirs autochthones. 2. (injurieux et raciste) Nord-Africain.—Travailleur Nord-Africain immigré. Par ext: étranger, paria" [1890 Esnault, "he who performs *corvée* service (compulsory service or duty)," slang. From Wolof bou-gnoul "black." 1. 1932. Name given by the whites of Senegal to native blacks. 2. (Derogatory and racist) North African—North African immigrant worker. By extension: foreigner, pariah] (106).

The fuller etymological treatment is to be found in the *Trésor de la Langue Française*: "Etymol.: Esnault. Individu corvéable; argot de la marine et l'infanterie coloniale. *Train bougnoul*, expression relevée à Brest pour désigner un train servant surtout aux paysans, aux 'indigènes' du département" [Etymology: Esnault. An individual subject to *corvée* service: colonial navy and infantry slang. *Bougnoul train*, an expression recorded in Brest to indicate a train used especially by peasants and those native to the region] (776).

The etymology indicates that the term came to be applied not just to rustics but to the backward "other," the others who were what defined backwardness. As Africans entered the picture in the 1930 usage, they became the Other. As North Africans emigrated to France in greater and greater numbers after World War II, they became the new *bougnouls*. The eventual assimilation, or departure, of other Southern Europeans in the past half-century left the Africans, and especially North Africans, as principal or sole Others to the French Same.

The fathers' attempts to learn to speak good French, their adaptation of French clothing, work patterns, food, and so on bespoke a certain degree of assimilation into that Same. For one of the fathers, Khémaïs, the French rejection that he experienced on his arrival in Marseilles was particularly painful, as he had built his dreams on the idealism embodied in Victor Hugo and the fraternity he had experienced with French comrades in Tunisia. His dreams were not those of the laborers, but of the intellectual—all the more "chimérique," as Christopher Miller establishes in his treatment of Ousmane Socé Diop's Fara in *Mirages de Paris* (1937).[6] For the others who came in order to work ("on est venu pour travailler"), the partial integration into French society was less wrenching. Their annual or bi-annual return trips home to family and village attested to the conditions of possibility for a continually divided subjectivity, to Bhabha's "hybridity." They foresaw something more for their children. Even when holding onto an Algerian or Tunisian or Moroccan identity, and to the religious identity of their children as Muslims, they saw assimilation and economic integration for their children as their eventual goals. In the end, they saw themselves as the sacrifice required for their children's success.

And as in a classical misrecognition of identity as wholeness, as a compensation for the fracturings that function in all acts of perception and enunciation, the children returned that gaze of their fathers in inversions. For Benguigui, the articulations of the children's positions were strikingly similar. They saw their fathers' efforts at assimilation as indications of their fear of rejection, fear of *refoulement* [being sent back], fear at being othered, of being Other. The children, ironically, proclaimed their otherness while simultaneously adhering to sameness. The "ados" [adolescents], spontaneously and without the bitterness of their thirty-year-old brothers and sisters, would return to this issue, this repression of the fathers, almost blithely.

This return was set up from the outset, when the policy of lodging was devised by the French ministries. To keep the families of the "cités" [housing projects] in line—"pour leur apprendre à ne pas casser, à ne pas faire trop de bruit, à ne pas jeter les eaux sales devant la porte et pour que leurs enfants acquièrent de la discipline" [to teach them not to break things, not to make too much noise, not to throw dirty water in front of their doors, so that their children would learn discipline] (Benguigui 133)—the decision was made to appoint strict disciplinarians as building managers, "genre anciens sergents-chefs qui connaissaient l'indigène" [the sort of old-time master sergeants who knew the native]! (133). Their charge was to enforce discipline, and the children soon learned the lesson: "Lorsque les enfants voyaient que leur père était quelquefois tabassé, traité de moins de rien, comme une bête, non seulement par le gestionnaire de la cité mais aussi par le flic du coin, nous en avons connu beaucoup qui, entre 17 et 20 ans, se révoltaient. Ils disaient que leur père avait perdu sa dignité et qu'ils voulaient le venger" [when the children saw that their fathers were smacked around sometimes, treated as less than nothing, like animals, not only by the manager of the projects but also by the corner cop, we encountered many who, between the ages of 17 and 20, revolted. They said that their fathers had lost their dignity and that they wanted revenge] (133–34).

For the second-generation singer-poet Mounsi, the revolt of the children led to a revision of the Oedipus. Interestingly, he does not portray this revision in terms of a displaced revolt against the newly substituted father figures, the "flics du coin" [corner cops], but rather as a thorough revision of the Oedipus itself. Rather than needing to kill the father, "au contraire, il nous faut le déterrer, il nous faut le faire revivre. Au lieu de le tuer," as he had already been destroyed by colonialism, the wars, and emigration, "il nous appartient à nous, les enfants, de le faire revivre, de lui faire redresser la tête, qu'il se tienne fier et droit comme il se faisait prendre en photo dans son beau costume pour l'envoyer et rassurer la famille restée au pays" [to the contrary, we must disinter him, bring him back to life. Instead of killing him . . . it is our job, we, the children's, to revive him, have his head held high, so that he might be proud and straight as he was made to appear in the photo, wearing his handsome suit, sent to reassure the family back in the home country] (163).

Two more of the second-generation respondents echoed Mounsi's words in striking images evoking the death of the fathers. Naima, who decided to take on the *hijab* [Muslim veil] as a visible sign of her adherence to Islam, described how her father's fears would render him invisible: "La grande peur de mon père était de se faire remarquer" [The great fear of my father was to be noticed]. We are not "chez nous" [at home], he would repeat. "Les Francais, ils nous regardent, ils nous surveillent, on va nous jeter ma fille, on va nous expulser" [The French look at us, keep an eye on us; they will throw us out my daughter, expel us] (186). Another woman, Warda, an activist who chose to work in social services, also saw the fathers as shadows whose self-effacement constituted a threat to the children. After leading a march on Paris, in protest of the killings of Maghrebians in France, she records their actions in contrast with their fathers' failures: "Nous étions épuisés mais triomphants. Nous avions montré que nous étions vivants, que nous refusions de n'être que des ombres, comme l'avaient été nos pères" [We were exhausted but victorious. We had shown that we were alive, that we refused to be only shadows, as our fathers had been] (208).

Mémoires d'immigrés begins and ends with the Oedipal assumptions of identity, projected, as in an analytical psychohistory, through the recuperation of memory and the orientation of the interlocutor. Identity and origin are the very substance of the world imposed on the "ados" and returned in their reactions. Deleuze and Guattari would describe this "desiring machine" as constrained by the Oedipus "family" structure as a fundamentally repressive mechanism whose functioning is cast inevitably in terms of identity: what were your parents? who are you?—origin, identity.[7] With the "ados" we are moving to the limits of the second generation: their responses here are prompted by the older second-generation teacher Wahib, who, like Naima and Warda, now concerns himself with the youth. Wahib asks: "Alors Yasmina, tes parents sont bien Tunisiens?" [So, Yasmina, your parents are Tunisians?] (170). She responds in the affirmative, and he asks, What are you?

> Yasmina: "Pff! Tunisienne, bien sûr" [Tunisian, of course] (171).
>
> Besma responds: "Comme je suis née en France, ça veut dire que je suis française, de nationalité, mais comme Yasmina, je suis tunisienne, quoi" [Since I was born in France, that means I am French, by nationality; but like Yasmina, I am Tunisian] (171).
>
> Farid: "Je te le dis franchement, si la loi française ne m'obligeait pas à posséder la carte d'identité française, à avoir la nationalité française, je garderais ma nationalité" [I will tell you frankly, if French law didn't force me to hold a French identity card, to have French citizenship, I would keep my (Algerian) nationality] (171). A blond girl responds: "Je ne retournerai jamais vivre en Algérie! Même si je sais que je ne suis pas tout à fait française, je suis née ici et c'est là que je me sens le mieux" [I will never go back to live in Algeria. Even if I know that I am not entirely French, I was born here and it's here that I feel the best] (171–72).

Wahid tries and fails to bring them into his subject position where creolization, configured in the form of a humanist reconciliation between diverse identity claims, could be realized. "Je m'appelle Wahid et j'ai épousé une Française, Corinne, et nous avons trois enfants, Rémy, Aurélie, . . . et Farah" [My name is Wahid and I married a French woman, Corinne, and we have three kids, Remy, Aurelia, . . . and Farah] (173). But they refuse him, as they do the shadow parents, the invisible fathers, the hosts of the conquered colonial past. "Ouah, la honte!" [Oh, how shameful] (173). As fights break out, which Wahid the teacher can no longer control with his whistle, the session is ended. Benguigui recounts how "[Wahib] baisse les épaules, comme s'il était épuisé" [Wahib's shoulders sag, as if he were exhausted] (175), but continues along the dogged path of struggle undertaken by Warda, Naima, Mounsi, and, we might add, the successful filmmaker Yamina Benguigui. For this older second generation, the base to their questions is always already provided by the Oedipal model of origin/identity. For the "ados," the assurances of the base are less certain; the responses set official identities against personal ones; and the result is an uncertain affirmation, "Je ne suis pas tout à fait française" [I am not entirely French].

The Angel of History

For Benguigui the arrival of the mothers in France was the condition for their liberation, for their access to speech. The most moving scenes in the film attest to this. But the parameters of this liberation are situated in a system in which the values, including the possibilities of self-liberation, self-expression, are framed entirely by the idea of modernity based on a Cartesian notion of progress. The model for those who were and still remain the dominant social class, masters of the knowledge of official history, is linked through command of the discourse in French to the old guard—those sustaining the political and social system in France. The masters remain the "masters of the word," those whose expositions in French translated the meanings of the "others'" private reflections, often recounted in nonstandard French or in Arabic. And it was that old guard who gave definition to the standard of modernity, along with the meanings of the events that are remembered.

The poor, those who were failures, among whom were to be counted primarily the Maghrebian fathers in this account, are marginal to this narrative of modernization whose language and point of view are placed before the lens of the camera. One of the anonymous mothers speaks, followed by explanations offered by a French social worker whose name we eventually learn is Isabelle Massin. The mother recalls her arrival and inscription in an evening class. "On était en retard," she states, "on était jamais à l'école. On ne savait pas comment lancer les mots" [We were backward, we had never gone to school. We didn't know how to launch words]. Intercalated between the scenes with this woman one finds enthusiastic and somewhat strained laughter in Isabelle Massin's responses as she recalls the work that had to be done when these uneducated families were lodged in the HLMs. Thus, if the Algerian woman felt herself to be "en retard" [backward], Massin recounts how everything had to be taught to the women and children: "toute une série d'explications" [an entire series of explanations] for which the reference point was "la famille française" [the French family]. Before launching into the description of the explanations of how to use a bathtub (not for slaughtering sheep, but for bathing, etc.), Massin stumbles over her words, revealing, most tellingly, the essential reference point, modernity, a term she shifts around. She states, "L'action sociale c'était au fond un travail d'assimilation, d'explication . . . explication pour être . . . euh" [Social work was, fundamentally, a work at assimilation, at explanation . . . explanation to be . . . uh], and at this point she shifts gears, and finishes, "pour vivre bon père de famille" [to live like a good father]. In the space of the "uh," the shift away from the apparent predicate, we can easily see where words like *civilisé* or *moderne* would have been in her mind. We then shift back to the Algerian woman, who elaborates on her earlier backwardness. "I couldn't read or write," she states, "and they taught us, they taught us . . ." At this point she too stumbles, and lamely finishes, "[O]n a appris beaucoup de . . . leçons" [We learned lots of . . . lessons]. She continues recounting how she had never been to a French or Algerian school; "alors je suis restée comme une bête" [so I stayed like an animal]. If our focus is on this woman's sense of her evolution, framed by the social worker's sense of what work had had to be done to bring these uncivilized people into the modern world, both remain totally oblivious to the counterpoint in this construction of backwardness: each needed the other to give definition to herself; the shame of the one had to be taught by the easy assumption of superiority of the other; the portrait of the one needed that of the other to be completed, and instead of a realization of complementary need, one follows the direction of the camera and the film's implicit narrative in recognizing a conventional trajectory of assimilation. This is a tale of "many lessons," and it is always the Maghrebians who are the students. In French, the word *maître* means "master" or "teacher."

All this shapes the drama constructed by Benguigui. But just as she is hidden from view, as the lens itself remains unperceived, so does the history present itself as if there were no relationship to modernism's grand project, as if the memories, the sighs, the tears, and the anguish of the displaced Algerians arose spontaneously, constructing by itself this triptych of fathers, mothers, and children.

In literary terms, we would term this project one of classic realism in which the work of mimesis is performed unreflexively, where the normalization of dominant social values appears to occur so naturally as to not be constructed. Classic realism brings closure to its narratives, and in the process resolves all contradictions raised in the narrative. At every point in Catherine Belsey's description of classic realism we can recognize the reigning ideological principles of *Mémoires*. Thus, the employment of an impersonal, third-person narrative whose authority "springs from the effacement of its own status as a discourse" (Belsey 72) has its equivalent in the effacement of the presence of Benguigui and of her questions in the film. The construction of history and truth have their parallels in the construction of the subject in classic realism where such subjects function as "the origin of meaning, knowledge, and action," while the governing ideology of liberal humanism works "to suppress the role of language in the construction of the subject" (67). The series of talking heads in the film function precisely as such subjects whose responses/memories provide "the origin of meaning." Most importantly, the reader in classic realism, like the spectator to Benguigui's classically realist documentary, is interpellated as a subject who is "invited to perceive and judge the 'truth' of the text, the coherent, noncontradictory interpretation of the world as it is perceived by an author whose autonomy is the source and evidence of the truth of the interpretation" (69). As the truth is assumed on all sides—by the act of remembering and eliciting memories, by the acts of enunciation and bearing witness, what is finally given closure is the assurance "not only of the truth of the text but of the reader's existence as an autonomous and knowing subject in a world of knowing subjects" (69). As Althusser and Lacan have shown, such "subjects supposed to know" work to reinscribe the dominant order, an order that Belsey claims preexists the events described in the text itself. The film gives us a truth that was always already there, and it is my claim that the name of that truth is modernism.

In terms of historical construction, we are closer to what Walter Benjamin calls historicism, rather than historical materialism. With historicism we have history described as a continuum with "homogeneous, empty time" (Benjamin 261). Like classic realism, historicism is concerned with explanations that function through the continuum of time. Thus, "historicism contents itself with establishing a causal connection between various moments in history" (263). Such a historian, for Benjamin, is like the believer who takes events in history "like the beads of a rosary" (263). This historical project results in "universal history" whose method is "additive" (262). The governing ideology here, as with classic realism, is a modernist notion of progress that requires homogeneous, empty time: "The concept of the historical progress of mankind cannot be sundered from the concept of its progression through a homogeneous, empty time" (261). Looking forward in time, like the sorcerer, social democratic theorists forgot about the connections to the violence and abuses of the past; looking back at the past, like Benguigui, the angel of history gets caught up in the blast of the storm that will sweep her into the future without her realizing it.

For Benjamin, historicism's flaws are to be contrasted with the knowledge of revolutionary historical materialists. Benjamin privileges key historical moments, monadic instances in which the break with the continuum occurs, and where the consciousness of the realities of suffering and exploitation is not obscured by the triumphalism associated with the victor and his spoils, his cultural treasures. Benjamin sets the victors in history over against the conquered, we might say the *bougnouls*, and regards the successes of the former with something of the dismay of the latter. The spoils of history, dubbed "cultural treasures," are to be regarded with caution: "without exception the cultural treasures [the historical materialist] surveys have an origin which he cannot contemplate without horror. They owe their existence not only to the efforts of the great minds and talents who have created them, but also to the anonymous toil of their contemporaries." He concludes with this powerful condemnation: "There is no document of civilization which is not at the same time a document of barbarism" (256).

So the angel of history is turned toward the past. "Where we perceive a chain of events, he sees one single catastrophe which keeps piling wreckage upon wreckage and hurls it in front of his feet." The angel wishes to stay and repair the damage, "make whole what has been smashed. But a storm is blowing from Paradise; it has got caught in his wings with such violence that the angel can no longer close them. This storm irresistibly propels him into the future to which his back is turned, while the pile of debris before him grows skyward. This storm is what we call progress" (257–58).

For the sorcerers of history, what is forgotten does not count, one might say. But the memories in *Mémoires* are solicited, while the unrecorded questions leave traces that can take on a totally new meaning only when uncoupled from the dominant narrative of the film. Forgotten is the life in Algeria during this period of immigration, and especially the circumstances of the lives of men who chose to immigrate to France during the war of liberation. Forgotten are the men for whom this adventure turned out to be successful, or even who returned definitively to Algeria, perhaps realizing their dreams. Forgotten, those who did not experience anguish at the need to affirm their identity, to choose between a French or an Algerian identity. One learns nothing of the history involving Maghrebian homosexuals, Maghrebian criminals, or *harkis*, those who collaborated with the French during the Algerian war. *Mémoires* constructs a monophonic History, as Glissant would term it, precisely because it is a history of the construction of identity, thus resting on a metaphysics of presence, yielding an identity politics, where the trajectory is invariably one of departure, voyage, resolution. The narrative's logic gives a meaning and a form to lives, to people—thus "identity." As such, the history is "originary" in Glissant's sense of the term: there is no prehistory.[8]

One can retain from Benguigui's *Mémoires d'immigrés* the detritus of history in the appearance of the faces, the sad words, and the gestures of anger and bitterness in which is contained Benguigui's vision of the truth of what their lives meant. But one ought always ask, Truth for what, and for whom? In this film it is clear that the history was constructed according to modernist criteria, the very criteria that serve the project of privileging notions of civilization and progress, and of justifying the lack of equilibrium between Europe and Africa, Europe and the Maghreb. The consequences of this are significant for the Algerians who felt their inferiority in terms of illiteracy, subaltern social and economic positions, and especially decent lodging. They accepted the logic of modernism without ever thinking of repudiating it; they boasted of their efforts to emerge from their "backward" condition, to educate themselves, to "advance" or "evolve." And in the film the images of well-placed French people who handled their affairs sustained this evaluation of difference.

The constructions of modernism serve to validate the relationships of difference, and it is in the construction of identity that these relationships are established. According to one of the "pères" [fathers] in the film, the word *bougnoul* was originally used by the Germans to designate the French. He adds this etymological gloss to the standard account: "En 1917, les Allemands quand ils sont entrés, il appelle les Français bougnouls, et maintenant, les Français il appelle bougnouls pour nous. C'est pas vrai ou quoi? Ils disent. Mais c'est pas nous les bougnouls, c'est les Français qui c'est les bougnouls" [In 1917, the Germans when they came, he called the French bougnouls, and now, the French he calls us bougnouls. True or not? They say. But it's not us the bougnouls, it's the French who's the bougnouls].

In a sense, one can conclude that these memories construct not only a past and identities, but especially races, classes—the word *bougnoul* indicating both meanings. The act of looking at the past corresponds to the act of creating ethnicities; but as the angel is blown by the wind from Paradise, the French too are swept up by the violence, their wings frozen in position.

The question for us is not what happened in the past, but what the project of modernism carries along with its subtle play of hide-and-seek, what mystifications are clothed in the act of remembering, and what images of the present and the future come to rest upon this foundation, thus serving to justify the relations of power that were at play in the past, and which still exist. The question is not "Who is a *bougnoul*?" but "Why *bougnoul?*"

Notes

1. See Michel Laronde's treatment of this question of Beur literature as sociology or French literature, i.e., "Literature": "Première manifestation de groupe d'origine exogène à se traduire au sein de la Culture par la Littérature, le discours beur n'a d'abord eu droit qu'à une dimension critique socio-politique" [As the first manifestation of a group to originate outside the country and to translate itself into the heart of the Culture through Literature, Beur discourse was at first treated to only a sociopolitical critical approach] (11).

2. The issues raised here parallel those discussed by Judith Butler in her exploration of the film *Paris Is Burning*. There it is a case of a white lesbian filmmaker who has also essentially "erased" her presence as filmmaker, while making a film about black gay dragsters, cross-dressers, and transsexuals. Butler cites bell hooks's review approvingly in establishing the problematic nature of the filmmaker's position:

> Jennie Livingston approaches her subject matter as an outsider looking in. Since her presence as white woman/lesbian filmmaker is absent from *Paris Is Burning*,

> it is easy for viewers to imagine that they are watching an ethnographic film documenting the life of black gay "natives" and not recognize that they are watching a work shaped and formed from a perspective and standpoint specific to Livingston. By cinematically masking this reality (we hear her ask questions but never see her) Livingston does not oppose the way hegemonic whiteness "represents" blackness, but rather assumes an imperial overseeing position that is in no way progressive or counterhegemonic. (hooks 61)

Though Benguigui is "part" of the culture she is filming, she is also distant from her subject as her education and status of filmmaker define her in counterdistinctive class terms. Thus, as Livingston shares a nonheterosexual orientation with her subjects, yet differs in terms of race, so does Benguigui share the cultural status of Beur, while differing in terms of profession, empowerment as filmmaker, and class. Most importantly, the issue of classic documentary filmmaking implies an alignment of the camera with the dominant perspective associated with that practice: "hooks is right to argue that within this culture the ethnographic conceit of a neutral gaze will always be a white gaze, an unmarked white gaze, one that passes its own perspective off as the omniscient, one that presumes upon and enacts its own perspective as if it were no perspective at all" (Butler 136).

All that needs to be added to this is the substitution of "mainstream French" for the mainstream American white implied in the above statement. Needless to say, that "mainstream French" is inflected white and male.

3. Much, though not all, of the dialogue in the film can also be found in the book version of *Mémoires d'immigrés* that Benguigui published with Canal + Editions in 1997.

4. In the course of this chapter, I use the term *modernism* to designate the reigning ideology of the period, the ideology Jameson has associated with late capitalism and with the colonial enterprise. It is grounded in the validation of Europe's sense of itself as having evolved into an advanced state of civilization, and sets itself off by contrasting itself with the traditionalism and "backwardness" of the colonized peoples. We can date modernism to the early twentieth century and mark its transition to postmodernism in the 1960s. Modernity, on the other hand, does not refer to a reigning ideological position, but to the advances associated with technology and the social infrastructure of an industrial, mechanized society.

5. As the cost of acquiring a slave in Africa rose over the long run, the relative price of slaves in much of the New World increased. By the eighteenth century, in many regions the price of slaves had risen to the point where it was less expensive to "breed" and raise a child than to purchase an adult slave. This was the case in the United States, where tropical diseases were less prevalent, where infant mortality rates declined, and where the slave trade was abolished in 1808.

6. The resemblance between Socé's character and Khémaïs's own account of his dreams is rather extraordinary. Writing his wife, Fara, a Senegalese who, like Khémaïs, dreamt of France, he states, "I am, as you say, a 'visionary' [*chimérique*], in love with a dream" (72, cited in Miller 85).

7. As one of many examples from *Anti-Oedipus*: "The oedipal operation consists in establishing a constellation of biunivocal relations between the agents of social production, reproduction, and antiproduction on the one hand, and the agents of the so-called

natural reproduction of the family on the other. This operation is called an *application*. . . . [I]t is a foregone conclusion that the collective agents will be interpreted as derivatives of, or substitutes for, parental figures, in a system of equivalence that rediscovers everywhere the father, the mother, and the ego"—what I have been terming, in this other context, origin and identity. Deleuze and Guattari continue:

> It is not at all surprising that only afterward is it discovered that all of this was the father and the mother, since this is assumed to be the case from the beginning, but is subsequently forgotten-repressed, though still subject to a later rediscovery in relation to more recent developments. Whence the magical formula that characterizes biunivocalization—the flattening of the polyvocal real in favor of a symbolic relationship between two articulations: so *that* is what *this* meant. Everything is made to begin with Oedipus, by means of explanation, with all the more certainty as one has reduced everything to Oedipus by means of application. (100–101)

8. Glissant develops this notion of originary thinking in his *Caribbean Discourse*. The argument is essentially a denial of the notion that one's identity is fixed and can be located in a trajectory that takes one back to a moment of origination that defined one's culture and people. In contrast, Glissant stresses the discontinuities that are glossed over or reduced to monophonic unitary thinking of the sort I am critiquing in *Mémoires d'immigrés*. Thus, Glissant states: "Histories of peoples colonized by the west have never since then been uniform. Their apparent simplicity, at least since the intervention of the west, and even more so in the case of 'composite' peoples like the Caribbean people, conceals the complex sequences where external and internal forces lead to alienation and get lost in obscurity" (92).

Works Cited

Barlet, Olivier. "*Mémoires d'immigrés*: entretien avec Yamina Benguigui." *Africultures* 2 (November 1997): 36–40.

Belsey, Catherine. *Critical Practice*. New York: Methuen, 1981.

Benguigui, Yamina. *Mémoires d'immigrés: l'héritage maghrébin*. Paris: Canal + éditions, 1997.

Benjamin, Walter. *Illuminations*. Trans. Harry Zohn. New York: Shocken, 1968.

Bhabha, Homi K. *The Location of Culture*. London: Routledge, 1994.

Butler, Judith. *Bodies That Matter: Questions of Appropriation and Subversion*. New York: Routledge, 1993.

Deleuze, Gilles, and Felix Guattari. *Anti-Oedipus: Capitalism and Schizophrenia*. Trans. Robert Hurley, Mark Seem, and Helen R. Lane. Minneapolis: University of Minnesota Press, 1992.

Glissant, Edouard. *Caribbean Discourse*. Trans. J. Michael Dash. Charlottesville: University Press of Virginia, 1992.

Le Grand Robert de la langue française. 2d ed. Vol. 2. Paris: Le Robert, 1986.

hooks, bell. "Is Paris Burning?" Z (June 1991): 61.

Jameson, Fredric. "Postmodernism and Consumer Society." *Postmodernism and Its Discontents*. Ed. E. Ann Kaplan. London: Verso, 1988. 13–29.

Laronde, Michel. "L'Ecriture décentrée." *L'Ecriture décentrée*. Ed. Michel Laronde. Paris: L'Harmattan, 1996. 7–14.

Mamdani, Mahmood. *Citizen and Subject*. Princeton, N.J.: Princeton University Press, 1996.

Miller, Christopher L. *Nationalists and Nomads*. Chicago: University of Chicago Press, 1998.

Séguy, Michel. Textes VEXILLA REGIS. <http://home.tiscalinet.be/vexilla/>, accessed August 2002.

Spivak, Gayatri Chakravorty. "Can the Subaltern Speak?" *Colonial Discourse and Post-Colonial Theory: A Reader*. Ed. Patrick Williams and Laura Chrisman. New York: Columbia University Press, 1994. 66–111.

Trésor de la langue française. Paul Imbs. Vol 4. Paris: Editions du Centre de la recherche scientifique, 1975.

8

French Interwar Cinema as Vernacular Modernism

Pabst's *Drame de Shanghaï* (1938)

Winifred Woodhull

Most of the intellectual work on French film of the interwar years focuses on avant-garde cinema of the 1920s and poetic realist films of the 1930s. This is so in part because many of these films have long been regarded, quite rightly, as important artistic achievements that give expression to the new perceptual, affective, and social experiences of modernity using a quintessentially modern industrial mode of cultural production. Another key reason for the focus on this body of work is that it appeared to offer a critical alternative to Hollywood cinema, which dominated global markets and was widely viewed as a conservative social force, one that naturalized an undemocratic social order in the west and constituted a crucial vehicle of cultural imperialism.

American classical cinema's distinguishing characteristics were (and still are) its continuity editing, its way of dissecting scenes (using mechanisms such as the shot/reverse shot formula) to create the illusion of a homogeneous, self-contained space, and its linear narratives, ordered by relations of cause and effect and driven by the psychologically motivated actions of the central characters. Until the late 1970s, American classical films were widely considered to lull mass audiences into passive acceptance of the status quo and to instill in them a taste for standardized, easily consumed entertainment rather than sparking a desire to resist the constraints of the present situation and invent other ways of being in the world. Although French commercial cinema had never been identical to Hollywood film (for example, it was less wedded to happy endings), it was widely considered to function much like its Hollywood counterpart—and like nineteenth-century realist fiction—in encouraging processes of identification that were consonant with bourgeois values and institutions.

Avant-garde and poetic realist films, on the other hand, were deemed more resistant to bourgeois social norms and more innovative aesthetically; in the world of film criticism, they were viewed less as entertainment than as art that demanded serious formal analysis. Moreover, the formal dynamics of the film texts were considered to determine the films' meanings and their effects on spectators—an assumption that prompted the coupling of formal analysis with psychoanalytic approaches to questions of desire and the unconscious, which were seen as fundamental to both subjective and social change.

Of course, in the past couple of decades, critics of French film, especially in the United States and the United Kingdom, have approached interwar cinema in new ways, notably by combining formal and psychoanalytic study with the analysis of the social contexts of the films' production and reception. Whereas attention to the social world (other than the realms of desire and questions of sexual difference) had largely fallen into disfavor in the heyday of structuralism and poststructuralism in the 1960s and 1970s, by the 1980s, the most interesting critics were beginning to consider cinema—including mainstream "commercial" film and popular genres such as melodrama—not as a mere reflection or reinforcement of a pre-given reality but as an active, potentially transformative engagement with social arrangements and subjective formations. For example, Dudley Andrew's study of poetic realist cinema interweaves nuanced formal analyses with reflections on the films' relation to literature, and on the ways in which both literature and film are embedded in the social history of interwar France. Yet although he acknowledges the films' appeal to a broad audience and their association with the Popular Front (which has been widely discussed by historians and film critics concerned mainly with the political issues treated in the film narratives), Andrew is primarily concerned with aesthetic matters such as poetic realists' remarkable use of mise-en-scène to create a certain atmosphere, often one of regret, pessimism, and fatality.

Other work, by contrast, places greater emphasis on the sociocultural stakes of the films' signifying processes. For example, Ginette Vincendeau looks at films of the same period in terms of gender and sexuality as they intersect with social class, race, and colonialism ("Melodramatic Realism," *Pépé le Moko*). Similar concerns are central in recent studies by Elizabeth Ezra and David Slavin, whose examination of French colonial cinema has broadened the range of films that are given serious critical attention. In addition to taking a fresh approach to the celebrated work of auteurs such as Jean Benoît-Lévy and Marie Epstein (*Itto*, 1934), Jacques Feyder (*Le grand jeu*, 1934), and Jean Grémillon (*Gueule d'amour*, 1938), these critics analyze unabashedly commercial "exotic" films such as Augusto Genina's *L'Esclave blanche* (1927) and Léon Mathot's *Bouboule 1er, roi nègre* (1933) as telling articulations of France's cultural imaginary and its complex relations with its colonies (Ezra; Slavin). They also take up questions of spectatorship and the contexts of film reception that shape the films' meanings, including aspects of film culture such as exhibition venues, advertising, film reviews, and fan magazines.

To date, French interwar cinema has been approached, then, mainly in terms of its national specificity (its concern with aesthetic innovation, its distinctive visual styles, its resistance to Hollywood norms) and, more broadly, in terms of its critique and/or legitimation of French colonial domination in Africa and Asia. Here, I would like to propose another approach to French film in this period, one that brings to the fore the transnational flows of capital, labor, commodities, and culture that shape its production and reception as well as the film texts themselves. The transnational dynamics of the interwar years compel us to consider the cinema of that period not just in terms of the genius of certain auteurs or of cinema's engagement with France's imperial project, but as one of many forms of "vernacular modernism" that, as Miriam Hansen shows, were developing worldwide in the 1920s and 1930s (10).

Hansen focuses on Shanghai silent film, claiming that, like classical American silent film, it is most productively understood as a form of modernism in its own right, rather than as low commercial fare that merely advances the cause of capitalists and mind managers, and as brain-numbing entertainment that stands in stark contrast to the critical masterworks of the modernist avant-garde. She writes: "This claim extends the scope of modernist aesthetics to include the cultural manifestations of mass-produced, mass-mediated, and mass-consumed modernity, a wide variety of discourses that both articulated and responded to economic, political, and social processes of modernization—fashion, design, advertising, architecture and urban environment, the changing fabric of everyday life, new forms of experience, interaction, and publicness" (11). I think Hansen's notion of a vernacular modernism is extremely useful for critics of French film, since historically, French intellectuals have granted even greater importance to elite culture, including art cinema, than have their counterparts in the United States and the United Kingdom, and have generally been resistant to sociocultural approaches to film, based on assumptions that these approaches preclude serious analysis of film aesthetics and that works of creative genius have a universal significance that transcends social determinants. As I suggested earlier, many critics of French film in the United States and the United Kingdom have tended to adopt this view as well, "privileging" avant-garde and poetic realist films while ignoring or disparaging both French popular cinema and American classical film (except that of *auteurs* such as John Ford and Alfred Hitchcock, which has been canonized by the *Cahiers du cinéma)*. As Hansen suggests, the idea of vernacular modernism emphasizes the "language, idiom, and dialect" that are specific to cultural forms such as film, while downplaying the negative connotations of "popular culture" in the history of film criticism (11). By displacing the elite/popular dichotomy, it clears a path for new modes of thinking about French cinema.

Shanghai is an important cultural and geopolitical site for the exploration that Hansen undertakes, since in the 1920s and 1930s it was the fifth largest city in the world (in terms of population) and the quintessentially modern city of Asia, often dubbed "the Paris of the Orient" (Lee 37). Shanghai's literary and cinematic modernism has been the subject of much exciting new work that disputes both the western view of modernism in Shanghai (and everywhere else outside the west) as imitative and inferior, as well as the nationalist assertion of its unique, *essentially* Chinese character (Shih; Zhang). These new studies emphasize the fundamental hybridity of Shanghai modernism, which, from the start, generated its own interpretations of such modernist icons as the Lumière brothers' first films, which premiered in Shanghai in August 1896, less than a year after they debuted in Paris. Far from "misunderstanding" western modernism, passively imitating it, or rejecting it in favor of new modes of artistic production that were deemed purely indigenous, Shanghai moderns—writers, filmmakers, and their audiences—actively engaged with modernism through processes of cultural translation that altered both the meanings of the art forms themselves and the individual subjects and collectivities that interpreted them. For Hansen, then, Shanghai is an important locus of vernacular modernism.

For the French in the interwar years, Shanghai had special significance as well; I will argue that France's real and imaginary relation to Shanghai in this period can enable us to begin thinking productively about France's own forms of vernacular modernism. André Malraux's *La Condition humaine*, winner of the 1933 Prix Goncourt, was the most influential "elite" literary text of the interwar period to deal with Shanghai, specifically Chiang Kai-shek's 1927 purge of communists from the Kuomintang (the Chinese nationalist movement), a bloody task he accomplished with the help of French, British, and Japanese forces. But Shanghai was the subject of myriad French dime novels as well, which spun tales of international political intrigue involving spies and gunrunners, gangsters and opium dealers, prostitutes and adventurers. One such novel (written by a Belgian) was Oscar-Paul Gilbert's *Shanghaï, Chambard et Cie*, which was adapted for the screen in Georg Wilhelm Pabst's *Le Drame de Shanghaï* (1938), a key object of analysis in this chapter. As Michael B. Miller tells us in his cultural history of the French-

Shanghai connection in these years: "For imaginations in the twenties and thirties Shanghai was the city of evocations and moods, its very name conjuring up a world of bandits, coolies, sampans, forbidden pleasures, traffickers, and spies. . . . Shanghai represented . . . sweep, globalization, crumbling worlds yet colonial pride, adventure joined to contemporary power struggles, and the pursuit of ambiance" (256–57). A cosmopolitan center of cultural ferment in republican China, Shanghai was integral to the vast global network spawned in the wake of World War I by what Miller calls "world-binding" (265) technologies such as long-distance flights, train and steamship travel, radio broadcasting, telegraph and telephone communications, and newspapers that employed armies of foreign correspondents, such as the French journalist who figures in Pabst's film.

Shanghai was also a semicolonial metropolis, at once an enclave for wealthy and powerful businessmen, a magnet for travelers and refugees, and a scene of poverty and squalor. The city contained the Anglo-American International Settlement that marked Britain's imperial domination there since the Opium Wars of the early 1840s. There was a French Concession as well, also dating from the nineteenth century, where not only the French but many other wealthy nationals lived, dining in elegant restaurants, dancing in swank nightclubs, listening to jazz in fashionable bars, and taking in the latest films at the many art-deco movie palaces constructed there in the early decades of the twentieth century.

The French were especially keen to protect their interests in Shanghai in the face of the rise of fascism in Germany, Spain, and Italy and the threat of war with Hitler's Reich, especially after the fall of the Popular Front in 1938. When Japan invaded China in 1937, occupying Shanghai and establishing its rule there, the French provided support for a battalion of Russian mercenaries charged with the task of protecting the Japanese from nationalist attacks (Witte 170). France was not the only western power to take such steps; there was a general build-up of U.S. and European troops in the city in response to worry over civil war in China as well as international strife.

Of course, Shanghai had not been exactly calm in the preceding years, since its governance consisted in political gangsterism, dominated by the infamous Green Gang. What is more, the city attracted large numbers of refugees from various parts of the world, notably White Russian royalists who left their country after the 1917 Revolution, Russian Jews fleeing pogroms, and later, western and central European Jews (mainly German, Hungarian, and Polish) who began arriving in Shanghai in 1938, when they could no longer get passports from the Reich and were refused visas by every country to which they had applied. Because of unusual circumstances in Shanghai at the time, having to do with the uneasy coexistence of the Chinese, the European powers, and the Japanese occupiers, there was no passport control after 1937. So the city became a refuge for thousands of Jewish refugees from Nazi Germany.

The experiences of these refugees have been movingly explored in *Shanghai Ghetto* (2002), a documentary film by Amir Mann and Dana Janklowicz-Mann, which features interviews with survivors who settled mainly in the United States, Israel, and Australia after World War II. While the story of Shanghai's Jewish ghetto is little known to this day, stories of White Russian refugees abounded in France in the 1930s and, as we shall see, figure centrally in Pabst's film as well. Guards in the czar's army, aristocrats, and others made their way to Shanghai, where many lived in desperate poverty, unable to rebuild their lives on a solid footing. This is the case with the "girls" in Pabst's film (designated as such, in English), young Russian women who work as dancers in a middle-class club and are forced to prostitute themselves to the Asian, European, and American clientele—sailors, students, and professionals. Participation in the skin trade is either written into their job description or a last resort for female workers who cannot get by on their meager wages.

More fortunate Russian women who immigrated to Shanghai managed (sometimes after years of struggle as showgirl/prostitutes) to become star performers in nightclubs. Pabst's protagonist in *Le Drame de Shanghaï* is such a figure, a Russian who goes by the stage name Kay Murphy (played by Christiane Mardayne [Christl Mardayn in her native Austria]). Kay performs at the Olympic, a nightclub run by an abusive ex-convict named Big Bill (Dorville). Despite her reliance on her employer and her function as a sexual fetish, Kay has achieved a considerable degree of economic independence and social dignity, relative to her earlier situation—enough to finance the education of her teenage daughter in a British boarding school in Hong Kong. In the trajectory she follows, Kay resembles the characters made famous by Marlene Dietrich a few years earlier in Josef von Sternberg's *Morocco* (1930) and *Blonde Venus* (1932).

A few Russian women made out considerably better than the Kay Murphy character and were able to lead respectable lives managing dancing schools. In the interwar years, learning the waltz, the foxtrot, and the tango became the rage in Shanghai, where social dancing became one of the marks of modernity. But those women were a small minority. As Andrew Field shows, many more women—Russians, Koreans, Chinese, Filipinas, Indians, and Vietnamese—worked as "dance hostesses" (taxi dancers) in seedy clubs that were mainly owned by Chinese and frequented by Chinese of the lower classes. These women, who were usually young and played an important role in supporting their families in the countryside or abroad, were often forced to provide sexual services to their clients as well as dance with them.

Field observes that "owing to a combination of commercial and cultural forces, the practice of cabaret-going and professional dancing quickly wove itself into Chinese culture, leading to an abundance of Chinese dance halls filled with women who earned their pay by fraternizing and dancing with a mostly male clientele" (107). According to Field, these dancing hostesses, as well as singing hostesses in tea houses, were key figures in Chinese print culture and in leftist films such as Yuan Muzhi's *Malu Tianshi* (Street Angel, 1937), which "illustrate the pathetic conditions of the Shanghai underclass. The singing hostess, the central figure in the story, symbolized the victimization of women in a callous, commercial society" (119). Such women—as well as the cultural practices with which they were associated—were important, too, in political debates about national identity and changing gender roles in modern urban life. From 1933 to 1937, nationalist denunciations of a "western tide," a "disease" infecting China's social body, were accompanied by "serious and consistent" threats on cabarets by zealots who rejected dance-hall culture as "unpatriotic" (Field 125).

Chinese singing and dancing hostesses, who so often appeared in fiction and film and were the subject of intense cultural-political debate in 1930s China, are closely related to a figure more familiar to western film viewers, namely, the American-bred Chinese prostitute Hui Fei (Anna May Wong) in Josef von Sternberg's *Shanghai Express* (1932). The action of Sternberg's film is set in republican China at about the same time as the events depicted in Malraux's *La Condition humaine*. Hui Fei is raped by a Chinese warlord (Warner Oland) while traveling by train from Peking to Shanghai during the civil war. In revenge, she stabs her attacker to death and frees the train's captive passengers, including the elegant, seductive adventuress Shanghai Lily (Marlene Dietrich), Hui Fei's western counterpart. Hui Fei's angry attack on the rapist of course doubles as an act of "Chinese" violence that the film associates, by means of racial stereotyping, with that of the armed rebels. Nonetheless, the murder is also coded as an act of valor insofar as it saves the Dietrich character, "the White Flower of the Chinese Coast," from being reduced to the status of a sex slave to the nefarious warlord, a fate she had accepted in order to spare her former lover, British Medical Corps captain Donald Harvey (Clive Brook) from being blinded by him. Beyond this, Hui Fei's murder of the warlord expresses a degree of solidarity between the women and even offers a glimpse of the ways in which female subordination and the skin trade play out in different geopolitical contexts, contexts that intersect and complicate one another in cosmopolitan cities such as Shanghai.

In addition to capitalizing on the international familiarity of figures such as those played by Wong and Dietrich, Sternberg's film clearly expresses western fears of miscegenation and loss of power on the world stage. It does so mainly through its emphasis on the female protagonists' sexual vulnerability to the brutal warlord, which is a key source of suspense in the plot. The warlord's identification as a Eurasian, like his initial disguise as a merchant named Henry Chang, at once tempers the sexual, political, and economic threat he poses and fuels the anxiety of western spectators by blurring boundaries between racial identities that, in the west, are heavily policed.

Needless to say, the cinematic evocation of fears of miscegenation and male powerlessness is not unique to *Shanghai Express*. As Michael Davidson shows, such fears figure prominently in films of the same period about the western United States, such as Alan Crosland's *Old San Francisco* (1927). The same is true of later films such as Orson Welles's *The Lady from Shanghai* (1948). Citing Michael Rogin's analysis of *Old San Francisco*, Davidson shows that a common textual strategy of California orientalism was to avoid racial ambiguity as much as possible and, instead, to displace fears of miscegenation by exaggerating racial differences and assigning members of each race to strictly segregated locales, such as San Francisco's Chinatown (350–51; 369 n. 5).

As it is depicted in *Old San Francisco*, Chinatown is as seedy, decadent, and dangerous as the China of the warlord period in *Shanghai Express*. The resemblance is underscored by the fact that the same actor, Warner Oland, plays both the cross-dressing villain in the former film and the mixed-race warlord in the latter. The fact that the Chinese villain in *Old San Francisco* is a cross-dresser seems to suggest that the film's strategy of defending against miscegenation and white males' loss of control is rather ineffectual: racial ambiguity is denied, only to resurface as sexual ambiguity. Small wonder that this character has to die, buried in the rubble of the Chinese ghetto during the 1906 earthquake.

There is no doubt that Pabst's *Le Drame de Shanghaï* lends itself to a reading such as Davidson's, based on a critique of orientalism, or to an interpretation that links orientalism to French colonialism, of the sort we find in discussions of other interwar films in the studies by Ezra and Slavin. In fact, *Le Drame de Shanghaï* was read in a similar way by many critics on the left in the 1930s who, according to Karsten Witte, dismissed it as a "cheap," "sensationalist" "exotic evasion" of serious political matters at hand. Subsequently, it was disparaged as well by film historians such as Georges Sadoul and Freddy Buache, who condemned its "kitschy orientalism" and its betrayal of politics in favor of commercial mediocrity and fatalism (various critics, cited by Witte 168–69, 260).

In what sense can the film be said to indulge in cheap orientalism? Apart from its themes of political intrigue, crime, and forbidden pleasures—themes that were already circulating widely in dime novels and commercial crime films—it follows a typical orientalist pattern common to many colonial films, that of using Shanghai (or Algiers or Baghdad) largely as a cipher for the preoccupations of disillusioned westerners, and as a setting for the dramas of European characters, who are the main subjects of the film narrative. Although the Chinese play a more significant role here than do "natives" in most colonial films (a point to which I will return later), their Shanghai drama is subordinated to that of the European protagonists: Kay Murphy, her daughter, Véra, and their friend André Franchon (Raymond Rouleau), the French journalist. Though we see shots of the nationalist leader Tcheng (My Linh Nam) addressing a large crowd of Chinese workers and denouncing the ills of colonialism, including child labor, hyper-exploitation of coolies, and poverty that forces mothers to sell their children as prostitutes, there is not a single shot that visually evokes the poverty of the Chinese masses, and no Asian "girls" figure in the film, only Russian ones. Instead, a single coolie stands in for the dispossessed in China.

The coolie falls victim to the Chinese gangster, Tse Pang (Valéry [Vladimir] Inkijinoff), in an experiment to test the poison with which the gang leader intends to kill Tcheng. The gaunt, scantily dressed coolie agrees to be injected in exchange for a silver dollar (which he accepts with childish delight) and dies seconds later from the lethal drug. Tellingly, the murder of the coolie, which symbolizes both colonial exploitation and class privilege, is perpetrated by a Chinese. Partly due to censorship, but largely due to ethnocentric cinematic conventions, the European violence depicted is mild by comparison.

Somewhat ironically, European violence is represented mainly through the character of Big Bill, whose apparently American identity serves, to some degree, to disguise and deny Europe's repressive force in Shanghai. He is shown spanking and berating the Russian "girls" who dance at his club, heartlessly throwing one of them out on the street when she dares to stand up to him. The other violent character is a White Russian, Ivan (Louis Jouvet), a former guard in the czar's army, who has fallen in with Tse Pang and adopted the gang leader's ruthlessness in exercising power over others. The film story tells us, though, that Ivan was once a good man (Kay's intimate friend in their youth), that the hardship of life as a refugee has driven him to these extremes, and that, unlike Tse Pang, he still has a shred of humanity: as he lies dying from a gunshot wound inflicted by Kay, Ivan is filled with self-loathing to the point of asking Kay why she didn't shoot him fifteen years earlier.

Another predictable orientalist feature of the film is that Pabst's narrative starkly pits "good" Chinese nationalists against "bad" Chinese gangsters, granting little complexity to any Chinese individual or group. Tse Pang and his thugs are greedy entrepreneurs with political ambitions to protect their turf at any cost, including war with Japan, which they deliberately provoke so that a Japanese victory may preserve their economic power from nationalist efforts to democratize China. The noble, idealistic, and handsome young nationalist leader Tcheng, who is always in western dress, is contrasted with the demonic Tse Pang, who is orientalized by means of "Chinese" costumes, props, and makeup that give him a sinister look, as well as by repeated acts of offscreen torture executed by his henchmen as he looks on with sadistic pleasure.

In a disquieting display of bizarre eroticism, Tse Pang sensuously rubs a glass globe against his cheek as his victims scream in agony. And when he is finally defeated by the nationalists, his decision to kill himself is rendered in a highly stylized manner that calls the gangster's sexual identity into question: Tse Pang, seen in closeup, signals his impending demise by passing a gold-rimmed black fan across his face, concealing it from the spectator's view. Tse Pang's sexual ambiguity functions here in much the same way as the warlord's racial ambiguity in Sternberg's *Shanghai Express*: both types of ambiguity code the Chinese antagonist as alien and evil, while at the same time associating him with sexual deviance and physical violence. However, in the remarkable shot just described, Pabst at least draws attention to both narrative and formal cinematic conventions in such a way as to dramatize their complicity with the political status quo in films like his own *Drame de Shanghaï*: the movement of the black fan across Tse Pang's face simulates the effect of a cinematic wipe, a gesture which in this instance marks not only the end of the scene, but also a key moment in the plot, when the "unmanly" villain is wiped out.

Taken together, the portrayal of Tse Pang as an oriental despot and of the Chinese people as a fairly undifferentiated, anonymous mass lend to Pabst's film an indisputably orientalist charge. The sexual ambiguity attributed to Tse Pang is also typical of orientalist cultural representations, as many critics have shown (Norindr; Eng). In certain key ways, at least, the film is indeed typical of "popular" cultural forms circulating in France and other western societies in the interwar years (Bernstein and Studlar). To a degree, then, it exemplifies an aspect of the phenomenon analyzed by Miller, "Shanghai on the Metro," that is, political intrigue, sex, and violence in the city of sin, imagined by real or armchair adventurers and served up to the French masses for easy consumption in the form of pulp.

But if *Le Drame de Shanghaï* is clearly orientalist in some respects, as critics have claimed, is it also an utter betrayal of politics? Pabst was an Austrian national who had made films in Berlin in the Weimar period and was noted both for his directorial artistry and for his political engagement, notably in films like *Die Freudlose Gasse* (The Joyless Street, 1925), which dealt with the poverty, emotional suffering, and moral and sexual vulnerability of young German women, but also their resistance to degradation at a time of uncontrollable inflation and economic hardship. By comparison with his Weimar cinema, the commercial films Pabst made while in exile in Paris in the first years of the Reich appeared to many critics to be both artistically and politically bankrupt. And naturally, the fact that Pabst returned to Nazi Germany after the fall of France and made films in the Reich retroactively prompted critics to judge his French films harshly.

Leftist critics considered *Le Drame de Shanghaï* to be a film so formulaic that, according to Siegfried Kracauer, one could see in it virtually no sign of Pabst's direction, other than some "brilliant photography" by Eugen Schüfftan (cited by Witte 168). Graham Greene echoed Kracauer's view. As for James Agee, he sniffed that Pabst's film was nothing more than Malraux's *La Condition humaine* "redone for the pulps" (qtd. in Rentschler, "Problematic Pabst," 18, 241 n. 49, n. 50). The crux of the matter though, regarding Pabst's supposed retreat from politics, was his abandonment of realism in favor of melodrama. To this day, many film critics, including Witte, dismiss melodrama on a number of counts, not least its recourse to stark binarisms, its simplistic affirmation of good over evil, and its ostensible reliance on the notion of fate in place of visual and narrative exploration of the root causes of evil, which lie in politics.

As feminist critics have been arguing for decades, however, male critics often scorn melodrama not because it inevitably betrays politics but because male intellectuals are able to see in it nothing but a lowbrow, escapist form that panders to the crowd by allowing sentiment to overwhelm critical judgment. The dismissive label "tearjerker" (whose French equivalent would be "larmoyant," lachrymose) speaks volumes regarding male critics' knee-jerk impulse to discount the significance of a film genre that appeals to a female audience by virtue of its attention to the concerns of women and its frequent focus on female characters. Melodrama's emotional excesses, the extraordinary coincidences that structure its plot (rather than logical cause and effect), and its attention to private life mark it as a feminine genre that is wrongly assumed to be inherently unsuited to serious political engagement (Gledhill; Petro).

In a consideration of a range of well-known French films of the 1930s, Ginette Vincendeau argues persuasively that there is in fact no clear distinction between interwar melodramas and the widely acclaimed films of poetic realism in terms of their use of plot, character, and above all, mise-en-scène to emphasize suffering, pessimism, and fatality ("Melodramatic Realism"). The main difference between the two, according to Vincendeau, is simply that while melodramas focus on the suffering of women, poetic realist films concern themselves with the suffering of men. For example, Vincendeau compares Marcel Pagnol's *Angèle* (1934) and Marcel Carné's *Jenny* (1936) to "masterpieces" such as Carné's *Quai des brumes* (1938). In *Angèle*, a young woman from the Provençal [southern French] countryside is beguiled by a sleazy city slicker, conceives an illegitimate child, and is rejected and imprisoned by her father before being reconciled to him in the end. Although Vincendeau argues persuasively that *Angèle* grapples with basic issues of pressing concern to women, including out-of-wedlock pregnancy, subjection to paternal authority, and new social identities that women are forging in the age of urban modernity, the film is generally considered to enact, in picturesque and sentimental terms, the private drama of a woman, one that has no significant or generalizable political dimension.

Vincendeau reads Carné's *Jenny* as a maternal melodrama in which the title character (Françoise Rosay), the world-weary madam of an escort service/"dancing-bar" ("L'endroit le plus gai de tout Paris" [The gayest place in all of Paris]), tries in vain to protect her daughter Dany, who has been in school in London, from the knowledge that her mother has made the girl's middle-class life possible by sacrificing herself, and other women as well, to the base appetites of the men who aspire to control them. For our purposes here, it is worth noting that the Jenny/Dany drama presents clear parallels with that of Kay Murphy and Véra in *Le Drame de Shanghaï* and drives home the point about the sexual exploitation of underclass women without recourse to "foreign" characters or exotic settings. In *Jenny*, the victims are French women in Paris rather than White Russian refugees in Shanghai (the latter being compatriots of the Russian producer of *Le Drame de Shanghaï*, Roman Pinès, an expatriate based in France).

By contrast with melodramas like *Angèle* and *Jenny*, *Quai des brumes* is celebrated as a high artistic achievement in no small part because it glorifies the suffering of a male hero (Jean Gabin), a deserter from the colonial army who can find no way to lead a decent life once he is back in France. His angst stems from sexual jealousy and the impossibility of protecting young Nelly (Michèle Morgan) from sexual exploitation by a dirty old man (Michel Simon). It stems equally from entrapment in a petty, violent world of gangsters, an oppressive situation that is visually rendered through the gloomy atmosphere of Le Havre, a port city that paradoxically offers no escape. Despite the common elements of organized crime, prostitution, entrapment, and world-weariness, *Quai des brumes* is labeled "art," whereas *Jenny*, *Angèle*, and *Le Drame de Shanghaï* are seen as categorically different, that is, as commercial fare. In *Quai des brumes*, the hero's suffering and pointless death are easily associated with existential dilemmas of grand proportions—

"man's fate," to recall Malraux—whereas the problems of Angèle, Jenny, and Kay are relegated to the private world of the family, when they are not written off altogether as "lachrymose" trivia.

I would like to suggest that much 1930s melodrama can be fruitfully considered as a form of vernacular modernism. I will argue that it situates France within the global network of relations that captured the French imagination in the interwar years. It can usefully be contrasted with poetic realism, a self-consciously "artistic" mode of cultural expression that privileges notions of directorial autonomy and "genius" while making of the male hero an emblem of social conflicts that play out on a national scale, or on the scale of the French colonial empire (as in *Le Grand jeu*, *Pépé le Moko*, and other colonial films). Interwar melodrama, on the other hand, has a different character and a different social function. However "commercial" and "formulaic" melodrama may be, it employs a cinematic idiom that has both national and international currency. Many melodramatic "women's films" use elements such as performance to inflect this idiom in ways that bring to the fore not only feminist concerns, but also points of intersection between social conflicts in France and those in other parts of the world. Pabst's *Le Drame de Shanghaï* is an important example of a melodrama that ties female insubordination to class struggles as well as anticolonial movements in various countries. Other examples, which limitations of space prevent me from discussing here, include well-made movies featuring stars such as Edwige Feuillère (in Jacques de Baroncelli's *Feu!*, 1937, and Raymond Bernard's *J'étais une aventurière*, 1938), as well as Marcelle Chantal, Fréhel, and Inkijinoff (in Fédor Ozep's *Amok*, 1933).

I want to emphasize that, in my view, the appeal of these films cannot be satisfactorily explained by their commonalities with classical Hollywood cinema (1917–60), if the latter is understood to please audiences all over the globe by virtue of having found the means to activate universal processes of perceiving and making sense of the world, as neoformalist, cognitivist critics claim (Bordwell et al., cited by Hansen 11). Rather, their appeal lies in their development of what Hansen calls "a sensory-reflexive discourse of the experience of modernity and modernization, a matrix for the articulation of fantasies, uncertainties, and anxieties" (14). It has to do, too, with a culture that, in Paris as in Shanghai, had "modernized in ways that exceeded the purview of literary and intellectual modernism"; both French and Chinese culture of the 1920s and 1930s "had developed responses to modernization in a wide range of media and on a mass scale, spawning a vernacular form of modernism" (Hansen 19).

In Pabst's *Le Drame de Shanghaï*, as in many other films of the period (and beyond), in France and elsewhere, the woman at the center of the narrative embodies the pressures of modernity and the anxieties they provoke, as well as the new possibilities they present. In Hansen's terms, women figure the ambivalence generated by processes of urbanization and new forms of publicness, and often function as emblems of the modern metropolis itself, "the city in its allure, instability, anonymity, and illegibility" (15). Women "may well be the privileged fetish of male/modernist projection and stereotyping," but they are also "the sites of greatest ambivalence and mobility, as traditional binarisms may be at once invoked and undermined through performance and masquerade" (16).

These things are certainly true of Kay Murphy in Pabst's film. On one level she embodies the allure and illegibility of Shanghai, especially for western viewers imagining an Asian city through the mediating figure of a *déclassée* White Russian nightclub performer. On another level she embodies "danger" as it is experienced by Tcheng when he is betrayed by her, and as it is defined by the cinematic convention of the femme fatale. In spite of himself, Tcheng is bewitched by Kay as she performs her act at the Olympic: he tells her that when she sings, he forgets "everything." The film, however, severely undercuts this association of Kay with the cinematic femme fatale by humanizing her as well as by conferring upon the spectators knowledge about her that Tcheng does not have. Viewers understand that Kay had no choice but to betray Tcheng: it was the condition set by Ivan when he agreed to free her from her ties to the secret organization led by Tse Pang, "le Serpent Noir" [the Black Serpent], ties that had been imposed by Ivan years before and that had kept Kay in a stranglehold. In exchange for her cooperation in capturing Tcheng, Kay would be allowed to leave Shanghai on a steamship bound for New York. If Kay had refused to cooperate with Ivan, he would have killed her and possibly her daughter as well.

The film makes clear that Kay sacrifices Tcheng in order to protect her daughter, not in self-interest. Her dependence on Ivan places her in an impossible bind rooted in sexual domination as well as the desperate circumstances in which she found herself in her first years as a refugee in Shanghai. Thus her "choice" to sacrifice Tcheng in order to save her daughter is no choice at all. In spite of the film's sympathetic rendering of Kay's impossible situation, however, it yields to the cinematic codes that structure melodrama, ultimately demanding punishment of the woman who embodies the insurmountable conflicts of modernity. As a figure for the painful, inextricably entwined experiences of sexual subordination, poverty, and exile, but also for women's increasingly visible and insistent demands, in many parts of the world, for a life that does not consist solely in service and sacrifice to others, Kay is deemed guilty and is condemned to death.

In addition to signifying the pleasure and danger of the city and of erotic bonds, Kay figures both racial ambiguity *and* the rigid racial distinctions that are drawn by westerners intent on preserving their sense of superiority over non-westerners in a world ordered by colonialism. She embodies the instability and insecurity of European identity in a colonialist yet cosmopolitan world. Kay is European, but her European identity is shaky in several respects. She is Russian, that is, she is from a country that lies in the easternmost part of Europe, on the border of Asia. Moreover, she is a White Russian who, in the wake of the revolution, has been forced to leave her homeland. She is a displaced person in Shanghai, a glorified female sex worker in a nightclub—in Kay's words, a "star" rather than an "artist."

Even critical thinkers and kind-hearted men like Tcheng and Franchon are fascinated by Kay because of the ethnic and cultural uncertainty she represents to and for them. In a moment of political crisis, however, when she is taken prisoner by Tse Pang on the eve of the Japanese occupation of Shanghai, Franchon decisively cuts through the ambiguity of her identity: "Kay Murphy est une blanche" [Kay Murphy is a white woman], he declares firmly, in an effort to impress upon Tse Pang the risk that he is running in holding her captive. In unequivocally declaring Kay a white woman, Franchon signals to the gang leader that the European powers will not tolerate his imprisonment and torture of Kay because of the threat these acts pose to western authority in Shanghai. Of course, Franchon simultaneously implies that the imprisonment and torture of one of Tse Pang's "own" Asian women would not be cause for European alarm, much less retaliation. Indeed, he also implies that Kay's public significance in this affair is determined by the political crisis at hand, and that under other circumstances Tse Pang's abuse of her would pass virtually unnoticed, since male control of women is a generally accepted social norm.

A related point is that in *Le Drame de Shanghaï*, Kay's ambiguous identity also makes her the bearer of westerners' fear of miscegenation. She is brutally exploited by two Americans or Europeans, Big Bill and Ivan, but because both these men answer to Tse Pang, Kay represents the "yellow peril" phantasmically operating in the field of sexuality. The instability of Kay's identity is doubled by that of Tse Pang himself. Tse Pang is stereotypically portrayed as an "inscrutable" Chinese, who is aligned with the Japanese against his own compatriots. What is more, he is played by Inkijinoff, a Russian actor from Kyrgyzstan, on the border of northwestern China. Familiar to French audiences through his many roles as criminals and sociopaths in films such as Julien Duvivier's *La Tête d'un homme* (1932) and Fédor Ozep's *Amok* (1934), the Russian expatriate actor blurs the boundaries of the conflicting Chinese, Russian, and French identities that figure prominently in Pabst's film.

Finally, to the extent that Kay embodies female mobility, not just as a downtrodden refugee who moves from one place to another in order to survive, but as a female performer whose economic success enables her to say to Ivan, "Je ne veux plus dépendre de toi" [I don't want to depend on you anymore], she holds out the promise of emancipatory changes in gender relations the world over. These changes are associated with Chinese nationalism, with women's demands for political equality in many parts of the world, and with new forms of public activity in a variety of contexts, including Shanghai and Paris.

In addition to Kay's declaration of independence from Ivan and the political gangsterism he has embraced, the film presents two striking enactments of Kay's demand not only for freedom, but for happiness as well. Both enactments call attention to performance and serve as examples of vernacular modernism's key means of adapting the formulas of interwar melodrama to particular purposes and cultural contexts. Likewise, both enactments anticipate the arrival of Kay's daughter, Véra, from Hong Kong after a seven-year absence. In the first one, Kay dresses in Russian garb in the presence of the elderly Niania, who had been her childhood nurse and Véra's as well. Anticipating the day when she will disguise herself as the Russian she "truly" is in order to leave Shanghai undetected, the glamorous star Kay Murphy masquerades as a decidedly unglamorous Russian woman, her head covered with a homely kerchief, and laughs with Niania about both the ruse and the happy end to which it is meant to lead.

The second enactment is Kay's performance of a children's song that reassuringly answers childish questions regarding familial and cultural origins, while also idealizing the past. We understand that this must be a song that Kay used to sing to little Véra before mother and daughter were separated. Kay's performance in this scene is remarkable because it occurs in her dressing room at the Olympic before an audience of only one person, Franchon. Her lively piano playing, cheerful singing, and smiling face clearly express her dream of happiness as well as freedom. This joyful, private, backstage performance contrasts sharply with the false gaiety of her nightclub performances, underlined in the film by shots of Kay, shown in profile before a backstage mirror, looking hatefully at Big Bill, then looking at herself in the mirror and pasting a smile on her face when she hears her musical cue to go on stage. Kay's happy singing in her dressing room contrasts too with her somnambulistic performance at the Olympic on the night when Big Bill, following Ivan's instructions, forbids her to leave the club the next day in order to meet Véra at the port when she arrives from Hong Kong. Finally, it contrasts with the performance in which Kay's nightclub act doubles as a seduction of Tcheng: Ivan forces Kay to use her powers of attraction to lure Tcheng into a trap, and in her subsequent conversation with Tcheng in a semiprivate alcove, Kay's identity as a sexual fetish clearly weighs heavily on her, as does her role as an accomplice in a repressive political act.

In sum, Pabst's protagonist dramatizes the social mobility potentially available to women in certain modern contexts, while keeping in view the ways in which it is severely limited by women's continued consignment to the category of sexual beings. Despite its conformity to convention in having Kay die—thereby symbolically purging the world of the contradictions and pain of modernity—*Le Drame de Shanghaï* nonetheless celebrates Kay's efforts to evade male domination and to grant priority to her relationship with Véra, the most important social bond she has. The film shows, too, though, that precisely because Kay represents modernity's threat to gender hierarchies the world over, authoritarian forces will do everything in their power to foreclose the possibilities open to her. The tragic significance of her death is amplified, rather than diminished, by the fact that it coincides with many defeats on the world stage, notably that of the Chinese nationalists, who were trying to combat the might-makes-right reign of Tse Pang as well as European colonialism and Japanese imperialism. For viewers in 1938, these events irresistibly called to mind fascist imperialism in Europe as well. Pabst produces a poignant and unsettling effect in a shot showing Kay being stabbed, unbeknownst to Véra and Franchon, who are walking with her through the crowded streets leading to the Shanghai harbor. Kay's upright corpse—clearly a figure for democratic politics as well as gender equality—is carried along by the European throng making its way to the port as the Japanese bombardment sounds the death knell of Chinese nationalism.

Kay Murphy, "le rêve de Shanghaï" [the dream of Shanghai], is dead and Shanghai itself is in flames. In the final sequence, the film retreats from the international perspective it had adopted earlier and withdraws into a European cocoon. Spectators see Shanghai now from the vantage point of the haggard Europeans in the harbor. Closeups of the French and British flags unsubtly invite viewers to identify with the social position of the Europeans fleeing the city and with their affective experience of the earth-shaking events that are unfolding. In this context, the odd but "reassuringly" heterosexual couple formed by the thirty-something Franchon and the sixteen-year-old Véra represents the only hope for a brighter future. Alongside the aged Russian nurse Niania, the formerly jaunty reporter, who is now very solemn, and poor, motherless Véra are shown on board a military ship against a bleak backdrop of gray steel. Like the commercial steamships that figure prominently in poetic realist films such as *Quai des brumes* and *Pépé le Moko*, as well as in Sternberg's *Morocco*, the vessel in *Le Drame de Shanghaï* may well take the protagonists nowhere. Pabst's film leaves its spectators more or less at sea, which is fitting considering that, according to my colleague Yingjin Zhang, the term "hai" in "Shanghai" literally means "sea" in Chinese.[1] The film thus declines to offer a clear resolution, even an imaginary or sentimental one, to the problems at hand.

Without doubt, *Le Drame de Shanghaï* is a pessimistic film, like many others made in the late 1930s. It bears witness to the grim mood of a period marked by economic depression and the rise of fascist imperialism in Asia and in Europe. However, it is not a "fatalistic" betrayal of politics, as many critics have claimed. I want to argue that although the film acknowledges the political reality of the day, namely that imperialist and homegrown gangsterism are preempting political responses to social conflict in Shanghai and elsewhere, it nonetheless articulates a critique of some of the worst features of international politics in the 1930s. Beyond its admittedly heavy-handed condemnation of gangsterism through its treatment of Tse Pang, it obliquely calls attention to French colonial domination in Indochina and to the prevalence of racialized forms of sexual and class exploitation, both in France's colonies and in semicolonial Shanghai.

I mentioned earlier that an important aspect of the film's orientalism was expressed through a contrast between the perversity and ruthless violence of Tse Pang and his thugs on the one hand and the relatively muted violence of American and European figures such as Big Bill and Ivan on the other. Here, I want to point out that, partly as a result of government censorship, the film does not depict any officially sanctioned violence on the part of France or any other European power; the villains are uprooted outlaws—Big Bill, the ex-convict who manages the Olympic, and Ivan, the alienated refugee from czarist Russia. Official malfeasance is shown to occur only in the realm of ideological manipulation through the international media, specifically "l'Agence internationale américaine télégraphique des nouvelles mondiales" [International American Telegraph Agency of World News], whose very name parodies the pretensions of the western powers.

The head of this agency, a plump man in late middle age, is a clownish figure who wears shorts and speaks nonsense—a parody of an American, but one whose Slavic last name (hard to decipher on the worn soundtrack) ends in "vich." He is a foil to the young, attractive, and responsible journalist, Franchon, who cleverly and amusingly deflates his boss's grandiosity and debunks his idiotic pronouncements. The media magnate is a mouthpiece for the chauvinism and wishful thinking of the western powers, which choose to ignore the rising tide of Chinese nationalism and to disbelieve Tcheng's claim that capitalist profiteering in Shanghai is weakening China and inviting Japanese aggression. Rather than dealing with the political crisis at hand, the boss tries to deny its very existence. He refuses to publish Franchon's report of

Tcheng's public denunciation of the *généraux* [generals], the *traficants d'armes* [gunrunners], the *profiteurs de guerre* [war profiteers], and the provocateurs who are preparing for war with Japan, destabilizing the Chinese economy, and preventing the Chinese people from constructing a viable future and living in peace. Indeed, the media magnate goes so far as to deny that developments in China could possibly bode ill or be of any consequence at all: "La Chine est un pays où il ne se passera jamais rien. Il n'y a pas de politique chinoise. . . . Il n'y a pas de Chine" [China is a country where nothing will ever happen. There is no Chinese politics. . . . There is no China].

The agency head's vaudeville-style performance, complete with hyperbolic raving and clownish gesticulations, renders him ridiculous. Again, performance is the vehicle through which the film uses the language of "commercial" cinema for its own purposes and articulates a critique of western hegemony in China. A related point is that Pabst mixes genres—melodrama, the gangster film, and vaudeville-style comedy—not simply because he has sold out to market forces, as some have suggested, but because in the political context in which he is working in 1938, his controversial messages about world events can be delivered and/or received only in a comic or melodramatic register. Generic flexbility is important in a time of censorship, political crisis, and widespread insecurity.

However mild a version of western hegemony and European violence finds expression in Pabst's film narrative, the circumstances of the film's casting and shooting present powerful testimony to French colonial domination in Asia, as well as to Pabst's complicity with it in making his film. With the exception of Tse Pang, the Chinese characters in *Le Drame de Shanghaï* are played by Vietnamese actors who speak fluent French, and the outdoor scenes are shot in Saigon. The few young "Chinese" women who appear in the film are in fact Vietnamese. They include Tcheng's beautiful sister (played by Mademoiselle Foun-Sen), who initially cooperates with Tse Pang (her husband) but is ultimately reconciled to her brother. They include as well some salt-of-the-earth working women who figure in the crowd scenes, listening to Tcheng's speech or marching in peaceful antiwar/national unity demonstrations. As we know from Field's study of dancing hostesses in Shanghai, young underclass Vietnamese women in that Asian metropolis are likely to be employed as taxi dancers and prostitutes, not unlike their counterparts in Saigon. In indirect ways, then, the Vietnamese actresses in *Le Drame de Shanghaï* point to the harms inflicted on the Indochinese by French colonialism and even hint at forms of sexual exploitation that are entirely absent from the film's narrative, that is, the prostitution of Vietnamese, Korean, Filipina, and other Asian underclass women in semicolonial Shanghai.

If the film obliquely reminds spectators of the racialized sexual and class exploitation that informs France's colonial rule in Indochina and its presence in Shanghai, it overtly invites sympathy for the female protagonist, Kay Murphy, and the Russian dancers at the Olympic. True, Kay and the Russian showgirls are sympathetic *because* they are European and because, to a certain extent, they stand in for the European underclass as a whole, not just for exploited women. As we have seen, they recall figures who appear in many French melodramas of the 1930s and who fulfill such a function, such as Carné's Jenny and, I might add, Carné's Clara (Arletty) in *Le Jour se lève* (1939), a music-hall performer who is mistreated by her stage partner and lover. Yet I do not think we can conclude that even so "simplistic" a film as *Le Drame de Shanghaï* focuses our attention exclusively on the misery of Europeans and ignores the plight of others. On the contrary, it makes use of the viewers' affective bond with the Russian women in order to extend their feelings of sympathy and solidarity to other groups as well, notably the Chinese nationalists and, by analogy, other democratic movements in Asia as well.

The association between the Russian showgirls and the Chinese nationalists is established through two basic textual strategies. One involves the configuration of characters in the narrative. The intelligent, handsome, and amusing young journalist, André Franchon, who is a genuine friend to Kay and her daughter, Véra, is also aligned with Tcheng as well as another educated nationalist figure, who, like Franchon, is a frequent customer at the Olympic. Franchon frees Kay, Véra, and Tcheng from Tse Pang's gang (although, as we have seen, Kay ultimately dies at their hands).

The other strategy for linking the Russian women and the nationalists is to juxtapose shots of these respective groups during the film's exposition and to underline the visual juxtaposition through verbal cues in the dialogue, which introduce the central themes of sexual, racial, and class exploitation. One shot sequence shows Big Bill firing a dancer who angrily rebukes him for fondling/spanking her, telling him she is revolted by his "sale officine" [dirty business]. Next there is a cut to a shot of Franchon and a Chinese nationalist friend who are watching the Russian women performing at the Olympic. The Chinese man urges Franchon to accompany him to the public meeting Tcheng is holding. In the following shot, Tcheng is haranguing a crowd of Chinese workers and denouncing various forms of colonial exploitation, including prostitution. Tcheng asserts that the multiform exploitation to which the Chinese people are subjected "n'est pas une forme de la barbarie, c'est un raffinement de la civilisation occidentale" [is not a form of barbarism, it is a refinement of western civilization]. Given the visual and verbal rhetoric in this shot sequence, Tcheng's observation acquires a double meaning: first, that the logic of instrumental rationality in western civilization has led to the domination of human beings the world over (as Max Horkheimer and Theodor Adorno would argue in 1944 in *Dialectic of Enlightenment*) and, furthermore, that sexual domination is a fundamental form of oppression: not only is it as important as the other forms mentioned by Tcheng, but it is inextricably bound up with them.

Contrary to popular belief, Pabst's woman-centered melodrama neither betrays politics nor dilutes politics to the point of meaninglessness. Instead, it presents the exploitation of women as an important lens through which other forms of oppression are to be examined and analyzed. Kay Murphy's feminist claim to independence and happiness resonates with Tcheng's demand that the "scandal" of colonial and class domination cease. It provides viewers with a powerful point of affective identification with the Chinese nationalists and with democratic movements in other locations. Far from simply confining oriental "others" to a separate, subordinate sphere in a doomed "exotic" city, Pabst's film interweaves several distinct but related Shanghai dramas whose meanings are to be deciphered in relation to that of Kay Murphy. Considered as an example of vernacular modernism, *Le Drame de Shanghaï* can be seen as something other than a mindless tearjerker, escapist fare for the masses who have not yet been enlightened by the political vanguard, and who supposedly lack the cultivation to engage with the innovative work of the artistic avant-garde. From the vantage point of vernacular modernism, Pabst's film can be understood as a medium that uses the cinematic lingua franca of the day to give expression to new forms of sensibility and social experience that are emerging in the interwar period, not only in France but around the world.

Note

1. E-mail communication, 25 February 2003.

Works Cited

Andrew, Dudley. *Mists of Regret: Culture and Sensibility in Classic French Films.* Princeton, N.J.: Princeton University Press, 1995.

Baroncelli, Jacques de. *Feu!* Société des productions cinématographiques F.C.L., 1937.

Benoît-Lévy, Jean, and Marie Epstein. *Itto*. Eden productions, 1934.

Bernard, Raymond. *J'étais une aventurière*. Ciné-Alliance, Georges Rabinovitch, 1938.

Bernstein, Matthew, and Gaylyn Studlar, eds. *Visions of the East: Orientalism in Film.* New Brunswick, N.J.: Rutgers University Press, 1997.

Carné, Marcel. *Jenny*. Réalisations d'art cinématographique, 1936.

———. *Le Jour se lève*. Productions Sigma, 1939.

———. *Quai des brumes*. Grégoire Rabinovitch Productions, Ciné-Alliance, 1938.

Crosland, Alan. *Old San Francisco*. Warner Brothers, 1927.
Davidson, Michael. "*The Lady from Shanghai*: California Orientalism and 'Guys Like Us.'" *Western American Literature* 4 (Winter 2001): 347–72.
Duvivier, Julien. *Pépé le Moko*. Paris-Films-production, 1936.
———. *La Tête d'un homme*. Vandal et Delac, 1932.
Eng, David L. *Racial Castration: Managing Masculinity in Asian America*. Durham, N.C.: Duke University Press, 2001.
Ezra, Elizabeth. *The Colonial Unconscious: Race and Culture in Interwar France*. Ithaca, N.Y.: Cornell University Press, 2000.
Feyder, Jacques. *Le Grand jeu*. Films de France, 1934.
Field, Andrew. "Selling Souls in Sin City: Shanghai Singing and Dancing Hostesses in Print, Film, and Politics, 1920–49." *Cinema and Urban Culture in Shanghai, 1922–1943*. Ed. Yingjin Zhang. Stanford, Calif.: Stanford University Press, 1999. 99–127.
Genina, Augusto. *L'Esclave blanche*. Société des films artistiques Sofar-Lothar Stark, 1927.
Gilbert, Oscar-Paul. *Shanghaï, Chambard et Cie*. n.p:n.d.
Gledhill, Christine, ed. *Home Is Where the Heart Is: Studies in Melodrama and the Woman's Film*. London: British Film Institute, 1987.
Grémillon, Jean. *Gueule d'amour*. U.F.A., A.C.E., 1937.
Hansen, Miriam Bratu. "Fallen Women, Rising Stars, New Horizons: Shanghai Silent Cinema as Vernacular Modernism." *Film Quarterly* 1 (2000): 10–22.
Horkheimer, Max, and Theodor Adorno. *Dialectic of Enlightenment*. Trans. John Cumming. New York: Continuum, 2000.
Lee, Leo Ou-Fan. *Shanghai Modern: The Flowering of a New Urban Culture in China, 1930–1945*. Cambridge, Mass.: Harvard University Press, 1999.
Malraux, André. *La Condition humaine*. Paris: Gallimard, 1933.
Mann, Amir, and Dana Janklowicz-Mann. *Shanghai Ghetto*. Independent Film, 2002.
Mathot, Léon. *Bouboule 1er, roi nègre*. Gaumont-Franco-Film-Aubert, 1933.
Miller, Michael B. *Shanghai on the Metro: Spies, Intrigue, and the French between the Wars*. Berkeley: University of California Press, 1994.
Muzhi, Yuan. *Malu Tianshi* (Street Angel). Mingxing (Star), 1937.
Norindr, Panivong. *Phantasmatic Indochina: French Colonial Ideology in Architecture, Film, and Literature*. Durham, N.C.: Duke University Press, 1996.
Ozep, Fédor. *Amok*. Pathé-Nathan, 1934.
Pabst, Georg Wilhelm. *Le Drame de Shanghaï*. Paris: Lucia film; Paris: Gladiator films, 1938.
———. *Die Freudlose Gasse*. Berlin: Sofar-Film-Produktion GmbH, 1925.
Pagnol, Marcel. *Angèle*. Films Marcel Pagnol, 1934.
Petro, Patrice. *Joyless Streets: Women and Melodramatic Representation in Weimar Germany*. Princeton, N.J.: Princeton University Press, 1989.
Rentschler, Eric. "The Problematic Pabst: An *Auteur* Directed by History." *The Films of G. W. Pabst: An Extraterritorial Cinema*. Ed. Eric Rentschler. New Brunswick, N.J.: Rutgers University Press, 1990. 1–23.
Shih, Shu-mei. *The Lure of the Modern: Writing Modernism in Semi-Colonial China, 1917–1937*. Berkeley: University of California Press, 2001.

Slavin, David Henry. *Colonial Cinema and Imperial France, 1919–1939: White Blind Spots, Male Fantasies, Settler Myths*. Baltimore: Johns Hopkins University Press, 2001.

Vincendeau, Ginette. "Melodramatic Realism: On Some French Women's Films in the 1930s." *Screen* 3 (Summer 1989): 51–65.

———. *Pépé le Moko*. London: British Film Institute, 1998.

Von Sternberg, Josef. *Blonde Venus*. Paramount, 1932.

———. *Morocco*. Paramount, 1930.

———. *Shanghai Express*. Paramount, 1932.

Welles, Orson. *The Lady from Shanghai*. Columbia Pictures, 1948.

Witte, Karsten. "China and Yet Not China: *Shanghai Drama* (1938)." *The Films of G. W. Pabst: An Extraterritorial Cinema*. Ed. Eric Rentschler. New Brunswick, N.J.: Rutgers University Press, 1990. 167–74.

Zhang, Yingjin, ed. *Cinema and Urban Culture in Shanghai, 1922–1943*. Stanford, Calif.: Stanford University Press, 1999.

III

Displacing *Francophonie*: Migration and Transcultural Identities

9

Quebec and France

La Francophonie in a Comparative Postcolonial Frame

Eloise A. Brière

France still sits squarely at the center of *la francophonie*, a concept born in the ashes of the French colonial empire.[1] It was the brain-child of assimilated postcolonial leaders, such as Léopold Sédar Senghor, who could not imagine a world without the linguistic ties created by empire. Beneath the claims of unproblematic linguistic partnership, the echo of assimilationist pretensions still remains today. The contradictions inherent in the unequal relationship between colonizer and colonized have simply taken on a new face. The stature of France on the international playing field is derived in part from its political and cultural involvement with *la francophonie*, which differentiates it from the rest of Europe. France's need for *la francophonie* in such places as the United Nations Security Council contrasts sharply with the situation within France itself, where there is little need for *la francophonie* and its literature.[2] Both are perceived as something quite external to France itself, detached from French concerns. This disjunction between France's role within *la francophonie* in its political guise and the marginalization of francophone writing within the French literary establishment is reflected in the marginal impact of postcolonial studies on literary debates in France. Though rooted in the work of "French" thinkers from Fanon to Foucault, postcolonial studies are viewed with great skepticism by the French.[3] For Abdelwahab Meddeb such skepticism is grounded in the fear of being deposed, "la peur de la destitution" (30). France would necessarily lose its central position if binarist paradigms were to be abandoned or the "universality" of French challenged (30). Since postcolonialism eschews the center-periphery model, this theoretical stance is a clear and present danger to the role France continues to enjoy at the center of *la francophonie*. Thus Paris continues to make or break literary careers much as it did for the first generation of writers produced by the colonial educational system. While these writers began the process of opening a new dialogic space within France's imperial center by contesting the colonial situation, this has not led to the kind of polycentrism we find in literatures of the postcolonial anglophone world. Leading French intellectuals such as Jean-Paul Sartre and André Breton helped to pave the way for Léopold Sédar Senghor, Aimé Césaire, and Frantz Fanon, whose writings addressed the French center but were unsuccessful in loosening the hold of the center-periphery model still prevalent in contemporary *francophonie*.

Like writers from Martinique, Senegal, Cameroon, and elsewhere, Québécois writers also sought to be anointed in France, seeking out publishers in Paris.[4] French or francophone writers were published in Montreal only when Paris was out of the question, such as during World War II or when a particular book was too risky for French publishers. For example, Mongo Beti's *Main basse sur le Cameroun* was published in Montreal by Editions Québécoises in 1974 after the 1972 Maspéro edition was seized by the French government. When Ahmadou Kourouma's iconoclastic prose in *Les Soleils des indépendances* was too unpalatable for Parisian publishers (it was turned down by both Présence africaine and Le Seuil), it was published by Editions de l'Université de Montréal in 1968. By then, however, Quebec had declared literary and cultural independence from France.[5] Montreal became the center of Quebec's cultural life as the Québécois government funneled unprecedented amounts of money into literature, the visual arts, theater, cinema, music, and dance.[6] Education reflected these changes, putting the literature and culture of Quebec at the center of the curriculum, displacing that of France and England.

Remapping National Identities: Quebec and France

In France it took a revolution and two centuries to create a modern national identity; in Quebec, it took a "quiet" revolution in the aftermath of World War II to unshackle the province from the Church and Anglo-American domination. The neocolonial, alienated society transformed itself throughout the 1960s and 1970s. Traditional elites were no longer able to control the forces at work in the province, particularly in the domain of information. Now substantial numbers of Québécois began to think of themselves as constituting a distinct society, different from the rest of Canada, thanks to the expansion of French-language newspapers and their allies, radio and television (Linteau et al. 387–416).[7] Literature became an important tool in this cultural revolution as Quebec recognized its colonized status and mentality, rejected the old thinking, and reformed the institutions that had perpetuated that status.[8] Michèle Lalonde's emblematic poem "Speak White" illustrates the new consciousness of those who understood why they lacked agency. The poem is also an ode to solidarity between the French-Canadian underdog and the rest of the world's oppressed or colonized peoples. The references to Haiti, the Congo, Vietnam, Algeria, and Little Rock allow the poet to easily establish parallels between Quebec's opposition to the Anglo-North-American domination and the resistance to colonial masters, dictators, and segregation. However, by the time Lalonde was writing "Speak White," Quebec had embarked on its own colonial conquest with the completion of the Manicouagan (Daniel Johnson) dam, one of the world's largest hydroelectric facilities at the time, situated near the Labrador border on the land of the Innu or Montagnais First Nations (Native Canadians). Hydroelectricity was at the heart of the modernization of Quebec, but whose water was it?

Emerging from its *Révolution tranquille* [Quiet Revolution] at the close of the 1960s, Quebec's Parti Québécois government behaved with increasing independence from Ottawa. Montreal became the cultural center of this new society, as the independence party pursued its ultimate goal of separation from the rest of Canada. As Quebec's view of itself evolved during the 1960s, 1970s, and 1980s, so too did its economic priorities. The first order of business was to reverse the conditions that excluded 80 percent of Québécois from economic power.[9] Nationalization of private companies for the development of natural resources on government-owned land provided the new economic impetus that revamped Quebec. Hydro-Québec is one of the more spectacular examples of how such privatization stanched the flow of capital out of the province and channeled it into development programs such as the transformation of the educational system. At the same time, such newfound economic independence allowed Quebec to play an increasingly central role in the francophone political arena, garnering the status of *government* within the main francophone cultural and technical agency, l'Agence de Coopération Culturelle et Technique (ACCT) [Agency for Cultural and Technical Cooperation]. This put Quebec on an equal footing with member countries such as Senegal and France.[10] Links to the other francophone nations were crucial for Quebec, in order to validate its intent to become a nation. Internally, greater control over immigration policy in Quebec after 1968 led to increased immigration from francophone areas. Thus, migrants from Haiti and the Caribbean, Lebanon, Morocco, and elsewhere reached Quebec, while the Québécois reengineered their society and economy to benefit from the general prosperity of the times.[11] They were ceasing to be subjected to others; *maîtres chez nous* [masters at home] became the watchword. Thus, a newfound sense of agency emerged as Quebec was increasingly successful in countering Anglo-American interests. While it had seen itself as occupying the periphery in relation to the United States, the rest of Canada, and France, it now began to place itself at the center of its own worldview. Given such a binary stance, who now would occupy the periphery to Quebec's center?

While Lalonde's poem discussed above shows Quebec's solidarity with oppressed others abroad, it does not include marginalized native peoples at home. The use of natural resources enabling Quebec to take charge of its economy and its identity rested on the idea that such resources belonged to the nation. Thus the Innu territory on which Hydro-Québec's Manicouagan dam had been built was seen as essentially "empty" territory, a *terra nulla* long ago abandoned by the First Nations. A popular song of the time, "La Manic," by the poet and songwriter Georges Dor, clearly shows a blind spot in Québécois thinking, illustrating the lack of awareness that this wilderness is the home of an aboriginal nation. As the words to Dor's song reveal, the territory is nothing more than a blank space for the hundreds of Québécois workers who realized the Herculean task of building the dam. In the song, one of them complains of boredom and longs for the excitement of city life. Real life, the one worth talking about, takes place in the province's cities, Quebec and Three Rivers; Manicouagan is a place of utter boredom and exile, an empty space to be filled with feats of engineering to ensure that homes in the South will be warm and well lit. Modernization of Quebec ushered in decades of conflict with the First Nations, whose formerly "worthless" land now held the key to Québécois independence.[12] Thus, before Quebec's new identity had crystallized, and more than a dozen years before the first referendum on sovereignty was held, part of the economic base on which it rested was being challenged by the First Nations. Another challenge to identity came from the very underdogs Lalonde had placed in the periphery, among the oppressed, in her 1968 poem. Immigrants were beating a path to Quebec's door at an unprecedented rate, just as in France, growing numbers of immigrants from the Maghreb and sub-Saharan Africa were bringing similar challenges to French soil.

While silence surrounds the Oka siege in Quebec, the Setif massacre in Algeria or—until recently—the World War II *Vel d'Hiv* roundup of Jews in Paris, other events, remembered and transmitted, become nodal points that define national identity as do other forms of collective remembrance, continually creating the nation.[13] What becomes of French and Québécois identities generated by such strategies, in the face of new citizens and immigrants whose memories bear the stamp of other national genealogies and iconographies? What of their histories and myths? Are they integrated into the national mix, or are they left to die a natural death? Or, perhaps more plausibly, are such histories relegated to a subterranean existence with only occasional outlets for expression in the new context? Glissant has argued that this underground existence offers a kind of freedom that generates *métissage*. This view of the culture of home being secretly—or not so secretly—transmitted as it binds with other cultures, is a question fundamental to our investigation of the remapping of cultures in contact. How do cultures map and remap themselves? Does remapping produce Bhabha's qualitatively different but not totally new object, the hybrid (see Papastergiadis 184)? Or does it on the other hand produce *transculturation*, the end result of deculturation and acculturation, as the Cuban Fernando Ortiz signaled in 1940 (qtd. in Lamore 19)? How does the presence of culturally different voices generate a remapping of the host culture? Remapping is as fundamental to the debate on integration, assimilation, and multiculturalism in France as it is in Quebec, where talk centers around *communautés culturelles*, cultural communities united by their use of French, essential to the survival of Quebec, but who maintain their cultural distinctiveness. As Jean-Loup Amselle argues, a similar kind of segmentation is fast becoming the norm in France, dealing a fatal blow to the republican ideal of equality: "La reconnaissance d'une multiplicité de groupes ethniques au sein du territoire français offre donc des conditions idéales pour l'essor du racisme. . . . [L]a recherche généalogique de la pureté de la race telle qu'elle est pratiquée par la Sécurité sociale . . . illustre bien le caractère de l'état français: Etat libéral mais également Etat communautaro-raciste" [Recognition of a multiplicity of ethnic groups within the French territory offers ideal conditions for the growth of racism. . . . Genealogical research on racial purity as it is practiced by Social security . . . illustrates the nature of the French state: a liberal government that is also a community-based racist government] (vii). To what degree is difference acceptable in the two francophone contexts under discussion?

Québécois identity is embedded in the "national" anthem made famous by Gilles Vigneault, "Mon pays," in which he equated Quebec with the winter season. Sung collectively, it is "the echoed physical realization of the imagined community" (Anderson 145). It sets the Québécois "nation" apart from the rest of Canada, as do the names of streets, squares, and bridges such as Jeanne Mance, Jacques Cartier, and Champlain. Their meaning is clear for those who have been systematically exposed to the "national" idea through education, the mass media, and administrative regulations. But how do others in Quebec construct the Québécois nation? How do they navigate the paradox of this smaller "nation" within the larger Canadian nation? By law, the children of immigrants in Quebec must be educated in French, presumably becoming tomorrow's Québécois, who now have the lowest birthrate in the Western Hemisphere.[14] Yet the distinction remains clear between *Québécois de souche* [Québécois people with Québécois ancestry], more popularly known as "pure laine" [100 percent pure wool], and *communautés culturelles* [cultural communities].[15] The former know why license plates in Quebec bear the motto "Je me souviens" [I remember]; the latter may also remember, but the referent is not the same: *pur polyester* versus *pure laine*.[16] The history-based collective identity that animated the Quiet Revolution can no longer purport to represent the collectivity.

Like the "pure laine" idea, the French nation rests on a nineteenth-century creation of collective memory and identity rooted in the myth of a single *Gaulois* origin, resting on one national idiom. Thus, French became the emblem of modernity and progress, relegating other regional languages to the realm of the backward and primitive. This is the same road to modernization France would offer its colonial subjects via education and assimilation. Given today's supra-national context of the European Union and the large numbers of visible minorities in France, the validity of the republican myth on which this road was built is being questioned. As the concept of "Français de souche" [French people with French ancestry] becomes synonymous with the *Gaulois* myth, the republic no longer integrates but splits contemporary society into multiple racial or ethnic groups. Thus, a remapping of the Republic is occurring. The recent transfer of Alexandre Dumas's remains to the Pantheon may be read as a sign of French cultural remapping at work. Long unrecognized as a great writer, despite his popular appeal, Dumas, the grandson of an enslaved African from France's richest sugar colony, Saint Domingue, has finally been laid to rest next to Voltaire, Rousseau, Hugo, and Zola in the very place where France buries its "great men," the Pantheon, itself an example of postrevolutionary cultural remapping. As the Republic's power trumped religious power, the church of St. Genevieve became a secular shrine devoted to the memory of the shapers of the nation. Does the attempt to include Dumas among them, righting an omission of history, mean that inclusiveness of visible minorities in French cultural discourse is at work? Or is this just one more case of France "naturalizing" what it sees fit to call French?[17] While in his speech, President Jacques Chirac recognized Dumas's African roots, he chose to portray Dumas as contributing to France's immortal identity, calling him "un fragment de la France éternelle" [a fragment of eternal France] wedded to republican ideals. "Avec lui, c'est notre mémoire populaire et notre imaginaire collectif qui entrent au Panthéon. . . . Alexandre Dumas trouvera enfin sa place aux côtés de ses frères . . . qui ont fait l'histoire de la République" [With him, our popular memory and our collective imagination enter the Pantheon. . . . Alexandre Dumas finally finds his place beside his brothers . . . who created the history of the Republic].[18] The recognition of Dumas as a participant in the creation of the French idea, despite nearly a century of exclusion, clearly illustrates that the mythmaking machine continues to spin out the republican idea of the nation, absorbing all value in its path. This is not tropicalization; this is naturalization.

Tropicalization?

Mirroring what is occurring in the streets of Paris or Montreal, francophone writers increasingly bring into focus the experience of difference in those francophone cities. The outsiders' gaze on French and Québécois culture is becoming part of the literary landscape. Theirs is not the bemused, detached view of the tourist soon to depart for other climes, but the critical and ironic gaze of those who assert their right to belong and to be allowed to create differently. New spaces of social discourse begin to open up through a sometimes reverse ethnographic gaze, as in *53 Cm*, a 1999 novel by Bessora, the Gabonese-Swiss writer. In it, she turns the ethnographer's eye, long focused on the empire's "primitive peoples," to the French. Following in the footsteps of Montesquieu, as did Bernard Dadié before her, she records the strange habits of Parisians that a struggling single black mother encounters in the French capital. She satirizes French beliefs and customs far more than did Dadié's bemused narrator in the landmark *Un Nègre à Paris* (1959). Similarly, Régine Robin's Jewish-French narrator in *La Québécoite* observes the Québécois as she wanders through Montreal, hearing French but not understanding, wondering how she will ever stake out a space where her French-Jewishness fits into late-twentieth-century *québécité*. Glissant tells us that such defamiliarization is to be expected in the postcolonial landscape because of colonization and the unpredictable effects of the machine of "Relation" that imperialism set in motion (Britton 13). The fact that Robin's Québécoite is from Paris, the heart of *la francophonie*, does not spare her from the condition of liminality in her new surroundings. If Bessora's and Robin's characters view defamiliarized French and Québécois societies from the margins, do such transcultural views contribute to French and Québécois cultural remapping?[19]

Remappings are inevitable because of the profound changes that postcolonial writing has introduced in literature. To describe this phenomenon, Milan Kundera uses the term *tropicalization*, since, in his view, writing from areas below the 35th parallel has revitalized the moribund novel form.[20] But as we have just seen in the case of Régine Robin's *La Québécoite*, change need not come from the South.[21] Transcultural, unpredictable, and most certainly not limited to South-North flows, transcultural writing transforms the novel as it plays with the myths of host cultures.[22] Its strangeness opens up new discursive space whether or not it hails from the tropics. As Michel Laronde has pointed out, such texts are decentered, existing in relation to a normed center where culture, language, and memory are constantly being constructed and kept in congruence by national mythmaking. The relationship between the host culture and the literary works produced by transcultural writers can make cultural displacements visible, as Jean-Marc Moura argues in *Littératures francophones et théorie postcoloniale* and as Bessora's *53 Cm* illustrates. But in what way do these displacements tug at the "host" culture's canonical forms and inherent messages, as Michel Laronde argues (7–8)? Does the untranslatable excess or supplement that transcultural writing brings operate as a critique of the principles of progress, homogeneity, and cultural organicism, as Homi Bhabha has pointed out (Papastergiadis 185)? Can these cultural displacements thus be harbingers of change, sites of remapping? Or on the other hand, does the lack of congruence function rather as an exotic mask, a response to expectations in the host culture? Are such works reinforcing hegemonic culture rather than opening up the canon? What goes on in the postcolonial francophone dialogic space? Does it differ in Montreal and Paris? This is what I aim to examine in the following pages by contrasting the reception of Dany Laferrière and Calixthe Beyala in the two different francophone contexts.

Writing: Portal to Acceptance?

François Duvalier's repression of dissenting voices is largely responsible for the existence of a world literary diaspora of Haitian writers and intellectuals. The first Haitian writers to arrive in Canada came to Montreal in the 1960s as the Duvalier regime stepped up its persecution of students and intellectuals.[23] Persecution took other forms but continued under Duvalier's son until he was ousted from power in 1986. Dany Laferrière left "Baby Doc" Duvalier's Haiti for Montreal in 1978, decisively opting for a life of exile in North America. His career as a writer was launched seven years later with his first novel, *Comment faire l'amour avec un nègre sans se fatiguer*. The novel ends as the main character, a budding writer, places all his dreams of success and fame on the novel he has just completed: "Mon roman. Ma seule chance. Va!" My novel, my only chance. Go, fly!] (177).

Cameroonian writers arrived in France in the 1950s, to pursue the next level of colonial education. Anticolonial writers such as Mongo Beti and Abel Eyinga became personae non gratae in neocolonial Cameroon after independence and were forced to live in exile in France.[24] When neither the political nor the economic climate improved after independence, writers such as Paul Dakeyo, Francis Bebey, Lydie Dooh Bunya, and others joined their ranks and took up residency in France.[25] A contemporary of Dany Laferrière, the

Cameroonian Calixthe Beyala is part of the third wave of Cameroonian writers to opt for life in France.[26] Calixthe Beyala launched her career from Paris in 1987 with *C'est le soleil qui m'a brûlée*. Interviewed about the French government's decision to transfer Alexandre Dumas's remains to the Pantheon, Beyala confided to journalists that the great Dumas was a model of cultural integration who proved that one could in effect become French by mastering the language of literary expression, in spite of racial handicaps.[27]

Calixthe Beyala may well look to Dumas as the embodiment of the symbolic power that literary success confers. The belief in the efficacy of writing as a way out of marginalization and powerlessness has long persisted in postcolonial areas of the world . . . at least since the loss of France's first colony to Haitian freedom fighters. Shortly after Haitian independence in 1804, it became clear to the new leaders that if they were to obtain the recognition they desperately needed on the international front, it would be through literature. If they were to counter their image of bloodthirsty black revolutionaries, it would be through literature. Literature would prove them human. In 1804 the Baron de Vastey, a nobleman in the kingdom of Haiti under King Henry Christophe, wrote in his *Réflexions*: "Has not our country, although still in its infancy, produced writers and poets to celebrate its name? In short, experience has proved to the world that we, as well as whites, had an aptitude for the sciences and arts. . . . The people of Haiti have . . . rights to the admiration of the universe and of posterity."[28]

Later, it was also the hope of acceptance through literary achievement that propelled Alain Locke's *The New Negro* and his first anthology of black poetry that were part of the Harlem Renaissance.[29] Similarly, black student movements in France in the 1930s, setting aside political demands made by earlier generations, sought advancement through cultural and literary recognition, eventually leading to the Negritude movement.[30] Thus, the seduction of *métropoles* through literature has been a longstanding portal to acceptance for those issuing from the margins of empire. An examination of Calixthe Beyala's *Les Arbres en parlent encore* will illustrate just how narrow that portal is in France today.

Calixthe Beyala, Masks and . . . Lies

In *Les Arbres en parlent encore* (2002), Calixthe Beyala's narrator, Edène, in the course of sixteen "veillées," or evenings of story telling, looks back at events that took place in her life more than half a century before (21), when France and Germany were at war (13).[31] In the course of her narration, Edène periodically signals her unreliability as a narrator. At the novel's outset, she affirms that masking is a common practice among her people and describes her father, Assanga Djuli, chief of the Etons, as bathed in "une lumière magnétique [qui] lui conférait le pouvoir de masquer ses vraies pensées" [a magnetic light that gave him the power to mask his true thoughts] (7).[32] A few pages later the narrator tells us, "Une confession écrite dans une langue étrangère est toujours un mensonge. C'est dans la langue de Baudelaire que nous mentons" [a confession written in a foreign language is always a lie. It is in the language of Baudelaire that we are lying] (9). Halfway through the sixteen "veillées," the narrator tells us: "[D]e ce qui va suivre . . . je m'en lave les mains. Je refuse d'assumer la maternité de cette histoire, par mesure d'honnêteté. . . . Si nous avons tous vécu un phantasme, je salue encore notre imagination!" [I wash my hands . . . of the following. I refuse to recognize this story as my own in the interest of honesty. . . . And if it was all a fantasy that we lived through, once again I salute our imagination!] (113). The narrator tells us her role is confined to simply repeating the oral tradition received from the "joueur de nvet" (113), the traditional bard. Whether or not such disclaimers can be attributed to the author's previous legal difficulties with plagiarism, the reader is forewarned that even though the novel is purportedly set at the time of the First World War, historical accuracy is not its objective.[33] Rather, masks and lies will be part of the telling.

History will be, as Scarpetta writes in *L'Impureté*, a reservoir of possibilities, blending with the most irrational of subjectivities.[34] Memory is fickle, the narrator tells us: "Quand nous essayons de nous remémorer le temps passé, de retrouver une date, un événement, nous mélangeons ce qui s'est passé avec ce qui n'a jamais eu lieu. Il nous arrive de faire du présent l'aboutissement imaginaire des moissons du souvenir" [When we try to remember the past, to find a date, an event, we confuse what occurred with what never happened. We sometimes turn the present into the imaginary culmination of memory's harvest] (145). Thus, anachronisms are commonplace in Edène's narration. For example, Michel Ange de Montparnasse, the French sergeant who appears in the Eton village before 1918, fathers several "café-au-lait" babies. The narrator tells us that the daughters sired by Michel Ange de Montparnasse would grow up to be the mistresses of French *coopérants* [development workers]. However, these girls would have been grandmothers by the time French *coopérants* appeared on the scene after 1960 in Cameroon. Kenneth Harrow has shown how similar chronological disjunctions in *Assèze l'Africaine* are the result of Beyala's borrowings from Paule Constant's *White Spirit*. In *Assèze*, village life does not ring true because the borrowed information has not been "relexified" and simply floats there, undigested (Harrow 229). However, in this novel, the messy chronology and inaccurate portraits of village life are the best the narrator can do with the materials at hand.

An Africa Made to Measure . . .

Despite the narrator's repeated warnings that the *veillées* of *Les Arbres* are not meant to reflect history, the book's jacket tells us that the book is "une page d'histoire de l'Afrique dont Calixthe Beyala ressuscite la mémoire" [a page of African history whose memory is rekindled by Calixthe Beyala]. The book jacket, meant for the French reader, underscores the difference between production (writing) and reception; books by francophone writers such as Beyala are read within parameters of French cultural and social practices that give them meaning.[35] Francophone writers who move from the margin to the center of *la francophonie*, as Beyala has done, can easily fall prey to the conflict not only between their writing and the context within which it is read, but also to the power of publishers over writers' careers. As Mongo Beti has pointed out, the African writer's success is entirely dependent on the literary institutions of the former master.[36] And the former master, like today's French reader, always already "knows" Africa and Africans. This "knowledge" resembles the commodification of the "natives" prevalent during colonial times: one "boy" is the equivalent of another, "they" are all the same. The process by which the "native" becomes a generic being is aptly described by Abdul JanMohamed: "Once reduced to his exchange-value in the colonialist signifying system, he is fed into the manichean allegory, which functions as the currency, the medium of exchange for the entire colonialist discursive system" (qtd. in Ezra 7). Beyala is France's "generic" African writer.

I have argued that France's use of *la francophonie* is an extension of colonial practice, under a new guise.[37] Thus African writers can be pressed into serving the French *neocolonial discursive system* exactly as earlier generations of writers were woven into the colonialist discursive system.[38] This postcolonial system is grounded in a "blank darkness" that originates in a collective desire to forget the colonial past, while feeding on images of the exotic "Other." As Elizabeth Ezra points out for the colonial period, French Africanist discourse "resists the desire for rational explanation. . . . [A]s it seeks . . . it searches, and insists on finding nothing" (10). In the neocolonial discursive system "nothing" is papered over with exotic images. Whether they be images from Belleville or Couscousville, they feed the French reader's desire for generic Africans, the ones he already knows from reading *Tintin au Congo* as a child. This empty exoticism is precisely what the French writer Jean-François Josselin, using metonymic stereotyping, emphasizes when he equates Beyala's writing with Africa itself: "[L]a langue de Calixthe [est] . . . [u]ne gazelle de la brousse, texte et contexte de son histoire, région mystérieuse, dure, triste et gaie. L'Afrique justement" [Calixthe's language (is) . . . a gazelle from the bush, text and context of its history, a mysterious place, harsh, sad and gay all at once. It is Africa].[39] Josselin sees "generic" African writing at work here.

Regardless of Beyala's narrator's pronouncements about the unreliability of her words, the text is congruent with France's Africa, that imagined community of exotic others, so that there is no need to look further. The abundance of colonialist clichés in the pages of Beyala's novel—grotesque black faces and bodies in caricatural poses, their blank stares, the mysterious beliefs Africans cling to, their ever present sexual appetites, wise chiefs, misguided missionaries and autocratic German soldiers—all reinforce the French reader's sense that the "Other" is alive and well in *Les Arbres*. Kenneth Harrow has noted the change from Beyala's early fiction, which depicted a universe in radical disarray, to one peopled with "Beverly Hillbillies," with the author comfortably arranging her depictions of Africa "so as not to disturb" (285). In the end, Beyala's use of stereotypes supports France's old binary view of the world, still sitting squarely at the center of *la francophonie*.[40] It also brings the writer up against the glass ceiling that maintains her in the "other" position as described by Bhabha, "a subject of difference that is almost the same but not quite" (qtd. in Ezra 7). Language is part of the glass ceiling's exclusionary practice, as can be seen in Jean-François Josselin's comment on *Les Arbres*. He makes a distinction between "notre langue à nous, le français, et sa langue personnelle" [our language, French, and her own personal language]; to him, Beyala's French is exotic, it is Africa itself (inside back jacket of *Les Arbres*). In spite of everything, her French seems to have developed in a void, having nothing in common with that of France. To Josselin this "tropicalized" version of French is merely an individual quirk ("sa langue personnelle"), not part of a wider transcultural phenomenon produced by colonization that is transforming literature written in French.

Knocking on the Door of the Republic

Lettre d'une Afro-française à ses compatriotes is a plea for a way out of the French postcolonial double bind created by the contradictory nature of French culture, based as it is on both universality and exclusion (Murphy 172). In the essay, Beyala lists half a dozen reasons why she loves France (12) and unequivocally affirms her loyalty to France: "Française je suis; française je reste; française je suis fière d'être" [French I am, French I shall remain; I am proud to be French] (30). She then also attacks the hypocrisy inherent in French universalism with rhetorical invocations of the Rights of Man. "J'ai cru au textes paraphés par tous les pays et qui reconnaissent aux êtres humains sans distinction de race, de couleur et de religion, le droit à la liberté d'expression, le droit à la liberté de la pensée, le droit à la protection des nations et tout simplement le droit à la vie" [I believed in the documents signed by all the countries that grant all human beings regardless of race, color and religion, the right to freedom of speech, the right to freedom of thought, the right to the protection of nations and quite simply, the right to live] (9–10). Beyala affirms: "Pour moi, femme noire, Française, l'espoir se diffracte. Une lueur s'éteint quelque part" [For me, a black French woman, hope is shattered. A light goes out somewhere] (45).

In this essay, Beyala considers the limited options the future holds for her children and others like them in tomorrow's France. She finds herself attacking the very system that facilitated her rise to stardom: "La puissance médiatique est telle aujourd'hui que l'on est ce qu'elle décide qu'on soit" [The power of the media is so strong today that you are what it decides you will be] (73). Not that Beyala renounces the Loukoums, Abdous, M'ams, Assèzes, Saïdas, and her other characters that often subtly reinforced French beliefs about Africans, especially immigrants. But she strikes out at the institutions that shape the public image of France: schools and the media whose failure to integrate minorities has made a sham of France's universalist and republican ideals. *Les Arbres* and *Lettre d'une Afro-française* are two halves of the same dilemma that illustrate the difficulty of subverting an existing order while reinforcing it. In France, Beyala's impact is circumscribed within the paradox of *la francophonie*: inside, yet never truly inside, nor truly congruent with an imagined notion of *francité*. Using a different approach, Dany Laferrière, on the other hand, has maintained a cautious distance from entanglements with the notion of *francité*, whether that of France or Quebec.

Deterritorialization and Remapping

The fear of neocolonial dependency caused Dany Laferrière to choose Quebec when exile became necessary for him. "Je ne voulais pas mettre mon destin entre les mains de la francophonie, c'est-à-dire de la France. . . . On ne doit jamais vivre dans un pays qui vous a colonisé . . . parce qu'alors on passe sa vie à être paranoïaque, à se croire attaqué, et on ressasse un seul débat, le débat racial, le débat de la colonisation" [I didn't want to put my destiny in the hands of *francophonie*, which stands for France. . . . You should never live in a country that colonized you . . . because then you spend your life plagued by paranoia, thinking you're being attacked, and you dwell on the same debates, the race debate, the colonization debate] (Sroka 10). Laferrière's ten novels are part of the growing body of works by francophone writers who, like him, have chosen to become Québécois. How do such works fit into the whole of the Quebec literary establishment? If we concur with Deleuze and

Guattari in their discussion of "minor literature" as exemplified by Kafka's works, minority literature is a distinct literature produced within a larger frame of a major world language. Such a definition would apply to Québécois literature.[41] As was mentioned earlier, the recentering of Quebec's culture during the Quiet Revolution put the literature and the arts of Quebec at the heart of the new national identity. But Quebec's writers from elsewhere, whether Haitian, Lebanese, Algerian, French, Chinese, Brazilian, or Italian, were themselves in a decentered relationship with the Quebec literary establishment. While Québécois writing is no longer deterritorialized, it is still a minor literature within the larger francophone context. This makes neo-Québécois literature a minority literature within a minor literature. Therefore, most neo-Québécois writing acts as counternarrative to the Quebec national narrative. However, Dany Laferrière bypasses this double minority status by means of a mask belonging to another minority. Laferrière uses an Afro-American mask to conceal the signs of his deterritorialization, so that he may stake his claim to North America. Like other neo-Québécois writers, Laferrière will stretch the boundaries of the Québécois national narrative, prying it away from its essentialist roots.

Peau Noire, Masque Noir . . . Dany Laferrière and the Conquest of North America

In his first novel, *Comment faire l'amour avec un nègre sans se fatiguer* (1985), Laferrière frees himself from the influence of earlier icons of Haitian literature such as Jacques-Stephen Alexis or Jacques Roumain. He consciously breaks with the past and actively seeks a new genealogy in this novel, by avoiding all images and references to Haiti, by eschewing the tropes that dot Haiti's cultural landscape, and by refusing all that smacks of the Caribbean. He himself says that *Comment faire l'amour* is an American novel that just happens to be written in French. In his view language is immaterial: the colonial past of English and French makes one just as objectionable as the other. "Qui choisir? Mon ancien colonisateur: le Français. Ou le colonisateur de mon ancien colonisateur: l'Anglais. Le Français fait pitié, mais je sais qu'il fut un maître dur. Finalement, je pris une décision mitoyenne. Je choisis de devenir un écrivain américain écrivant directement en français" [Which one should I choose? My former colonial master, French, or the colonial master of my former colonizer, English? I feel sorry for French, but I know that it was a tough master. Finally I opted for the middle of the road. I decided to become an American writer who would write directly in French] (Laferrière, *J'écris* 3).

What is important, however, is location. Being in North America is what matters. In this way, the language Laferrière chooses enables him to exit not only the deterritorialized migrant condition but also the realm of *la francophonie*. By reterritorializing his language in North America, he clearly affiliates his writing with its American and Afro-American lineages. This new genealogy is symbolized by the main character's typewriter. It once belonged to Chester Himes and has now become the main character's tool for writing, Afro-American writing, that is. As he enters into the Afro-American psyche, James Baldwin and Richard Wright figure prominently in his new genealogy. Recordings of Charlie Parker, Ella Fitzgerald, and John Coltrane play as Vieux, the novel's protagonist, types out his novel, *Paradis d'un dragueur nègre*. The immense creativity of Afro-America, barely known in Quebec, is the reservoir used by Vieux. Not only do his cultural references establish his Afro-American affiliation, they also enable him to reject cultural ghettoization. He lays claim to the art, films, literature, and philosophy of the west. The innumerable references to western literature and art make it clear that Vieux's conquest of America is not limited to Afro-America.

White women become the icons of this conquest, for when he is not at the typewriter, he lays claim to an array of WASP princesses, mainly McGill University students. Laferrière may be writing an Afro-American novel devoid of Caribbean tropes, but his use of black/white sexual relationships ushers the ghost of Fanon into his Afro-American fantasy. Vieux's numerous sexual adventures act out over and over again the passage in *Peau noire, masques blancs* where Fanon describes a black man's thoughts during his sexual conquest of a white woman: "J'épouse la culture blanche, la beauté blanche, la blancheur blanche. Dans ces seins que mes mains ubiquitaires caressent, c'est la civilisation et la dignité blanches que je fais miennes" [I am united with white culture, white beauty, white whiteness. With these breasts that my ubiquitous hands caress, white civilization and dignity become mine] (71). However, Vieux is not pursuing cultural lactification when he has sex with young white college women in Montreal's upper-class neighborhoods. He is at home here precisely because he has a score to settle with colonization and slavery: "Je suis, en quelque sorte, à ma place, moi aussi. Je suis ici pour baiser la fille de ces diplomates pleins de morgue qui nous giflaient à coups de stick" [This is somehow my place too. I'm here to fuck the daughter of these arrogant diplomats who used to beat us with sticks] (113). Laferrière uses sex with the daughters to avenge the deeds of the fathers, deliberately choosing what he has called the most explosive imagery possible: interracial sex from a male perspective.

Quebec, having limited familiarity with Afro-America and only a small black population of its own, had never before produced a novel like *Com-*

ment faire l'amour, with its ironic voice, often violent or provocative, and always graphic as it played with all of the major racial stereotypes. As Laferrière tells an interviewer, "The topic of interracial fucking hit them right in the solar plexus" (Coates 912). As a result, *Comment faire l'amour* was indeed the portal of acceptance for Laferrière, enabling him to leave the factory where he had worked for eight years. He became a television announcer and eventually was able to write full-time.[42] Two other novels in the same vein followed, *Eroshima* and *Cette Grenade dans la main du jeune nègre est-elle une arme ou un fruit?* Having become too much of a celebrity in Quebec, Laferrière moved to Miami, where he could write incognito.[43] In Miami, Laferrière wrote *L'Odeur du café* and the six other novels that constitute the autobiographical portion of his oeuvre. His objective achieved, Laferrière's Afro-American mask lost its usefulness: he had gained the freedom to be a writer. However, Québécois literature would never be the same again. It had been tropicalized in the extreme by *Comment faire l'amour*. While the heterogeneity of neo-Québécois writing had chipped away at the self/other binarism of post–Quiet Revolution writing in Quebec, Laferrière's Afro-American mask forced Quebec to confront something entirely different: not the exotic south of Brazilian Sergio Kokis or the Italy of Marco Micone, or the Algeria of Nadia Ghalem, but the North American racial question. It could be argued that Laferrière did for Quebec literature what writers like Jacques Poulin or Jacques Godbout had attempted to do: provide it with a novel that was undeniably North American. And how did he do this? By venturing into Afro-American territory, bypassing *la francophonie*.

Remappings?

While aporias concerning the inclusion of "foreign" cultures are common to both France and Quebec, it is clear that remappings and inclusions within the literature of Quebec are quite different from those within the literature of France. In France, where postcolonial critical theory has made few inroads, the map is in the hands of a powerful literary establishment that decides what will or will not be included in "French" literature.[44] At the same time, the myth of *la francophonie* and the dream of celebrity continue to attract writers to Paris like moths to a flame, inviting them into the macabre dance between margin and center. There, the time-honored knowledges of Africa burn bright, shedding their yellow light on the counternarratives by African writers, ensuring that writers like Beyala are "correctly" read and then relegated to the category of francophone, never French, literature. Perhaps it is because Quebec itself was colonized that its repertoire of such knowledges is limited, leaving its solar plexus unprotected, subject to blows from the counternarratives of neo-Québécois writers. Perhaps it is simply the newness of the Quebec national idea, its precariousness. Clearly, though, the inclusiveness that characterizes Québécois literature has roots in its own postcolonial stance, developed during the Quiet Revolution, when the works of Césaire, Fanon, and Memmi were read and discussed by writers as opposition to Anglo-America grew.[45] Today, Québécois identity evolves on the new terrain created in part by the neo-Québécois. Quebec has recovered from the blow to its collective solar plexus dealt by *Comment faire l'amour*. As for Dany Laferrière, now published in France and beginning to make the literary circuits there, he still claims to be an American writer who happens to use French.

Notes

1. The "imagined reality" of *la francophonie* began with mapmaking and the use of color to signal empire. Maps represented the French colonial empire as lavender-hued, distinctly apart from the pink British Empire, each appearing as autonomous entities around the globe, seemingly fully detachable from their geographic context. Thus it became possible for the geographer Onésime Reclus, creator of the word *francophonie*, to actually "see" this imagined reality in maps of the late nineteenth century. This was the first time the map was not a "compass to the world," but to a nascent imagined linguistic community. This abstract image of the French colonial empire is still in use in the present-day logo of the Agence de la Francophonie. Benedict Anderson points to the role of color and abstraction in maps to create logos of empire in *Imagined Communities* (175–78).

2. David Murphy shows how francophone literature is excluded from the category of French literature. "Foreign" writers such as Ionesco and Beckett, Milan Kundera and Andreï Makine, are integrated into the French canon, while writers of French nationality, but of African origin, such as Azouz Begag, Mongo Beti, Tierno Monenembo, and Mehdi Charef are considered "Francophone" (173).

3. Published in 1999, the first French study of postcolonial theory that attempted to open the field of francophone studies to such an approach was *Littératures francophones et théorie postcoloniale* by Jean-Marc Moura. Following a seminar on that topic, Bessière and Moura published *Littératures Postcoloniales et Francophonie*. One of the earliest looks at postcolonialism is the special issue of *Dédale* (1997), in which Abdelwahab Meddeb brings together a variety of writers and thinkers, from Rushdie, Todorov, and Glissant to Leiris and Alain Rey. Similarly, *Africultures* (2000) established an inventory of the debates on postcolonialism.

4. The Québécois writers Ringuet (Philippe Panneton's pseudonym) and Gabrielle Roy were heralded at home thanks to success in France. Ringuet's *Trente arpents* was published in 1938 by Flammarion, and Gabrielle Roy's *Bonheur d'occasion* was awarded the Prix Fémina in 1947.

5. Francois Paré states that France ceased to be a key reference point in Québécois self-perception (18).

6. Linteau et al. indicate that cultural spending increased in Quebec nearly a hundredfold in just over twenty years. The increase was from $5.9 million in 1957 to $24.6 million in 1967 to $197.4 million in 1977. By 1981 it was spending $428.2 million annually (for a population of approximately 6 million) (798).

7. Nationalism was not successful in French Canada in the nineteenth century, the period of world history in which the nation was becoming an international norm. Prior to 1867 the British colony was administered from Westminster. Then the British North America Act established the confederation and served as Canada's constitution until 1982. Canadians did not see themselves as being independent of Great Britain, but only as being self-governing of their domestic affairs.

8. Linteau et al. stress that "à aucune autre époque peut-être la littérature et les écrivains n'auront occupé une position aussi centrale dans la vie culturelle du Québec, ni n'auront joui d'un tel rayonnement. Par eux passent directement les débats, les prises de conscience, les inquiétudes et les attentes qui définissent l'esprit des nouvelles élites cultivées" [at no other time perhaps have literature and writers occupied such a central position in Quebec's cultural life, nor have they exerted such influence. The debates, the consciousness raising, the worries and the expectations that define the concerns of the new educated elites are articulated through them](780).

9. Taras Grescoe states that in 1959 three-quarters of the province's financial institutions were in non-Québécois hands and that only 6.5 percent of the huge mining sector was Québécois (246).

10. Léopold Sédar Senghor of Senegal and Hamani Diori of Niger invited Quebec to be a founding member of l'Agence de Coopération Culturelle et Technique (ACCT). This followed on the heels of General de Gaulle's "Vive le Québec libre!" [Long live a free Quebec!], a speech given on a state visit in 1967, enjoining the Québécois to free themselves from Anglo neocolonial domination. For over thirty years, the ACCT, whose headquarters are in Paris, has been the clearinghouse and source of funding for the majority of francophone cultural and technical projects taking place in the nearly fifty nations and regions of the world that are members. A Québécois, Jean-Marc Léger, was named its first head in 1969. Such provincial visibility on the international francophone scene forced Ottawa to develop its own policy towards francophone countries (Linteau et al. 748).

11. Taras Grescoe states: "In Quebec, modernity came like a dam burst. . . . [T]he idea of being Québécois, as opposed to French-Canadian, became fashionable, as did the notion of forming a distinct nation, one defined by language and culture rather than religion" (270). "Quebec has transformed itself from one of the most morally oppressive, ethnically homogeneous, and backward corners of the continent into a modern and relatively diversified society. It's among the most tolerant and liberal parts of North America" (266–67). See also Sherry Simon's discussion of this transition in *Le Trafic des langues* (29–33).

12. During the planning of a conference on the planned expansion of Hydro-Québec and its impact on the Cree community in 1991, conversations by the author with Cree representatives and the Cree Grand Council revealed a fully modern and sophisticated approach to public relations as well as to business among leaders. The awareness they

generated eventually caused New York State to cancel a $19 billion contract with Hydro-Québec.

13. The development of a golf course at Oka encroached on land of the Kanesatake native-owned reservation and threatened Mohawk burial grounds, leading to a three-month standoff that at first pitted the Mohawks against Quebec provincial police (leading to the death of one *Sureté Québec* corporal) and then against Ottawa, with the intervention of over 4,000 Canadian soldiers. The standoff is generally viewed as successful by the Mohawks. In 1997 the federal government bought contested land at Oka and gave it to the Mohawk community. French forces killed several thousand Algerians during a demonstration of the PPA (Algerian Popular Party) at Setif in 1946, deepening the chasm that would lead to the Algerian war of independence. In July of 1942 thousands of French police rounded up 13,000 French Jews. Some women and children were sent to the French "transit" camp at Drancy; those held in the *Vel d'Hiv* (*vélodrome d'hiver*) [indoor bicycle racing track] were sent directly to Auschwitz. In July 2002, at the *Vel d'Hiv*, Prime Minister Jean-Pierre Raffarin laid a wreath in honor of the Jews who died as a result of French collaboration.

14. Legislation closed the doors to English-language schools for immigrants (save for those with one English-speaking parent) as a way of stemming the tide out of the province to the rest of Anglo-Canada/America. After two centuries of minority status, French became the province's official language in 1977.

15. Prime Minister Pariseau's attribution of the loss of the Parti Québécois referendum on sovereignty in 1995 to Quebec's "ethnic" vote, while it shocked many Québécois, is an illustration of this "Québécois de souche" thinking.

16. "Pur Polyester" is the title of a short story focusing on immigrant life, by Lori Saint-Martin in *Mon père, la nuit*.

17. In Pierre Nora's *Lieux de mémoire*, Mona Ozouf describes the symbolic impact of the Pantheon's location, at the very center of French territory, the heart of the nation.

18. The excerpts are from a speech delivered by President Chirac during the celebration of Dumas in front of the Pantheon.

19. Bennetta Jules-Rosette affirms that writers play a key role in the French national landscape, particularly in the debates around incorporation of immigrants and the desire for inclusion that "resonate[s] across their works" (174).

20. Kundera introduces the concept in *Les Testaments trahis* (35–46). Taking up the term, the Québécois critic Pierre Nepveu tells us that Montreal is becoming tropicalized as Haitian and other francophone writers increasingly become part of Quebec's cultural landscape (337). A more ironic use of the term can be found in Latin American studies, where it is equivalent to the specific traits, images, and values used to construct Latin Americans and Latinas/os in U.S. hegemonic discourse.

21. Marco Micone, Flora Balzano, Fulvio Cacci, Antonio d'Alfonso, all of Italian descent, Alice Parizeau from Poland, and Jacques Folch-Ribas from Spain are other neo-Québécois writers who do not come from below the 35th parallel.

22. Jack Kerouac's French Canadian cultural roots expressed in *unitedstatesian* terms, left indelible marks on the novel of the United States; see *Dr. Sax* and *Visions of Gerard* in particular.

23. Opposition to oppression became particularly intense in the Haitian post-colony during what amounted to recolonization by the United States in 1915. Such opposition has become a characteristic of Haitian writing since that time.

24. See Richard Bjornson's discussion of the Ahidjo government's suppression of writing in Cameroon (144–45).

25. Bjornson states that Dakeyo's exile was "from a homeland to which he felt he could not return until it had been liberated from its neocolonialist masters" (365).

26. Gaston-Paul Effa, Victor Bouadjio, and Simon Njami are also part of this third wave.

27. Beyala underscores the handicaps Dumas faced as a mulatto writer, describes the suffering he experienced at the hands of critics who called him a "stinking negro," and claims him as a model: "Pour une quarteronne comme moi et pour les jeunes qui rêvent d'intégration, il est un modèle: s'intégrer envers et contre tous. . . . Dumas est la preuve que l'on peut être d'origine africaine, devenir français malgré les handicaps et les vents contraires au point de maîtriser mieux que personne cette langue" [For a halfblood like me, and for young people who dream of integration, he is a model for integration no matter what the odds. . . . Dumas is proof that you can be of African origin, become French despite the handicaps and difficulties and even master the language better than anyone else]("On le traitait" 6).

28. *Réflexions sur une lettre de Mazères, ex-colon français, adressée à M. J. C. L. Sismonde de Sismondi, sur les noirs et les blancs, la civilisation de l'Afrique, le royaume d'Haïti* (Cap-Henry [Haïti] P. Roux, imprimeur du Roi, 1816), quoted in the January 1821 issue of the periodical *Hayden's Geological Essays* 132. The writings of Africans had just been used by Henri Grégoire, the famed French abolitionist, in his *On the Cultural Achievements of Negroes*, as a foil for the arguments of those who vilify the Negroes.

29. Alain Locke, who taught philosophy at Howard University, published *The New Negro*, an anthology demonstrating the genius of Afro-Americans, in 1925. The New York Public Library's Schomburg Collection was built upon a core of books and documents that were the personal collection of Arthur Schomburg, a black American of Caribbean origin. Schomburg was motivated by a similar need to demonstrate the acceptability of blacks through their literature.

30. See Lilyan Kesteloot for a discussion of the influence of U.S. movements on those who later developed the Negritude movement (60–63). Philippe Dewitte discusses the political thrust of the black movements that preceded Negritude in *Les Mouvements nègres en France* (347–49).

31. Calixthe Beyala has become a familiar figure in the French national limelight. Since 1987, she has published eleven novels and two essays, won several coveted French literary awards, and has managed to remain in the public eye through much-publicized legal trials accusing her of plagiarism. More recently, she has become a spokesperson for France's black community, leading the struggle for black representation in television programming. In addition to persevering despite accusations of plagiarism, Beyala has managed something quite rare among francophone women writers. She supports herself and her family by means of her writing by following a rigorous self-imposed work schedule, aiming to publish a book every two years.

32. Beyala's Eton ethnic group of south-central Cameroon is part of the larger Fang-Beti-Bulu Bantu group.

33. In 1996, Beyala was found guilty of plagiarism in *Le Petit prince de Belleville* for incorporating numerous passages from translations of the novels of two American writers, Howard Buten and Charles Williams. Other "sources," from Paule Constant and Alice Walker to Ben Okri, have nourished subsequent works. A disputed passage from Okri is in *Les Honneurs perdus,* the novel that won the *Grand Prix du roman de l'Académie Française* in 1996. See Mongo Beti and Kenneth Harrow.

34. "L'Histoire perçue non comme une accumulation figée d'événements, mais comme un précieux réservoir de virtualités" [History perceived not as an accumulation of events, but a precious reservoir of potential] (20). "Un champ de possibilités . . . où les hasards, les postures subjectives les plus irrationnelles jouent un rôle parfois déterminant dans l'accomplissement des destinées" [A field of possibilities . . . where chance, the most irrational of subjective positions play a role that sometimes determines the fulfillment of destiny] (280).

35. See Roger Chartier's discussion of reception in *The Cultural Uses of Print in Early Modern France* (183).

36. "Peu de peuples se sont trouvés, comme nous autres d'Afrique dite francophone, dans une situation historique de dépendance contraignant leurs créateurs à utiliser non seulement la langue, mais surtout l'appareil culturel d'une nation étrangère, qui de surcroît les avait colonisés" [Few peoples have found themselves in the situation that characterizes those of us in so-called francophone Africa, in a situation of historical dependency that obliges their writers to use not only the language, but especially the cultural institutions of a foreign nation, which, moreover, has colonized them] (41).

37. Christopher Miller in *Blank Darkness* shows how Africa functions as an empty trope, to be filled with Africanist discourse, rather than with knowledge (see Ezra 9–10).

38. This is the well-known charge levied against Camara Laye by Mongo Beti in "Afrique noire, littérature rose," accusing the Negritude writer of turning a blind eye to colonialism's ravages.

39. From the inside back jacket of *Les Arbres en parlent encore.*

40. Calixthe Beyala was among the candidates in the contest to replace Boutros Boutros-Ghali at the head of the Organisation Internationale de la Francophonie [Francophone International Organization], claiming she would create a "Francophonie populaire." The contest was won in October 2002 by the former Senegalese head of state, Abdou Diouf. See Dioh.

41. This is—in part—the point of departure of François Paré's excellent study of such literatures in *Les littératures de l'exiguïté.*

42. In an interview with Bernard Magnier, Laferrière states, "[C]e livre allait me donner une chance. Celle de sortir de l'usine" [This book was going to give me a chance. The chance to leave factory work] (Laferrière, *J'écris* 152).

43. "A Montréal je suis un écrivain connu. Les gens m'accostent dans la rue pour me parler de mes livres. Je cours les fêtes. Je suis constamment à la télé. . . . A Miami, personne ne me connaît. A Montréal, le douanier me demande s'il y a un film sur le feu ou un nouveau livre à déclarer" [In Montreal I am well known. People come up to me on the street to talk about my books. I'm always at parties. I am constantly on television.

. . . In Miami, no one knows me. In Montreal the customs officer asks whether I have a film on the back burner or a new book to declare] (Laferrière, *J'écris* 48).

44. Murphy, citing Compagnon, writes that French theoretical questioning about literature has not evolved since the 1970s in France. He also notes Moura's critique of the French literary establishment: "The standards of French literature are assumed to be the norm and francophone literatures are assessed on their ability to match up to these standards" (176).

45. See my discussion of this in "*Mère-Solitude* d'Emile Ollivier."

Works Cited

Africultures 28 (May 2000). Special issue on "Postcolonialisme: inventaire et débats."

Amselle, Jean Loup. *Vers un multiculturalisme français*. Paris: Flammarion, 1996.

Anderson, Benedict. 1983. *Imagined Communities: Reflections on the Origins and Spread of Nationalism*. Reprint, London: Verso, 1995.

Bessière, Jean, and Jean-Marc Moura, eds. *Littératures postcoloniales et francophonie: conférences du séminaire de littérature comparée de l'Université de la Sorbonne Nouvelle*. Paris: H. Champion, 2001.

Bessora. *53 Cm*. Paris: Le Serpent à plumes, 1999.

Beti, Mongo. "L'Affaire Calixthe Beyala ou comment sortir du néocolonialisme en littérature." *Palabres: revue culturelle africaine* 1:3–4 (1997): 40–48.

———. "Afrique noire, littérature rose." *Présence africaine* 1–2 (April–June 1955): 133–45.

———. *Main basse sur le Cameroun: Autopsie d'une décolonisation*. Paris: Peuples Noirs, 1984.

Beyala, Calixthe. *Les Arbres en parlent encore*. Paris: Albin Michel, 2002.

———. *Assèze l'Africaine*. Paris: Albin Michel, 1994.

———. *C'est le soleil qui m'a brûlée*. Paris: Stock, 1987.

———. *Lettre d'une afro-française à ses compatriotes*. Paris: Editions Mango, 2000.

———. *Le Petit prince de Belleville*. Paris: Albin Michel, 1992.

Beyala-Milady, Calixthe. "On le traitait de nègre qui pue." *Paris Match* 2774 (25 July 2002): 6.

Bjornson, Richard. *The African Quest for Freedom and Identity: Cameroonian Writing and National Experience*. Bloomington: Indiana University Press, 1991.

Bonn, Charles, ed. *Littératures des immigrations*. Paris: L'Harmattan, 1995.

Brière, Eloise A. "*Mère-Solitude* d'Emile Ollivier: apport migratoire à la société québécoise." *International Journal of Canadian Studies/Revue Internationale d'Etudes Canadiennes* 13 (Spring 1996): 61–70.

Britton, Celia M. *Edouard Glissant and Postcolonial Theory: Strategies of Language and Resistance*. Charlottesville: University Press of Virginia, 1999.

Chartier, Roger. *The Cultural Uses of Print in Early Modern France*. Trans. Lydia G. Cochrane. Princeton, N.J.: Princeton University Press, 1987.

Chirac, Jacques. Televised speech celebrating Alexandre Dumas. Transmitted live in France on Saturday, 30 November 2002. Channel TV5.

Coates, Carroll F. "An Interview with Dany Laferrière." *Callaloo* 22.4 (1999): 910–21.
Cohen, William B. *The French Encounter with Africans: White Response to Blacks, 1530–1880*. Bloomington: Indiana University Press, 1980.
Dadié, Bernard. *Un Nègre à Paris*. Paris: Présence africaine, 1959.
Dédale 5–6 (Spring 1997). Special issue on "Postcolonialisme, décentrement, déplacement, dissémination."
Deleuze, Gilles, and Felix Guattari. "La Littérature mineure." *Kafka: pour une littérature mineure*. Paris: Editions de Minuit, 1975. 29–53.
Dewitte, Philippe. *Les Mouvements nègres en France: 1919–1939*. Paris: L'Harmattan, 1985.
Dioh, Tidiane. "Une Candidate pas comme les autres." *Jeune Afrique/l'intelligent* 2124 (September 25–October 1, 2001): 105.
Dor, Georges. "La Manic." 1964. *Le Québec par ses textes littéraires (1534–1976)*. Montreal: France-Québec, 1979. 251–52.
Ezra, Elizabeth. *The Colonial Unconscious: Race and Culture in Interwar France*. Ithaca, N.Y.: Cornell University Press, 2000.
Fanon, Frantz. *Peau noire, masques blancs*. Paris: Seuil, 1961.
Glissant, Edouard. *Poétique de la relation*. Paris: Gallimard, 1990.
Grégoire, Henri. *On the Cultural Achievements of Negroes*. Trans. Thomas Cassirer and Jean-François Brière. Amherst: University of Massachusetts Press, 1996.
Grescoe, Taras. *Sacré Blues*. Toronto: McFarlane, Walter and Ross, 2001.
Harrow, Kenneth W. *Less Than One and Double: A Feminist Reading of African Women's Writing*. Portsmouth, N.H.: Heinemann, 2002.
Kerouac, Jack. *Dr. Sax*. New York: Grove Press, 1959.
———. *Visions of Gerard*. New York: McGraw-Hill, 1963.
Kesteloot, Lilyan. *Histoire de la littérature négro-africaine*. Paris: Karthala, 2001.
Kourouma, Ahmadou. *Les Soleils des indépendances*. Montreal: Université de Montréal, 1968.
Kundera, Milan. *Les Testaments trahis*. Paris: Galllimard, 1993.
Jules-Rosette, Bennetta. *Black Paris: The African Writers' Landscape*. Urbana: University of Illinois Press, 1998.
Laferrière, Dany. *Cette Grenade dans la main du jeune nègre est-elle une arme ou un fruit?* Montreal: VLB Editeur, 1993.
———. *Comment faire l'amour avec un nègre sans se fatiguer*. Paris: Bellefond, 1989.
———. *Eroshima*. Quebec: Typo, 1998.
———. *J'écris comme je vis. Dany Laferrière: Entretien avec Bernard Magnier*. Montreal: Lanctot. Paris: Editions la Passe du vent, 2000.
———. *L'Odeur du café*. Montreal: VLB Editeur, 1991.
Lalonde, Michèle. "Speak White." *Le Québec par ses textes littéraires (1534–1976)*. Montreal: France-Québec, 1979. 298.
Lamore, Jean. "Transculturation: naissance d'un mot." *Vice versa* 21 (1987): 18–19.
Laronde, Michel. "L'Ecriture décentrée." *L'Ecriture décentrée: la langue de l'Autre dans le roman contemporain*. Ed. Michel Laronde. Paris: L'Harmattan, 1996. 7–14.
Linteau, Paul-André et al. *Histoire du Québec contemporain*. Montreal: Boréal, 1989.

Locke, Alain LeRoy. *The New Negro: An Interpretation.* New York: Arno Press, 1968.

Meddeb, Abdelwahab. "Dans le post-colonialisme, il y a l'enjeu du décentrement." *Africultures* 28 (May 2000): 30–33.

Moura, Jean-Marc. *Littératures francophones et théorie postcoloniale.* Paris: Presses universitaires de France, 1999.

Murphy, David. "De-centring French Studies: Towards a Postcolonial Theory of Francophone Cultures." *French Cultural Studies* 13.2 (June 2002): 165–85.

Nepveu, Pierre. *Intérieurs du Nouveau Monde.* Montreal: Boréal, 1998.

Nora, Pierre, ed. *Les Lieux de mémoire.* 3 vol. Paris: Gallimard, 1997.

Ortiz, Fernando. 1940. *Contrapunteo cubano del tabaco y azucar.* Barcelona: Ariel, 1973.

Ozouf, Mona. "Le Panthéon." *Les Lieux de mémoire.* Vol. 1. Ed. Pierre Nora. Paris: Gallimard, 1997. 155–78.

Papastergiadis, Nikos. "Ambivalence in Cultural Theory: Reading Homi Bhabha's *Dissemination.*" *Writing the Nation: Self and Country in the Post-Colonial Imagination.* Ed. John C. Hawley. Amsterdam: Rodopi, 1996. 176–93.

Paré, François. *Les Littératures de l'exiguïté.* Ottawa: Nordir, 1994.

Ringuet. *Trente arpents.* Paris: Flammarion, 1991.

Robin, Régine. "A propos de la notion kafkaienne de 'littérature mineure': quelques questions posées à la littérature québécoise." *Paragraphes* 2.2 (1990): 6–14.

———. *La Québécoite.* Montreal: Typo, 1993.

Roy, Gabrielle. *Bonheur d'occasion.* Montreal: Boréal, 1993.

Saint-Martin, Lori. *Mon père, la nuit.* Quebec: L'instant même, 1999.

Scarpetta, Guy. *L'Impureté.* Paris: Grasset, 1985.

Simon, Sherry. *Le Trafic des langues.* Montreal: Boréal, 1994.

Sroka, Ghila. "Conversation avec Dany Laferrière: de la francophonie et autres considérations." *Tribune juive* 16.5 (August 1999): 8–16.

Vigneault, Gilles. "Mon pays." *Littérature québécoise.* Ville La Salle, Quebec: Hurtubise, 1996. 282.

10

Displaced Discourses

Post(-)coloniality, Francophone Space(s), and the Literature(s) of Immigration in France

Michel Laronde

The literatures of immigration create a specific type of intersection between what has been conventionally called the francophone diaspora and postcoloniality. Their presence in contemporary France raises the question of the nature of the postcolonial discourse, or discourses, they represent. In turn, their postcolonial quality within the borders of the French nation demands a necessary displacement of the concept of *francophonie* and a redefinition of the geopolitical and linguistic limits of what constitutes a francophone diaspora, with France as part of it on equal terms with other francophone cultures, and their literatures.

Arabo-French literature, the literature of immigration that emerged in the 1980s with *beur* fiction, and Afro-French literature, a recent corpus that emerged in the 1990s, now form the bulk of postcolonial literatures written in France. They pose the question of the place of postcolonial literatures in general in relation to French literature, particularly on the ideological and institutional levels. Theorizing the location of this growing body of texts starts with the acknowledgment of an institutional void. As literature produced within France by a group of writers ethnically and culturally identifiable as postcolonial subjects, *beur* literature has no space within "French" literature. Promoting a distinction by using the label "*beur* fiction" had a connotation of displaced status with regard to "French" literature, while calling it "North African" or "Algerian" literature signaled rejection. The oppositional discourse within the French institution on *beur* literature either refused to acknowledge its existence as a singular discourse with a specific body of texts or reduced it to a "minor literature." In the first instance, it becomes assimilated into the supremacy of "French" literature. It is reduced to near silence as a postcolonial literary discourse from within French culture, and the assimilatory supremacy of "French" literature is preserved. If the "*beur*" label is accepted, institutional discourses (those of the media and the publishing world) reduce it to a "minor" literature.[1]

To skirt the ideological impasse of an "either/or" discourse of non-belonging or assimilation (a possible remnant of colonial ideology), *francophone* will be considered as a possible third term to represent *beur* literature: it does not have to be recuperated as French literature, rejected as Algerian literature, or decentered to a peripheral position. To bring the term *francophone* to represent a literary discourse within France, the geographical, political, and cultural content of the term *francophone* need to be displaced from an outside to an inside position in relation to a "French" space. As a consequence, the displacement will lead to a reevaluation of the place of France and of its culture within an enlarged francophone diaspora. Therefore, the main argument is that, in a postcolonial context, a French cultural space no longer stands alone with regard to, and in opposition to, a francophone diaspora with its many cultures, but it has become part of a larger francophone space that now includes it. This should dramatically impact the hegemonic perception of French literature within French culture and of French literary institutions for other French-speaking cultures. I hope to illustrate how the body of postcolonial literatures produced in France creates an ideological shift that allows francophone and French spaces to be merged in literature. As a ripple effect, this merging will further displace the referential status of French literature with regard to other francophone cultures that already have developed a strong presence through their literature in academic institutions in western countries of Europe and in North America.

Three examples of strategies for dehegemonizing French culture from the inside will be examined here: (1) defining *post-colonial* written with a hyphen as a historical discourse-in-progress and acknowledging how it takes part in the construction of a postcolonial mentality specific to French culture; (2) proposing a three-term paradigm to establish a parallel between "Arabo-French," "Afro-French," and "Franco-French," as a strategy to decanonize the literature from France on an institutional level; (3) proposing to revisit the limits of *francophonie* in relation to the specific French-speaking space of France and to its particular postcolonial mentality.

Definition: The "Post" of a Post-coloniality within France

I find it important to insist on a distinction between two meanings for the coined word *post-colonial*, based on the presence or absence of a hyphen between the two terms of the word. Written with a hyphen after the "post,"

post-colonial signifies the impossibility of separating the historical quality of a concept—coloniality—from a situation—colonialism. Associated with *colonial*, the prefix "post" maintains a purely temporal dimension, where the hyphen inscribes the term as the sign of a diachronic separation between two spaces of the History of France and its (former) colonies, that of a colonization and a post-colonization stage.[2] The separation of the "post" from the word *colonial* establishes meaning along a historical paradigm ideologically attached to a "colonial" period as a central term. The "post-colonial" period is the one that comes after the independence of countries colonized by the language and culture of France. Homi Bhabha states that, when used strictly as a diachronic marker, "the popular use of the 'post' to indicate sequentiality—*after*-feminism; or polarity—*anti*-modernism" ("Introduction" 4) would not bring much meaning to the question of postcoloniality, other than a change of politico-ideological status for the colonies. I am not so easily convinced that a postcolonial mentality (what I refer to as "postcoloniality") does not fundamentally rest on its "sequential" dimension. I still contend that the "post" as a marker of time and History remains a fundamental cornerstone of "postcoloniality" as a concept, once the concept has integrated its sequential element, once the hyphen no longer distinguishes the "post" from the "colonial." The sequential quality participates in a concept that lies *beyond* the purely referential politico-historical context; it remains an integral part of it, especially in a situation of migration from a former colonized space to the symbolic space of a colonizer culture. The sequential quality of the literatures of immigration is crucial to the postcolonial mentality in France, when it is produced by post-colonial subjects and their descendants who emigrated from North Africa to France. It is especially significant in the case of Algeria, because of the traumatizing experience of de-colonization and independence for both parties.[3] A postcolonial mentality *within France* necessarily has its roots in History and Politics between France and its former colonies. A post-colonial ideology, inherited through History, is part of the concept of postcoloniality and constitutes a major discourse in its literature. Ignoring the post-colonial dimension of the literatures of immigration in the development of a postcolonial mentality is akin to performing an act of amnesia. Revisiting History through anamnesis and memory through discourses of, and on, exile, is a post-colonial initiative that forces France, as a western nation, to confront its post-colonial histories uncovered by an influx of "postwar migrants and refugees" telling "an indigenous or native narrative internal to its national identity" (Bhabha, "Introduction" 6).

The concept of postcoloniality as a mentality necessarily includes post-colonial components. Because a historical background cannot be denied to the concept of postcoloniality, cannot be forgotten, or cut off, the concept may include post-colonialism as an active set of practices (in politics, language policies, cultural initiatives) that are the consequences of History. The "post," then, acts more like a principle of continuity between the two periods, the colonial and the post-colonial, rather than one of separation. In that sense, postcoloniality is inscribed in a continuum and retains ties with the fields of politics and colonialism, and with coloniality as a mentality. Because its roots are embedded in colonialism understood as a set of political and cultural practices specific to the colonial period, the discourse of postcoloniality reacts on instances of colonial ideological content.

The literatures of immigration in France have to be considered in a historical perspective, as texts written by authors born from parents who (e)migrated from North and sub-Saharan Africa to France as part of postcolonial migratory movements. The study of a literary postcoloniality within France takes into account the ethno-cultural origins of authors who have direct or indirect ties with colonial History. The distinction that has been made between the terms *post-colonial* and *postcolonial* as representing a mentality that has matured during the aftermath of liberation efforts by former colonies—the process is still ongoing—allows us to separate "technical" from sociocultural criteria. The ethnic origins and politico-legal situations of authors are technicalities. Sociocultural criteria ground texts in a literary mentality specific to the authors' post-colonial situations as exiles and first-, second-, or third-generation residents, nationals, and clandestines educated in French culture.

As a matter of fact, it is impossible to read Arabo-French texts without paying attention to their post-colonial dimension. Signs of the presence of the "sequential" are written all over Arabo-French fiction, from the 1980s to the present. The strongest symbol of the post-colonial in postcolonial literature that has emerged recently is (for the time being) "October 17, 1961."[4] But other signs are recurrent: the politico-cultural fate of *harkis* after the independence of Algeria, memories of the war of independence, the dream of erasing the situation of exile by "returning" to the motherland by the generations of Algerians who emigrated to France in the 1950s, 1960s, and 1970s. Explicit post-colonial references are especially present in *beur* novels from the 1980s. With more recent Arabo-French texts, the grounding of fiction in a postcolonial dimension "assimilates" the historical content as a historical *quality* that shares in a more sophisticated construction of a postcolonial mentality at the intersection of the two meanings of the "post" in the "post-colonial." This view is very close to the one expressed by Jean-Marc Moura as the difference between a "historical concept" and an "analytical concept": "'Post-colonial' désigne donc ici le simple fait d'arriver après l'époque coloniale, tandis que 'postcolonial' se réfère à toutes les stratégies d'écriture déjouant la vision coloniale, y compris durant la période de la colonisation" [Here, "post-colonial" designates the mere fact of coming after the colonial period, when "postcolonial" refers to any writing strategy that destabilizes a colonial vision, including during the period of colonization] (Moura 4, my translation).

Arabo-French and Afro-French Literatures: Decentering a Canon

When it emerged in the 1980s, the literature written by "second-generation" Maghrebis raised and educated in France created an institutional tension. Attempts at situating this new corpus within the diaspora of literatures written in French tended to associate it with one of two existing and distinct literary entities, that of French literature as a unified corpus written within the national borders of the French Literary Nation, or that of a recently identified corpus of National Algerian Literature. Both "imagined" official literary entities were inadequate to absorb the literatures of immigration. Intellectuals from the Maghreb rejected *beur* literature from their national literature as being "French" literature, while French intellectuals and the media rejected it as not belonging to a French "national" literary tradition. The double rejection may be best understood in the perspective of the emergence of a postcolonial literary consciousness both in France and in Algeria, the two main protagonists of this post-colonial discourse. Still today, French literary institutions either treat *beur* literature as a "minor literature" or place it on the shelves with "the literatures of the Maghreb" in major bookstores (like the FNAC, for example, which may be considered as reflecting a general institutional attitude). Institutionalizing it qualitatively "below" French literature, and spatially "beside" it, signals both a rejection of that new corpus as an intruder in a protected space, that of French Culture and a French Canon, and an inclusion in an area on the margins of French literature, that of a francophone literature. On the other hand, when the Algerian intelligentsia also rejects *beur* writers from their own corpus of a new National Algerian Literature written in French, the message seems to be that this new corpus produced by second-generation residents in the former colonial "mother" culture is considered closer to the tradition of French literature, not to the recent postcolonial National Literature they themselves produce. The fact is that inscribing this new field *exclusively* in the French literary tradition or, by default, in a new postcolonial Algerian literary culture that are both strongly defined as national, is not satisfactory, and denies the possibility of a postcolonial literary mentality generated by both nations.

From this perspective, postcolonial studies has carefully avoided treating the corpus as an extension of French literature or of a new national Algerian literature in French (Moura 7). Calling it "*beur*" (a term used by the media in the 1980s as a reversal of the French term *arabe*) was an attempt at carving a space for the corpus within the institution while saving it from being made anonymous as "French" literature or expelled as its institutional opposite, as non-French literature that belonged to another national space, that of a new francophone literature, the national Algerian literature written in French. If "*beur* fiction" was to represent the emergence of a literary mentality, it had to include all texts that could be linked to the presence of Maghrebian culture in French culture, including texts written by authors not identified by their ethnic origins (like Michel Tournier or Leïla Sebbar), but whose fiction could be inscribed "around" the presence of a Maghrebian culture and a postcolonial mentality (Laronde, *Autour*). In that sense, "*beur* fiction" was meant to open up a new space in the French literary institution that was likely to play a major role as a *parasitic* discourse, leading to displacements in the perception of the institutional value and role of a national literature (Moura 58).

Today, the literatures of immigration are essentially made up of two corpuses, Arabo-French literature, a continuation into the 1990s of "*beur* fiction" from the 1980s, and Afro-French literature, which first appeared in the early 1990s. The introduction of a term shift from *beur* to *Arabo-French* suggests an internal evolution of the initial corpus of *beur* literature. Texts written by the sons and daughters of North African (im)migrants to France in the 1980s are mainly collective, ethnographic, autobiographical fictions. Ethnographic references by authors are to their Maghrebian origins. The fiction emphasizes the sociological gap between their exiled parents and their own modes of integration, assimilation, or resistance to French society. Recurrent markers of spatial location are the *banlieues*—the peripheral areas of French cities or "suburbs"—*bidonvilles* (slums), and HLMs (large-scale public housing projects). Early education in the French school system is a near constant motivation for the narrative. In the 1990s, ethnographic content is still traceable in Arabo-French fiction, but most texts have moved away from merely recording the collective experience of immigration. Instead, ethno-auto-biographical fiction (Laronde, "Evolution") gives a more creative account of that particular postcolonial experience of displacement. The shift from *beur* to *Arabo-French* has led me to create a paradigm that develops its meaning around three terms: "Arabo-French," "Afro-French," and "Franco-French." The term *Afro-French* imposed itself naturally after I coined *Arabo-French*, probably from a similar usage in American culture (Afro-American literature, Afro-American studies). First, the two prefixes "Arabo" and "Afro" make a distinction between two discourses that diversify the literary production by post-colonial subjects (hence the plural for literatures of immigration), while grafting the suffix "French" onto them establishes a link to a common cultural and linguistic core. Further expanding the paradigm to include the concept of "Franco-French" literature establishes a second parallel between each of the two branches of the literatures of immigration and the general corpus of French literature. The terminological shift from *French* to *Franco-French* suggests a more dramatic institutional repositioning of the corpus of "French" literature in relation to the totality of the literatures from France, which include the literatures of immigration. The strategy suggests a new institutional agency whereby three distinct yet related literary productions are put on a disjointed footing. It is meant to destabilize the notion of a unique and undivided Canon of French literature.

Discursively, introducing *Arabo-French* and *Afro-French*, two terms that refer to ethnicity as a community of language but a difference of culture, to account for the evolution of contemporary literature in France, challenges the hegemony of a French Literature, and of a French Language as a model and a norm (here, Language is understood as *Langue*, not as *Langage*). The suggested ethnic connotation of the coined term "Franco" is, of course, a cultural myth grounded in an imagined homogeneous ethnic reality for the Nation. Conversely, the ethnic references of *Arabo-French* and *Afro-French* are toned down by the linguistic and cultural parallel with *Franco-French*. In addition, "Arabo," referring to North African cultures from Algeria, Morocco, and Tunisia, is a generic term that does not take into account ethnic differences (the most obvious being Berbers). "Afro," referring to all francophone cultures from sub-Saharan West Africa, is an even more outrageous generic term that transcends ethnic references. The key to this reading is the presence of the second term, "French," with each term of the paradigm, that makes all three terms function on the same discursive level, thus bringing *Franco-French* to signify in relation to the other two terms and collapsing a pyramidal structure of hegemony. The paradigm can be read as the institutional presence of a post-colonial literary discourse in France, and as the harbinger of a postcolonial mentality in the literary culture.

Toward a Postcolonial Mentality in/of French Culture

On the level of a macro-structure of francophone literatures, the concept of postcoloniality is not monolithic. The literary diversity that flourishes now, during the post-colonial period, has developed from historico-cultural ties established by France during the colonial period with (present) French-speaking countries of the world. In an effort to organize postcolonial literatures according to the post-colonial nature of their ties with the French nation, with its literature and with the French language, I have proposed three categories that correspond to three different mentalities: the new national literatures, the literatures of "postcontact," and the literatures of immigration (Laronde, "Littératures").

(1) The new national literatures are produced by the nations of the Maghreb and sub-Saharan Africa. I call "intersection" the particular dialectics that have developed with each corpus during the post-colonial period through different cultural and linguistic ties to French literature and a common language.

(2) The literatures of "postcontact" are produced mainly by the French Caribbean DOMs (Départements d'Outre-Mer [French Overseas Departments]) of Guadeloupe and Martinique. They maintain a dialectics of "parallelism" with French national literature, since they belong to a postcolonial mentality while maintaining neocolonial institutional ties with France.

(3) The literatures of immigration that have developed within the French nation since the 1980s occupy a special dialectical position with regard to French national literature, which I call "interpenetration." The dialectics share characteristics of both the new national literatures and the literatures of "postcontact." The literatures of immigration are in a cultural and linguistic position of insider with regard to French literature. They share the same cultural background, since the authors are the first generation to have been educated in France. But at the same time, the literatures of immigration are in a position of intersection with the new national literatures of the Maghreb (for Arabo-French literature) and sub-Saharan Africa (for Afro-French literature), since they have established variable modes of interaction with a common language, based on residual traits from the cultures "of origin." They have also established a dialectics of parallelism of their own that is different in nature from the one that characterizes the literatures of "postcontact." On the one hand, they do belong to the same ambiguous post-colonial period, in a historical sense, where a national culture generated by the (former) colonial institution still feeds the authors' literary background (this is the role of the national system of education, the *Education Nationale*); on the other hand, the literatures are motivated by different postcolonial mentalities and different cultural backgrounds.

Therefore, at the level of a macro-structure of all literatures written in French, literatures of immigration appear to be in a situation of cultural and literary *doubling*, since they are connected to the French domain and to postcolonial domains constituted by other francophone categories, the new national literatures and the literatures of "postcontact." A situation of doubling suggests that a postcolonial mentality in France is generated at the junction of two fields: French literature and at least one other post-colonial literary field, be it one or more of the new national literatures, or one or more of the literatures of "postcontact." But the term "doubling" is insufficient to map out a more subtle and wider network of relations between the three fields that make up the diversity of postcolonial mentalities. The three terms used here, *interpenetration*, *intersection*, and *parallelism*, suggest other possibilities for "rhyzome"-like (Deleuze and Glissant) interactions between mentalities, which impact differently on the form and content of certain bodies of francophone literatures.

As an example, to account for the presence and evolution of a postcolonial mentality in/of French literature, it may be beneficial to consider a corpus organized as "the literatures of exile." Just as literatures of immigration are articulated in the field of History, that of post-coloniality with a hyphen, so are "the literatures of exile." Using 1962, the year of the coming of age of the Algerian nation, is a symbolic marker of the start of a historical post-coloniality and of the end of a colonial situation between France and Algeria in particular, as the last (latest) colony to have gained independence from France. Having a post-colonial corpus called "literatures of exile" would make that date all the more elastic. Retrospectively, the presence of a literary postcolonial mentality in France could go back to the colonial period with texts written mostly in the 1950s. Although the "literatures of exile" may precede the literatures of immigration in a historical diachrony, certain texts support a double postcolonial discourse, that of "exile" and that of "immigration." For example, the fiction of Franco-Guadeloupean author Gisèle Pineau builds a bridge between the literatures of "postcontact" and the literatures of immigration. In *L'Exil selon Julia* and *Un Papillon dans la cité*, the physical organization of the text between two spaces, Guadeloupe and France, is symbolic of a dialectic of exile, a dialectic and a structure one finds in several Afro-French novels. Along the same lines, Leïla Sebbar establishes a bridge between the literatures of immigration and the national literature of Algeria in much of her fiction.

Looking at a more detailed periodization of the historical frame of the post-colonial, it seems possible to identify two discourses of exile. During the first period, straddling the colonization period and the period of independence, a discourse of exile is produced by Africans writing from inside the colonizer's place (just as the discourse of immigration will be twenty years later). Camara Laye's *L'Enfant noir*, Ousmane Sembène's *Le Docker noir*, or Bernard Dadié's *Un Nègre à Paris* embody a discourse of exile marked by a certain postcolonial mentality. It recriminates against France and laments a loss of identity with regard to the African culture that has been left behind. During the next period, that of the literatures of immigration, starting in the 1980s, a discourse of exile embedded in a number of texts embodies a different postcolonial mentality. The discourse of exile expressed in *beur* fiction becomes that of the aborted experience of return to the country of origin (with Leïla Houari, Sakinna Boukhedenna, Akli Tadjer, or Nacer Kettane), and exile is denounced as a false discourse. Sakinna Boukhedenna's *Journal "Nationalité: Immigré(e)"* claims exile as a position to be defended against alienation. Kassa Houari's *Confessions d'un immigré* might be a text on exile as well as others, such as Malika Mokeddem's *L'Interdite*, which takes us to the 1990s (*L'Interdite* was published in 1993). During the same period (1990s), the discourse produced by Afro-French fiction offers a different postcolonial point of view, where exile is considered from within France and from within the cultural context of the African country as well. J. R. Essomba's *Le Paradis du nord* and Alain Mabanckou's *Bleu-Blanc-Rouge* are striking examples of a double discourse that recriminates against both discourses, since they are tied to the colonial—thus they remain two post-colonial discourses in a historical sense—as well as being discourses produced by Africans, one from within France, one from within Africa.

The discourse of exile from the first period is generally marked by recrimination against the (former) colonial power. The discourse of exile from the second period seems to add an interesting touch to that particular postcolonial mentality by supplementing recrimination against contemporary (post-colonial) French culture with recrimination against the post-colonial culture of the African country of origin. For example, a text like *Bleu-Blanc-Rouge* is even organized in a format that suggests the entire dialectics, since half of the novel takes place in the Congo (Brazzaville) and half in Paris, while the characters move from one space to the other. The African who carries the general point of view criticizes, accuses, denounces, demystifies, and deconstructs two discourses: the one that Congolese exiles living in France (the "Parisians") produce on French culture while in France and the one on French culture they bring back to the Congo. The second discourse has maintained within Congolese culture a colonial stereotype that perpetuates the myth of "*le prestige de la France*." The novel is therefore a testimony to Congolese culture during the post-colonial era. The Republic of the Congo is presented as living under a sort of self-induced cultural and economic neocolonialist dependence. Through the denunciation by the main character, a rhetoric of *revendication* (in the sense of claiming, or reclaiming) that demands an evolution toward a postcolonial mentality is ultimately inscribed in the rhetoric of recrimination. The discourse of exile in *beur* novels is represented by the mythical return of the first generation of immigrants to the country of origin, to Algeria or Morocco. During that second period, the cultural myth is also denounced, and recrimination against France and against the country of origin is already present in several *beur* novels. In recent Arabo-French novels, like Paul Smaïl's, ruminating against both cultures has taken over large portions of the text, and the argumentative dimension of the discourse is more pronounced.

The understanding of the postcolonial mentality at work within French culture is enriched when it is examined with the concept of exile as being part of it, not as preceding it, as a strictly historical colonial/post-colonial periodization would have us believe. Leïla Sebbar's extended discourse on and of exile and its discursive ramifications is a good example of the various directions that the discourse on/of exile can take. In her early fiction, *métissage*, uprootedness, alterity and difference, the language of the Other, and multiple racial and cultural crossings and hybridizations are ever present lines that represent exile. The rich treatment of the subject is probably the reason why her texts "intersect" with different domains of postcolonial writing, that of the Arabo-French literature of immigration, and that of Algerian literature as a new national literature (as in *Fatima, ou, Les Algériennes au square,* but also in a recent collection of short stories like *La Jeune fille au balcon*), as well as the wider domain of francophone, "migrant" literature. Recent collections of her own short stories, such as *La Négresse à l'enfant*, *La Jeune fille au balcon*, *Le Baiser,* and *Soldats*, and edited collections of short fiction pieces (*Une Enfance outremer, Une Enfance algérienne*), approach the postcolonial questions of History, memory, and identity that are also part of the first period of the situation of exile, a period I perceive more as a discourse of recrimination, with a much stronger sense of *revendication.* Themes like amnesia, the wars of decolonization and their consequences, and post-colonial migrations now make up a more powerful discourse throughout the postcolonial mentality that has shaped the literatures of immigration. The most recent development is the question of anamnesis with regard to the Algerian war of independence, which has been fictionalized so eloquently by Leïla Sebbar in her 1999 novel, *La Seine était rouge*, as a discourse that is clearly focused on a circulation between recrimination and *revendication.*

Francophonie and Post(-)*Francophonie*

> Il y a une grande différence entre parler *en* français et parler *le* français, clamait-il sans développer sa pensée.
>
> [There's a big difference between speaking *in* French and speaking French, he claimed, without developing his thinking further.]
> **Mabanckou 63, italics in text**

The presence of postcolonial literatures in France questions the ideology of "the prestige of the French Language" that has endured since the eighteenth century through colonial situations and, in post-colonial times, still perniciously maintains the hegemony of France over its former cultural subjects in the domain of literature. Backed by realpolitik in the form of institutions, *francophonie* is the post-colonial continuation of politics of acculturation through education that established the literary prestige of France during colonial times. It still promotes the same mentality on the international scene today. The fact that *francophonie* has been, and still is, understood as the presence of the French language *beyond the borders of the French nation, at the exclusion of the territory of the French nation*, is symbolic of the hegemonic mentality France has maintained over other French-speaking countries. Suggesting that France belongs to a francophone world from a linguistic standpoint, based solely on an extended use of the French language, is not that revolutionary. But it is still a new proposition to suggest that *the world of francophone literatures should also include French literature.* Moving from the notion of a linguistic community to that of a literary diaspora rekindles the controversy over the "prestige" of the French language and displaces it onto that of the preservation of a national literature as a corpus and a Canon.

The suggestion that France is part of the francophone diaspora is a crucial postcolonial step that has to be taken seriously. Literature, as a bridge between language and culture, has introduced a postcolonial discourse into France that originates in the nation's own linguistic and cultural margins. Now that diglossic practices are developing within the French nation, both the geo-cultural and symbolic borders of *francophonie* have to be reconsidered. Discussed from a colonial/post-colonial perspective, a set of binary paradigms establishes the position of French literature as follows: when characterized as "classical and modern," it is in opposition to "post(-)colonial" literatures, as "canonical" to "minor" or "dialectal," as "French" to "francophone," as "central" to "peripheral" or "decentered." The French "classical and modern" literary canon is challenged by a contemporary postcolonial literary production from within French culture that can be called francophone in all domains except for the *territorial* reference. The presence of a postcolonial mentality within the sanctuary of French literature becomes manifest when the literatures written by post-colonial subjects are more or less institutionalized. Symbolically, the presence within French culture of literatures that can be established as francophone in a conventional sense (they refer to cultures outside France) undoes the hegemonic position of "French" literature as nonfrancophone. The Afro-French branch of literatures of immigration gives the literature of exile from French-speaking sub-Saharan Africa a new postcolonial twist. Postcolonial literatures of the French Caribbean, mainly the literatures of "postcontact" from Guadeloupe and Martinique, contribute further to the diversification of a postcolonial cultural and literary mentality in France.

Decentering is a two-step process. A first step claims that the literatures of immigration are francophone. Therefore, the concept of literary postcoloniality, understood as the various francophone literatures produced outside France, is displaced to include that part of the literatures produced in France that is postcolonial. As a second step, the nature of the displacement questions the perception of a monolithic "French" literary identity and constitutes the basic element for a definition of French postcoloniality. Introducing a distinction between Arabo-French and Afro-French literatures and between both corpuses and another corpus called Franco-French literature constitutes the claim to that particular postcolonial literary mentality. Franco-French literature *also* occupies a portion of the literary space that makes up a francophone literary discourse within the borders of the French nation.

It has been commonly understood that *francophonie* refers to differential uses of the language outside France. Supporting the proposition that the literatures produced in France are postcolonial *and* francophone is the enormous work that has been done especially by Arabo-French authors on, and through, language. It compares with parallel (but different) decentering strategies that have marked other francophone literatures. Especially sophisticated in Caribbean writing, these strategies are also present to various degrees in all francophone literatures. The same logic applies to the literatures of immigration where language does not precede writing, but is part of a negotiation between two cultures, the culture "of origin" and the culture "of migration" *at the time of writing.*[5] This negotiation is probably more significant here than it is with other francophone, postcolonial literatures, because of the ideological urgency and impact that are at stake when it takes place within the former "master" culture. The study of Arabo-French literature where the language is decentered in its form and meaning clearly shows distortions that are characteristic of the presence in France of a postcolonial mentality and a postcolonial literary production, which goes well beyond the sole linguistic domain and permeates the culture. Azouz Begag's fiction is exemplary in that respect. Sustained by textual irony, a continuous process of de-writing and re-writing infiltrates language through the manipulation of (French) literary and cultural clichés. Techniques such as *verlan* (where syllables of words are reversed), the introduction of decentered glossaries, the use of distorted Arabic and French words and phrases, are devised as a strategy, *at the time of writing*. Displacements in the practice of a common language with postcolonial literatures in France lead us to reconsider the limits of the concept of *francophonie*.

It may be along these lines that one should consider a *post-francophonie* period (as in *post-colonial*, the hyphen here is the mark of the sequential) when the hegemonic position of the French language *as a linguistic and liter-*

ary norm would be diluted in a more expansive and diverse francophone diaspora. In that case, it may be possible to conceptualize a literary *post-francophonie* as well, as a mentality where the architecture of the literatures written in French is reorganized. Franco-French literature is in a situation of parallel, of intersection, or of interpenetration with other francophone literatures and no longer stands as a referential value system. The suggestion opens onto a complete revaluation of the "classico-centrist" mentality already denounced by Roland Barthes in 1969 (*Le Bruissement*), which still dictates choices for programs in French literary studies. In that sense, what the "post" in *post(-)francophonie* suggests is a dismissal of the neocolonial discourse maintained by the presence of francophone institutions around the world. It acts very much the way dismissing the hyphen does with *post-coloniality*. It removes the largely historical quality of a discourse that makes it political in nature (the paradigm may include colonialism, neocolonialism, post-colonialism, and *francophonie*), and it allows post(-)*francophonie* to evolve toward a mentality that takes into consideration cultural hybridization within France.

In French academic circles, change is apparent in a certain split between teachers of "classical" and "modern" French literature ("modern" meaning twentieth-century French literature *only*) and teachers of "francophone literatures," a term that excludes twentieth-century literature from France. Understandably, change is coming from outside. It is clearly visible in North American universities, where the positioning of "francophone studies" or "postcolonial studies" alongside "French studies" causes important shifts in programs. These moves seem to indicate a change in what constitutes literature, in its institutional, ideological, and esthetic sense, a change that is not unusual in literary History (Barthes, *Le Grain* 208). In France, the recent questioning of a canon for "French literature," seems to come from the introduction of a postcolonial mentality in the 1980s with the corpus of *beur* literature. It challenges the historical notion of a national literature, a literature of the Nation. A postcolonial perspective acknowledges that new modes of writing are generated by a political sense of what literature is (Moura 6–7). Francophone literatures have all devised writing strategies that liberate them from formal linguistic constraints propagated by the French literary Canon. This makes it impossible to treat the literatures of immigration as mere extensions of "classical" French literature. Quite to the contrary, with the literatures of immigration, the "Language of the Other" (Laronde, "Ecriture") metaphorically "postcolonizes" the French Language and Culture.

The time for the liberation of postcolonial writing within France translates into an *in-between* (literary) space that disrupts the continuities of a French national literary tradition. The position of cultural interiority occupied by postcolonial literatures authorizes a mechanism of dialectical inversion to take place. The displaced literary discourse is no longer the one that is produced at the margin, but the one that has been at the center, through peripheral subversion. The language of the center is controlled by the periphery, transformed, and restructured to be used differently in its form and content. The carrier of a hybrid identity is no longer the discourse at the periphery but the discourse at the center. In *L'écriture décentrée*, I call the phenomenon a process of "decentering" writing. In this chapter, it is presented on the institutional level with the coined terminology: "Franco-French literature." "Franco-French," acting in parallel, in intersection, or in interpenetration with the other two coined terms, "Afro-French" and "Arabo-French" literatures, represents "the inscription and articulation of culture's *hybridity*" (Bhabha, "Commitment" 38, italics in text). Probably the last frontier of resistance, and the most defining boundary, for a true (as in "complete") postcolonial literary francophone diaspora is when the site of communication is situated *within* the former center. The demythifying/demystifying role played by the literatures of immigration has to be acted out from within through subversive maneuvers and counterdiscursive strategies leveled specifically at the cultural reference, the French literary canon, in a radically alternative inscription of power.

The 1980s reactions of ostracism against *beur* fiction may well have been defense mechanisms against the "deterritorialization" of the French literary canon that introduced diglossia *inside* French literature. In a situation of post-*francophonie*, *francophonie*, considered in its linguistic dimension as a variety of spaces outside the Hexagon [France], and therefore outside "the French Language of France," exceeds its original space. The linguistic "reterritorialization" of the French language that has been taking place in francophone literatures during the *francophonie* period has promoted multilingualism (or "heterolinguism," Moura 73) outside France. During the post-*francophonie* period, "deterritorialization" will denounce monolinguism as a myth *inside France as well*; it will deter the artificial language that has long been the support of and reference for conventional literature, and it may promote a "reterritorialization" of literature—or literatures—in France through a "third code" or "third codes," an "*interlangue*" (Chantal Zabus in Moura 147) or *interlangues*, which are the linguistic equivalents of a "third space" (Bhabha) as a cultural signifier for a complete (as in "true") postcolonial post*francophone* mentality.

Notes

1. *Beur* literature, as an ethnic literature and a literature of immigration, corresponds to the definition of a "minor literature" proposed by Deleuze and Guattari: "Une littérature mineure n'est pas celle d'une langue mineure, plutôt celle qu'une minorité fait dans une langue majeure. . . . Les trois caractères de la littérature mineure sont la déterritorialisation de la langue, le branchement de l'individuel sur l'immédiat-politique, l'agencement collectif d'énonciation" [A minor literature is not the literature of a minor language, rather it is the literature written in a major language by a minority. . . . A minor literature has three characteristics: the deterritorialization of language, its immediate political value, and its collective value] (*Kafka* 29, 33, my translation).

2. The capitalization of History in this chapter refers to the official, western-told (here, by France) history of the francophone world. It stands in opposition to marginalized post-colonial "histories" that are painfully unearthed by writers as postcolonial subjects (see infra). Politics, Nation, Culture, Canon, Literature, and Language are capitalized for the same reason.

3. Should not the act of folding former colonized countries into large geopolitical units be considered a dangerous neocolonial gesture? Are not francophone West Africa, the Caribbean, the Indian Ocean, cultural artifacts created during colonial times and being "imagined" as (francophone) "communities," taken for granted as frames of reference for large contemporary cultural systems? The problem with talking of cultures as nonindividualized entities is that the study of their literatures is also lumped together into categories reproduced by Western institutions of learning that correspond to these large geopolitical units. Should not one of the major tasks of serious postcolonial-*ists* be to unfurl larger categories and uncover individual (francophone) cultural and literary practices? Malagasy literature and the literature from Reunion are quite apart. We know now that the literature of Guadeloupe and Martinique is not that of Haiti. Despite a common historical background, should we not ask ourselves if it is (still) appropriate to consider the literature from Guadeloupe and Martinique as one? As for North Africa, drastically different historical, cultural, and political interaction with France as a colonial and neocolonial power has made twenty-first-century North African nations quite different from one another. If I generally refer to Algeria only when I discuss the literature of immigration from North Africa, it is because the literature from Tunisia is nonexistent, and there are few authors with origins in Morocco. Likewise, choosing 1962, the end of the war of independence for Algeria, as a historical divider between a colonial and post-colonial mentality, is a symbolic gesture that could not be performed with reference to Morocco or Tunisia. On a macrohistorical level, 1962 is also highly symbolic of Algeria as the last country to have gained independence from France, therefore marking the end of colonial times. It is then that the question of "imagined communities" returns, with neocolonial anachronisms such as Guadeloupe and Martinique as contemporary French Overseas Departments, or even Corsica, as a French Department with manifest desires for emancipation.

4. Anamnesis is the strongest sign of the presence of the "sequential" in post-colonial times and in a postcolonial mentality. Leïla Sebbar's novel *La Seine était rouge* and Anne Donadey's book, *Recasting Postcolonialism*, are significant contributions to anamnesis

about the war of independence in Algeria. (In Paris on 17 October 1961, an unknown number of North Africans were killed after a peaceful demonstration in favor of the independence of Algeria, and many bodies were thrown into the Seine).

5. "La langue ne précède pas l'oeuvre postcoloniale. L'écrivain y négocie un code langagier, propre à sa culture et à son individualité. . . . [É]crire est un véritable acte de langage, le choix d'une langue d'écriture engageant de fait toute une conception de la littérature. A cause de sa situation, l'écrivain francophone est condamné à *penser la langue*" [Language does not precede postcolonial writing. A writer finds in it a linguistic code appropriate to her/his own culture and individuality. . . . Writing is a true act of language since the choice of a language for writing involves in fact a comprehensive conception of literature. Because of her/his situation, a francophone writer is forced to *think the language*] (Moura 71, my translation, my emphasis).

Works Cited

Anderson, Benedict. 1983. *Imagined Communities: Reflections on the Origin and Spread of Nationalism*. London: Verso, 1991.

Barthes, Roland. 1969. *Le Bruissement de la langue: essais critiques IV*. Reprint, Paris: Seuil, 1984. 45–56.

———. *Le Grain de la voix: entretiens 1962–1980*. Paris: Seuil, 1981. 204–11.

Begag, Azouz. *Le Gône du Chaâba*. Paris: Seuil, 1986.

Bhabha, Homi K. "The Commitment to Theory." In *The Location of Culture*. London: Routledge, 1994. 19–39.

———. "Introduction: Locations of Culture." In *The Location of Culture*. London: Routledge, 1994. 1–18.

Boukhedenna, Sakinna. *Journal "Nationalité: immigré(e)."* Paris: L'Harmattan, 1987.

Dadié, Bernard. *Un Nègre à Paris*. Paris: Présence africaine, 1955.

Deleuze, Gilles. *Mille plateaux*. Paris: Editions de Minuit, 1973.

Deleuze, Gilles, and Felix Guattari. *Kafka: pour une littérature mineure*. Paris: Editions de Minuit, 1975.

Donadey, Anne. *Recasting Postcolonialism: Women Writing between Worlds*. Portsmouth, N.H.: Heinemann, 2001.

Essomba, J. R. *Le Paradis du nord*. Paris: Présence africaine, 1996.

Glissant, Edouard. *Poétique de la relation*. Paris: Gallimard, 1990.

Houari, Kassa. *Confessions d'un immigré: un Algérien à Paris*. Paris: Lieu commun, 1988.

Houari, Leïla. *Zeïda de nulle part*. Paris: L'Harmattan, 1985.

Kettane, Nacer. *Le Sourire de Brahim*. Paris: Denoël, 1985.

Laronde, Michel. *Autour du roman beur: immigration et identité*. Paris: L'Harmattan, 1993.

———. "L'Ecriture décentrée." *L'Ecriture décentrée*. Ed. Michel Laronde. Paris: L'Harmattan, 1996. 7–14.

———. "Evolution de la littérature arabo-française." *Vives Lettres* 1 (2000): 161–75.

———. "Les littératures des immigrations en France. Question de nomenclature et directions de recherche." *Le Maghreb littéraire* 1.2 (1997): 25–44.

Laronde, Michel, ed. *L'Ecriture décentrée: la langue de l'Autre dans le roman contemporain*. Paris: L'Harmattan, 1996.
Laye, Camara. *L'Enfant noir*. Paris: Plon, 1953.
Mabanckou, Alain. *Bleu-Blanc-Rouge*. Paris: Présence africaine, 1998.
Mokeddem, Malika. *L'Interdite*. Paris: Grasset et Fasquelle, 1993.
Moura, Jean-Marc. *Littératures francophones et théorie postcoloniale*. Paris: Presses universitaires de France, 1999.
Pineau, Gisèle. *L'Exil selon Julia*. Paris: Stock, 1996.
———. *Un Papillon dans la cité*. Paris: Sépia, 1992.
Sebbar, Leïla. *Le Baiser*. Paris: Hachette Livre, 1997.
———. *Fatima, ou, Les Algériennes au square*. Paris: Stock, 1981.
———. *La Jeune fille au balcon*. Paris: Seuil, 1996.
———. *La Négresse à l'enfant*. Paris: Syros-Alternatives, 1990.
———. *La Seine était rouge*. Paris: Thierry Magnier, 1999.
———. *Soldats*. Paris: Seuil, 1999.
Sebbar, Leïla, ed. *Une Enfance algérienne*. Paris: Gallimard, 1997.
———. *Une Enfance outremer*. Paris: Seuil, 2001.
Sembène, Ousmane. *Le Docker noir*. Paris: Présence africaine, 1956.
Smaïl, Paul. *Ali le Magnifique*. Paris: Denoël, 2001.
———. *Casa, la casa*. Paris: Balland, 1998.
———. *La Passion selon moi*. Paris: Robert Laffont, 1999.
———. *Vivre me tue*. Paris: Balland, 1997.
Tadjer, Akli. *Les A.N.I. du "Tassili."* Paris: Seuil, 1984.
Tournier, Michel. *La Goutte d'or*. Paris: Gallimard, 1986.

11

The Francophone Postcolonial Field

Jacques Coursil and Delphine Perret

In order to grasp the purpose of a francophone postcolonial critique, is it necessary to revisit the categories of history and to undertake a study of discourse production.[1] The history in question is that of colonization, decolonization, and globalization; the language of the discourse is French in its relationship with regional and other international languages. The first area of inquiry interrogates the epistemological necessity of a critique of history; the second calls into question discourse itself in its ambiguities, its contradictions, and its inherent tropisms.

One could represent the francophone postcolonial field as the intersection of two domains: postcolonial discourse theory and francophone literary studies. However, such an intersection is not a simple object to construct. As simple as it might seem, the translation of the English word *postcolonial* into French is a very tricky proposition, both intellectually and culturally. In French-speaking countries, this word is not in common use, neither on the street nor in the press and is seldom used even in academic circles, where it is viewed as an anglicism.

It is not very difficult, in French, to make sense of a word whose translation is a literal transcription. Nevertheless, unlike the derivative *postmodern*, which has actually made its way into the French language, the word *postcolonial* and the interrogative corollaries that accompany it have been resisted in francophone literary studies despite the powerful interest the postcolonial paradigm has raised in anglophone countries. This resistance (in a Freudian sense) is particularly interesting since much of the theoretical apparatus of postcolonial studies is drawn from French work in philosophy and related critiques, such as structuralism, poststructuralism, and psychoanalysis, and since the colonial paradigm functions through similar discursive principles. In other words, the methodologies of francophone studies and postcolonial theory are not symmetrical. Postcolonial discourse theory, to a greater extent than francophone studies, stresses forms of language use. "Language is a fundamental site of struggle for post-colonial discourse because the colonial process itself begins in language" (Ashcroft, Griffiths, and Tiffin 283).

The materiality of colonization, including its corollaries of violent territorial appropriation, genocide, the slave trade, and its related exploitation of entire peoples is not to be denied. However, there is another dimension that continues to this day, one we encounter in the writing of the revolutionary, essayist, and psychoanalyst Frantz Fanon. Colonization also entails a psychic alienation, for which language is the only medium. What is named "blessure sacrée" [blessed wound] by Césaire (233), "plaies indélébiles" [indelible wounds] by Fanon (299), "coupure radicale" [radical split] and "névroses" [neuroses] by Glissant (*Discours antillais* 133), is what remains after five centuries of colonial history. Thus, postcolonial discourse theory emphasizes the necessity of reading both language and the commonplace representations that underlie discourses, discourses of the ex-colonizers as well as the ex-colonized. Both, in the crucial diversity of their respective experiences, share analogous psycho-clinical patterns, and both use the same language patterns in equally conflicted ways.

Every stick, every whip has two ends, and at each end there is a subject. Each one offers his or her fragmentary, and thus imaginary, version of a real and shared drama; Prospero and Caliban, the master and the slave (whose conflict has so effectively been used as a metaphor for anticolonialism and resistance), must also be viewed as two broken characters occupying roles in the same drama, in the same theater, where their antagonistic discourses are performed. As Memmi wrote: "For if colonization destroys the colonized, it also rots the colonizer" (*Colonizer* xvii). Not surprisingly, postcolonial discourse theory takes its themes primarily from the poetics of writers, and from formerly colonized nations. As Said notes: "None of us would disagree, I think, if in the first instance we were to interpret the great mass of recent non-European literature as expressing ideas, values, emotions formerly suppressed, ignored, or denigrated by, and of course in, the well-known metropolitan centers" ("Figures" 3). It was specifically with the publication of Edward Said's landmark work *Orientalism* (1978) that the discursive aspect of colonial representation first appeared as a paradigm shift in literary criticism. In it, Said wrote: "The Orient has helped to define Europe (or the west) as its contrasting image, idea, personality, experience. Yet none of this Orient is merely imaginative. The Orient is an integral part of European material civilization and culture" (1–2).

Since 85 percent of the world has been affected by western hegemony, colonial and postcolonial questions concern almost all societies, and every particular history is but one account in that common history. Even a country that is only a point on the map contains a part of the history of the whole world.

The Advent of the Globalized Representation of the Earth

The European navigators of the sixteenth century, including Columbus, da Gama, and Magellan, achieved a monadic enclosure of the world. The journey around the world and the shock of the ensuing encounters made possible the advent of its global representation (see Koyré).[2] For these Europeans, everything added up consistently: metaphysics declared it (as early as Parmenides, sixth century B.C.), the newly born mathematical physics demonstrated it (Copernicus, Galileo, sixteenth century), and planetary travels showed that the earth was neither flat nor the fixed center of the universe but rather a globe orbiting the sun. As this radical transformation of the representation of the planet was taking over, older representations were displaced and progressively began to fade away: no longer were there infinite spaces or forbidden abysses on earth.

Before the emergence of this globalized conception of the earth, there were different worlds, some in contact with each other and yet others unaware of each other. In the representations that preceded the "discoveries," revealed by European cartography of the time, the world in its physical reality, its proportions, its human and cultural diversity, had not yet appeared. With Christopher Columbus and the other navigators, one moved from a plurality of worlds, each one living its own history, to a fully global perception; a unique representation emerged, Earth. The shock of this advent entailed the end of the autonomy of many "worlds," and sometimes also the end of their very existence (Glissant, *Intention* 12).

History is a discourse that presupposes a represented object. Thus, the history of the world (as the whole world) could not begin before its representation was established in human consciousness. As such, the history of the global world is only as old as its representation, which is to say only five centuries old. Commenting on Glissant, Michel-Rolf Trouillot notes: "The world became global five centuries ago. The rise of the west, the conquest of the Americas, New World slavery, and the Industrial Revolution can be summarized as 'a first moment of globality'" (8).

The Western World: A Place or a Project?

> L'Occident n'est pas à l'ouest. Ce n'est pas un lieu, c'est un projet.
> [The western world is not in the west. It is not a place, but a project.]
> **Edouard Glissant**

Glissant's formulation of the western world as not a place but a project (*Discours antillais* 12 n. 1) turns an improper geographic representation of "the west" (which is neither in the west nor the east, any more than it is in the north or south) into a narrative of a global project that he calls *La Relation* (*Intention* 17).[3] This "western project," born in Europe at the end of the Renaissance, is without doubt the most formidable enterprise of conquest in the history of humanity. One can conceive of it as a permanent world war that lasted for five centuries. In the resistances it met, the rivalries between conquerors, its reversals of fortune, and its incomplete nature, the project was always meant to be a global one. In its very structure, it could not limit its scope to anything less than the whole world and all of humanity, and this systematic hegemonic propensity is still obvious in the complex questions of today's globalization.

The culture of hegemony on a global scale stemmed in Europe from the geographical experience of the globe and its astronomical and geometrical representations. In the sixteenth century, possessing ocean fleets and guns, Europeans were further ahead in military technology than all the people they met. After five centuries of resistance and submission of colonized peoples and conflicts between the conquerors, the flexibility of such powers of intervention in all areas of the globe has resulted in the remnants of fragmented empires that correspond to the world as we know it today.

The west as a project does not represent a specific people or a specific place, but a global political (economic, juridical, cultural) intention, which has continued to maintain itself, in all periods and under all political regimes (Wallerstein, *Modern*, "Rise"). To date, none of the revolutions in western countries, which have been numerous and often radical, has succeeded in derailing this hegemonic goal to be everywhere at once (for lack of being everything). In other words, the western project is an autonomous system; its only dynamics are its expansion, the resistance it encounters, and its internal implosions.

The enterprise and execution of this western project of global conquest has been a crucial event at one moment or another in the history of all the people of the earth. Local histories across the worlds have all gone through the concrete advent of this unification of the world. It is because of this political shock that all human societies share a common history, lived and told in as many ways as there are protagonists and points of view. National historiographies, especially those of the former colonizers as well as those of the formerly colonized, often mask this common tale of the history of the world intrinsic to each society, for the sake of political identity.

Rhetoric in the Field

> Nous pensons un univers que notre langue a d'abord modelé.
> [We think of a universe that was first modeled by our language.]
> **Emile Benveniste**

The term *post-colonial* in its literal chronological meaning has been used by historians and critics to discuss decolonization and the postindependence period. However, in the wake of global capitalism, the term tends to be used today to point out the cultural and subjective effects of colonization and their consequences.[4] Thus, postcolonial theory should not be viewed as a theory of decolonization, but rather as an intellectual attitude that studies the traces of the psychic experience (and trauma) of colonization through representation. Ashcroft, Griffiths, and Tiffin write: "'Post-colonial' as we define it does not mean 'post-independence,' or 'after colonialism,' for this would be to falsely ascribe an end to the colonial process. Post-colonialism, rather, begins from the very first moment of colonial contact. It is the discourse of oppositionality which colonialism brings into being. In this sense, post-colonial writing has a very long history" (117).

Colonization and Decolonization, with Special Reference to France

The rhetoric surrounding the use of the words *colonial* and *postcolonial* shows that the methodology of classification by dictionaries or nomenclatures is not refined enough to give an accurate account of a language at work within history.[5] Colonial power is by definition external and implies a metropolitan center ruling it. Thus, a conquest with settlement is a colony as long as it is commanded and controlled by a distant metropolitan center. This settling, which is always an act of war, implies the resistance and finally the submission of the original inhabitants, but must also be effected in the name of an external center of power. Thus, the conquest of territories and the submission of their inhabitants are not sufficient to define colonization. One knows, for example, that Duke William of Normandy became king of England by his conquest of it, but we also know that King Louis Philippe of France did not become bey of Algiers by conquering Algeria. In other words, England (which had been a Roman colony) has never been a Norman colony, while Algeria became a French colony.

Imperialism imposes its control on states, but colonialism destroys them; it destroys even their names and their borders, destabilizes their social relations and previous land allocations. As a result, the decolonization of a state does not necessarily presuppose its prior colonization. For instance, Upper Volta (today Burkina Faso) did not exist before colonization and in fact came into being only during the dismantling of what was then the "Soudan Occidental Français" [French Western Sudan].[6] Thus, the decolonization of Burkina Faso did not follow the colonization of its territory. Similarly, the Republic of Mali is not located on the foundations of the ancient empire of Mali; the symbolic appropriation of the name does not erase the colonial origin of the drawing of its borders. It is the same for all the other states directly or indirectly created from the Berlin Conference (1885), which ordered the distribution of African territories between the main European powers. One therefore understands that the national perception of the citizens of these new states is different, for instance, from that of the Egyptian citizens whose territory, often invaded and colonized, was never dismantled. The term *postcolonial* can thus be applied to states that were born out of decolonization itself. Such is the sophistry: the prefix "post" does not have in these cases a symmetrical anteriority: before being "post," these states did not exist.

In the Caribbean islands, the French conquered Martinique in 1635 and completed the genocide of the Carib Indians around 1658. In the literal meaning of the word, one can observe that during this first period of colonization, the ones who were "colonized" were the Caribs, and not the Africans who were later captured, sold, and deported through the slave trade. But in the middle of the nineteenth century, capitalist colonialism replaced colonial slavery as the predominant social order. As abolition took place, the slaves, not without irony, became the "colonized people" without having being colonized initially. A century later, in the French West Indies, the law of departmentalization (1946) abolished the colonial order through the assimilation of the "colonized" population as full French citizens. In this particular case, decolonization consists, then, not in independence but in an "assimilation" of the colonized by the colonizer.[7] We could give many more examples showing that the words *colonial* and *postcolonial* should not be read as theoretical concepts, but rather as historical tropes.

The Snag of Loose Usage

The word *postcolonial* seems vague from a positivist viewpoint, since its reference is not unequivocal. However, both the philosophy of language and psychoanalysis insist on the fact that there is nothing truly vague in human speech (precisely when it is considered to be such). J. L. Austin calls this point "the snag of Loose . . . Usage" (183).[8] As such, the word *postcolonial* is not vague but rather is used to catch meanings that can only be given by tropisms. In postcolonial discourse theory, the tropological figures of rhetoric constitute the only conceptual tools available, since logical classifications and nomenclatures have shown their limitations as discussed above. Thus, postcolonial theorists have been particularly concerned with the tropisms of historical discourse when applied to colonialism. As Spivak notes:

> Postcolonial studies, unwittingly commemorating a lost object, can become an alibi unless it is placed within a general frame. Colonial Discourse studies, when they concentrate only on the representation of the colonized or the matter of the colonies, can sometimes serve the production of current neocolonial knowledge by placing colonialism/imperialism securely in the past, and/or by suggesting a continuous line from that past to our present. This situation complicates the fact that postcolonial/colonial discourse studies is becoming a substantial subdisciplinary ghetto. In spite of the potential for cooptation, however, there can be no doubt that the apparently crystalline disciplinary mainstream runs muddy if these studies do not provide a persistent dredging operation (1).

The failure of meta-definitions in postcolonial discourse theory does not imply the lack of a precise object (a "lost object"). Indeed it shows that while the domain is heterogeneous, it is not deprived of its order. On the contrary, the postcolonial question constitutes a very clear and important aspect of the crisis of contemporary humanism and culture: a crisis in western certainties and values, as identified by Sigmund Freud or Hannah Arendt.

Postmodern Asteism

The prefix "post" is one of the key concepts of the postmodern paradigm from which postcolonial discourse derives (Lyotard, Jameson, Bongie).[9] The rhetoric of "post" is recursive; it displaces the predicate "modern" in a loop. After modernity, it is still modernity, as after today's present, it will still be the present. The expression *post/modern* frees itself from this circle, as it is not a descriptive concept but a trope. This trope is called asteism, which consists in transgressing an absolute limit: in our case a limit of time.[10] Postmodern asteism enacts the closure of modern times on itself. It criticizes modernism, for which the future will be by definition more modern than today's present, making this present always late in relation to social time. Modernism is shown as a prophetic discourse between a present that is always outdated and a future whose signs are just beginning to appear; "modern man" is on the brim of time.[11]

Analogously, the word *postcolonial*, like *postmodern*, is caught in a loop: it contains some past but no future in its definition. In other words, *postcolonial* designates a concept in which the beginning can be shown, but not the end, since there is no criterion to indicate when a society should no longer be considered postcolonial. Displaying this sophistry shows that *post-colonial* is not an operational concept, but a trope as mentioned earlier.

The Francophone Paradox

> Je n'ai jamais pu accepter la sorte de vague ralliement
> qu'est la francophonie.
> [I have never been able to accept the sort of vague assemblage that is Francophonie.]
> **Edouard Glissant**

For Salman Rushdie, the category of Commonwealth literature is a false construct, one both confused and suspicious from a political viewpoint. Moreover, the idea of postcolonial literature is not compatible with the idea of literature itself: "South Africa and Pakistan, for instance, are not members of the Commonwealth, but their authors apparently belong to its literature. On the other hand, England, which, as far as I'm aware, has not been expelled from the Commonwealth quite yet, has been excluded from its literary manifestation. For obvious reasons. It would never do to include English literature, the great sacred thing itself, with this bunch of upstarts, huddling together under this new and badly made umbrella" (Rushdie 62).

With a few analytical differences, Rushdie's argument with regard to the Commonwealth can be transposed to the field of francophone literatures, although the classification of the literatures in the English language under the expression "English literature" (Rushdie) does not have an equivalent in French. On account of a complex range of uses, the classification of francophone literatures under the name of French literature would be meaningless; and the opposite, the classification of French literature under the rubric francophone worldwide literatures, has yet to be adopted.

In the French language, the expression "francophone literature" is not only restricted to (non)-French but, in a greater sense, to (non)-European; "traditionally"[12] the literatures from French-speaking Switzerland, Belgium, Luxembourg, etc., are not termed "francophone" in France; this is also true for philosophy, songs, and cinema (Rousseau, Verhaeren, Michaux, Brel, Godard). On the other hand, Césaire, Fanon, Glissant, and Condé, who are French citizens, are classified as "francophone" writers. Use does not ignore history. What is termed "francophone" has to be related one way or another to colonial history, that of Canada, the Cajuns, the Antilles, sub-Saharan Africa, Madagascar, the Maghreb, or Lebanon, but does not apply to neighboring European nations that have never been colonized by France. As an example, a special "francophone" show on French television on letters and word games is expected to present non-European French-speaking persons. The irony here, as Hargreaves indicates, is that European writers who immigrated to France from nonfrancophone countries, such as Samuel Beckett, born in Ireland, or more recently Andrei Makine, born in Russia, have their books classified as "French" literature by librarians and booksellers, while writers of Maghrebi or similar origin, such as Mehdi Charef, Azouz Begag, and Farida Belghoul, who were raised and often born in metropolitan France, do not find their books appearing in anthologies of "French" literature. This latter point shows the difficulty in defining/redefining French identity. Herein lies the francophone paradox: is Rousseau (who was from Geneva but is always presented as a French philosopher) francophone?

Rule of the Attribute and the Epithet

In order to explain this apparent semantic shift, grammar proposes a rule (the rule of the attribute and of the epithet) that distinguishes two uses for the same word.[13] In the first one, *francophone* subsumes all subjects who speak French; *francophone* is then an attribute of these subjects. In the second one, besides asserting "the use of French language" (as an attribute), the epithet *francophone* is a mode of nomination. In this case, it is used by the French (European) "center" to distinguish itself from its peripheral "Others." Thus, the use of postcolonial presupposes stories or experiences shared by the speakers and is clearly understood as an epithet, evoking, in a subtle but imperative way, a history and a status.

Francophone as an epithet is defined by three characteristic features described (in French / non-French (non-European) / cultural) as germane to "francophone literature," "francophone songs," "francophone cinema," etc. It remains an attribute in all other cases, as in "francophone communication" or "francophone business," where it only means "in French." This use of *francophone* as a French epithet has been shaped by colonial history, and the word takes on its meaning only within this history, integrating the entire colonial and postcolonial paradigm.

Worldwide Languages and Demography

The English, Spanish, and French languages, leading participants and competitors in globalization, are spoken by 600 million, 350 million, and 135 million speakers respectively.[14] The number of speakers of Portuguese (180 million) is larger than that of French speakers; however, the worldwide status of both languages is not equivalent. The same applies to Russian (285 million), Hindi Urdu (450 million), and Mandarin (1 billion). Measuring the number of speakers of these languages does not translate into equivalent weight in today's worldwide culture, though one can agree on the necessity of a critical minimum size for a worldwide language. The cultural power of languages is not directly linked to the birthrate. A greater number of speakers of a language may be an apparent reason for satisfaction but is a poor indication of its political, economic, and cultural strength. Clearly, the quantitative measure of languages is too simple a means for inferring their scope. To define the political, economic, and cultural status of a language, accounting methods are not enough; one needs a history.

If one compares French to English and Spanish as the three current finalists of the same colonial epic, one can observe, beyond differences in status, a basic opposition. Where English and Spanish are spoken as mother tongues, neither the British, in the case of the English language, nor the peninsular Spanish, in the case of the Spanish language, are the depositories of their idiom. The main international languages do not depend on a metropolitan linguistic monopoly. Their planetary propensity is not compatible with a fantasy of linguistic ownership. In France, however, French tends to be considered as a national cultural possession. Thus, while French has a tendency to remain a North-South-oriented language, English and Spanish have taken on a more global orientation.

Francophone communication is structured around the center-periphery model, rather than being effected through translateral networks. In other words, although some works may also be published in Strasbourg and Marseille, in French-speaking European countries, Algeria, Senegal, the Caribbean islands, and above all, Quebec, the cultural prestige of francophonie is centered squarely in Paris. Paris is still the place where most literary production happens and where it is showcased. The former metropolis, though caught in the francophone paradox, has become the cultural center of the entire francophone world.

Multilateral exchanges, although very desirable, are very difficult to achieve in the present economic form of neoliberal globalization. It is a known fact that neoliberalism has accelerated the process of connecting the economies of the peripheral countries to the global market.[15] Therefore, countries sharing the same language, in the same area, and at the same level of development become competitors and lose the economic complementarities that would have encouraged their economic exchanges and consequently their verbal and cultural exchanges. Since francophone communication is regulated by this imperative direct transit through the world market, multilateral relationships lose their basis. The schemas of translateral exchanges are then destructured by the obligatory economic reference to the center, preferably the former colonizing metropolis, which belongs to the group of the seven or eight richest nations in the world.

Conclusion: "Dissensions That Always Existed in the City"

It would be erroneous to look for critics of the imperial west only outside of its borders. Like the "Dissensions that always existed in the City" evoked in Montesquieu's Rome, the western world, whose intention has always been a complete conquest of the earth, has gone through internal conflicts and contradictory tensions since the very beginning.[16] From Montaigne's time to current times, western societies have been producing their own counterdiscourses. It would be vain to ignore the huge critical questioning that took place in all domains of knowledge during the twentieth century and that initiated a crisis in positive reasoning and values. Scientific disciplines in their present epistemologies do not want to, and can no longer, be used as metaphysical frameworks for discourse. Today, positivism is no longer a sufficient criterion for the sciences themselves, and such concepts as universal truths have tended to become dubious notions. For the most part, fundamental disciplines, in each of their respective fields, have criticized or criticize determinism (nonstandard mathematics and logic, studies of unstable systems, etc.). And one may notice that the sciences do not declare themselves "western" so comfortably anymore. However, despite this thoroughgoing and forceful critique, common sense remains strongly logocentric in modern societies. We are aware that this logocentrism has been one of the most powerful means of construction of colonial representations.

At each step of our examination of the francophone postcolonial field, we have exposed the difficulties engendered by the conceptual tools and methods originating from positivist rationalism concerning issues such as the global representation of the earth, semantic definitions in the field, communicative activities in an international language and more specifically in the francophone world. These conceptual tools are commonplace in modern societies; however, they are overly simplistic and in the long term hinder critical analysis. The representations they create hide the real complexity of the field and its constantly renewed wealth of information beneath a simple logic. We have stressed that tropes are, today, the only way to address the complex issues raised by the francophone postcolonial field, as well as the implications of using these tropes. More specifically, we have seen that the francophone paradox explains why the word *postcolonial* is not used in French. French people from France, who are francophone by attribute, do not designate themselves by the epithet *francophone*. This epithet, with the exception of

French-speaking Europeans, covers de facto the postcolonial field. It is a fact that the word *francophone* has been mostly shaped by its use within the French political world, whereas *postcolonial* has been shaped by its relationship with the anglophone academic world. What both reveal is that changes in semantics are good indicators of similar, or even parallel, changes taking place in representation. For this reason, the way in which the word *francophone* evolves will continue to be of critical interest.

Notes

1. We want to thank Steve Arkin, Michèle Praeger, Tsitsi E. Jaji, and Duane Rudolph, who contributed to this work by their comments and suggestions concerning the documentation and issues under discussion, as well as establishing the text in English.

2. The writings of Koyré are essential in the study of cultural and social representations and their transformations. They constitute a major theoretical reference in francophone studies. In *Etudes galiléennes*, Koyré studies the effect of the heliocentric revolution on people's representations and cultures in the late European Renaissance.

3. In French, the word *relation* means both "link" and "relater" [telling a story].

4. Arif Dirlik notes: "The term *postcolonial* in its various usages carries a multiplicity of meanings that need to be distinguished for analytical purposes. Three uses of the term seem to me to be especially prominent (and significant): (*a*) as a literal description of conditions in formerly colonial societies, in which case the term has concrete referents, as in postcolonial societies or postcolonial intellectuals; (*b*) as a description of a global condition after the period of colonialism, in which case the usage is somewhat more abstract and less concrete in reference, comparable in vagueness to the earlier term *Third World*, for which it is intended as a substitute; and (*c*) *as a description of a discourse on the above-named conditions that is informed by the epistemological and psychic orientations that are products of those conditions*" (emphasis ours) (331–32).

5. See Shohat on this topic.

6. The colonization of Western Sudan corresponds to the destruction of the Mossi kingdom, of the Toucouleur empire of El Hadj Omar Tall, of the Wolof empires, etc.

7. The assimilation of a colonized population in the citizenship of a colonizing state marks the legal end of the colonial order. The colony is abolished *de juris*, the territories and the populations are absorbed in the republic. One can thus understand—as is the case for the DOM (Départements d'Outre-Mer [French Overseas Departments])—that the questions of autonomy, independence, and identity, can be articulated only on the basis of the assimilation process.

8. Austin notes: "Well, people's usages do vary, and we do talk loosely . . . [b]ut first, not nearly as much as one would think . . . a genuinely loose or eccentric talker is a rare specimen to be prized" (183–84).

9. "The entangled condition that I am gesturing toward in the word 'post/colonial' can be read in parallel with Lyotard's more recent uses of the word 'postmodern,' in which it signals not a 'new age' following upon modernity (as was suggested in his

earlier, and implicitly avant-gardist, formulations of the concept in the 1979 *La condition postmoderne*) but a self-reflective component of that modernity: 'neither modernity nor the so-called postmodernity can be identified and defined as clearcut historical entities'" (Bongie 13).

10. Example of asteism: "This girl is too beautiful, too intelligent, and too charming." In each use, *too* goes beyond the limits of an absolute.

11. The meaning of *modern*, from *modernus*, meaning what belongs to "the time of the one who speaks," or to a recent time, began to change in the middle of the nineteenth century with the appearance of *modernité*, which started closing the present as a historical reference appearing at the same time absolute, impossible to outdate, but always outdated; the term *modernism*, born in the early twentieth century, aggravated the problem.

12. We can observe that, in other contexts, such as in American universities, the expression *francophone studies* can be used to refer to the study of all cultural productions in the French language.

13. Thus, languages distinguish two semantic uses of adjectives, as attributes and as epithets: "My friend is old" (attribute), "an old friend" (epithet), "Platanov is crazy" (attribute), "This crazy Platanov" (epithet). An attribute predicates a property of an object that can be true or false; an epithet is a way to designate it. Some epithets are flattering and others not so, some are innocent and others embarrassing.

14. These numbers from Malherbe are approximate and include speakers using these languages as a second language. Ager estimates that there are 110 million French speakers in the world.

15. A minority during the Keynesian years that followed the Second World War, 1945–50, neoliberalism (F. Von Hayek, Milton Friedman) was progressively imposed as a mode of thought, transforming in particular the institutions of Bretton Woods (World Bank, IMF), which were, when they were created, tools of intervention for governments and central banks. Free trade, the minimal intervention of public powers, the theory and the myth or the fable of an economy without regulations, even without states, is now presented as the only alternative to its radical and disastrous opposite, planned collectivism. Many contemporary economists such as Salama-Valier, political science specialists, and historians such as Susan George, as well as a number of world movements of the civil society, resist this "neo-Darwinian" conception of economic relations. Neoliberalism is a caricature of modernity based on the most obscure myths, such as "the fight for life," analogous to the "state of nature." The concept of conflict is understood as the human telos: competition between states, regions, enterprises groups, and individuals. Ultra-competition profits only the center and ruins the periphery that cannot follow the race, mostly the countries from the postcolonial Third World that did not go through the process of accumulation of industrialization.

16. In *Considerations*, Montesquieu shows in his main chapter, "The Dissensions That Always Existed in the City," that Rome, "owner of the world," was not monolithic, but organized around its inner conflicts.

Works Cited

Ager, Dennis. *Identity, Insecurity and Image: France and Language.* Clevedon, U.K.: Cleveland Multilingual Matters, 1999.

Arendt, Hannah. 1954. *Between Past and Future: Eight Exercises in Political Thought.* New York: Viking, 1968.

———. *La Crise de la culture.* Trans. Patrick Lévy. Paris: Gallimard, 1972.

Ashcroft, Bill, Gareth Griffiths, and Helen Tiffin, eds. *The Post-Colonial Studies Reader.* London: Routledge, 1995.

Austin, J. L. 1961. "A Plea for Excuses." *Philosophical Papers.* Ed. J. O. Urmson and G. J. Warnock. Oxford, U.K.: Clarendon Press, 1970. 175–204.

Bongie, Chris, *Islands and Exiles. The Creole Identities of Post/Colonial Literature.* Stanford, Calif.: Stanford University Press, 1998.

Césaire, Aimé. "Moi laminaire, calendrier lagunaire." *Aimé Césaire: anthologie poétique.* Ed. Roger Toumson. Paris: Imprimerie nationale, 1996. 233–34.

Dirlik, Arif. "The Postcolonial Aura: Third World Criticism in the Age of Global Capitalism." *Critical Inquiry* 20 (Winter 1994): 328–56.

Fanon, Frantz. 1961. *Les Damnés de la terre.* Paris: Gallimard, 1991.

Freud, Sigmund. 1929. *Civilization and Its Discontents.* Trans. James Strachey. London: Norton, 1961.

Glissant, Edouard. *Caribbean Discourse: Selected Essays.* Trans. J. Michael Dash. Charlottesville: University Press of Virginia, 1989.

———. *Le Discours antillais.* Paris: Seuil, 1981.

———. *L'Intention poétique.* Paris: Seuil, 1969.

———. *Traité du Tout-Monde.* Paris: Gallimard, 1997.

Hargreaves, Alec G. "Francophonie and Globalisation: France at the Crossroads." *Francophone Voices.* Ed. Kamal Salhi. Exeter, U.K.: Elm Bank, 1999. 49–57.

Jameson, Fredric. *Postmodernism or the Cultural Logic of Late Capitalism.* Durham, N.C.: Duke University Press, 1992.

Koyré, Alexandre. *Études galiléennes.* Paris: Herman, 1939.

———. *Galileo Studies.* Trans. John Mepham. Atlantic Highlands, N.J.: Humanities Press, 1978.

Lyotard, Jean François. *La Condition postmoderne.* Paris: Editions de Minuit, 1979.

———. *The Postmodern Condition: A Report on Knowledge.* Trans. Geoff Bennington and Brian Massumi. Minneapolis: University of Minnesota Press, 1984.

Malherbe, Michel. *Les Langages de l'humanité.* Paris: Seghers, 1983.

Memmi, Albert. *The Colonizer and the Colonized.* Trans. Howard Greenfeld. New York: Orion Press, 1965.

———. *Portrait du colonisé, précédé du portrait du colonisateur.* Paris: Buchet/Chastel, 1957.

Montesquieu, Charles Louis de Secondat. 1734. *Considerations on the Causes of the Greatness of the Romans and Their Decline.* Trans. David Lowenthal. New York: Free Press, 1965.

———. *Considérations sur les causes de la grandeur des Romains et de leur décadence.* Ed. Gabriel Compayré. Paris: Armand Colin, 1917.

Rushdie, Salman. 1983. "'Commonwealth Literature' Does Not Exist." *Imaginary Homelands: Essays and Criticism 1981–1991*. London: Granta, 1991. 61–70.

Said, Edward W. "Figures, Confirmations, Transfigurations." *Race and Class* 32.1 (1990): 1–16.

———. *Orientalism*. New York: Pantheon, 1978.

Shohat, Ella. "Notes on the 'Post-Colonial.'" *Social Text* 31–32 (1992): 99–113.

Spivak, Gayatri Chakravorty. *A Critique of Postcolonial Reason: Toward a History of the Vanishing Present*. Cambridge, Mass.: Harvard University Press, 1999.

Trouillot, Michel-Rolf. "The Perspective of the World: Globalization Then and Now." *Beyond Dichotomies: Histories, Identities, Cultures, and the Challenge of Globalization*. Ed. Elisabeth Mudimbe-Boyi. Albany: State University of New York Press, 2002. 3–20.

Wallerstein, Immanuel. *The Modern World System: Capitalist Agriculture and the Origin of the European World-Economy in the Sixteenth Century*. New York: Academic Press, 1974.

———. "The Rise and Future Demise of the World Capitalist System: Concepts for Comparative Analysis." *Comparative Studies in Society and History* 16.3 (1974): 387–415.

IV

Theorizing the Black Atlantic

12

Borders, Books, and *Points de Repère*

Renée Larrier

> One needs to be vigilant against simple notions of identity which overlap neatly with language or location.
> **Gayatri Spivak**

> La migration est une position de parole.
> [Migration is a speech position.]
> **Joël Des Rosiers**

> The Dyaspora are people with their feet planted in both worlds.
> **Jean Dominique (qtd. in Edwidge Danticat, *The Butterfly's Way*)**

One highlight of La Fête de l'Internet in March 2002 was the historic live meeting that reunited Aimé Césaire in Fort-de-France and Joseph Zobel in Paris in an event honoring Léopold Sédar Senghor. New technology permitted these two old friends to interact despite their location on two different continents. Border crossings in which passports, visas, work permits, and the knowledge of a foreign language are necessary involve Edouard Glissant, Maryse Condé, and Assia Djebar, who are distinguished professors at prestigious universities in New York City and yet continue to produce books in French. For Haitian writers, however, the situation is usually more complicated. Because of their particular experience of exile and displacement, since the 1960s especially, another dimension of the language issue is imposed. While authors who left Haiti more than thirty years ago continue to write in French or Creole, some who relocated to the United States more recently or were raised here have begun to publish in English and thus disturb the francophone studies frame. How are these writers classified, and how should they be? Does and should the francophone/postcolonial studies frame accommodate them? What are the implications for our research and teaching? Can we justify reading these writers in our French courses?

Border crossing involving Haitian writers also raises broader questions of identity. With so many residing outside of Haiti,[1] what are the criteria for inclusion in the designation of Haitian writer: birthplace? nationality? country of residence? language? Who decides? Due to the accessibility of texts, contemporary Haitian literature produced abroad is more familiar to those of us teaching at U.S. universities. Drawing on various discourses of identity, I will examine the situation of the contemporary Haitian writer whose language of production often depends on his or her location. I argue that the conventional inside/outside division of Haitian literature is inadequate. Haitian literature is produced in different languages—French, Creole, English, and Spanish—in different locations, and to read it solely within the francophone frame is to do it a disservice. Haitian literature is truly a transnational one.

In some respects, national borders have become more and more permeable. Single-currency systems in francophone West Africa, the anglophone Caribbean and, most recently, in western Europe are just a few examples. Satellite television, the Internet, and e-mail not only make information more accessible, but facilitate connections among people around the world. To describe the kind of thinking that recognizes the importance of intercultural exchange or Relation, Edouard Glissant, in *Introduction à une poétique du divers*, borrows a trope—"la pensée archipélique" [archipelago thought]—from the topographical configuration of the Caribbean. The islands connecting the continents of North and South America (which have also been likened to an umbilical cord by the "créolistes") serve as a model for the world in which Relation is the norm. When Glissant asserts that "la notion de nation prend un contenu beaucoup plus culturel qu'étatique, militaire, économique ou politique" [the idea of nation is much more culture-based than state, military, economic or political] (*Introduction* 132), he hints at the formation of a borderless nation in which culture is the unifying, but not universalizing, factor. Jean Bernabé, Patrick Chamoiseau, and Raphaël Confiant take Glissant's ideas even further in *Eloge de la créolité*, proclaiming an identity founded on the Creole language and culture that could extend beyond the Caribbean to the Indian Ocean.

These theories of interchange and extended kinship, however, coincide with an atmosphere of isolationism in which more stringent immigration requirements have been put into place by various governments. At the same time that information is more readily accessible and long-distance bonds among individuals rendered easier (with the resulting exchange of ideas), international travel and border crossing for certain people from developing countries have become more difficult. Boats carrying Haitian refugees fleeing poverty and political uncertainty are intercepted by the United States Coast Guard. These refugees seeking a better life are either incarcerated in detention camps in Florida and Guantanamo Bay or sent back to the island, where, ironically, American popular culture and English-language usage are becoming more and more widespread.

Migration and exile notwithstanding, Haitians all over the world sustain a permanent link to the "pays natal" [native land] in the form of an extraordinarily powerful allegiance to and pride in the revolutionary origins of the nation. Even if national citizenship is relinquished, Haitian identity is not. There are several words designating an expatriate who remains attached to the land of his or her birth. *Tenth department*, *dyaspora*, *viejo*, *vyaje*, and *nonvyaje* are all self-assigned. *Tenth department* refers to the fact that Haiti is divided into nine administrative districts, and the tenth department encompasses those residing elsewhere without regard to class, color, or gender divisions that operate within society. Dyaspora with a *y* has similar connotations, as Edwidge Danticat explains: "The tenth department is not concrete land. It is not a specific place, but an idea to which Haitians can belong, no matter where we are in the world. We of the Haitian dyaspora maintain a very long umbilical cord with our homeland" ("AHA!" 42). Yet nuances in the tone that an individual uses in pronouncing *dyaspora* can have the desired effect of accentuating differences between insider and outsider.[2]

In the postcolonial context, social scientists utilize terms like *transnational citizen*, *transborder citizen*, and *transmigrant*. In his study *Diasporic Citizenship: Haitian Americans in Transnational America*, Michel Laguerre defines "diasporic citizenship" as: "the situation of the individual who lives outside the boundaries of the nation-state to which he or she had formerly held primary allegiance and who experiences through transnational migration (or the redesigning of the homeland boundaries) the subjective reality of belonging to two or more nation states. . . . It presupposes some level of integration in the country of residence and some kind of attachment with the homeland. The intensity of these relationships may vary over time from one individual to another and from one generation to the next" (13). It is significant that Laguerre focuses in his study on *rerootedness* rather than *uprootedness* or *disruption* that can characterize immigrant life (4).

While in a bookstore in Miami, Edwidge Danticat was introduced to yet another distinct label, one that carefully inscribes the new location. A young man approached her, proudly identifying himself and her as "AHA," an acronym for "African, Haitian, American," "a new way for young Haitians who had been in the United States for a while to define themselves, partly to combat the negative labels they were bombarded with, among them 'boat people' and the 'AIDS people'" ("AHA!" 39–40).[3]

Whether created by academics or members of the younger generation, the above-mentioned categories embody identities without the hyphen. Plural and multiple identities supersede the in-betweenness and divided subjectivities experienced by people from the French DOMs (Départements d'Outre-Mer [French Overseas Departments]). According to H. Adlai Murdoch: "French West Indians must enact a daily double gesture that splits their subjectivity between metropole and department" (6). For Haitians abroad, on the other hand, identity is not a simple question of either/or, but of both, simultaneous, and fluid. For example, an individual as a citizen of the host country can still, to some degree, engage in activities across national boundaries: from sending money to relatives to backing candidates seeking elective office, from building schools to participating in medical missions. Such activities not only demonstrate a strong obligation to family in Haiti and a desire to invest in a better future, but can involve thousands of people controlling millions of dollars. The economic power of the combined Haitian population in New York, Miami, and Boston, whose numbers surpassed that of Haiti's second largest city, Cap-Haïtien, has not been lost on high government officials (Laguerre, *Diasporic* 29).[4] In 1994, President Jean-Bertrand Aristide created the Ministère des Haïtiens Vivant à l'Etranger [Ministry of Haitians Living Abroad; also referred to as the Ministry of the Diaspora], to coordinate relationships between individuals and groups inside and outside the country (Laguerre, *Diasporic* 162–64).

What is the impact of transnationalism on Haitian writers in particular? As Patrick Chamoiseau laments in *Ecrire en pays dominé*, Martinican writers are not immune to the dynamic of power, place, language, and imaginary: "Comment écrire alors que ton imaginaire s'abreuve, du matin jusqu'aux rêves, à des images, des pensées, des valeurs qui ne sont pas les tiennes? Comment écrire quand ce que tu es végète en dehors des élans qui déterminent ta vie? Comment écrire, dominé?" [How do you write when your imaginary drinks, from morning until night, from images, thoughts, and values that are not your own? How can you write when what you are vegetates outside of the momentum that determines your life? How can you write within a system that dominates you?] (17).

While in-betweenness can be a dilemma for the "domiens" [people from the French overseas departments], it does not appear to be one for Haitian writers who were an integral part of the unprecedented flight of intellectuals from the island beginning in the 1960s. Settling in Europe and Africa, as well as North America, they who were "writing outside the nation"—an expression I am borrowing from Azade Seyhan, who used it in another context—produced more literary works than writers inside the country who were silenced or censored. Citizenship notwithstanding, they still identify themselves and are identified as Haitian writers. Liliane Dévieux, for example, states without ambiguity that she is a Haitian writer: "Il n'y a aucun doute, même si je ne vis pas en Haïti" [There is no doubt, even if I do not live in Haiti] (qtd. in Jonassaint, *Pouvoir* 50). She, along with Emile Ollivier, Nadine Magloire, Gérard Etienne, Anthony Phelps settled in Canada; Jean Métellus and Jean-Claude Charles, in France; Paul Laraque and Marie Vieux Chauvet, in the United States; and Roger Dorsinville, Jean Brierre, Gérard Chenet, and Jacqueline Scott, in Senegal.[5] Roger Dorsinville saw no contradiction in the fact that he served as an officer in the Association des écrivains du Sénégal [Association of Senegalese Writers] (Jonassaint, *Pouvoir* 35–36).

For Joël Des Rosiers, arriving in Montreal as a child, migration is a privileged position of speech: "La migration est une position de parole" [Migration is a speech position] (150). In *Théories caraïbes*, he equates the word *island* with his Haitian identity: "Comme le mot île, notre identité est instable, précaire cependant intense d'une conscience du lieu, du paysage, des odeurs, une façon non réductible de sentir et d'exister" [Like the word *island*, our identity is unstable, precarious nevertheless intense from an awareness of place, landscape, smells, an irreducible way of feeling and existing] (71).

Writers sometimes become immersed in identity politics because the literary enterprise forces them to. Where should their works be placed on library shelves, for example? Emile Ollivier understands the process very well: "Dans l'institution littéraire, il faut nécessairement qu'on soit typé, catalogué, rangé, rangé sur une étagère; alors, je suis tantôt un écrivain haïtien, tantôt un écrivain québécois d'origine haïtienne, tantôt un écrivain caraïbe ou un écrivain montréalais! J'aimerais être considéré comme écrivain seulement, mais il faut bien assumer le fait qu'on vient nécessairement de quelque part" [As part of the literary institution one has to be typed, catalogued, arranged, put on a shelf; thus, I am sometimes a Haitian writer, sometimes a Quebec writer of Haitian origin, sometimes a Caribbean writer or a Montreal writer! I would like to be considered simply as a writer, but one must accept the fact that one surely comes from somewhere] (qtd. in Pauyo 8). Indeed, in most library systems in American universities, Haitian writers regardless of location share shelf space.

While Ollivier is ambivalent about literary categories, Dany Laferrière vigorously resists them. The word *francophone* even gives him pause, a position with which I concur, in that it defines and categorizes utilizing one single element—language, in effect, conflating difference without a space for specificity.[6] As for origins, he declares, "Je subis l'outrage géographique" [I am subjected to geographical insult] (86). He consciously distances himself from Haitian literary traditions, preferring rupture with the past in order to forge his own way (Coates 910–11). Though he lives in the United States, he continues to publish in French. His ten-volume autobiographical oeuvre traces his/the narrator's journey from Port-au-Prince to Miami, leading Alvina

Ruprecht to characterize his as "borderless text[s]" (251). Another writer of Laferrière's generation, Joël Des Rosiers, speaking of others like him who were born in Haiti and grew up in Canada—"half-generation"—claims an identity embracing multiple elements: "Nous sommes haïtiens québécois. . . . Notre travail consiste à tester les identités. Notre identité est plurielle" [We are Quebec Haitians. . . . Our job is to test identities. Our identity is plural] (182).

Frantz Fanon reminds us that speaking a language assumes a culture (17), and in "Political Geography of Literature" Réda Bensmaïa theorizes the implications of the "bi-langue," which is predicated on Abdelkebir Khatibi's notion of the "bi-langue," that is, the gap between writing in one language and speaking in another.[7] What happens, then, when a Haitian writer, already bilingual in Creole and French, settles in a non-French-speaking area and adopts a third language? Micheline Dusseck published short stories in magazines in Spain prior to her first novel *Ecos del Caribe* in 1996, and Edwidge Danticat has achieved fame writing prose in the United States. In fact, most of the younger generation of Haitian writers residing in the United States, that is, the half-generation or first generation, now publish in English and thus are positioned outside of the standard francophone/creolophone literary frame.[8] One wonders what their relationship is to English. Marilene Phipps, raised in Haiti and France, transitioned to writing poetry in English with some difficulty: "I had to redefine my sense of self, my way of relating to the world. I realize as I am saying it how much the way we speak and, perhaps, write influences the way we experience the world. . . . I realized how much was tangled up in how I wrote, how I spoke, how language is what we use to experience and also to express what we experience—the two are intertwined in ways that are very complex" (qtd. in Shea, "A Prayer" 18). Danticat considers English her stepmother tongue, but not in a negative way. It is the language she adopted due to her family circumstances (Shea, "Dangerous" 387–88).

Danticat is a representative figure in this regard in that she does not fit neatly into conventional linguistic or national categories. Born in Haiti, she joined her parents in Brooklyn at age twelve. Considered half-generation, that is, born in Haiti and raised there and elsewhere, her work is greatly informed by her Haitian literary ancestors as well as contemporary African American writers.[9] On the one hand, her work is included in courses offered in English departments on African American, Caribbean, women, and immigrant writers. On the other hand, I have taught *Breath, Eyes, Memory*, *Krik? Krak!*, and *the farming of bones* in both undergraduate and graduate French courses on Caribbean literature and culture.[10] It is fitting that Danticat's characters travel, migrate, and renegotiate their identities. Furthermore, her 1998 novel *the farming of bones* is set in Haitian and Dominican border towns, intersections themselves, "contact zones," sites where Relation is experienced and performed. Her displaced characters are constantly in search of landmarks or *points de repère* that prove to be illusory. Coincidentally, Joël Des Rosiers has commented that this era is characterized by the loss of such markers (166).

That Edwidge Danticat's texts are translated into French—*Le Cri de l'oiseau rouge* [*Breath, Eyes, Memory*] and *La récolte douce des larmes* [*the farming of bones*]—soon after their publication in English and that she has read short stories from *Krik? Krak!* in Creole over the radio in Haiti testify to a desire to reach the French-reading and Creole-speaking Haitian audiences. These are just two examples of the ways in which books circulate across borders in hard copy, through translations, and in broadcast and electronic form. CARAF Books of the University Press of Virginia counts among its translations five by Haitian writers.[11] *Open Gate: An Anthology of Haitian Creole Poetry*, a bilingual anthology edited by Paul Laraque and Jack Hirschman encompassing pioneer Félix Morisseau-Leroy along with younger authors living in Boston, New York, Port-au-Prince, Montreal, Miami, Cuba, and Senegal, crosses generational boundaries in its aim to promote poetry written in Creole. Transnational projects such as the joint venture between presses in Montreal and Port-au-Prince that are responsible for the publication of Marie-Célie Agnant's novel *Le Livre d'Emma* (2001) and Patrick Lemoine's narrative *Fort-Dimanche, Fort-la-Mort* (1996) are another form of border crossing. Under the leadership of Rodney St. Eloi, Editions Mémoire in Port-au-Prince is republishing several of Maximilien Laroche's books of literary criticism that originally appeared in Canada. The *Prix des Amériques insulaires et de la Guyane* [American Islands and Guiana Prize], established in 2001, also has a transnational dimension. Intended to be awarded every two years to a Caribbean writer no matter where he or she is located or in what language he or she writes, the honor could conceivably be bestowed on a Haitian author living abroad and writing in a language other than French or Creole.

In fact, Haitian literature has always been transnational. While some early poems appeared in local periodicals in Port-au-Prince, such as *L'Abeille haïtienne*, or in single-author volumes, such as Coriolan Ardouin's *Poésies* (1881), due to the paucity of the book-publishing infrastructure inside the country, the majority of texts in the nineteenth and early twentieth centuries were published in France: from Emeric Bergeaud's novel *Stella* (1859) to Louis Morpeau's *Anthologie d'un siècle de poésie haïtienne 1817–1925* (1925).[12] Haitian literature has also long been transnational in content and audience, in that a few nineteenth-century novels were not even set in Haiti.

Poems crossed the border to the United States in 1934, the year that marked the end of the American occupation, in Edna Worthy Underwood's *The Poets of Haiti 1782–1934*, a compilation of translations of fifty male writers.[13] A corollary development is in the area of critical discourse, which has evolved from 1980s-style journal articles about writers grouped by location—Max Dorsinville's "les écrivains haïtiens à Dakar"—to publications that consider the global reality, such as Pierre-Raymond Dumas's *Panorama de la littérature haïtienne de la diaspora* (1996), Jenner Desrocher's *Prolégomènes à une littérature en diaspora* (2000), or Paul Laraque and Jack Hirschman's *Open Gate* (2001).

Haitian literature is produced in multiple sites. Its authors span the globe, have their choice of languages, and yet do not relinquish their identity as Haitian writers. One would have expected that these border crossings would have resulted in a problematized or contested identity. On the contrary, it is renegotiated, an issue explored in any number of texts. The writers who remained in Haiti, those long exiled, those who returned, and the younger generation raised overseas justify Depestre's "multiple ailleurs d'Haïti," which, I believe, is a more proper perspective than the traditional inside/outside binary.[14] The way in which Depestre articulates his own personal profile is also appropriate for these writers, some of whom have been displaced several times.[15] Comparing his identity to a banyan tree with multiple roots, whose principal root is located in Haiti, he echoes Glissant in his theorization of rhizomatic identity in *Poétique de la Relation*.[16]

What about the younger and future generations born, raised, or living abroad? Unlike their parents, rarely do they see themselves as exiles, yet they do avow a powerful Haitian identity despite their location. Typical is critic Myriam Chancy, who asserts: "I am claiming my Haitianness in the United States, an identity made especially suspect in this country by racism and xenophobia" ("Lazarus" 237). It is significant as well that college students routinely organize a campus Haitian association whose linguistic identity is Creole, not French, a language only some of them speak. They, along with those whose Haitian Creole is weak, are united in asserting a common cultural identity. These factors, in the case of Haiti, subvert the premise of *francophonie*, which envisions a global community solely based on language. These circumstances would exclude this population, which still identifies itself as Haitian. Yves Déjean is one individual who, twenty-five years ago, refuted the notion of Haiti as a francophone country. Considering that French is spoken by only a small minority (5 to 10 percent of the population), Déjean asserted that "francofolie" better describes the kind of thinking that would incorporate Haiti into the group of French-speaking nations (11–13).

Haitian literary production is intimately linked to the historical circumstances that led to the various locations of its authors, sometimes rendering a disjuncture between national identity and place. Border crossings have indeed enriched the literary corpus, which can be inserted into not only the francophone frame, but the creolophone, anglophone, and hispanophone as well. *The Butterfly's Way: Voices from the Haitian Dyaspora in the United States* is just one publication acknowledging, recognizing, and promoting one model of the linguistic and geographical diversity of the literature. As Réda Bensmaïa posits, one must accept that bilingual writers belong to more than one history, culture, and space (295). Still, Haiti has traditionally been included in the francophone studies field, which then should accommodate this nation's literature in all its guises, that is, encompassing *dyaspora*. Consequently, professors of French should relish the opportunity to read, study, and teach Jacques Roumain, Yanick Lahens, Georges Castera, Félix-Morisseau-Leroy, Maude Heurtelou, Jean Méttelus, Louis-Philippe d'Alembert, Marie-Célie Agnant, and Edwidge Danticat, without neglecting the attendant implications and tensions of crossing borders of generation, location, and language.

Notes

1. An exact number of writers is impossible to quantify, but there are currently more published Haitian writers living outside the republic than inside. A history of intimidation, repression, and censorship at home, coupled with the legacy of the lack of local publishers who specialize in developing creative writers, severely limits opportunities.

2. Danticat mentions an incident in which she was made to feel uncomfortable and guilty (*Butterfly's* xiv–xv). Francie Latour writes about a similar experience: "'You were made outside.' This is the way many Haitians speak of those of us who were born or grew up in the United States. It is as much a badge of pride as it is a stinging resentment. The ones made outside have proven how well Haitians can flourish in the land of opportunity. But, in all our successes, we have also abandoned them. For Haitians who have struggled through the poverty and terror of daily life, there is no room for hyphens in a person's identity. Because I have not suffered with them, I can never be of them" (Danticat, *Butterfly's* 131).

3. The media's use worldwide of "boat people" (without translation into other languages) has class-specific connotations and has provoked emotions ranging from compassion to derision. We can add "Fugees" to the list of self-assigned names, the young music group having appropriated the word *refugee*.

4. For a discussion of Haitians in the United States see Schiller, Wah, Catanese, Stepick.

5. See Max Dorsinville, "Les Ecrivains haïtiens à Dakar," and Jean Jonassaint, "Des récits haïtiens au Québec."

6. The same argument has been articulated around the word *postcolonial.*

7. I thank the editors for calling to my attention the link between my discussion of this issue and Réda Bensmaïa's work on Khatibi.

8. I would like to acknowledge the work of three women in this area. Myriam Chancy includes a chapter on Danticat and Anne-Christine d'Adesky in her study *Framing Silence: Revolutionary Novels by Haitian Women* (1997); Kathleen Balutansky published an article on Haitian American women poets in 1998; and Edwidge Danticat assembled thirty-five poets and essayists who address issues of childhood, migration, return, and the future in a 2001 anthology called *The Butterfly's Way*.

9. Danticat's admiration for Marie Vieux Chauvet and Jacques Stephen Alexis is evident. *Krik? Krak!* is modeled on *Romancero aux étoiles*. For a discussion of intersections with Alexis, see Larrier (58 n. 7). Danticat credits Maya Angelou and Paule Marshall for influencing her work, in an interview with Shea ("Dangerous" 386–87).

10. I am retaining the typography of Danticat's title, *the farming of bones*, as it appears on the cover and title page of the first edition. I believe that the lack of capital letters intensifies the metaphor implicit in "farming" and "bones," that is, that which is under the surface, hidden from view, like the massacre's victims and their stories. Dany Bébel-Gisler uses a similar trope in her blending of gender and Guadeloupean history in her title *Léonora: l'histoire enfouie de la Guadeloupe* [*Leonora: the Buried Story of Guadeloupe*].

11. René Depestre, *Festival of the Greasy Pole*; Lilas Desquiron, *Reflections of Loko-Miwa*; Jacques Stephen Alexis, *General Sun, My Brother* and *In the Flicker of an Eyelid*.

12. See Naomi Garret's bibliography, 235–47.

13. The poets comprising the collection are: Emile Roumer, Léon Laleau, Etzer Vilaire, Carl Brouard, Philippe Thoby-Marcelin, Charles Pressoir, Jean Brierre, Clément Magloire-fils, Maurice Casséus, Milo Rigaud, Jacques Roumain, Roland Chassagne, Robert Lataillade, Victor Mangonès, Pascal Casséus, Pierre Mayard, Jean-Joseph Vilaire, Constantin Mayard, Damoclès Vieux, Tertullien Guilbaud, Luc Grimard, Volvick Ricourt, Christian Regulus, Ignace Nau, Massilon Coicou, Edgard Numa, Louis-Henri Durand, Oswald Durand, Louis Borno, Macdonald Alexander, Justinien Ricot, Dominique Hippolyte, Louis Morpeau, Christian Werleigh, Timothée Paret, Fernand Ambroise, Edmund La Forest, Duraciné Vaval, Frédéric Burr-Reynaud, Adrian Carrénard, Georges Lescouflair, Charles Moravia, Léon Louis, Normil Sylvain, Georges Sylvain, Arsène Chevry, Paul Lochard, and Isaac Toussaint-Louverture.

14. While critics Laroche, Lahens, Jonassaint, and Barthélémy engage in the inside/outside discourse, they favor a broad definition of Haitian literature, opting for inclusion rather than exclusion. The recent anthology *150 Romans antillais* lists writers born in Haiti, regardless of current residence.

15. Félix Morrisseau Leroy lived for many years in Senegal and the United States; René Depestre, who resided in Cuba for many years, also lived in France, Italy, and Brazil; Dany Laferrière travels between Canada and the United States. Novelist Louis-Philippe Dalembert has had multiple sites of residence spanning North America, South America, Africa, and Europe, as well as the Caribbean and the Middle East. Some writers returned to the island republic after the fall of Jean-Claude Duvalier; others

travel back and forth, thus making the inside/outside dichotomy not always the best description of the situation.

16. See interview with Depestre (550); and Glissant, *Poétique de la Relation* (23).

Works Cited

150 Romans antillais. Sainte-Rose, Guadeloupe: ASCODELA, 2001.

Agnant, Marie-Célie. *Le Livre d'Emma*. Montreal: Editions du Remue-ménage and Port-au-Prince: Editions Mémoire, 2001.

Alexis, Jacques Stephen. *Compère Général Soleil*. Paris: Gallimard, 1955.

———. *L'Espace d'un cillement*. 1959. Paris: Gallimard, 1998.

———. *General Sun, My Brother*. Trans. Carrol F. Coates. Charlottesville: University Press of Virginia, 1999.

———. *In the Flicker of an Eyelid*. Trans. Carrol F. Coates and Edwidge Danticat. Charlottesville: University Press of Virginia, 2002.

———. *Romancero aux étoiles*. Paris: Gallimard, 1960.

Ardouin, Coriolan. *Poésies*. Port-au-Prince: Imprimerie Ethéart, 1881.

Balutansky, Kathleen. "The Muse Speaks a New Tongue: New Perspectives On Language and Identity in Haitian American Women's Texts." *MaComère* 1 (1998): 115–33.

Barthélémy, Gérard. "La Société haïtienne et sa littérature." *Notre Librairie* 132 (October–December 1997): 8–18.

Bébel-Gisler, Dany. *Léonora: l'histoire enfouie de la Guadeloupe*. Paris: Seghers, 1985.

———. *Leonora: The Buried Story of Guadeloupe*. Trans. Andrea Leskes. Charlottesville: University Press of Virginia, 1994.

Bensmaïa, Réda. "Political Geography of Literature: On Khatibi's 'Professional Traveller.'" *French Cultural Studies: Criticism at the Crossroads*. Ed. Marie-Pierre Le Hir and Dana Strand. Albany: State University of New York Press, 2000. 295–308.

Bergeaud, Emeric. *Stella*. Paris: Dentu, 1859.

Bernabé, Jean, Patrick Chamoiseau, and Raphaël Confiant. *Eloge de la créolité*. Paris: Gallimard, 1989.

Berrouet-Oriol, Robert. "Interview." Trans. Paulette Richards. *Callaloo* 15.2 (1992): 518–21.

Catanese, Anthony V. *Haitians, Migration and Diaspora*. Boulder, Colo.: Westview, 1999.

Chamoiseau, Patrick. *Ecrire en pays dominé*. Paris: Gallimard, 1997.

Chancy, Myriam J. A. *Framing Silence: Revolutionary Novels by Haitian Women*. New Brunswick, N.J.: Rutgers University Press, 1997.

———. "Lazarus Rising: An Open Letter to My Daughter." *The Butterfly's Way: Voices from the Haitian Dyaspora in the United States*. New York: Soho, 2001. 223–39.

Coates, Carrol F. "An Interview with Dany Laferrière." *Callaloo* 22.4 (1999): 910–21.

Danticat, Edwidge. "AHA!" *Becoming American: Personal Essays by First Generation Immigrant Women*. Ed. Meri Nana-Ama Danquah. New York: Hyperion, 2000. 39–44.

———. *the farming of bones*. New York: Soho Press, 1998.

———. *Krik? Krak!* New York: Random House, 1996.

Danticat, Edwidge, ed. *The Butterfly's Way: Voices from the Haitian Dyaspora in the United States*. New York: Soho Press, 2001.

Déjean, Yves. *Dilemme en Haïti: français en péril ou péril français?* New York: Connaissance d'Haïti, 1975.

Depestre, René. *The Festival of the Greasy Pole*. Trans. Carrol F. Coates. Charlottesville: University Press of Virginia, 1990.

———. "Interview." *Callaloo* 15.2 (1992): 550–54.

———. *Le Mât de cocagne*. Paris: Gallimard, 1979.

———. "Le Multiple ailleurs d'Haïti." *Boutures* 1.4 (March–August 2001): 42.

Desquiron, Lilas. *Les Chemins de Loco-Miroir*. Paris: Stock, 1990.

———. *Reflections of Loko Miwa*. Trans. Robin Orr Bodkin. Charlottesville: University Press of Virginia, 1998.

Desrocher, Jenner. *Prolégomènes à une littérature haïtienne en diaspora*. Montreal: Editions du Centre International de Documentation et d'Information Haïtienne Caraïbéenne et Afro-Canadienne (CIDIHCA), 2000.

Des Rosiers, Joël. *Théories caraïbes: poétique du déracinement*. Montreal: Triptyque, 1996.

Dorsinville, Max. "Les Ecrivains haïtiens à Dakar." *Etudes littéraires* 13.2 (August 1980): 347–56.

Dumas, Pierre-Raymond. *Panorama de la littérature haïtienne de la diaspora*. Port-au-Prince: Imprimeur II, 1996.

Dusseck, Micheline. *Ecos del Caribe*. Barcelona: Lumen, 1996.

Fanon, Frantz. *Black Skin, White Masks*. Trans. Charles Lam Markmann. New York: Grove Press, 1967.

Glissant, Edouard. *Introduction à une poétique du divers*. Paris: Gallimard, 1996.

———. *Poétique de la Relation*. Paris: Gallimard, 1990.

———. *Traité du Tout-Monde: Poétique IV*. Paris: Gallimard, 1997.

Itzigsohn, José. "Immigration and the Boundaries of Citizenship: The Institutions of Immigrants' Political Transnationalism." *International Migration Review* 34.4 (Winter 2000): 1126–54.

Jonassaint, Jean. *Le Pouvoir des mots, les maux du pouvoir.* Paris: L'Arcantère, 1986.

———. "Des Productions littéraires haïtiennes aux Etats-Unis (1948–1986)." *Journal of Haitian Studies* 5–6 (1999–2000): 4–19.

———. "Des Récits haïtiens au Québec (1937–1995), repères pour une histoire." *Neue Romania* 18 (1997): 81–104.

Khatibi, Abdelkebir. *Maghreb pluriel*. Paris: Denoël, 1983.

Laferrière, Dany. *J'écris comme je vis. Dany Laferrière: entretien avec Bernard Magnier*. Genouilleux, France: La Passe du vent, 2000.

Laguerre, Michel S. *Diasporic Citizenship: Haitian Americans in Transnational America*. New York: St. Martin's Press, 1998.

Lahens, Yanick. "Exile: Between Writing and Place." Trans. Cheryl Thomas and Paulette Richards. *Callaloo* 15.3 (1992): 735–46.

———. *L'Exil entre l'ancrage et la fuite, l'écrivain haïtien*. Port-au-Prince: Deschamps, 1990.

———. "Littérature haïtienne: problématiques." *Notre Librairie* 132 (October–December 1997): 62–75.

Laraque, Paul, and Jack Hirschman, ed. *Open Gate: An Anthology of Haitian Creole Poetry*. Willimantic, Conn.: Curbstone Press, 2001.

Larrier, Renée. "'Girl by the Shore': Gender and Testimony in Edwidge Danticat's *the farming of bones*." *Journal of Haitian Studies* 7.2 (Fall 2001): 50–60.

Lemoine, Patrick. *Fort-Dimanche, Fort-la-Mort*. 2nd ed. Port-au-Prince: Editions Regain; Montreal: Editions du Centre International de Documentation et d'Information Haïtienne Caraïbéenne et Afro-Canadienne (CIDIHCA), 1996.

Morpeau, Louis, ed. *Anthologie d'un siècle de poésie haïtienne 1847–1925*. Paris: Editions Bossard, 1925.

Murdoch, H. Adlai. *Creole Identity in the French Caribbean Novel*. Gainesville: University Press of Florida, 2001.

Pauyo, Eric. "L'Exil et le royaume: entretien avec Emile Ollivier." *Spirale* (January–February 2002): 8–9.

Ruprecht, Alvina. "'L'Amérique c'est moi': Dany Laferrière and the Borderless Text." Ed. Alvina Ruprecht and Cecilia Taiana. *The Reordering of Culture: Latin America, the Caribbean, and Canada in the Hood*. Carleton, Ontario: Carleton University Press, 1995. 251–67.

Schiller, Nina Glick, and Georges Eugene Fouton. *Georges Woke Up Laughing: Long-Distance Nationalism and the Search for Home*. Durham, N.C.: Duke University Press, 2001.

———. "Transnational Lives and National Identities: The Identity Politics of Haitian Immigrants." *Comparative Urban and Community Research* 6 (1998): 130–61.

Seydan, Azade. *Writing outside the Nation*. Princeton, N.J.: Princeton University Press, 2001.

Shea, Renée H. "The Dangerous Job of Edwidge Danticat: An Interview." *Callaloo* 19.2 (Spring 1996): 382–89.

———. "'A Prayer for Haiti': A Conversation with Writer and Painter, Marilene Phipps." *MaComère* 4 (2001): 14–24.

Spivak, Gayatri Chakravorty. *The Post-Colonial Critic*. New York: Routledge, 1990.

Stepick, Alex. *Pride against Prejudice: Haitians in the United States*. Needham Heights, Mass.: Allyn and Bacon, 1998.

Underwood, Edna Worthy, ed. *The Poets of Haiti 1782–1934*. Portland, Maine: Mosher Press, 1934.

Wah, Tatiana K. "Expatriate Reconnection: An Alternative to Expatriate Recovery and Engagement for Homeland Development—The Case of Haiti." Ph.D. dissertation, Rutgers University, 2001.

Zéphir, Flore. *Haitian Immigrants in Black America: A Sociological and Socio-linguistic Portrait*. Westport, Conn.: Bergin and Garvey, 1996.

13

Francophone Studies / Postcolonial Studies

"Postcolonializing" through *Relation*

Anjali Prabhu and Ato Quayson

> Thought of the Other is the moral generosity disposing me to accept the principle of alterity . . ., [b]ut [it] can dwell within me . . . without "prizing me open," without changing me within myself. As an ethical principle, it is enough that I not violate it.
>
> The other of Thought is precisely this altering. Then I have to act [and] change my thought. . . . I change, and I exchange. This is an aesthetics of turbulence whose corresponding ethics is not provided in advance.
>
> **Edouard Glissant, *Poetics* 154–55**

In this piece, we bring together some key theoretical reflections on the question of hybridity in postcolonial theory. We look, particularly, at the movement from francophone studies to the more general field of postcolonial studies that, for better or for worse, is defined in English and dominated by the North American and British, and to some extent the Australian, academy. We wish to pursue, by juxtaposing and closely studying aspects of these different versions of hybridity, an othering process, suggested by Glissant's quotation above, from the location of hybridity in postcolonial theory. Our interest in this preliminary working through of the issue is to conceive of it as a movement toward "postcolonializing."

"The process of postcolonializing . . . would mean the critical process by which to relate modern-day phenomena to their explicit, implicit or even potential relations to th[e] fraught heritage [of the colonial aftermath]" (Quayson 11). But this is done within the framework of "postcolonialism [which] must be seen as a project to correct imbalances in the world, and not merely to do with the specific 'postcolonial' constituencies" (Quayson 11).

Hybridity, in recent postcolonial discourse from all language backgrounds, gestures toward the impossibility of purity as both a theoretical category and especially as a cultural phenomenon. While the concept of hybridity is readily linked to culture (particularly through the notion of "ethnicity"), the ambiguous relationship between culture and race becomes implicated, either explicitly or implicitly, in any discussion of hybridity. The proliferation of theoretical writing on this subject in the last few decades is an indication of the importance of the concept to postcolonial studies. We can also clearly recognize it to be a result of the opportune translation of various theoretical writings into English (e.g., Benitez-Rojo or Glissant). Significantly, in the movement from French to English, it has also been accompanied by the "arrival" of major critics on the U.S./U.K. academic scene: Françoise Lionnet and Françoise Vergès, who employ the French term *métissage* while writing in English. These intellectuals have served as crucial conduits for the movement of notions of hybridity (through their interest in métissage) between francophone postcolonial theory and the larger field of English language-based postcolonial studies. However, it is to the critic Homi K. Bhabha that, in postcolonial studies, the term *hybridity* inevitably leads.

Specifically here, we wish to present an approach to culture and difference in the spirit of Glissant's more radical notion of the other of thought that this chapter seeks to validate. Considering Bhabha, one of the many fine points made by him regarding hybridity is its positing as a discursive space whence there arises a possibility to figure difference. For him, hybridity is located at the limit of authoritative discourses, thus questioning both their coherence and their internal difference. On the question of difference, Bhabha states: "If cultural diversity is a category of comparative ethics, aesthetics or ethnology, cultural difference is a process of signification through which statements *of* culture or *on* culture differentiate, discriminate, and authorize the production of fields of force, reference, applicability, and capacity" (Bhabha 34). It is the hybridity arising from difference, rather than from diversity, as defined above by Bhabha that becomes pertinent to our theoretical pursuit. It is through difference that there is an active processual quality to the generation of hybridity, while diversity allows the coexistence of fixed categories. In much the same way, Glissant qualifies "thought of the other" as stemming from a "moral generosity," while the "other of thought" implies the kind of alteration that requires an ethics of action (*Poetics* 154–55). For us, this kind of qualified difference and alteration constitutes a move toward the larger project of postcolonializing to which we subscribe.

Salient readers of Glissant who first put him on the map from the francophone to the anglophone context were his translator J. Michael Dash and

Françoise Lionnet. More recently, of course, reference to Glissant in writing in English has increased (see Bongie, Murdoch, Britton, for example only). Lionnet's first major work and Dash's translation of *Le Discours antillais* came out the same year. This was a decisive moment for Glissantian thought entering postcolonial theory for a wide audience in a significant way. It was also a significant moment for the coming together of Bhabha and Glissant. In the following pages, we will discuss some specific aspects of this movement from French to English in relation to hybridity.

The signifying power of race in any conception of hybridity is not always evident in reading Bhabha. Robert Young's introduction to his book *Colonial Desire* is an important reminder of this entanglement. He sifts through some of the terminology relating to hybridity, including Bakhtin's linguistic hybridity as a subversive strategy, Bhabha's interest in hybridity in the colonial and postcolonial framework, and some important historical points regarding the uses of the terms *hybridity* in English and *métissage* in French, and their contexts. Françoise Lionnet reminds us that the slippage between race and culture is perhaps easier in English than it is in French. In the introduction to Lionnet's *Autobiographical Voices*, she relies on the then-forthcoming translation of *Discours antillais* by J. Michael Dash as *Caribbean Discourse*. In a note she explains that while Dash translates the French *métissage* from Glissant as "creolization," she herself will retain the French *métissage*, as *creolization* is not really suggestive of the racial undertones of the term (4). Upon close examination of Dash's translation, one notes that he frequently translates the term *Relation* as *creolization*. Celia Britton, in her recent *Edouard Glissant and Postcolonial Theory*, notes that Dash translates *Relation*" by using *creolization*, *cultural contact*, and *cross-cultural relationships* ("A Note on Translation"). Our purpose here, however, is not to question the accuracy or the adequacy of specific translations of Glissant's work. We want, instead, to distinguish Glissant's use of *métissage*, *créolisation*, and *Relation* in a succinct manner that we believe illustrates the importance of their alterity and their difference in the weighted significance we have given these latter terms following Glissant and Bhabha, respectively. For this purpose, we work from Glissant's more recent *Poétique de la Relation*. Following this, we will unearth the differences in the single term *métissage* taken up by Lionnet and reappearing in Vergès.

For Glissant, if *métissage* is the initial *choc* [shock] or *rencontre* [encounter] that anticipates a *synthèse* [synthesis], creolization is the more active (altering, differentiating) process that *diffracte* [diffracts] (*Poétique* 46/*Poetics* 34). From this understanding, *métissage* refers to a relatively simple, though essential, point. It is the encounter that serves as a cognitive shock that can then allow us to track difference; it is also a moment in a process in reality that opens up the possibility of creolization. However, métissage does not necessarily lead to the complex process that Glissant describes and admires. Métissage could lead toward a process that privileges synthesis by the erasure, or at least the recuperation, of difference. Creolization, though, is a dynamic process in which difference continues to function and proliferate as a constitutive reality and as a basis for thought and action.

For Glissant, creolization is the earthly approximation of his idea of total *Relation* (of everything to everything else, simultaneously and equally): "What took place in the Caribbean, which could be summed up in the word creolization, approximates the idea of *Relation* for us as nearly as possible" (*Poetics* 34). A fuller appreciation of the complexity that Glissant wants to preserve emerges upon close examination of his description of *Relation* itself: "[W]hen we speak of a poetics of Relation, we no longer need to add: relation between what and what? This is why the French word *Relation*, which functions somewhat like an intransitive verb, could not correspond, for example, to the English term *relationship*" (*Poetics* 27). The impossibility of even considering *Relation* outside itself is where we can identify the radical nature of Glissant's proposition. It is clear, though, that *Relation* cannot be conceived of without reference to the "real" world. It is the instance of Caribbean creolization with which Glissant is most familiar that allows him to conceive of *Relation* in totality. Still, it is also evident that as a theoretical paradigm for understanding and transforming reality, this instance has to be reworked into the larger framework of an all-encompassing *Relation* (that he sometimes calls a *chaos-monde*). He suggests the impossibility of grasping *Relation* in terms of anything but itself. "We must . . . abandon this apposition of Being and beings: renounce the fruitful maxim whereby Being is relation, to consider that Relation alone is relation" (*Poetics* 170). Clearly, then, particular instances of being do not somehow all together simply become Being; likewise, in order to understand *Relation*, it is not enough to figure various instances of particular relations. Therefore, while examining *Relation* always implies the relation of all possible things and their interrelations, it is impossible to name that totality, capture it, or descry, once and for all, its boundaries. This impossibility of fixedness and definitive circumscription in *Relation* will become evident as we further examine this concept.

It is, perhaps, this doggedness about relation (not *to* anything, but relation as an absolute, as a totality) that makes Glissant's work seem removed from reality and that has haunted him in many critical evaluations of his work, the most significant of which comes from his Martinican compatriot *créolité* critics, especially following their earlier collaborative work. Even the reader's thought process must, if at times in desperation, follow this resolute relationality as process. When, finally, some semblance of a definition is provided, it is done with the ruse of the most cunning conductor of the orchestra of *Relation*: "But Relation is not to be confused with the cultures we are discussing nor with the economy of their internal relationships nor even the intangible results of the intricate involvement of all internal relationships with all possible external relationships. Nor is it to be confused with some marvelous accident that might suddenly occur apart from any relationship, the known unknown, in which chance would be the magnet. Relation is all these things at once" (*Poetics* 170–71).

In fact, it would probably be more apt to refer to Glissant as the poet of *Relation* that he is. Quite clearly, there are several aspects of *Relation* that Glissant specifies: it has to do with the real world and the identifiable cultures within it; it includes the relationships within them as well as the results of these relationships and the connections of these results; it encompasses what are seen as relationships within particular cultures to the elements and their interrelations external to them; it includes unforeseen and unforeseeable events that spring up seemingly out of unidentifiable processes; however, the most important point we come away with is that the conception of *Relation* has to include all these aspects *at the same time*. In the passage quoted, the reader is forced to keep in mind, in the space (breath?) of one paragraph the negation of all that *Relation* is *not*. There appears an incremental repetition in which no single element can stand on its own, nor be privileged. The differences within the repetition of the idea of relation in this definition are at times subtle in form but, like in poetry, radical in meaning. Like the accumulative meaning in the repetition of a refrain in a ballad, the residue is sometimes marginal and can be missed.

Once this mental exercise on not-*Relation* is performed, the last sentence of the paragraph instructs you, now that you are holding them all in your head, to figure them simultaneously in order to attempt *Relation*. Of course, this would have been impossible as an instruction at the beginning of the paragraph. This definition of *Relation* approximates, to the closest degree, the enactment of a mental *Relation* that strives to deny sequence and hierarchy.

Creolization, in this active form for Glissant, is opposed quite specifically to creoleness, whose principles "regress toward negritudes, ideas of Frenchness, of Latinness, all generalizing concepts—more or less innocently" (*Poetics* 89). Writing thus quite explicitly contra the *créolité* critics' *Eloge de la créolité*, Glissant once again stresses the centrality of diffracting alterity that opposes the kind of generalization that a synthesis could provide—what we have found close to Bhabha's notion of difference (as opposed to diversity). It might, therefore, be useful to preserve the distinction that Glissant establishes in his use of the terms *métissage*, *creolization*, and *Relation*. At the very least, this distinction needs to be properly recorded as we move from French to English if we are serious about engaging with his work for a more subtle analysis that can account for the processes of contact and relation we are concerned with in much of postcolonial theoretical work.

The practice of translation and the movement between spaces are crucial to the forms of postcolonializing that the notion of hybridity, in its various guises in postcolonial theory, has been employed to examine and/or promote. Given the importance of the process of translation to Glissant's thought (see the quotation mentioned above regarding the inadequacy of the English term *relationship* to Glissant's project of relation), we pause at an emblematic consideration of the more prosaic, but daunting, task of translating Glissant from French to English.

Betsy Wing's careful and sensitive translation of Glissant's *Poétique de la Relation* as *Poetics of Relation* gives us some clues regarding just how difficult it is to conceptually hold (which suggests a form of stasis) this idea of process. "Observons qu'il y a métissage là où auparavant s'opposaient des catégories, qui distinguaient leur essence. Plus métissage se réalise, plus la notion s'en efface" (*Poétique* 106). The translation reads: "Note that *métissage* exists in places where categories making their essences distinct were formerly in opposition. The more *métissage* became realized, the more the idea of it faded" (*Poetics* 92). The movement in the French version from the past tense (*s'opposaient*, *distinguaient*) in the second part of the first sentence to the present tense of the second sentence (*se réalise*) that goes back to the established present (*il y a métissage*) is not insignificant. For along with this shorter and somewhat more dramatic second sentence that pronounces the paradox of *métissage* in the present of the reader's reality, the pronominal use of the verb *se réalise* places *métissage* closer to an idea of an execution or a performance than to a completed action in the past that the English translation *became realized* suggests. From these remarks, the choice of the verb *to exist* (*métissage exists* as a translation of *il y a*, which in itself is perfectly reasonable) here can be reexamined. *Métissage*, whose shock can engender creolization rather than a synthesis, as we have seen, in Glissantian thinking, does not "exist." This would place it closer to the idea of creoleness as a constituted form. Wing herself is aware of this as she carefully discusses Glissant's quarrel with the Martinican critics in their conception of creoleness as a state versus his more active creolization as process. Therefore, his use of "il y a métissage" would correspond more closely to something such as "métissage occurs" (rather than "métissage exists").

What emerges from these sentences further illuminates this idea of *métissage* only as possibility of creolization, and its retroactive calling up of difference. It also points to the fact that the importance of *métissage* resides less in the moment it is lived than in what follows it and allows it to be tracked backward. The analytical processes that a society can generate in producing images of itself involve the hazard of collapsing the metaphors that allow it to reach the reality it has lived and that it lives, and that reality itself. In fact, it is also the relation between thought and reality that is central to the process that Glissant follows. Glissant is obviously interested in instances when creolization as a diffracting process follows the moment of contact. His narration of the process mimetically rehearses, as well, its apprehension as an operation of cognition. *Métissage*, when it progresses as synthesis, though, cannot be brought back as the moment of shock in all its signifying power. Its accomplishment in the form of synthesis, then, would retroactively render it less robust—the idea of *métissage* cancels itself out, is erased or "fades," in Wing's translation (see the quotation above). Its progress as creolization, however, as we have seen earlier, figures the moment of *métissage* more strongly as a collision of differences.

This account of hybridity, proceeding from Glissant, indicates the particular importance of dialogism to its central avatars of *métissage*, creolization, and *Relation*. It also suggests that there is no definitive translation as we excavate a path toward *Relation* that is necessarily reconstructed and renegotiated constantly. There is no formula (or translation) that would provide, for example, a clear methodological path to follow in an analysis of *Relation*. Translations of Glissant (understandings of *Relation*) must indispensably follow the idea of a Poetics—as creations themselves in process. An easy assimilation of *Relation* is counter to its basic poetics. One definition of *Relation* we have considered above is a clear illustration of how the speed and rhythm of thought itself and the oscillatory movement of translation (between languages as well as between the general and the particular, between reality and thought process) are all intrinsic to Glissant's endeavor.

Some of these suggestions anticipate the next understanding of *métissage*. We move now to two other uses of the term *métissage* as it is retained in writing in English (by Lionnet and Vergès) but clearly informed by its French sociolinguistic and historical nuances. For Lionnet, "*Métissage* is a form of *bricolage*, in the sense used by Claude Lévi-Strauss, but as an aesthetic concept it encompasses far more: it brings together biology and history, anthropology and philosophy, linguistics and literature. Above all it is a reading practice that allows me to bring out the interreferential nature of a particular set of texts, which I believe to be of fundamental importance for the understanding of many postcolonial cultures" (*Autobiographical Voices* 8). This definition makes of *métissage* an interdisciplinary and countercanonical strategy. Here, Lionnet privileges a particular aspect of Glissant's *Relation* that works in the accomplishment of her project. *Métissage* allows Lionnet to validate perspectives from "small places" (the Mauritian-born Marie-Thérèse Humbert and the Guadeloupean Maryse Condé, for example), alongside canonical autobiographies. Drawing from Bhabha as much as from Glissant, Lionnet constructs a method she terms *métissage* that can account for surprising dichotomies and clears a space for a feminist perspective on St. Augustine and Nietzsche. In a later formulation, Lionnet develops her idea of *logiques métisses* (the term is derived from the title of Jean-Loup Amselle's book) that can understand how "[t]he global mongrelization or métissage of cultural forms creates complex identities and interrelated, if not overlapping, spaces" ("Logiques" 7). A firm believer in the impossibility and inadequacy of assimilation, Lionnet proposes, in this work, "a theoretical argument about postcolonial culture" (7) by pursuing, through women writers, subject-agents in the construction of hybrid identities. We also believe, with Lionnet, that "[w]hat is needed, then, is a new vocabulary for describing patterns of influence that are never unidirectional" ("Logiques" 11). Suzette Henke remarks, in her review of Lionnet's *Autobiographical Voices*, that "the term [*métissage*] itself is so multi-faceted and polyvalent, so all-consuming and potentially subversive, that it sometimes skids on protean linguistic practices" (110). Glissant's work provides a subtle theoretical distinction of *métissage* from creolization, in his elaboration of a poetics of *Relation*. Following Lionnet, it is, to our minds, also crucial to build a *shared* and sufficiently differentiated vocabulary that can track some of these movements in the myriad spaces of postcoloniality.

Françoise Vergès's work on *métissage* in La Réunion, *Monsters and Revolutionaries: Colonial Family Romance and Métissage*, explores this term in its full colonial significance: specifically as signaling a taboo that indicated the colonial obsession with the purity of race as well as its attraction to the (racial) other. *Métissage* in La Réunion is, no doubt, inscribed as a temptation within "the reactive strategies of discipline and control developed by the French state and its representatives on the island" (*Monsters* 2). Vergès notes her discomfort with the currency of hybridity: "the social organization of slavery and colonialism produced métissage, that is, an intermixing of groups, new cultural forms, new languages, and an identity that remained indecisive. Now global capitalism has adopted métissage as a new cultural commodity" (10). It is important to indicate a rather obvious point: *métissage* exists as a word in standard French. It refers to the mixing of different "races" and, in a more "figurative" meaning, refers to the mixing of cultures. In the context of zoology or botany, such mixed entities are termed hybrids. To a layperson, something or someone with a mixed identity (*métis* or *métisse*) is made of two halves, which can be traced to two distinct and different wholes. Contrarily, even if deriving from this, the use of the term *métis-*

sage within Glissant's poetics of *Relation* takes on the very particular valence that we have specified. We might say that Glissant's technical use of the term has a weight that is registered only within a particular political and theoretical framework—what we have identified here as within the project and process of postcolonializing. Vergès examines the role of individuals and the group of the *métis* within the history of La Réunion. For example, she has a very illuminating chapter on "Blood Politics and Political Assimilation" (72–122); also interesting is her psychoanalytical reading of the 1844 novel *Les Marrons*, following a historical reading of the trial of its *métis* author, Louis-Timagène Houat, who offers *métissage* as "a utopian project of coexistence to compensate for the actual conflictual existence in Bourbon [the colonial name for La Réunion]" (*Monsters* 36). Among her other accomplishments in this book, Vergès considers *métissage* in its full historical, and linguistically and socially specific, meaning in La Réunion, providing insights regarding how this identity has been constructed and how a certain *métis* group has functioned politically. Her interest in *métissage* is located within the larger project of studying the intellectual and political history of the anticolonialist struggles of La Réunion, where the group of recognizable *métis*, disinherited most often by their white fathers, formed part of the educated nonwhite population. It is therefore a historically specific study of interracial identity and the politics of such an identity in a particular history of colonialism.

In her more recent "Post-Scriptum" to Goldberg and Quayson's *Relocating Postcolonialism*, Vergès ends with a section entitled "Diaspora, Hybridity, Creolization." In this piece, her objection is to the recuperation of the idea of mixedness in the fashion of Benetton advertisements and some cities that proclaim to be "hybrid," where the suggestion is a coexistence of radically other, exotic cultures for the consumption of, again, a largely white consumer, deriving from a history of colonialism. Her historical study of *métissage* in the context of La Réunion's relationship with France and its anticolonial struggle clearly stands out as an example against a careless or vague use of the notion of hybridity. In many ways, Vergès studies the hybrid as it is given to us in its material reality; through history. In fact, her work on La Réunion reminds us that, upon careful examination, the hybrid, in reality, records a history of slavery and colonialism. She ends her short essay with a dry criticism of the proliferation of positive and exuberant notions of the hybrid, where an ideal has more currency than reality: "The idea of humanity is more appealing than the actual 'disappointing' human beings. I prefer 'disappointing human beings and their demystifying acts'" (357).

Her main assertion with regard to hybridity in postcolonial studies is that we "should constantly rework the radicality [*sic*] of hybridity and métissage" ("Post-Scriptum" 357). While in complete agreement with Vergès's proposal, we find, though, that it is precisely this radical potential of hybridity that is lost as a result of a formulation such as that of her section title, "Diaspora, Hybridity, Creolization." It is unclear if they all mean the same thing; if they are arranged in a particular sequence indicating a hierarchical significance or one that has theoretical consequences; or if it is indeed the lack of distinction in recent theory that Vergès wants to critique through an ironic presentation that mimics this dubiousness. She notes that "[t]hough distinctions have been made between them, their consequences can be compared: the process of displacement and flexible identities, the position of in-betweenness and impurity, and the experience of transnationalism and cosmopolitanism" (356). Even though Vergès is skeptical of the idea that "a good humanity could perhaps be imagined métisse, hybrid, and diasporic" (357)—once again the ways in which these different adjectives are linked and/or differentiated remain unclear—this fusion and the suggested interchangeability of the terms accomplished in her short piece are a disservice to the very trend that she is deeply committed to correcting.

The radical possibilities for an idea of hybridity and its accomplishment as a form of postcolonializing lies, in our view, in never losing from sight (or thought) the absoluteness of *Relation* proposed by Glissant and in the important distinctions he makes when considering the approximations of it upon which he draws. We believe, in sympathy with Vergès's position regarding the primacy of material history, that, proceeding from Glissant's *métissage*, there is a theoretical space to be cleared, which can encompass the historical processes that Vergès studies as well as the type of analysis that Lionnet employs.

We propose, as a first step toward a more effective form of postcolonializing in the context of hybridity, to attend to Glissant's idea (or ideal) of absolute *Relation* as a principle that provides the direction of movement. In proceeding, we also suggest that to describe concepts and realities that bear upon hybridity and its theorization in postcolonial studies, we work toward a more rigorous and collaboratively established distinction of terms—rather than different inventions and uses that do not dialogue with one another. *Métissage* might be considered by some as residing in the object of analysis itself. To others, it might mean a political practice of interpretation. To some, it might build upon destabilizing ambiguities as conceived by Bhabha. From our reading, we wish to suggest that *métissage* and its radical "potential" for creolization, so clearly recognized by Glissant, retain its connection, as a theoretical term, to *Relation* as an engagement with totality. Reaching (for) the idea of *Relation* itself is always an attempt at putting into play a process that incrementally dissolves hierarchies even while registering the moments and residues of such hierarchies. Clearly, this short intervention can only begin the dialogue we propose in forging "an aesthetics of turbulence," as

Glissant suggests, without providing, in advance, the "corresponding ethics" (*Poetics* 154–55).

Works Cited

Benitez-Rojo, Antonio. *The Repeating Island: The Caribbean and the Postmodern Perspective*. Trans. James Maraniss. Durham, N.C.: Duke University Press, 1992.

Bernabé, Jean, Patrick Chamoiseau, and Raphaël Confiant. 1989. *Eloge de la créolité / In Praise of Creoleness*. Trans. M. B. Taleb-Khyar. Paris: Gallimard, 1993.

Bhabha, Homi K. *The Location of Culture*. London: Routledge, 1994.

Bongie, Chris. *Islands and Exiles: The Creole Identities of Post/Colonial Literature*. Stanford, Calif.: Stanford University Press, 1998.

Britton, Celia M. *Edouard Glissant and Postcolonial Theory: Strategies of Language and Resistance*. Charlottesville: University Press of Virginia, 1999.

Glissant, Edouard. *Caribbean Discourse*. Trans. J. Michael Dash. Charlottesville: University Press of Virginia, 1989.

———. *Le Discours antillais*. Paris: Seuil, 1981.

———. *Poetics of Relation*. Trans. Betsy Wing. Ann Arbor: University of Michigan Press, 1997.

———. *Poétique de la relation*. Paris: Gallimard, 1990.

Henke, Suzette. "Françoise Lionnet: *Autobiographical Voices: Race, Gender, Self-Portraiture*." *Canadian Review of Comparative Literature* 16.1 (1991): 109–12.

Lionnet, Françoise. *Autobiographical Voices: Race, Gender, Self-Portraiture*. Ithaca, N.Y.: Cornell University Press, 1989.

———. "Logiques métisses: Cultural Appropriation and Postcolonial Representations." *Postcolonial Representations: Women, Literature, Identity*. Ithaca, N.Y.: Cornell University Press, 1995. 1–21.

Murdoch, H. Adlai. *Creole Identity in the French Caribbean Novel*. Gainesville: University Press of Florida, 2001.

Quayson, Ato. *Postcolonialism: Theory, Practice, or Process?* Cambridge, U.K.: Polity Press, 2000.

Vergès, Françoise. *Monsters and Revolutionaries: Colonial Family Romance and Métissage*. Durham, N.C.: Duke University Press, 1999.

———. "Post-Scriptum." *Relocating Postcolonialism*. Ed. David Theo Goldberg and Ato Quayson. Oxford, U.K.: Blackwell Publishers, 2002. 349–58.

Young, Robert J.C. "Hybridity and Diaspora." *Colonial Desire: Hybridity in Theory, Culture, and Race*. London: Routledge, 1995. 1–28.

14

Intersections and Trajectories

Francophone Studies and Postcolonial Theory

Dominic Thomas

They ruled over us, ran the country, exploited us, taught us their language, sent us to their schools, and gave us new ancestors called Gauls. That's why we still speak French, love French food, and still like to spend our vacations in France, even if these days it is easier to get a visa to the moon than to that country.
Emmanuel Dongala, *Little Boys Come from the Stars*

What kind of phrase is this: "So what?" Is that English? That is not English. Only the immigrants can speak the Queen's English these days.
Zadie Smith, *White Teeth*

France 0 Senegal 1
Nous n'oublierons JAMAIS.
[We shall NEVER forget.]
FIFA World Cup, May 31, 2002, bumper sticker widely available for sale in Dakar, Senegal

"Let's start at the very beginning, a very good place to start." With a playful intertextual gesture to the celebrated musical *The Sound of Music*, so opens Mark Behr's second novel, *Embrace*. Whereas the young children in the aforementioned film had been shielded from the atrocities of the Second World War that provide the subtext, so too is the young protagonist in Behr's novel as he navigates his way through what constitutes a challenging, compelling, and disquieting landscape of complicity and collaboration in the context of South African apartheid. In both cases, a heuristic reading unveils a troubling narrative that is similar to the one that one encounters in a consideration of the relationship between francophone studies and postcolonial theory itself. The violent and dehumanizing project that was colonialism generated a corpus of African texts anchored primarily in the linguistic realm of European cultural traditions, generating in subsequent years theoretical models that endeavored to explore and explain colonial and postcolonial circumstances. Therefore, in order to juxtapose francophone and postcolonial studies, chart their autonomous trajectories, and delineate their points of intersection, it remains essential to take into consideration the different yet nevertheless imbricated transcolonial histories in which a plethora of theoretical apparatuses have been deployed.

The agendas I propose will consist in: (1) interrogating France's long and complicated history with Africa; (2) foregrounding the African components of and contributions to francophone studies; (3) addressing and highlighting the contradictory nature of ongoing debates in France concerning multiculturalism and postcolonial theory; (4) underscoring the importance of African theoretical models from Negritude to the more recent work of theorists such as Achille Mbembe; (5) adhering to the guiding spirit of this volume of essays by exploring and questioning the manner in which francophone and postcolonial studies have shared, contested, and even enjoyed promiscuous discursive grounds under the aegis of a broad range of disciplinary alignments in the United States; (6) and finally, charting the new coordinates and intellectual routes of these fields in order to gauge their usefulness and pertinence in the process of unpacking diverse cultural phenomena.

En-Countering Modernity

French colonial expansionism was premised on the adherence to the concept of modernity. Progress was accordingly understood as a gravitational force toward the assimilation of a specific set of universal ideals that served as indicators of this movement. As Bill Ashcroft has argued in his book *Post-Colonial Transformation*, "Modernity was seen to be a distinctive and superior period in the history of humanity . . . and 'introduction' into modernity became the right and obligation of the European powers" (210). However, in his book *Branchements*, French anthropologist Jean-Loup Amselle suggests that we attempt to move away from "modernism" as the defining factor, and explore instead the idea of "branchements" [connections]:

> Le fil conducteur de cet ouvrage s'ordonne autour de la thématique du "branchement": par là on a souhaité s'éloigner de celle du "métissage," qui représentait notre problématique antérieure et qui nous paraît aujourd'hui trop marquée par la biologie. En recourant à la métaphore électrique ou informatique du branchement, c'est-à-dire à celle d'une dérivation de signifiés particularistes par rapport à un réseau de signifiants planétaires, on parvient à se démarquer de l'approche qui consiste à voir dans notre monde globalisé le produit d'un mélange de

cultures vues elles-mêmes comme des univers étanches, et à mettre au centre de la réflexion l'idée de triangulation, c'est-à-dire de recours à un élément tiers pour fonder sa propre identité.(7)[1]

[This work is organized around the notion of "connections." Whereas the concept of "métissage" had previously been useful, it now seems too closely linked to a biological component for our purposes today. Through recourse to the electronic or computational metaphor of the connection, a framework emerges in which a derivation of particular signifiers is juxtaposed with a network of planetary ones. This allows for a move away from the perception of our globalized world as the product of a mixing of cultures that are themselves seen as impervious universes, and the foregrounding instead of the idea of triangulation, that is to say recourse to a third component in order to establish one's identity.]

Through the examples of the process of Islamicization in the tenth century, Amselle effectively provides a compelling precursor to the phenomenon that is commonly understood today as globalization. According to this way of interpreting intercultural dynamics, colonialism finds itself relocated as a mechanism that proceeds from globalization, rather than the other way round. In turn, this framework offers us the occasion to adequately assess the complex manner in which populations and histories have become imbricated or creolized, rather than analyzing these entities as somehow autonomous, closed, and threatened with eradication by globalization. The implications of this recontextualization are tremendously helpful in delineating the objectives of this chapter and in illustrating how this theoretical apparatus could be put into practice toward achieving an understanding of the dynamics of colonialism, transcolonialism, transnationalism, and what I would describe as transpostcolonialism.

If indeed we are willing to agree that colonialism, as a state-sponsored project that was deployed in the aftermath of the 1884–85 Berlin Conference, provided the discursive *encounter* with modernity, then, arguably, African responses generated subsequent to that historical moment must be understood as having been conceived and designed as attempts at countering and demystifying the foundational tenets of that project.[2] To this end, the work and activities of such important figures as Alioune Diop (founder of the journal *Présence africaine* in 1947), Cheikh Anta Diop, Léopold Sédar Senghor, and Albert Memmi become central to any consideration of francophone and postcolonial studies given the various ways in which they have countered western intellectual supremacy and hegemony by recontextualizing and foregrounding African contributions to the arts, philosophy, and sciences.[3] For while some texts by Cheikh Anta Diop (primarily *Nations nègres et cultures*) and Senghor (essentially the various poetry anthologies currently available) continue to receive critical attention, others are being ignored, at the very least insufficiently exploited in curricular offerings or overlooked in scholarly works (notably *L'Afrique noire précoloniale*, *L'Unité culturelle de l'Afrique noire*, *Antériorité des civilisations nègres*, and *Civilisation ou Barbarie* by Diop, and the *Liberté* I–IV series by Senghor). This is especially evident when one considers the remarkable body of research that has been devoted to the content and form of the Caribbean experience—Aimé Césaire (*Discours sur le colonialisme*), Frantz Fanon (*Black Skin, White Masks*, *The Wretched of the Earth*, and *Toward the African Revolution*), Edouard Glissant (*Caribbean Discourse*), and Jean Bernabé, Raphaël Confiant, and Patrick Chamoiseau (namely their collective volume, *Eloge de la créolité*). Indeed, francophone and postcolonial studies could considerably enhance their validity and authenticity by continuing to insist on the need for a model that is as democratic and inclusive as possible with regard to the various geographic zones in which thinking is generated. For if the Senegalese response to its national soccer team's victory over France in the 2002 FIFA Japan/Korea World Cup I, included as one of the epigraphs to this chapter, is any indication (widespread celebrations in the streets of Dakar, capitalization of the word *jamais* [never] on the bumper sticker), sub-Saharan African populations continue to harbor transgenerational resentment toward French reductive discourse concerning Africa. To underestimate the significance of this is to profoundly misunderstand the complex and tenuous relationship between former francophone sub-Saharan African colonies and the metropole.[4]

This chapter is located primarily within a *francophone* context, and the term itself naturally serves to underline the historical connections and intersections between the Hexagon [France] and areas of the world that were once colonized or that remain occupied—such as the Départements d'Outre-Mer (DOM) and Territoires d'Outre-Mer (TOM)—and that continue to be subjected to French hegemonic practices under *la francophonie* (of course, the irony of the French Antilles being an "integral" part of France needs to be underlined here). In many ways, the symbiotic link between French literature and francophone sub-Saharan African literature has its origins in French discourse on Africa in several texts and literary traditions, such as the eighteenth-century *Encyclopédie* project, the work of Arthur Gobineau, Prosper Mérimée, and the Abbé Grégoire, among others, and the representations that emerged from this thinking. Indeed, one could argue that these representations provided much of the justification for colonial expansionism, increased missionary activity, assimilationist practices, and of course the *mission civilisatrice* [civilizing mission] as an ideological project.[5] Colonial and imperial expansionism provided some of the more striking historical examples of the totalitarian impulses of universalizing tendencies—notably the implementation of standards on the communities colonial powers were collectively and indiscriminately engaged in fracturing. If *assimilation* is understood as a process of merging, then the notion of merging is not appropriate in the colonial context, given that colonizing mechanisms were invested in the reduction of the other toward *sameness*—that is, to the molding of cultural prototypes embracing colonial ideologies. The rationale behind the actual *merging* of cultural elements contains the implication that *métissage* would be theoretically possible, a dimension that would be contrary to the ideals of French *assimilation*, given that the justificatory rhetoric for expansionism was provided by the *civilizing* imperative's objective of compensating for the perceived cultural, linguistic, political, religious, and social inadequacies of the colonized. French colonial mechanisms were erected on an ethnocentric assimilationist paradigm that refused to interpret culture as a dynamic process and, accordingly, to incorporate African cultural elements. Instead, French actions themselves serve as testimony to efforts aimed at dismissing, repudiating, dismantling, and systematically erasing African contributions from some kind of universal entity. My position is that France's treatment of multiculturalism and postcoloniality, and in turn the various ways in which French and francophone studies have explored cohabitation in the American academy, reflect this colonial history. I shall return to this question later in this chapter. To a certain degree, this is a perspective that was developed by Emily Apter in her essay "French Colonial Studies and Postcolonial Theory," in which she signaled that "many French intellectuals seem to have difficulty in grasping the pertinence of postcolonial theory to the contemporary politics of culture" (169).

Within the framework of this chapter, I suggest we go one step further in order to distinguish between cultural and economic issues in global contexts. Ashcroft has characterized recent trends as a kind of "recolonization" (208) but insisted we acknowledge that while the International Monetary Fund, World Bank, and multinational companies "have a heavy influence on the domestic policies of countries" (209), an important distinction has to be made, given that these organizations are not imperial in that they do not operate as autonomous states (an important transition can be recorded here from western colonial and neocolonial influence). Nevertheless, various cultural practitioners have concentrated their work on denouncing these latest trends as mere rearticulations and reconfigurations of previous exploitative traditions—the Senegalese filmmaker Djibril Mambéty Diop's film *Hyènes*

(*Hyenas*, 1992) and Glen Ellis's documentary film denouncing the activities of the Shell Corporation in Nigeria, *The Drilling Fields* (1994), provide striking examples of the kind of direction recent work has taken in its effort to demonstrate how these organizations function in similar ways as states, remaining unaccountable in their behavior, often enlisting the help of private militias, and insisting that their activities are beneficial to the membership of indigenous populations in modernity-based modes of existence.

Hexagonal Resistance: Multiculturalism and Postcoloniality

France's rejection of multiculturalism is precisely due to what it perceives as the term's historical indebtedness to and indissociability from the American context in which the accompanying discourses on civil and individual rights are considered to protect citizens above and beyond the communitarian imperatives of the republican state. In France, the primary concern remains the integrational, assimilationist drive toward that ambiguous ideal that is Frenchness. As I have already argued, the colonial civilizing mission was premised on the attempt at creating French cultural prototypes. Newly formed French-Africans soon realized that this stated objective was unattainable. Their status as colonized subjects and constructs inscribed by a hyphenated identity forever precluded their access to some distant evolutionary point, much in the same way that today's ethnic minorities are relegated to topographic zones outside of the parameters of Frenchness. Yet, paradoxically, American blackness has for decades been recuperated and imported into France—from Josephine Baker and Richard Wright to recent television commercials that have capitalized on the sociocultural currency this offers by featuring young black Americans rather than the local resources offered by African minorities residing in France's postcolonial diasporic communities. This latter category remains inseparable from a broader social discourse linking African minorities to criminal behavior. Such discourse is anchored in age-old colonial projections and stereotypes that symbiotically link diasporic Africans with what the media and certain politicians perceive as the "non-civilized" and "barbarous" practices associated with polygamy, excision, and arranged marriages. These stereotypes in turn serve to justify the marginalization of these communities to the peripheries of urban centers. Ironically, the marginalization of these groups creates the very ghettos that the French perceive as the inevitable outcome of U.S. multicultural politics. Yet, for the French authorities, the collapse into the supposed invisibility of Frenchness remains paramount, and the need for individual "special rights" on French soil is seen as unnecessary. Naturally, for individuals who are reminded of their perceived non-Frenchness (because of indelible nonwhite somatic markers), as violence is visited on them on a quotidian basis by educational, employment, housing, police, and legal discrimination, conclusions differ considerably. The end result of these disparate policies is similar, thus reducing the validity of French critiques of U.S. multiculturalism.

A number of global signifiers of blackness—what Amselle might call a "signifiant flottant" [floating signifier] (15)—recuperated outside of nationalist and nationalizing discourses allow us today to consider, for example, the way in which American rap music (by established or more recent artists and groups such NWA, Public Enemy, Eazy-E, Ice-T, Tupac, Notorious BIG), films produced by black artists (such as Spike Lee or John Singleton), or young black actors (Will Smith, Chris Rock, Martin Lawrence), are revered in a country such as France that simultaneously rejects multiculturalism at the state level. In fact, this influence is currently reflected in language as well, since the "in" term to refer to blacks in France today is the English *black* rather than *noir*.[6]

Ashcroft has provided a summary of the two main approaches informing the definition of globalization: "On the one hand culture is seen to be essentially territorial, the possession of a particular society or social group; on the other hand it is seen to be a malleable array of strategies for negotiating a group's reality, a *translocal* learning process. According to these positions culture is either . . . formed by societies and nations or transformed by diasporas and intercommunication" (214). Thus, for Ashcroft, globalization is either homogenizing/hegemonic or heterogenetic/interpenetrating (214). If globalization is indeed an "interpenetrative" phenomenon, then perhaps the local may not in fact be closed and the diaspora *could* have a role to play in redefining the local outside of those universalizing tendencies indebted to the west. However, this will *not* be possible until we distance ourselves from the dangers inherent in the reformulation of the "modernity" argument, according to the tenuous parameters of current discourse that synonymously links "nurture" and "exploitation" (212). Furthermore, France's insistence on protecting the "French exception" in the cultural realm is itself problematic in its hegemonic antimulticulturalist agenda, particularly when one considers the concerted effort that is made by the French Cultural Services in the United States to promote *francophonie* as an indicator of France's supposed openness to cultural diversity. The Summit of Francophone Heads of State initially agreed in 1986 that its membership include "those countries having in *common* the usage of French" [avoir en commun], and while the criterion for inclusion later shifted to "countries *sharing* the usage of French" [partager], perhaps offering a paradigm that could challenge the legitimacy of canon formations in decentralizing linguistic hegemony in order to generate a more inclusive model, one should insist that these measures in no way imply that metropolitan domination of *francophonie* has ceased.[7]

Africa at the Crossroads

As Christopher L. Miller has argued, "The study of black African literature in French requires an approach that is sensitive both to local, ethnic differences and to the homogenizing effects of the French language. The part that 'theory' has to play therein should be cautiously determined by asking to what degree it is appropriate" (24).[8] The work of the most well-known postcolonial theorists, Homi Bhabha, Edward Said, and Gayatri Chakravorty Spivak (among others, of course), have been accorded the critical attention they deserve. Yet, as I mentioned a little earlier, many African authors remain insufficiently read compared to their anglophone and Caribbean counterparts, thereby voiding the potentialities of truly inclusive models. While Miller insists on the need "to reconsider with skepticism the applicability of all Western critical terms and to look to traditional African cultures for terms they might offer" (25), perhaps the most effective way of achieving this end is to bring to the attention of scholars the work of these African theorists that is silenced by the economy of words—distribution of knowledge, economics of publication, circulation of human resources in the global academy.[9]

When I first read Leila Gandhi's book *Postcolonial Theory*, I was somewhat struck by the definition she provided for *postcolonial theory*: "a contentious category which refers, somewhat arbitrarily, to 'literatures in English,' namely those literatures which have accompanied the projection and decline of British imperialism" (141). I initially reflected for some time on the deeper significance of this observation, rejecting its veracity at first, locating the origins of its formulation in what I conceived of as the author's unawareness of the vast body of literature and critical responses generated in francophone, lusophone, and other linguistic sites. Then, returning to what I identified as perhaps the key word in her observation—"arbitrarily"—I began to think that she was perhaps onto something—on the one hand, that other modes of inquiry may in fact be performing what we commonly refer to as postcolonial theory without actually utilizing that term, and on the other, that disciplinary and institutional alignment may in fact be hindering discussion and dialogue across the various real and imaginary boundaries that have been erected to stifle their porous qualities. A cursory overview of the most important contributions to postcolonial theory in fact confirms that this discursive realm has been dominated, almost exclusively, by work produced in Australia, New Zealand, India, Britain, Canada, and the United States in departments of English, literature, cultural studies, and comparative literature, and focusing accordingly, almost exclusively, on primary texts that have emerged from the cultural traditions of those areas. There are of course exceptions that include frequently read texts by Ngùgì wa Thiong'o, Frantz Fanon, texts on the question of Negritude, and to a certain extent by Léopold Sédar Senghor. *The Post-Colonial Studies Reader*, edited by Bill Ashcroft, Gareth Griffiths, and Helen Tiffin, *Colonial Discourse and Post-Colonial Theory*, edited by Patrick Williams and Laura Chrisman, *Dangerous Liaisons*, edited by Anne McClintock, Aamir Mufti, and Ella Shohat, along with *Postcolonial Theory* by Bart Moore-Gilbert, all perform this gesture.[10] Clearly, issues of exclusiveness and limited perspective are in question here, although this is more as a result of disciplinary training than an indictment of the agenda informing these volumes—such a gesture would in fact be futile. Rather, in underlining the important contributions these works make to the recognition of rich and diversified cultural productions, I am merely endeavoring to underscore the fact that what is excluded often leads us to the sad realization and recognition that we all have colleagues, often even working in the same institution, from whom we have so much to learn in terms of collaborative exchanges.

Postcolonial theory has not talked sufficiently about the work of African theorists and writers. This has much to do with language boundaries of course, but more significantly with the nature of departmental configurations in the American academy, an analysis of which can take us a long way toward understanding current circumstances as well as to determining the task with which we are confronted in order to correct and rectify the situation. A number of scholars have already made significant inroads in redressing this imbalance. In the volume edited by Georg M. Gugelberger, *Marxism and African Literature*, contributions reflected a supranational and multilinguistic (anglophone, francophone, and lusophone) approach, and works by authors from such distinct countries as Kenya, Mozambique, South Africa, Nigeria, and Mali were examined. Chidi Amuta's book, *The Theory of African Literature*, adopted a transcolonial framework in order to explore African texts by Cabral, Neto, Ngùgì, and Sembène, while Christopher L. Miller, in his *Theories of Africans*, broadened the field of inquiry considerably, insisting that "the task is to seek a better understanding of francophone African literature by placing it within its historical, political, but especially anthropological context" (5). In turn, Françoise Lionnet demonstrated the potentialities of comparative and transnational investigations (Algeria, Botswana, Egypt, Guadeloupe, Jamaica, Mauritius), in *Postcolonial Representations*. More recently, work by prominent francophone theorists working at the intersection between literature, philosophy, political science, and sociology—most notably Achille Mbembe's remarkable *On the Postcolony*—have been increasingly read—in some instances only as their works have become available in translation.

My objective in this chapter is not to provide an exhaustive and in-depth analysis of the most important African theoretical models, but rather to identify some of the key paradigms that have emerged and that by implication speak to postcolonial theory. Foremost among these stands the project of Negritude itself, the originality of which emerged from what Senghor has described as the attempt to "l'élaborer comme arme de combat, instrument de libération à l'Humanisme du XXème siècle" [develop the concept into a weapon of combat, an instrument of liberation toward a twentieth-century Humanism] (*Liberté III*, 69). As I stated earlier, the assumption of identitarian consciousness constituted an early stage in the struggle against the reductive hegemonic discourse that both justified and remained an intrinsic component of the colonial project. The works of Senghor himself, along with those of a plethora of francophone sub-Saharan African novelists addressed these issues through their consideration of various aspects of colonialism and its respective impact on African culture, philosophy, psychology, and religion. The most convincing articulations of these questions were first formulated by Camara Laye, Mongo Beti, Ferdinand Oyono, Cheikh Hamidou Kane, Bernard Dadié, Tchicaya U Tam'si, and Ousmane Sembène during the 1950s and 1960s. They were later recontextualized according to the changing political circumstances associated with postcoloniality by Alioum Fantouré, Aminata Sow Fall, Massa Makan Diabaté, Ahmadou Kourouma, Henri Lopes, Emmanuel Dongala, Mariama Bâ, and Sony Labou Tansi. At the crossroads of the new millennium, these questions were raised again in the new generation of strikingly original texts produced by Abdourahman Waberi, Eugène Ebodé, Nangala Camara, Daniel Biyaoula, Alain Mabanckou, and Boris Boubacar Diop. Tangential to the concerns of these writers have been the critical responses they have generated—organized around questions of gender, literary influence, ideology, historiography, national literatures, postcoloniality, and of course the discourses generated from both the circumstance of exile and the assumption of residency in various African diasporic communities.[11]

Arguably, the most challenging thinking about these questions is to be found in the work of Achille Mbembe. The following lengthy quotation from his book *On the Postcolony* serves to underline the manner in which Africa and western discourse remain imbricated. In many ways, this contextual framework echoes my own positionality concerning the manner in which both francophone studies and postcolonial theory *and* French and francophone studies remain necessarily symbiotic. For Mbembe:

> In the very principle of its constitution, in its language, and in its finalities, narrative about Africa is always pretext for a comment about something else, some other place, some other people. More precisely, Africa is the mediation that enables the West to accede to its own subconscious and give a public account of its subjectivity. . . . The central assumption that guides what follows is that the peculiar "historicity" of African societies, their own raison d'être and their relation solely to themselves, are rooted in a multiplicity of times, trajectories, and rationalities that, although particular and sometimes local, cannot be conceptualized outside a world that is, so to speak, globalized. From a narrow methodological standpoint, this means that, from the fifteenth century, there is no longer a "distinctive historicity" of these societies, one not embedded in times and rhythms heavily conditioned by European domination. Therefore, dealing with African societies' "historicity" requires more than simply giving an account of what occurs on the continent itself at the interface between the working of internal forces and the working of international actors. It presupposes a critical delving into Western history and the theories that claim to interpret it. (3–9)

These observations lead us then to further reflect on the relationship between francophone studies, postcolonial theory, and African studies, while also affording us the opportunity of suggesting ways in which we might begin to chart the trajectory of future curricular alignments. Indeed, there has already been much thinking in this direction, and my argument merely constitutes a further contribution to what should be an ongoing debate.[12] Clearly, though, alternative discourses are being generated here. The next section will address some of the political and curricular implications of these transitions.

When one looks at the history of French departments in the United States—faculty profiles and training, mission statements, curricular orientation—one finds that departmental configurations for the most part mirrored the structure of their counterparts across the Atlantic (indeed, this was the case in Britain as well until the 1980s, a situation that is best exemplified by the refusal of certain scholars at the prestigious colleges of Cambridge and Oxford to teach living authors—there are in fact accounts circulating of students celebrating the premature death of Albert Camus in 1960!). There are of course numerous ways in which the American context has afforded scholars a perspective and distance with regard to the various texts they have studied, and that in turn has generated the wealth of scholarly output from America-based scholars—from structuralism to deconstruction, Queer theory, gender studies, and so on. This scholarly output, rather than having created what I have heard described as a *lite* version of French studies (to indicate the term used in France to designate diet beverages), has instead provided the field with the vitality and dynamic energy that has maintained its status at the forefront of the humanities. I share the fundamental belief that French departments are being transformed by new scholarly approaches and fields, but my reasons for reaching this conclusion differ considerably from the implied critique contained in the allusion to the term *lite*. The resistance to francophone studies (and by association to postcolonial theory itself) in French departments aligns itself with the objections I registered above to certain conceptions of what French studies should look like, but more significantly to a rejection of those literatures produced in Africa north and south of the Sahara, in Canada, the Caribbean, the Indian Ocean, the Near East, Asia, the Pacific region, European countries with French-language traditions, and of course in those postcolonial communities in France. Yet, the situation is slowly changing and most French departments (some have even changed their name to departments of "French and Francophone Studies" in order to reflect this additional orientation) now have at least one specialist faculty member. However, given the geographic areas such specialists are called upon to teach, the question clearly remains as to whether *one* francophone specialist per department in fact suffices. These positionalities parallel France's own failure to adequately incorporate the literatures of the francophone world in their institutional frameworks precisely because of their complicated origins in colonial histories—racial/ethnic contexts and mind-sets—with which France has yet to come to terms.

Analysis of curricular orientation and alignment in American institutions provides an interesting road map for a journey into the world of francophone and postcolonial studies, and it is with deliberate intent that I use the notion of an intersection in the title of this chapter as a way of underlining this relationship. For, if African nations emerge as a consequence of European colonialism and imperial expansionism, as is indeed evidenced by current cartographic alignments, then so too are the various linguistic influences and subsequent publications a testimony to this legacy of western influence. Africa (and other areas of the nonwestern World) has been marginalized in the curriculum, through its relegation to area studies, centers, and programs.[13] Interdisciplinarity has been stifled in French studies due to the closed nature of the field, and it is not surprising that more significant advances have been made in many comparative literature departments that—at least in principle—are defined by the built-in structure they offer for exploring cultural phenomena across various boundaries. Yet one of the exciting ways in which connections between anglophone, francophone, and other postcolonial cultures could be established is precisely through transcolonial and transnational approaches, in which the relationship of these fields with other cultural influences such as the Arabic and Islamic ones could be foregrounded. Of course, broader interdisciplinary frameworks are characteristic today of the most engaging research in the field of French studies, from the medieval period to contemporary times, as evidenced most recently by David Lee Rubin and Julia Douthwaite's coedited volume of *EMF: Studies in Early Modern France*.

France's colonial histories, along with the history of decolonization, post–Second World War immigration, and the expansion of the European community (among a range of other sociocultural factors), have of course transformed the demographic, institutional, and political structure of France. Lawrence Kritzman's 1995 edited volume of *SubStance* challenged the agenda of Pierre Nora's seven-volume *Les Lieux de mémoire*, a project framed as "the result of an imaginary process that codifies and condenses a national consciousness of the past" (13). Instead, Kritzman's volume illustrated how collective memory today enjoys radically different coordinates (13). Indeed, a well-read alien observer, newly arrived in the Nevada desert, might think that Pierre Nora had been contracted to design Paris-Vegas, an architectural site that is a testimony to the outdated, stereotypical vision of what France corresponds to—Eiffel Tower, Arc de Triomphe, and Louvre—with which we are regularly confronted in our contact with students, and in articles on France.[14] Similarly, Mbembe makes the following observations relative to continued western interference (simultaneously through the exercise of power by governmental and multinational organizations) in the governance of sovereign African nations. In this context, a country such as Congo "is an example of extraterritorialization. Here, the model is not that of partition proper, but rather of a vortex. Violence is cyclical, and its epicenter is the capital. Located in the hinterland, the capital itself has its center of gravity outside itself, in the relation the state maintains with the oil companies operating offshore" (282). Mbembe's observations could serve as an example of how French studies could begin to deterritorialize by fostering methodological innovation that would stand to impact the future of interdisciplinarity.

The Economy of Words and Mapping New Routes

It has become common knowledge that Paris and, to a lesser degree, London remain the publishing centers for writers originating in territories with colonial ties to France and Britain. The long list of authors who in recent years have been either shortlisted or the actual winners of the most coveted literary awards in France (the Goncourt and Renaudot) and Britain (Booker) is impressive. These include Tahar Ben Jelloun and Patrick Chamoiseau, in the case of the Goncourt (Aminata Sow Fall was shortlisted in 1979), and Ahmadou Kourouma, for the Renaudot, while the Booker has been awarded to J. M. Coetzee (twice!), Nadine Gordimer, Salman Rushdie, Ben Okri, and Arundhati Roy. To this end, the ironic and subversive dimension of Zadie Smith's words, which I included as an epigraph to this chapter, seem all the more relevant: "What kind of phrase is this: 'So what?' Is that English? That is not English. Only the immigrants can speak the Queen's English these days" (151). This extraordinary work by such a young, English-Jamaican writer, who published at age twenty-four this magnum opus, whose white, Bangladeshi, and Jamaican protagonists address the challenges and paradoxes confronting a multicultural Britain, daringly traces the "New England" in a humorous and forthright manner. The novel was extremely popular, generated much public debate, and was adapted for television in September 2002.

There is, nevertheless, something a little more ambiguous and even sinister about these trends. The French case is perhaps the most revealing, since most francophone African authors are published in France. Specialized publishing houses such as Présence africaine and L'Harmattan carry the bulk of these authors (in fact, once their work has achieved a certain notoriety, writers often move to larger publishing houses—Henri Lopes started with CLE and Présence africaine and moved to Seuil in 1990, and Alain Mabanckou left Présence africaine in 2002 for Le Serpent à plumes), while the larger publishers insist that they are able to concentrate only on a select number of writers. Only rarely do these publishers promote new voices, and little effort is being made to establish and assist independent African publishing houses.[15] One of France's largest bookstores, FNAC, continues to segregate authors writing in French according to the geographic regions from which the authors originate—France, Maghreb, Afrique noire, Antilles, etc., while one of the most important publishers, the Editions Gallimard, recently launched a new series, *Continents noirs*, in one of the most blatant examples of the center recuperating the periphery and thereby maintaining the hierarchy and status quo. Yet, paradoxically, while one may argue that these efforts at least afford certain writers the opportunity to be read, another perspective might suggest that institutions awarding literary prizes may in fact need these writers far more than they need them. Indeed, Sony Labou Tansi once argued, "Il faut dire que s'il y a du français et de moi quelqu'un qui soit en position de force, ce n'est pas le français, c'est moi. Je n'ai jamais eu recours au français c'est lui qui a recours à moi" [One must say that if between myself and French there is anyone who is in a position of strength, it is not French, but I. I have never had recourse to French, it is rather French that has had recourse to me] (30). With this thought in mind, I propose to outline some of the ways in which French studies in America should insist on a more democratic and inclusive model to ensure its very survival as a field of study.

This is not a debate concerning disciplinary territoriality, but rather the expression of the precarious position of French in American institutions, and a concerted attempt to articulate how one may secure the continued relevance of French studies in the humanities. Without serious thinking on this question, French departments run the risk of becoming mere service providers for other units on campus and the training ground for the acquisition of vocational linguistic competency outside of a cultural context. The curriculum should better reflect both the realities of institutional missions in the twenty-first century and the interests of students, but perhaps more importantly the needs, exigencies, and realities of employment prospects for undergraduate and graduate students beyond the university. Rather than heralding the demise of French departments, these changes suggest instead new ways of thinking about education, defining the role French could, and should, play in the future. While safeguarding healthy enrolments, student interest, and so on, these changes contain the promise of enhancing interest in language study as well as the internationalization of the student experience, while simultaneously better preparing students for postuniversity education and training.

One of the ways of enacting change is to begin by taking stock of the presence of French studies on campus in general. Rather than constantly having to justify and establish criteria for new faculty hires, language departments *should* be recuperating relevant courses offered on campus that could become central to the department mission. Why, for example, should the work of French anthropologists, historians, filmmakers, sociologists, artists, etc., remain the privileged domain of other campus departments? Why should Gramsci be taught in sociology and not in Italian? Why should Marx be restricted to philosophy and political science, and not *also* available in German departments (in the original *and* in translation)? Given the colonial context of France's rise to centrality, this should not be seen as an attempt to colonize interdisciplinarity—cross-departmental dialogue, team-teaching, and the cross-listing of courses should be encouraged in every way possible in order to strive to create truly interdisciplinary offerings—but rather as an indication as to how the defense of a traditionally conservative version of French studies will inevitably result in its disappearance. Language departments need to offer these types of courses and be actively engaged in recruiting faculty with training and Ph.D.'s in related fields. Furthermore, these measures would not be designed to eliminate other institutional units, but rather to enrich the work that is done across departments and pedagogic practices. As Dominick LaCapra has argued in his "Reconfiguring French Studies":

> A third challenge involves the movement or expansion of the field of interest from literature to culture, society, and history, including francophone cultures, societies, and histories. With this shift the civilization course is no longer a makeshift delegated to an overly gullible, unguardedly good-natured, insufficiently high-powered, or otherwise theory-impaired colleague. It becomes a truly demanding undertaking that epitomizes the entire problem of expanding the field from a study of literature in the restricted sense to a concern with culture in a broader anthropological, theoretical, and historical sense. . . . In other words the civilization course or text becomes an exemplary site for an attempt to rearticulate and reframe the field of French studies and critically explore the demanding problem of the interaction among theory, criticism, historiography, ethnography, and the study of literature or other forms of art—a problem that may deceptively be taken as a solution called cultural studies. (193–94)

I wholeheartedly embrace LaCapra's insistence on broader approaches and agree that "this reproblematization is, I think, necessary if the field is to be vital and in a viable position to make a place for itself in a configuration of disciplines that is being redefined in the face of both intellectual and economic demands" (226).

These reforms are *not* in any way designed to generate antagonistic exchanges or promote conflict—but rather to underscore the mutually constitutive nature of differing approaches to cultural phenomena. In both acknowledging and responding to the reality of increased English language hegemony, there is an urgent need to foreground the many ways in which all approaches to culture and literature, whether so-called traditional approaches or those that employ more recent critical tools, have to benefit from cooperation. This is not about winners and losers, regular, *lite*, leaded, or unleaded agendas, but rather about fostering productive dialogue that begins with accepting that reinterpretation and recontextualization are necessary. As Apter has suggested, "French postcolonial criticism could reinvigorate the links between political philosophy and literary/cultural analysis. It could broaden the parameters of translation to encompass a polyglot identity in the arts. . . . [P]ostcolonialism could foster the inclusion of Francophone Studies within a framework other than that of 'enlightened' assimilationism, thus leading to broader interest in French studies abroad" ("French" 172). Furthermore, effective foreign language instruction has a key role to play in this, since without the competence to access new theoretical approaches and understand current sociopolitical events, we subject ourselves to a dependency on translations.

Of course, there has already been some progress in this direction, although the United States is behind Britain, where for some time now French departments have hired specialists in film, philosophy, European studies, media, and history (see, for example, the curricular offerings at the universities of Edinburgh, Bristol, Nottingham, London, Leeds, and Southampton). While the expression of a certain openness to these ideas has been evidenced through faculty hires in these areas in some departments, and while this constitutes, of course, a step in the right direction, these measures are *not* sufficient unless they are accompanied by a genuine willingness and commitment to acknowledge that these reorientations are not temporary—reflecting some sort of popular trend—but rather more permanent ways of rethinking, rejuvenating, and realigning curricular orientation. Paradoxically, rather than threatening disciplinary alignment, these new paradigms should be embraced as the guarantors of French studies as a field. The objective should not be hospitality or cohabitation, but the formulation of pedagogic philosophies that reflect the closely imbricated colonial origins of these fields and their continued potential for cross-pollination. Of course, interdisciplinarity itself must avoid at all costs the pitfalls inherent to any kind of institutionalization, a precondition to protect and ensure the revitalizing and dynamic exigencies that keep subjects alive.

Teachers have the responsibility of designing innovative syllabi across centuries and fields of specialization and training that underline the relationship between French and francophone studies, probing the links between: the surrealist André Breton and the Martinican poet Aimé Césaire, Sartre prefacing Senghor's, Fanon's, and Memmi's works; France and the United States—Jean-Loup Amselle on multiculturalism, the work of Jean Baudrillard; *francophonie* and globalization—the Dreyfus Affair and antisemitism in France today; medieval literature and African folktales; and finally, perhaps, explorations of the question of tolerance through readings of works by Voltaire and Tunisian author Abdelwahab Meddeb's *La Maladie de l'Islam*—the possibilities and configurations are endless.[16] Graduate students have the opportunity to explore these new alignments across boundaries delineated between the humanities and social sciences, but also through transcolonial and transnational frameworks. Our task will consist in assisting them in breaking new ground, mapping new routes, and delineating new pathways to the future. With boundless energy, enthusiasm, imagination, and resourcefulness, it is they who will provide the coordinates for the road ahead. Their projects might explore the work of Hanif Kureishi and Azouz Begag, Zadie Smith and

Calixthe Beyala, Abdourahman Wabéri and Nuruddin Farah, Ousmane Sembène and Ngùgì wa Thiong'o, but also that of theorists such as Bhabha and Mbembe. Students should be encouraged to break new ground in their research without feeling compelled to formulate dissertation projects that fit into neatly compartmentalized boxes, for the simple reason that departments should not look the same tomorrow as they do today. For if the role of teachers and scholars is to lead students out of the darkness—and I say this in a purely figurative sense, with neither religious implications nor patronizing intent—then it is their pathbreaking projects that will lead us toward the light.

Notes

1. Amselle is the author of a number of works that have emphasized the urgency of deploying new research paradigms in order to relocate anthropology as a productive discipline for cross-cultural investigations. See his *Logiques métisses* and his collaborative work with M'Bokolo in *Au coeur de l'ethnie*. For a meticulous reading of Amselle's notion of "logiques métisses," see Lionnet. Whatever positionality one may subscribe to in our critical explorations, Lionnet underlines the fact that "Amselle's remarks force us to rethink some of the fundamental notions that we are beginning to take for granted as literary and cultural critics: the respect for multiculturalism, the vexing questions of separatism and cultural autonomy, and the need for contemporary societies to respect difference without falling into a situation of apartheid. . . . To follow Amselle is to come to the conclusion that it is not the existence of *different* cultures which induces a comparative (ethnographical) approach; rather, it is the critic's (or anthropologist's) stance as a comparatist which creates an arbitrary and singular object (be it 'Bambara culture,' or 'Francophone' or 'postcolonial' studies) and thus imposes constraints on a determinate set of particularisms" (17–18).

2. For a historical perspective on the question of contact between France and Africa see Cohen.

3. See Mudimbe, ed. *The Surreptitious Speech*. Indeed, the work of the Beur writer Mehdi Charef serves to further complicate this relationship in its attempt to point out ways in which western historiography has often conveniently erased various African contributions to thinking. The title of Charef's novel, *Le Thé au harem d'Archi Ahmed*, recuperated the text's otherness in the hexagonal diasporic context by foregrounding the "thé," "harem," and Maghrebi dimension, while the 1985 film adaptation insisted instead (in a clever variation and corruption of the original title) on a play on words that transformed Archi Ahmed into "Archimède," *Le Thé au harem d'Archimède*, thereby introducing the reference to the mathematician Archimedes. For a more in-depth discussion of this, refer to the two most significant books on Beur culture by Hargreaves and by Laronde (88–89).

4. Indeed, one of the most striking examples of this was provided on 7 October 2001 during a friendly match between Algeria and France played in France. Thousands of

Maghrebi spectators whistled, thereby disrupting the performance of the French national anthem prior to kickoff. See Kédadouche.

5. For French discourse on Africa, see Miller, *Blank Darkness*.

6. An article published in France during the summer of 2002 by Valérie Zerguine, indicated a shift in this trend, yet nevertheless signaled certain behavioral patterns that were accorded more value through the attribution of the distinctive labels "black" and "nègre": "Vous êtes un black quand vous tapez dans un ballon ou rappez dans un micro et un nègre quand vous cherchez du boulot" [You're a black when you kick a ball or rap into a microphone and a negro when you look for a job] (8). Significantly, the article addresses the recurring issue in the French context concerning the balance between multiculturalism and social segregation: "Au sein de la vaste communauté noire française, des voix s'élèvent pour demander plus de représentativité et moins de mépris dans notre société. Des revendications qui pourraient, si rien ne change, conduire à un repli identitaire" [From the very heart of France's black community, people are calling for increasing representation and less contempt in society. Unless things begin to change, these claims could in turn result in a withdrawal into identity politics] (7).

7. See Senghor, *Ce que je crois*, and Tétu.

8. Many of these questions have been raised in a different context by Gates, and Appiah explored related questions in his landmark essay, "The Postcolonial and the Postmodern." See also Mateso; Chinweizu, Onwuchekwa Jemie, and Ihechukwu Madubuike; and Irele, *The African Experience in Literature and Ideology*. It goes without saying that the work of Towa, Hountondji, Masolo, and of course Mudimbe would be foregrounded as central works in securing an accurate representation of African contributions to thinking.

9. The question of translation is, of course, central to these issues. On this, see Apter, "On Translation."

10. As I mentioned, this is only a very general list of some of the volumes and works that include essays by the most well known and respected "postcolonial theorists." Individual works by such leading scholars as Arjun Appadurai, Timothy Brennan, Dipesh Chakrabarty, Partha Chatterjee, Seamus Deane, David Lloyd, would, of course, have to be added to a more complete list.

11. See, for example, Hitchcott, Volet, Green et al., Huannou, Midiohouan, Bjornson, Mongo-Mboussa, Fonkoua and Halen. These questions are addressed at length in Thomas. See also the recent contributions of the following scholars: Rosello, Diawara, and Irele.

12. More recently, the question of the future cohabitation of French and francophone studies has been the subject of numerous conferences and panel discussions. The conference held at Yale University in November 1999 is perhaps the most significant example of this and is the subject of a special issue of *Yale French Studies* (ed. Laroussi and Miller). See also Laronde, "Les Littératures des immigrations."

13. For a more in-depth exploration of some of these questions, see Miller, "Literary Studies and African Literature."

14. See, for example, Knox.

15. This applies to translations of anglophone authors as well. Leading South African authors J. M. Coetzee, Nadine Gordimer, Beyten Breytenbach, and André Brink are

divided up between Seuil (Coetzee), Grasset (Gordimer and Breytenbach), and Stock (Brink).

16. See also *Yale French Studies* (ed. Sarkonak).

Works Cited

Amselle, Jean-Loup. *Branchements: anthropologie de l'universalité des cultures*. Paris: Flammarion, 2001.

———. *Logiques métisses: anthropologie de l'identité en Afrique et ailleurs*. Paris: Payot, 1990.

———. *Vers un multiculturalisme français: l'empire de la coutume*. Paris: Flammarion, 2001.

Amselle, Jean-Loup, and Elikia M'Bokolo. *Au coeur de l'ethnie: ethnies, tribalisme et état en Afrique*. Paris: La Découverte, 1985.

Amuta, Chidi. *The Theory of African Literature: Implications for Practical Criticism*. London: Zed, 1989.

Appiah, Kwame Anthony. "The Postcolonial and the Postmodern." *In My Father's House: Africa in the Philosophy of Culture*. New York: Oxford University Press, 1992. 137–57.

Apter, Emily. "French Colonial Studies and Postcolonial Theory." *SubStance* 76–77 (1995): 169–80.

———. "On Translation in a Global Market." *Public Culture* 13.1 (Winter 2001): 1–12.

Ashcroft, Bill. *Post-Colonial Transformation*. London: Routledge, 2001.

Ashcroft, Bill, Gareth Griffiths, and Helen Tiffin, eds. *The Post-Colonial Studies Reader*. London: Routledge, 1995.

Bâ, Mariama. *Une Si longue lettre*. Dakar: Nouvelles éditions africaines, 1979.

Baudrillard, Jean. *Amérique*. Paris: Grasset, 1986.

Behr, Mark. *Embrace*. London: Little, Brown, 2000.

Bernabé, Jean, Raphaël Confiant, and Patrick Chamoiseau. *Eloge de la créolité*. Paris: Gallimard, 1989.

Beti, Mongo. *Le Pauvre Christ de Bomba*. Paris: Robert Laffont, 1956.

Biyaoula, Daniel. *L'Impasse*. Paris: Présence africaine, 1996.

Bjornson, Richard. *The African Quest for Freedom and Identity: Cameroonian Writing and the National Experience*. Bloomington: Indiana University Press, 1991.

Camara Laye. *L'Enfant noir*. Paris: Plon, 1953.

Camara, Nangala. *Le Printemps de la liberté*. Paris: Le Serpent à plumes, 2000.

Césaire, Aimé. *Discours sur le colonialisme*. Paris: Présence africaine, 1955.

Charef, Mehdi. *Le Thé au harem d'Archi Ahmed*. Paris: Mercure de France, 1983.

Chinweizu, Onwuchekwa Jemie, and Ihechukwu Madubuike. *Toward the Decolonization of African Literature*. Enugu, Nigeria: Fourth Dimension, 1980.

Cohen, William B. *The French Encounter with Africans*. Bloomington: Indiana University Press, 1984.

"Conference on the Relation between English and Foreign Languages in the Academy: Constructing Dialogue, Imagining Change." *PMLA* 117.5 (October 2002): 1233–94.

Dadié, Bernard. *Climbié*. Paris: Seghers, 1956.

Diabaté, Massa Makan. *Le Lieutenant de Kouta*. Paris: Hatier, 1979.

Diawara, Manthia. *In Search of Africa*. Cambridge, Mass.: Harvard University Press, 2000.

Diop, Boris Boubacar. *Le Cavalier et son ombre*. Paris: Stock, 1997.

Diop, Cheikh Anta. *L'Afrique noire précoloniale*. Paris: Présence africaine, 1960.

———. *Antériorité des civilisations nègres*. Paris: Présence africaine, 1967.

———. *Civilisation ou barbarie*. Paris: Présence africaine, 1981.

———. *Nations nègres et cultures*. Paris: Présence africaine, 1954.

———. *L'Unité culturelle de l'Afrique noire*. Paris: Présence africaine, 1960.

Diop, Djibril Mambety. *Hyènes*. Senegal: Kino International, 1992.

Dongala, Emmanuel. *Le Feu des origines*. Paris: Albin Michel, 1987.

———. *Little Boys Come from the Stars*. Trans. Joël Réjouis and Val Vinokurov. New York: Farrar, Straus and Giroux, 2001.

Ebodé, Eugène. *La Transmission*. Paris: Gallimard, 2002.

Ellis, Glen. *The Drilling Fields*. Catma Films, U.K., 1994.

EMF: Studies in Early Modern France 6 (2000). Special issue on "Cultural Studies 1: A State of the Question." Ed. David and Julia Douthwaite.

Fall, Aminata Sow. *La Grève des Bàttu*. Dakar: Nouvelles éditions africaines, 1979.

Fanon, Frantz. *Black Skin, White Masks*. Trans. Charles Lam Markmann. London: MacGibbon and Kee, 1968.

———. *Toward the African Revolution*. Trans. Haakon Chevalier. New York: Grove Press, 1967.

———. *The Wretched of the Earth*. Trans. Constance Farrington. New York: Grove Press, 1963.

Fantouré, Alioum. *Le Cercle des tropiques*. Paris: Présence africaine, 1972.

Fonkoua, Romuald, and Pierre Halen, eds. *Les Champs littéraires africains*. Paris: Karthala, 2001.

Gandhi, Leila. *Postcolonial Theory: A Critical Introduction*. New York: Columbia University Press, 1998.

Gates, Henry Louis, Jr. *The Signifying Monkey: A Theory of Afro-American Literary Criticism*. New York: Oxford University Press, 1988.

Glissant, Edouard. *Caribbean Discourse: Selected Essays*. Trans. J. Michael Dash. Charlottesville: University of Virginia Press, 1989.

Green, Mary Jean, et al. *Postcolonial Subjects: Francophone Women Writers*. Minneapolis: University of Minnesota Press, 1996.

Gugelberger, Georg M., ed. *Marxism and African Literature*. London: James Currey, 1985.

Hargreaves, Alec G. *Immigration and Identity in Beur Fiction: Voices from the North African Community in France*. Oxford, U.K.: Berg, 1991.

Hitchcott, Nicki. *Women Writers in Francophone Africa*. Oxford, U.K.: Berg, 2000.

Hountondji, Paulin. *Sur la philosophie africaine*. Paris: Maspéro, 1976.

Huannou, Adrien. *La Question des littératures nationales en Afrique noire*. Abidjan, Ivory Coast: CEDA, 1989.

Irele, Abiola. *The African Experience in Literature and Ideology*. London: Heinemann, 1981.

———. *The African Imagination: Literature in Africa and the Black Diaspora*. New York: Oxford University Press, 2001.
Kane, Cheikh Hamidou. *L'Aventure ambiguë*. Paris: Julliard, 1961.
Kédadouche, Zaïr. *La France et les Beurs*. Paris: La Table ronde, 2002.
Knox, Edward C. "The *New York Times* Looks at France." *French Review* 75.6 (May 2002): 1172–80.
Kourouma, Ahmadou. *Les Soleils des indépendances*. Paris: Seuil, 1970.
LaCapra, Dominick. "Reconfiguring French Studies." *History and Reading: Tocqueville, Foucault, French Studies*. Toronto: University of Toronto Press, 2000. 169–226.
Laronde, Michel. *Autour du roman beur: immigration et identité*. Paris: L'Harmattan, 1993.
———. "Les Littératures des immigrations en France. Question de nomenclature et directions de recherche." *Maghreb Littéraire* 1.2 (1997): 25–44.
Lionnet, Françoise. "*Logiques métisses*: Cultural Appropriation and Postcolonial Representations." *Postcolonial Representations: Women, Literature, Identity*. Ithaca, N.Y.: Cornell University Press, 1995. 1–21.
———. *Postcolonial Representations: Women, Literature, Identity*. Ithaca, N.Y.: Cornell University Press, 1995.
Lopes, Henri. *Le Pleurer-Rire*. Paris: Présence africaine, 1982.
Mabanckou, Alain. *Bleu-Blanc-Rouge*. Paris: Présence africaine, 1998.
Masolo, D. A. *African Philosophy in Search of Identity*. Bloomington: Indiana University Press, 1994.
Mateso, Locha. *La Littérature africaine et sa critique*. Paris: ACCT/Karthala, 1986.
Mbembe, Achille. "At the Edge of the World: Boundaries, Territoriality, and Sovereignty in Africa." Trans. Steven Rendall. *Public Culture* 12.1 (Winter 2000): 259–84.
———. *On the Postcolony*. Berkeley: University of California Press, 2001.
McClintock, Anne, Aamir Mufti, and Ella Shohat, eds. *Dangerous Liaisons: Gender, Nation, and Postcolonial Perspectives*. Minneapolis: University of Minnesota Press, 1997.
Meddeb, Abdelwahab. *La Maladie de l'Islam*. Paris: Seuil, 2002.
Memmi, Albert. *The Colonizer and the Colonized*. Trans. Howard Greenfeld. Boston: Beacon Press, 1965.
Midiohouan, Guy Ossito. *L'Idéologie dans la littérature négro-africaine d'expression française*. Paris: L'Harmattan, 1986.
———. "Le Phénomène des littératures nationales." *Peuples noirs, peuples africains* 27 (1982): 57–70.
Miller, Christopher L. *Blank Darkness: Africanist Discourse in French*. Chicago: University of Chicago Press, 1985.
———. "Literary Studies and African Literature." *Africa and the Disciplines*. Ed. Robert H. Bates, V. Y. Mudimbe and Jean O'Barr. Chicago: University of Chicago Press, 1993. 213–31.
———. *Theories of Africans: Francophone African Literature and Anthropology*. Chicago: University of Chicago Press, 1990.
Mongo-Mboussa, Boniface. *Désir d'Afrique*. Paris: Gallimard, 2002.

Moore-Gilbert, Bart. *Postcolonial Theory: Contexts, Practices, Politics*. London: Verso, 1997.

Mudimbe, V. Y. *The Idea of Africa*. Bloomington: Indiana University Press, 1994.

———. *The Invention of Africa: Gnosis, Philosophy, and the Order of Knowledge*. Bloomington: Indiana University Press, 1988.

Mudimbe, V. Y., ed. *The Surreptitious Speech: Présence Africaine and the Politics of Otherness, 1947–1987*. Chicago: University of Chicago Press, 1992.

Nora, Pierre. *Les Lieux de mémoire*. Paris: Gallimard, 1984–92.

Orisha, Ifé. "Sony Labou Tansi face à douze mots." *Equateur* 1 (October–November 1986): 29–32.

Oyono, Ferdinand. *Une Vie de boy*. Paris: Julliard, 1956.

Rosello, Mireille. *Postcolonial Hospitality: The Immigrant as Guest*. Stanford, Calif.: Stanford University Press, 2001.

Sembène, Ousmane. *Les Bouts de bois de Dieu*. Paris: Le Livre contemporain, 1960.

Senghor, Léopold Sédar. *Ce que je crois: Négritude, francité et civilisation de l'universel*. Paris: Bernard Grasset, 1988.

———. *Liberté I: Négritude et humanisme*. Paris: Seuil, 1964.

———. *Liberté II: nation et voie africaine du socialisme*. Paris: Seuil, 1971.

———. *Liberté III: Négritude et civilisation de l'universel*. Paris: Seuil, 1977.

———. *Liberté IV: socialisme et planification*. Paris: Seuil, 1983.

Smith, Zadie. *White Teeth*. New York: Vintage, 2001.

Sony Labou Tansi. *L'Etat honteux*. Paris: Seuil, 1981.

SubStance 76/77 (1995). Special issue on "France's Identity Crises." Ed. Lawrence D. Kritzman.

Tétu, Michel. *La Francophonie: histoire, problématique perspectives*. Montreal: Guérin littérature, 1988.

Thomas, Dominic. *Nation-Building, Propaganda, and Literature in Francophone Africa*. Bloomington: Indiana University Press, 2002.

Towa, Marcien. *Essai sur la problématique philosophique dans l'Afrique actuelle*. Yaounde, Cameroon: Editions CLE, 1971.

U Tam'si, Tchicaya. *Le Mauvais sang*. Paris: Caractères, 1955.

Volet, Jean-Marie. *La Parole aux Africaines ou l'idée de pouvoir chez les romancières d'expression française de l'Afrique sub-Saharienne*. Amsterdam: Rodopi, 1993.

Waberi, Abdourahman. *Cahier nomade*. Paris: Le Serpent à plumes, 1994.

Williams, Patrick, and Laura Chrisman, eds. *Colonial Discourse and Post-Colonial Theory: A Reader*. New York: Columbia University Press, 1994.

Yale French Studies 100 (2001). Special issue on "France/USA: The Cultural Wars." Ed. Ralph Sarkonak.

———. 103 (2003). Special issue on "French and Francophone: The Challenge of Expanding Horizons." Ed. Farid Laroussi and Christopher L. Miller.

Zerguine, Valérie. "Fier d'être noir." *de l'air: reportages d'un monde à l'autre* 11 (June–July 2002): 7–15.

Afterword

Francophonie, Postcolonial Studies, and Transnational Feminisms

Françoise Lionnet

> Une morale de l'ambiguïté, ce sera une morale qui refusera de nier à priori que des existants séparés puissent en même temps être liés entre eux, que leurs libertés singulières puissent forger des lois valables pour tous.
>
> [An ethics of ambiguity will be one which will refuse to deny a priori that separate existants can, at the same time, be bound to each other, that their individual freedoms can forge laws valid for all.]
>
> **Simone de Beauvoir, *Pour une morale de l'ambiguïté***

With this volume, H. Adlai Murdoch and Anne Donadey have assembled a timely collection of essays that illuminates the points of intersection between two fields of research that have much in common yet do not speak the same "language." The editors offer new and comprehensive ways of reconfiguring the dialogue between these fields, and their much-needed revision of theoretical agendas will be inspiring to scholars in these expanding academic domains. In our increasingly internationalized curricula, the editors' focus on questions of language and translation is a salutary reminder that the "*imperium* of English" (Spivak, "Scattered Speculations" 277) has led to uneven development and unfortunate misreadings of the fundamental critical and cultural parameters of *francophonie*. Conversely, as they point out, the translation of influential postcolonial theorists into *French* also lags behind and results in their neglect both in France and the broader francophone world. By making such gaps clearly visible, this collection is an important step on the road to more productive conversations and comparisons.

In the introduction, the editors note that "the point of entry of postcolonial theory into francophone studies has been primarily through postcolonial feminist theory" even if "few francophone studies scholars" have taken up the term *postcolonial* as a theoretical rather than as a temporal marker. This insightful remark goes a long way toward explaining some of the difficulties that have delayed the rapprochement of the two fields. Indeed, if feminism has been the ground of their mediation in the U.S. academy, such a foundation is no longer available in French and francophone critical practice in France, where feminism no longer plays a central role. Due to the theoretical fortunes of "French feminism" in the 1970s and 1980s, scholars of French literature everywhere were attuned to feminist research even as it evolved and interacted with Anglo-American and other "ethnic" feminisms, thus creating an ideal terrain for the rise of interdisciplinarity in the U.S. academy. If the three main "French" feminist critics, Cixous, Irigaray, and Kristeva, continue to be studied by U.S. scholars, their own work has since moved in new, and sometimes unexpected, directions, whereas vocal critics of their poststructuralist and dialectical methods have pointed to the limitations of these approaches in a multicultural or multiracial context. Their focus on language and psychoanalysis, in particular, led to charges that these theories ignored history as well as social realities, and could not account for agency in the individual subject.[1]

During the 1980s and 1990s, intellectual and political engagements between different "schools" of feminist theory and the fields of "postcolonial, indigenous, and emergent" feminisms played themselves out in the pages of such journals as *Yale French Studies*, *Signs*, *Genders*, *Critical Inquiry*, *differences*, *L'Esprit créateur*, *Studies in Twentieth-Century Literature*, or *Callaloo*, to name but a few.[2] Today, "feminism" continues to expand as an academic discipline in the United States. In many institutions, women's and gender studies have large undergraduate majors and important M.A. programs. Furthermore, doctoral programs are being instituted in a growing number of research universities, such as UCLA. Women's studies was the first successful program of serious interdisciplinary study to be developed, and it continues to offer courses that attract students anxious to study, say, the science of gender and the gender of science as well as the histories through which they can begin to acquire the "courage and tools" needed for sustained critical analysis of our prevailing sex and gender regimes in a variety of cultural or national contexts.[3]

In France, by contrast, many intellectuals today take a very negative view of "feminisms," as evidenced by Elisabeth Badinter's 2003 *Fausse route*, in which the former women's rights activist now accuses feminists of seeing "victims" everywhere, arguing that this tendency is in part the result of twenty-five years of (damaging) radical American feminist influence (*à la* Andrea Dworkin and Catharine MacKinnon).[4] Badinter thus seems unaware of the vastly more complex debates that have since flourished in gender studies, from the focus on performance and performativity to the widely negative reviews of universalizing tendencies implied by some western versions of feminism, not to mention Judith Butler's 1994 critique of MacKinnon's "structurally static account of gender, its pro-censorship position, and its falsifying cultural generalizations about the eternally victimized position of women" (15).[5]

There is only one program of "études féminines" in France: Hélène Cixous's at Paris VIII-Vincennes and its future is in question. All too often, due to the time lag (and disinterest) in translating the most current theoretical works of U.S. feminists and postcolonial theorists, French intellectuals are "en retard d'une guerre" [one step behind], as we say, when it comes to understanding the issues and engaging with the existing debates and internal critiques within these disciplines, whether the topic is the "war of the sexes" or the "culture wars." Like feminism, "ethnic studies" is viewed in France as a political field, based in narrow communitarian ideologies, too earnest and too "PC" to be worth the intellectual efforts required to understand what it has contributed to the transformation of our contemporary *mentalités*.[6]

When postcolonial and ethnic studies have made inroads in the French academy, it has been in departments of English and American studies. There, the intellectual, literary, and cultural history of the English-speaking world is part of the curriculum, and scholars are better informed about U.S. multiculturalism and British, Indian, or Australian postcolonial contexts. It is thus worth noting that several scholars of *la francophonie* working today in the United States were first trained in departments of English and American studies in France, and then arrived in the United States already familiar with American ethnic literatures and the political theories and critical methodologies that differ markedly from those used most often by scholars trained in departments of "French" literature, in France or elsewhere. The paradox and difficulty, therefore, for francophone studies arise from its natural "affinity" with a broad range of debates about nationalism, colonialism, immigration, diaspora, identity, orientalism, "subalternity," and transnationalism, debates that have so far had little or no purchase in France, where for mainstream French studies formalism is still pretty much de rigueur. The tendency in France seems to be more toward "integrating" the complex ethnic, cultural, and discursive patterns of both the French and the francophone corpus under the broader umbrella of *francophonie*, as does an influential anthology.[7] Francophone writers who get anointed by Parisian publishing houses and receive critical acclaim followed by major literary awards are the ones who make it into the canon of contemporary literature, and their works generally get subsumed under established national, aesthetic, or formal categories.

That is, they become legible in terms of such categories instead of providing an opportunity for a radical rethinking of the existing parameters of formal, let alone cultural, analysis.

But, as Edward Said has taught us, it has become imperative, in a multipolar world, "to think through and interpret together experiences that are discrepant" (*Culture* 32). As he explains in *Culture and Imperialism*, a "comparative, or . . . contrapuntal perspective" can illuminate connections between seemingly disparate entities. He advocates a move "beyond insularity and provincialism . . . to see several cultures and literatures together . . . [as] an antidote to reductive nationalism and uncritical dogma" (43). The present volume provides just such an important "antidote" while emphasizing the lasting contributions made by francophone scholars to the critical and comparative study of literature and culture in languages other than English.

One area in which this volume does not offer new insights, however, is that of feminist theory. How interesting that the discipline that provided the mediation between postcolonialism and *francophonie* no longer seems to play an active role in their mutual reconfigurations. To be sure, some of the contributors to this volume focus in part on women's texts: Brière on Beyala, Harrow on Benguigui, Larrier on Danticat, and Scharfman on Cixous, whereas Woodhull brings a transnational feminist perspective to bear on Pabst's films. But there is no sustained engagement with feminist discourses as such, and no major attempt to investigate the new avenues opened up by transnational feminist ethics, a rubric under which much innovative "First" and "Third World" feminist theorizing is now being done.[8] Is it because French and francophone studies are no longer in dialogue with such a field? Are there no new French or francophone "feminist" writers and theorists to inspire the critics and bridge the gap between western theories of the subject and new approaches to feminist ethics in our globalized academies? Or have these two modes of inquiry become too "discrepant" in view of the now widespread indifference to gender studies within metropolitan France or in the Départements d'Outre-Mer, where some research paradigms get set?[9] Will the logical next step for francophone studies be a rethinking of the place of gender studies within its midst, now that this volume makes clear that transnational feminism is at once a source of "blindness *and* insight" for French and francophone studies in general? If so, then this volume deserves to become a long-lasting or "classic" point of reference for scholars in these interdisciplinary fields.

Taking my cue from Said's call for a "contrapuntal" reading of "discrepant" spheres of experience, I would like to dwell on the current "disconnect" between feminism and francophone studies, since each indeed has its own "particular agenda and pace of development, its own internal formations, its internal coherence and system of external relationships, all of them co-existing and interacting with others" (Said, *Culture* 32). By describing the "discrepant experiences" of empire in the preceding terms, Said points to the logic internal to each experience, and to the networks that can either connect them or keep them on parallel tracks. If gender studies and francophone studies now pursue "parallel tracks," the phrase Donadey and Murdoch use in the introduction to describe the trajectories of postcolonial and francophone studies, it may be interesting to ask why, and to think about ways of foregrounding their respective blind spots. Such a task cannot be mine here, for it would require yet another volume. But the time will no doubt come when it will be useful to revisit the gendered contexts of francophone studies, and to shift the emphasis onto this currently missing link.

What I would like to do in the rest of this brief essay, then, is to make a first stab at bringing together some elements for further research in that direction. I would like to use an example from contemporary French cinema to explain what I have in mind.

What I find especially compelling in Said's description of "discrepant" spheres is the strong echo that it creates for me with the interpersonal "ethics of ambiguity" formulated by Simone de Beauvoir some fifty years earlier (in 1947). Taken together, Said's and de Beauvoir's perspectives may help to demarcate a fertile terrain for rethinking feminist questions within a transnational or globalized francophone frame. As de Beauvoir states in the epigraph I used above, "[a]n ethics of ambiguity will be one which will refuse to deny *a priori* that separate existants can, at the same time, be bound to each other, that their individual freedoms can forge laws valid for all" (*Ethics* 18). Her emphasis on "separate existants" resonates with Said's description of "discrepant" experiences, although she is more concerned, as a philosopher, with the individual and the personal, whereas his focus is on culture, intellectual history, and the disciplines. Nonetheless, de Beauvoir's contention that separate or distinct entities can also be "bound to each other" in a way that may subject them to the same "laws valid for all" is an important one for thinking through an ethics of coalition and solidarity in a global context. Transnational feminism attaches much value to questions of solidarity, for such an ethics implies that we remain respectful of differences while arguing for universal human rights in a multicultural world. I was thus especially gratified to discover that the recent Coline Serreau movie *Chaos* (2001) is a witty "case study" of a French bourgeois woman who cannot go on with her "normal" life once she has witnessed the appalling indifference to suffering that characterizes her class.

Serreau's film provides a "transnational" feminist perspective by dealing humorously with serious questions of women's rights. She vigorously denounces the dehumanizing global forces that now contaminate all aspects of our private and public lives. She crafts a tale of friendship and selflessness that foregrounds an ethics of relationality across multiple sites of encounter in which differences are not blurred but become the ground upon which solidarity can begin to be conceived. As a deft manipulator of emotions, images, and situations, Serreau gingerly elicits a recontextualization of some important ethical questions faced by postcolonial and feminist theorists today. Using her film as my guide, I propose that we take seriously her portrayal of feminine solidarity and appropriate it for French and francophone studies in a transnational frame.

In the final scene of the movie, we see four women sitting together in silence on a bench in front of a beautiful house, set on what appears to be the coast of Normandy. They are facing the sea, and their faces express different emotions. Two of them are French, and two of them are Algerian-born French citizens. The two immigrant sisters are sitting between the Frenchwomen. The youngest, Zohra, is frowning and appears puzzled while her sister, Malika, has a serious, determined, and thoughtful look. The middle-aged French woman, Hélène, has a vacant stare, while Mamie, her mother-in-law, appears, by contrast, to be quietly blissful. The camera lingers on each face in turn and finally comes to rest on a close-up shot of the beaming, white-haired and blue-eyed grandmother, played with understated style by the veteran actress, Line Renaud.

The country house in the background might appear to connote the ultimate Franco-French traditional "home" of nationalist literary and cultural history (Balzac's, Flaubert's or Proust's), as it attempts to "integrate" into its midst the immigrant women framed here by Hélène and Mamie. But this venerable mansion is not what it seems. True to Serreau's style of reversing stereotypes and playing with our *idées reçues* [commonly held beliefs], the final shots succinctly make fun of nationalist rhetoric, bourgeois domesticity, and fundamentalist familial arrangements.[10] Indeed, the house does not belong to the Frenchwomen. Rather, it was just purchased by Malika. She has brought all the women here, and they seem to be facing together an uncertain, hazy, but wide-open horizon of possibilities in the soft light of the setting sun. Granted, the Frenchwomen "frame" the immigrants, but they are also in the debt of the latter, especially Malika, who has provided companionship and shared stories.

As she recounts it to Hélène in her autobiographical narrative embedded in the film, Malika has freed herself from a grueling experience of sexual bondage, drug addiction, and prostitution that has allowed her to amass a considerable fortune, thanks to her resourcefulness, her fleecing of rich old clients, and her investment wizardry on the Internet. Having escaped barely alive from a brutal beating at the hands of her Russian pimps, she is nursed back to health by Hélène (who witnessed the attack but was prevented by her insensitive and ruthlessly egocentric Parisian husband from intervening in the situation). Malika completes her convalescence with the help of Mamie and subsequently rescues her teenage sister from the stifling patriarchal immigrant familial milieu that destined them both to arranged marriages with older Algerian men, back in their other "home" country. *Chaos* is a biting social satire that indiscriminately stereotypes men, Frenchmen as well as Eastern European and Maghrebian immigrants, who are, without exception, uncaring monsters.[11] But Serreau's female characters are not their "victims": they take charge, fight back, leave "home" in order to create this new and temporary community in a world depersonalized by greed and callousness, globalization and the Internet. Malika is the one who is now in control. She has fulfilled her dream of owning a house by the sea. Serreau's final images seem to suggest that theirs is now a "postcolonial" and "feminist" future. But what that future may be made of is left to our (amused) imagination at the conclusion of this charming, fast-paced, and gynocentric movie that mixes slapstick comedy with humane dramatic vignettes.

The frantic opening scene of *Chaos* features the upper-class bourgeois couple, Paul and Hélène, as intimate strangers going through their high-velocity morning routine on a background of jazzy techno music by the group St Germain. By contrast, the peaceful and quiet final shot of transgenerational and transnational "sisterhood" is underscored by the music of J. S. Bach. The Aria from the *Goldberg Variations* plays on. The movie hints hesitantly and amusingly at the dream of a common feminist future in which tradition is not what it seems and women might achieve a provisional form of solidarity that transcends age, race, class, culture, and history. Their very different facial expressions and affects reveal, however, that Serreau's vision is by no means a utopian construction of postcolonial and postpatriarchal harmony. As Simone de Beauvoir might indicate, the women here are presented as "separate existants," "bound to each other," but each with her own particularities and reactions to this unusual state of newfound freedom from alienating familial, sexual, social, or professional relations. As the camera moves from one face to the next, we take in the irreducible subjectivity of each woman, captured in each one's singular look: emptiness (Hélène), puzzlement (Zohra), weariness (Malika), or contentment (Mamie).

The uncertainty and weariness expressed by Malika is contrasted by the peacefulness conveyed by Bach's music as the final still shot of Mamie concludes the film and the credits roll on. Even though Serreau chose to use only the Aria, one cannot help but think of Bach's fugues, of what Edward Said has called music's utopian vision and its ability to dissolve difference and to underscore a secular form of humanism (*Musical Elaborations*).[12] Funk and Wagnalls *New International Dictionary of the English Language* and *Le Petit Robert*, in English and French respectively, define *fugue* exactly the same: both (1) a musical "form in strict polyphonic style in which a theme is introduced by one part, harmonized by contrapuntal rule, and reintroduced throughout" and (2) an episode or "an interval of flight from reality." This "contrapuntal" quality of the music evokes Edward Said's own use of the term, his call for "contrapuntal criticism" in postcolonial studies in order to achieve a better form of mediation between the west and its Others, the First World and the Third. I would argue that French filmmakers such as Serreau (but Brigitte Roüan and Claire Denis also come to mind) contribute a broad view of postcolonial and gender issues, and that they struggle with an *ethical* understanding of their own positionality in relation to the cultures they traverse. To take up Spivak's well-known phrase, Serreau suggests that the subaltern can indeed speak, so long as the transnational encounters occurring on uneven thresholds of power and knowledge (Hélène is a lawyer, Malika "just" a prostitute with business savvy) do not repress differences, if only for the moment of a "fugue."

It is significant that Malika's physical injuries initially leave her paralyzed and speechless—a situation treated with (much respectful) good humor by the filmmaker. After Malika recovers the full use of her faculties, Serreau makes her tell her *own* story, bearing witness and sharing her tale in one of the many moments of physical proximity that become a metaphor for what Ronnie Scharfman, in this volume, calls the "coming home of solidarity." Hélène's privileged difference (note the homonymy with Cixous's own first name) does not preclude the possibility of being "bound to" another whose individuality, freedom, and agency are separate and radically *other*. Serreau's film, like Cixous's *Les Rêveries de la femme sauvage* (to a certain extent) or de Beauvoir's *Ethics of Ambiguity*, does not advocate the loss of boundaries between distinct subjects. Rather, it calls for new ways of imagining solidarity and coalition. I propose that this might well be a model for our own disciplinary practices as scholars working at the intersection of postcolonial, francophone, feminist, ethnic, and transnational studies, and as scholars who care deeply about the shape of knowledge in a broad context of rights. As Serreau says in an interview, "[M]ost people just don't care. If you take five people on this planet, one is on a diet and four are starving. Yet that doesn't seem to prevent us from going on. What I'm showing in this movie is one person who can't go on in the old way. She's stopped in her tracks. And right beside Hélène is Paul, who's oblivious. We see his blindness through her eyes. And that's where the comedy comes in. It's also tragedy. Because we're all doing what Vincent [Lindon, the actor who plays Paul] does" (Abeel). Serreau's creative insights add a funny twist to recent scholarship in the fields of gender and transnationalism, and to the comparative perspectives of scholars who worry about the ethical dimensions of personal and professional encounters. These efforts are all geared to forestalling the homogenization of our identities, be they personal, professional, or cultural. The present volume contributes to these efforts while opening exciting new academic and cultural directions for interdisciplinary francophone studies in the twenty-first century. By giving us new ways of considering this field, and by remaining attuned to questions of feminist practice, the editors of this volume provide useful models for French and francophone studies on both sides of the Atlantic.

Notes

I wish to thank the editors for inviting me to write this afterword, and for their careful readings and invaluable suggestions. Thanks also to Alison Rice for her advice.

1. The first influential anthology of French feminism in the United States was Marks and de Courtivron's *New French Feminism*. See also Moi, *Sexual/Textual Politics*; Fraser and Bartky, *Revaluing French Feminism*; Grosz, *Sexual Subversions*; and Scott, "Universalism."

2. For example, Spivak, "French Feminism in an International Frame"; a special issue of *Signs* on "Postcolonial, Indigenous, and Emergent Feminisms"; a special issue of *Yale French Studies* on "Post/Colonial Conditions: Exiles, Migrations, and Nomadisms"; a special issue of *L'Esprit Créateur* on "Postcolonial Women's Writing"; Woodhull, "Unveiling Algeria"; a special issue of *Studies in Twentieth-Century Literature* on "Contemporary Feminist Writing in French"; a special issue of *Callaloo* on "The Literature of Guadeloupe and Martinique"; and a special issue of *Callaloo* on Maryse Condé.

3. I borrow this phrase from the title of the collection edited by Glasgow and Ingram, *Courage and Tools*. A second volume on feminist scholarship from 1989 to 2003 is forthcoming.

4. Badinter also critiques contemporary French feminist sociology influenced by Bourdieu's concept of male domination. For a scathing review of *Fausse route*, see de Champs, "Femmes." For a more nuanced report, see Remy, "Le *J'accuse*," and her interview with Badinter, "L'homme."

5. See also other contributors to this special issue of *differences* edited by Butler. An important volume on *Pleasure and Danger*, published more than twenty years ago, testifies (contrary to Badinter's views) to American feminism's lasting engagement with questions of sex, passion, and pleasure.

6. See Lionnet, "Performative." For a controversial and critical engagement with postcolonialism in the arts, see Amselle, "Primitivism."

7. Jean-Louis Joubert (and a team of collaborators) use this approach in the major anthology *Littérature francophone*. This volume includes works from the sixteenth to the twentieth century, and covers all areas of the francophone world.

8. See the articles by Donchin, Nussbaum and Nnaemeka in *Signs*; Lionnet and Shih, *Minor Transnationalism*; a special issue of *Signs* on "Globalization and Gender"; Mo-

hanty, Russo, and Torres, *Third World Women and The Politics of Feminism*; Fuss, *Essentially Speaking* and *Inside/Out*; Cheng, *The Melancholy of Race*; Khanna, *Dark Continents*; Stoler, *Race and the Education of Desire*; Alexander and Mohanty, *Feminist Genealogies*; Springfield, *Daughters of Caliban*; Smith, *Global Feminisms since 1945*; DeKoven, *Feminist Locations*; Kaplan, Alarcón, and Moallem, *Between Woman and Nation*.

9. See, for example, the *créolistes*' position on feminism in their interview with Taylor.

10. For another look at Coline Serreau's use of stereotypes, see Rosello.

11. Several women characters are also stereotypes: for example, the busy, chatty, and distracted nurses or the female university students. One could argue that the main female characters too correspond to particular "types"; but my point here is that Serreau never sees any one of them as simply "victims" even as she denounces the sexual exploitation of immigrant women. Her "feminist" vision is thus at odds with Badinter's simplistic view of feminist ideology.

12. I thank Susan McClary for drawing my attention to this point.

Works Cited

Abeel, Erica. "Fast-Paced Feminism; Coline Serreau Talks about *Chaos*." <http://www.indiewire.com/people/people_030130serreau.html>, accessed May 2003.

Alexander, M. Jacqui, and Chandra Talpade Mohanty, eds. *Feminist Genealogies, Colonial Legacies, Democratic Futures*. New York: Routledge, 1997.

Amselle, Jean-Loup. "Primitivism and Postcolonialism in the Arts." Trans. Noal Mellott and Julie Van Dam. *MLN* 118.4 (September 2003): 974–88.

Badinter, Elisabeth. *Fausse route: réflexions sur trente années de féminisme*. Paris: Odile Jacob, 2003.

Beauvoir, Simone de. *The Ethics of Ambiguity*. Trans. Bernard Frechtman. Secaucus, N.J.: Citadel Press, 1980.

———. *Pour une morale de l'ambiguïté*. Paris: Gallimard, 1947.

Butler, Judith. "Against Proper Objects." *differences: A Journal of Feminist Cultural Studies* 6.2–3 (Summer–Fall 1994): 1–26.

Champs, Emmanuelle de. "Femmes: fausse route ou marche arrière?" *Le Monde*, 17 May 2003, available on the website of the organization Mix-Cité. <http://www.mix-cite.org/communique/index.php3>, accessed May 2003.

Callaloo 15.1 (1992). Special issue on "The Literature of Guadeloupe and Martinique." Ed. Maryse Condé.

Callaloo 18.3 (1995). Special issue on Maryse Condé. Ed. Delphine Perret and Marie-Denise Shelton.

Cheng, Anne. *The Melancholy of Race: Psychoanalysis, Assimilation and Hidden Grief*. New York: Oxford University Press, 2001.

DeKoven, Marianne, ed. *Feminist Locations: Global and Local, Theory and Practice*. New Brunswick, N.J.: Rutgers University Press, 2001.

Differences: A Journal of Feminist Cultural Studies 6.2–3 (Summer–Fall 1994). Special issue on "More Gender Trouble: Feminism Meets Queer Theory." Ed. Judith Butler.

Donchin, Anne. "Converging Concerns: Feminist Bioethics, Development Theory, and Human Rights." *Signs: Journal of Women in Culture and Society* 29.2 (Winter 2004): 299–324.

L'Esprit Créateur 33:2 (1993). Special issue on "Postcolonial Women's Writing." Ed. Elisabeth Mudimbe-Boyi.

Fraser, Nancy, and Sandra Bartky, eds. *Revaluing French Feminism: Critical Essays on Difference, Agency, and Culture*. Bloomington: Indiana University Press, 1992.

Funk and Wagnalls. *New International Dictionary of the English Language*. Chicago: J. G. Ferguson and World, 1995.

Fuss, Diana. *Essentially Speaking: Feminism, Nature, Difference*. New York: Routledge, 1989.

Fuss, Diana, ed. *Inside/Out: Lesbian Theories, Gay Theories*. New York: Routledge, 1991.

Glasgow, Joan, and Angela Ingram, eds. *Courage and Tools: The Florence Howe Award for Feminist Scholarship, 1974–1989*. New York: Modern Language Association, 1990.

Grosz, Elizabeth. *Sexual Subversions: Three French Feminists*. Sidney: Allen and Unwin, 1989.

Joubert, Jean-Louis, et al., eds. *Littérature francophone*. Paris: Nathan, 1992.

Kaplan, Caren, Norma Alarcón, and Minoo Moallem, eds. *Between Woman and Nation: Nationalisms, Transnational Feminisms, and the State*. Durham, N.C.: Duke University Press, 1999.

Khanna, Ranjanna. *Dark Continents: Psychoanalysis and Colonialism*. Durham, N.C.: Duke University Press, 2003.

Lionnet, Françoise. "Performative Universalism and Cultural Diversity." *Terror and Consensus: The Cultural Singularity of French Thought*. Ed. Jean-Joseph Goux and Philip Wood. Stanford, Calif.: Stanford University Press, 1998: 119–32.

Lionnet, Françoise, and Shu-mei Shih, eds. *Minor Transnationalism*. Durham, N.C.: Duke University Press, forthcoming.

Marks, Elaine, and Isabelle de Courtivron. *New French Feminism*. Amherst: University of Massachusetts Press, 1980.

Mohanty, Chandra Talpade, Ann Russo, and Lourdes Torres, eds. *Third World Women and the Politics of Feminism*. Bloomington: Indiana University Press, 1991.

Moi, Toril. 1985. *Sexual/Textual Politics: Feminist Literary Theory*. London: Taylor and Francis, 2002.

Nnaemeka, Obioma. "Nego-Feminism: Theorizing, Practicing, and Pruning Africa's Way." *Signs: Journal of Women in Culture and Society* 29.2 (Winter 2004): 357–85.

Nussbaum, Martha C. "Women's Education: A Global Challenge." *Signs: Journal of Women in Culture and Society* 29.2 (Winter 2004): 325–55.

Le Petit Robert: Dictionnaire alphabétique et analogique de la langue française. Vol. 1. Paris: Le Robert, 1972.

Remy, Jacqueline. "Le *J'accuse* d'Elisabeth Badinter." *L'Express*, 24 April 2003. <http://www.lexpress.fr/Express/Info/Societe>, accessed May 2003.

———. "L'Homme n'est pas un ennemi à abattre." Interview with Elisabeth Badinter.

L'Express, 24 April 2003. <http://www.lexpress.fr/Express/Info/Societe>, accessed May 2003.

Rosello, Mireille. *Declining the Stereotype: Ethnicity and Representation in French Cultures*. Dartmouth, N.H.: University Press of New England, 1998.

Said, Edward W. *Culture and Imperialism*. New York: Knopf, 1993.

———. *Musical Elaborations*. New York: Columbia University Press, 1991.

Scott, Joan Wallach. "Universalism and the History of Feminism." *differences: a Journal of Feminist Cultural Studies* 7.1 (Spring 1995): 1–14.

Serreau, Coline. *Chaos*. Films Alain Sarde, 2001.

Signs: Journal of Women in Culture and Society 29.2 (Winter 2004). Special issue on "Development Cultures: New Environments, New Realities, New Strategies." Ed. Françoise Lionnet, Obioma Nnaemeka, Susan Perry, and Celeste Schenck.

Signs: Journal of Women in Culture and Society 26.4 (Summer 2001). Special issue on "Globalization and Gender." Ed. Amrita Basu, Inderpal Grewal, Caren Kaplan, and Liisa Malkki.

Signs: Journal of Women in Culture and Society 21:1 (Autumn 1995). Special issue on "Postcolonial, Indigenous, and Emergent Feminisms." Ed. Iris Berger, Elsa Chaney, VèVè Clark, Joanna O'Connell, Françoise Lionnet, Angelita Reyes, and Mrinalini Sinha.

Smith, Bonnie G., ed. *Global Feminisms since 1945*. New York: Routledge, 2000.

Spivak, Gayatri Chakravorty. "Can the Subaltern Speak?" *Colonial Discourse and Post-Colonial Theory: A Reader*. Ed. Patrick Williams and Laura Chrisman. New York: Columbia University Press, 1994. 66–111.

———. "French Feminism in an International Frame." *Yale French Studies* 62 (1981): 154–84.

———. "Scattered Speculations on the Question of Culture Studies." *Outside in the Teaching Machine*. New York: Routledge, 1993. 255–84.

Springfield, Consuelo López, ed. *Daughters of Caliban: Caribbean Women in the Twentieth Century*. Bloomington: Indiana University Press, 1997.

Stoler, Ann Laura. *Race and the Education of Desire: Foucault's History of Sexuality and the Colonial Order of Things*. Durham, N.C.: Duke University Press, 1995.

Studies in Twentieth-Century Literature 17 (Winter 1993). Special issue on "Contemporary Feminist Writing in French: A Multicultural Perspective." Ed. Laurie Edson.

Taylor, Lucien. "Créolité Bites." *Transition* 74 (1998): 124–61.

Vance, Carole, ed. *Pleasure and Danger: Exploring Female Sexuality*. Boston: Routledge and Kegan Paul, 1984.

Woodhull, Winifred. "Unveiling Algeria." *Genders* 10.1 (1991): 112–31.

Yale French Studies 82–83 (1993). Special issue on "Post/Colonial Conditions: Exiles, Migrations, and Nomadisms." Ed. Françoise Lionnet and Ronnie Scharfman.

About the Contributors

Eloise A. Brière is associate professor of francophone studies at the State University of New York at Albany. Articles and chapters by her have appeared in *Quebec Studies*, *Fictions Africaines et le postcolonialisme* (2002) and *Encyclopedia of Postcolonial Studies* (2001).

Jacques Coursil is professor of philosophy of language at the University of the Antilles–Guyane in Martinique. He is visiting professor of postcolonial francophone literatures at Cornell University and has published *La Fonction muette du langage* (2000).

Anne Donadey is associate professor in the departments of European studies and women's studies at San Diego State University. She is the author of *Recasting Postcolonialism: Women Writing between Worlds* (2001).

John D. Erickson is professor of French and francophone studies at the University of Kentucky. He is founder and editor of *L'Esprit Créateur*. He has coedited three books and is the author of three, among them *Islam and Postcolonial Narrative* (1998).

Alec G. Hargreaves is director of the Winthrop-King Institute for Contemporary French and Francophone Studies at Florida State University. His publications include *Post-Colonial Cultures in France* (1997), coedited with Mark McKinney.

Kenneth W. Harrow is professor of English, with a focus on African literature and cinema, at Michigan State University. He is the author of *Less Than One and Double: A Feminist Reading of African Women's Writing* (2002).

E. Anthony Hurley is associate professor of francophone literature in the Africana studies department at Stony Brook University, State University of New York. He is the author of *Through a Black Veil: Readings in French Caribbean Poetry* (2000) and editor in chief of *Migrating Words and Worlds: Pan-Africanism Updated* (1999).

Michel Laronde is associate professor of French at the University of Iowa. He is the author of *Autour du roman beur* (1993) and editor of *L'Ecriture décentrée* (1996) and *Leïla Sebbar* (2003).

Renée Larrier is associate professor of French at Rutgers University, New Brunswick, New Jersey. She is author of *Francophone Women Writers of Africa and the Caribbean* (University Press of Florida, 2000) and coeditor of *Migrating Words and Worlds: Pan-Africanism Updated* (1999).

Françoise Lionnet is professor and chair of French and francophone studies and professor of comparative literature at the University of California, Los Angeles. Her recent essays include "Reframing Baudelaire" (*Diacritics* 1998), "The Mirror and the Tomb" (*African Arts* 2001), and "National Language Departments in the Era of Transnational Studies" (*PMLA* 2002). She is also coeditor, with Dominic Thomas, of a special issue of *MLN* on "Francophone Studies: New Landscapes" (September 2003). She coedited a special issue of *Signs* (Winter 2004) as well as a forthcoming book collection, *Minor Transnationalism* (with Shu-mei Shih).

Elisabeth Mudimbe-Boyi is professor of French and comparative literature at Stanford University. She has edited two volumes of essays, *Beyond Dichotomies: Histories, Identities, Cultures, and the Challenge of Globalization* (2002) and *Remembering Africa* (2002). She was president of the African Literature Association, 2002–03.

H. Adlai Murdoch is associate professor of French and francophone literature at the University of Illinois at Urbana-Champaign. He is coeditor of a forthcoming special issue of the *Journal of Caribbean Literatures* on "Migrations and Métissages." His book, *Creole Identity in the French Caribbean Novel*, was published by the University Press of Florida in 2001.

Delphine Perret is professor of French at San Francisco State University. She is author of *La Créolité: espace de création* (2001).

Anjali Prabhu is assistant professor of French and francophone studies at Wellesley College. She is completing a book manuscript on hybridity and has most recently published articles in *Research in African Literatures* and *Studies in Twentieth-Century Literature*.

Ato Quayson is director of African Studies, University Lecturer in English, and Fellow of Pembroke College at the University of Cambridge. His most recent book is *Calibrations: Reading for the Social* (2003).

Ronnie Scharfman is professor of French and literature at Purchase College, State University of New York. She is author of a book on Aimé Césaire and of numerous articles on francophone Caribbean and North African writers. She coedited a special edition of *Yale French Studies* on postcolonial conditions (1993) and an anthology of French and francophone women writers, *Ecritures de Femmes* (1996).

Dominic Thomas is associate professor of French and francophone studies at the University of California, Los Angeles. He has published *Nation-Building, Propaganda, and Literature in Francophone Africa* (2002). He is also coeditor, with Françoise Lionnet, of a special issue of *Modern Language Notes* on "Francophone Studies: New Landscapes" (September 2003).

Winifred Woodhull is associate professor of French and cultural studies at the University of California, San Diego. She has published widely on gender, ethnicity, and cultural politics in French and francophone literatures, including literatures of immigration.

Index